Natural Space In Literature
Imagination and Environment in Nineteenth and Twentieth Century Fiction and Poetry

By Tom Henighan

Golden Dog Press
Ottawa - 1982

Canadian Cataloguing in Publication Data

Henighan, Tom
    Natural Space in Literature

ISBN 0-919614-44-2

1. Literature — Philosophy.   I. Title

PN45.H46   801   C83-090007-1

The Golden Dog Press gratefully acknowledges the assistance accorded to its publishing programme by the Ontario Arts Council and The Canada Council.

This book has been published with the help of a grant from the Canadian Federation for the Humanities using funds provided by the Social Sciences and Humanities Research Council of Canada.

To my mother, Helen Smith, and to

the memory of my father

TABLE OF CONTENTS

(v)

PREFACE

This study of the image of nature in modern literature was conceived from the start as an overview of the ways in which poetry and fiction since the beginning of the nineteenth century have reflected the natural environment. Literature, I believe, is one distinct strand of psycho-social evolution, but it is important to recall its connections with those other systems of knowledge man has created in making himself what he is. I think what follows sufficiently demonstrates how the study of the image of nature in literature can lead us into the heart of those "secondary worlds" devised by many great writers, and how their insights make a unique contribution to our knowledge of the natural environment and to human self-knowledge in that evolutionary journey largely charted for us now by the visionary explorations of modern science.

So far as I know, this is the first attempt at a comprehensive investigation of the image of the natural environment in modern literature, and in order to deal with this neglected area of study in the widest possible way, I have decided to pay some attention to the theoretical and historical contexts, while undertaking as well that close analysis of texts that must be the final demonstration of the relevance of such an approach.

Part One introduces some basic notions on literature's rendering of natural space and provides a brief overview of the idea of nature in western thought up to the Romantic period. Some contemporary evaluations of Romanticism are then scrutinized and it is suggested that the realistic note in Romantic nature description has been undervalued, and that this provides a link to the equally undervalued struggle for order and meaning in Naturalism. These two ways of perceiving nature are dealt with in a variety of texts in Part Two, which is an historically-grounded survey of some of the chief modes in which modern writers have expressed their visions of the natural environment. Wild nature, the cultivated nature of the field and the natural paradise are examined from an environmental frame of reference, and modern literature's vision of man in the biosphere is defined and traced to the point at which an ecological perspective becomes visible. (An appendix cites other examples in a wide variety of texts, allowing the reader to undertake further exploration of the concepts introduced). Part Three is a detailed analysis of the image of nature in the fiction of Thomas Hardy, H.G. Wells and

D.H. Lawrence, and makes use of the ideas already developed in order to attempt a definitive study of this important aspect of the work of these writers.

Since my analysis is most often conceptual, and is not based on the assumption that I am uncovering a tradition in which one writer always directly influences another, there need be, perhaps, no apology for the important figures left out of my discussions. Given that modern poetry has moved away from the traditional art of description and is seldom a realistic genre to the degree that the novel is, my chief emphasis is on fiction, yet I wanted to examine the image of nature in the important texts of each age, and believing as I do that many great Romantic poems develop important concepts of the environment I could hardly avoid dealing with these, even if it had to be accomplished at the expense of other relevant prose examples, such as the novels of George Eliot and E.M. Forster, and some of the writings of Carlyle and Ruskin.

Throughout the first two parts I have played down somewhat the valid critical perspective that takes close account of national traditions and concentrated instead on the universal aspects of the ecological basis of literature. When a writer produces a vision of men and women in the field, or describes an aspect of wild nature, there exists a point of connection with other writers who have dealt with such themes, beyond questions of national traditions. In the third part, I have tried to redress the balance somewhat by dealing with three writers from a specific tradition whose work nearly overlaps in time. I agree entirely with the emphasis of such theorists as René Dubos on the immense significance of specific locales and on regional perspectives as a primary foundation for artistic creation (not to mention viable cultural life in general). I should also point out that in this study I have intentionally dealt with both topography and with the more general idea of ''nature'', trying to strike a balance between an analysis of the ''spatial'' and the ''natural'' aspects of any given work.

The first encouragement to write such a book came more than ten years ago from the late Peter Ure of the University of Newcastle. I am grateful to him and also to R.S. Woof, also of Newcastle, and Professor W.W. Robson of Edinburgh for specific suggestions. Four other academic readers must be credited with a major role in improving the form, tone and scholarship of this essay (none of them to be held responsible for any errors or infelicities that remain) — Dr. E.A.J. Honigmann of Newcastle, Professor A.T. Tolley of Carleton, Professor W.J. Keith of the University of Toronto and Professor W.T. Foster of the University of British Columbia.

Others have been very helpful as well. Terry Cheney of Ottawa, with a good knowledge of both the sciences and the arts, contributed ideas, as did many of the students in the special graduate courses I have given at Carleton over the years. Among these latter I should like to mention

Marie-Lynn Hammond, Dorienne Wilson, Fraser Sutherland, Tara Cullis, Ariadna Ochrymovych, Earl Coulas, Ria Kinzel, Alan Sierolowski, Roger Brunet, Duane Macmillan, Stan Macmullen, Murray Richardson, Dale Reagan, Brian Reagan and Graham Smart. Susan Gervers, from New Mexico, and Pamela Rooks, from England and Africa, provided frequent inspiration, encouragement, and expert knowledge of Lawrence. I owe a special debt of thanks to Dr. René Dubos, both for his writings and for encouragement during my research.

Finally, I would like to thank my wife, Marilyn Carson, for many substantive insights and criticisms along the way, Michael Gnarowski, director of the Carleton University Press, for invaluable assistance on this and other projects, and also Mrs. Margaret Jones whose excellent work on a typescript that has been re-written many times has made a difficult job easier.

Tom Henighan
Carleton University
Ottawa, Canada

"As far as we are concerned, the real environment is that which we can perceive by our senses or which affects our bodies. The only world that is real for us is the primary phenomenal world in which the sun moves from east to west, the stars are hung in the skies, the reference of measurement is the human body. We remain Ptolemaic because this is the way we perceive the world during our early years, with the result that our reasoning, shaped by our senses, proceeds according to this initial way of thinking. Whatever road to progress he takes man will reach a desirable destination only if he is guided by the direct perception of his senses, and by the yearning for elemental modes of life."

René Dubos, *A God Within*

PART ONE

Natural Space in Literature: The
Critical and Historical Perspective

CHAPTER ONE
Natural Space in Literature

1. Introduction and Overview

In an essay on Lucretius, George Santayana expresses his doubt about the ability of poetry to create a landscape. Any attempt to render the natural scene, Santayana argues, would "encounter the insuperable difficulty which Lessing long ago pointed out, and warned poets of". This difficulty is connected with "the unfitness of language to render what is spatial and material; its fitness to render only what, like language itself, is bodiless and flowing — action, feeling, and thought".[1] Despite Lessing's and Santayana's difficulty with the concept, literature from the earliest times is full of place-descriptions: man demands to know *where* he is, and some of the most memorable and famous passages of the greatest works of prose and poetry are descriptions of place. Eighteenth century theories of language notwithstanding — human beings have memory, and can visualize a quite definite scene from word symbols. The investigation of natural space leads us to the center and not the periphery of many significant works.

Our human orientation in real space is primarily visual; man's vertebrate eyes have developed binocular stereoscopic vision, and we live our lives in a "hemispheric transparent shell whose distance from us we fixate".[2] Yet our sense of spatial relation and distance is partially a function of the environment we inhabit. As.R. L. Gregory points out in his book *Eye and Brain*, "people living in the Western world have a visual environment rich in perspective clues to distance".[3] He mentions the case of the members of a tribe living in dense forest, who, when taken out of their forest habitat and shown distant objects, see them not as distant, but as small. Since our "visual environment" may be taken to include not only the actual physical world, but also the cultural inheritance, we have three factors to consider in thinking about real visual perspectives: first, biological possibilities, second, experience in habitats, and third, cultural determinants. In dealing with visual perspec-

3

tives we should avoid both extreme ethno-centricism, which assumes that our culture's way of seeing is universal, and extreme relativism, which under-estimates the compelling force of the biological substratum all humans share. If western culture has learned to see in a particular way, its seeing is nonetheless part of the history of mammals moving in a variety of natural environments. Man's original habitat was arboreal, and he later moved into open grasslands and savannahs where culture may in fact have first developed. Learning to face life in open spaces, man retained perhaps a vestigial preference for enclosures, and while working so as to modify his natural environment, preserved in all of his artifacts a relation, subtle or symbolic, to the enveloping natural scene. To separate elements in the complex inheritance of western man in order to describe what specifically occurs in a given visual act is a task for the specialist. Generally speaking, we may sum up by saying that we see what our environment (in the widest sense) makes it necessary for us to see; our brain interprets sensory clues toward the solution of a given problem, and our eyes signal pleasure in the physical satisfaction of seeing, and in the emotional evaluation of the patterns the brain registers.

The visual perception that dominates our encounter with real space is important for literature. In our actual experience of the environment (as Paul Shepard suggests in *Man in the Landscape*) the world is organized into shapes that hold and is populated with forms that are "rich in perceptual meaning."[4] Art objects, including literary works express this emotional connection of man to place. They convey meaningfulness, and yet, at the same time must be, in any given case, a product of man's understanding of place: always they exhibit this Janus-like quality. A natural description in modern literature, then,will usually be partially the result of a real "seeing" process which includes as a shaping factor other literary works, even those unread by the writer, which are nonetheless active in creating the "vision" of the culture he lives in.

This power of a certain visual tradition to affect seeing has been better documented in art history than in literature. Perspective, or the representation on two-dimensional surface of three-dimensional objects in space, has its own historical line of development. The growth of specifically linear perspective in European art from the fifteenth century onward is a good example of how a way of seeing can be passed on from artist to artist, even though it involves the acceptance of a highly artificial system of perception. Our eyes, we know, can with experience learn to make use of perspective clues. Visual illusions and tricks of *trompe l'oeil* can appear once a system of seeing is established. The famous example of non-Western people who make little or nothing of drawings or photographs reminds us how in the visual arts, and therefore in literature too, we must learn to respond to hints suggesting the illusion of spatial depth and complexity. A painter creates perspective not by depicting the world as it "is" but rather by mimicking the retinal images, which are scaled by

4

the perceptual process known as "constancy" to compensate for viewing distance.[5] A photograph gives true geometrical perspective, but if compared with a drawing sometimes looks "wrong" because it lacks the retinal constancy scaling of the artist's depiction. If the artist wishes to achieve spatial rendering he must invoke the viewer's constancy scaling by using selected "depth" clues.

The exchanges between western art and literature have been sometimes fruitful, but often critically confounding, and it would be unwise to go to art for a basic theory of natural space in literature.[6] We may learn from art, however, the power of tradition to affect seeing, and be reminded that in literature too the reader is often invited to translate specific clues into a kind of spatial understanding, though not of course as instantaneous perception. A good literary description will use verbal suggestion to give the reader a sense of spatial order; it will do justice in some way to the reader's visual sense. At the same time, a description of a specifically *natural* setting will be conveying some impression of the environment. Natural space in literature must be understood as the expression of men who occupy a certain place in and have a certain perspective on, the real space of nature; traditions of rendering landscape could not change unless a man standing in a landscape felt a certain tension between a given tradition and the actual experience of being where he is, an experience in which biological possibility and the fact of specific habitat, loom large.[7] Furthermore, one clear function of literature is to create man's image of the biosphere, and while that image may involve a great deal more than primary "realism", or Frye's "art of implicit simile", it involves that too.[8] "Nature" in literature may ultimately mean such an elaborate re-ordering of elements derived from man's environmental origins that the question of tradition will become all-important. But what is being studied here is that kind of natural image in which nature, or landscape, is still being understood in relatively "realistic" terms. While such a tradition is strongest in the nineteenth and twentieth centuries (despite countervailing forces), it exists as far back as *The Odyssey*. For in *The Odyssey*, while certain landscapes are clearly the product of tradition (Hades, for example) and others very probably a blend of various "traditional" landscapes (Circe's Island), others still (the harbour of the Laestrygonians is one) are described in such specifically realistic detail that they seem to be based on personal visitation, or mariner's accounts of a Mediterranean port.[9] The point is, that while there are degrees of realism in the image of nature in literature, the kind of landscape we refer to here leads us quickly back to man's activities in the environment. The natural base that underlies the artifice of tradition must not be forgotten and should inform any construct we devise to sum up the image of nature in literature.[10]

As a human product, the word-symbols of literature always render natural space from the human viewpoint, even when no figure is

5

specifically visible in the landscape. The "scale" of a given literary landscape remains significant whether the human presence is expressed directly, or only implied. Scale depends upon the degree to which the landscape is subdued to man, and this is connected with the possibilities of what might in general be called "the inner life". Two elements must be considered, then, in evaluating any description of natural space: first, and most obviously, the contours of the landscape itself, and secondly, the kind of feelings generated by the human presence in the landscape.

Man lives at first in wild nature, establishing his presence in what is at the beginning alien territory. Being mobile, he masters a wide variety of environments, and slowly wins a certain freedom from the tyranny of instinct and the necessity of the struggle for existence. He transforms nature first through agriculture, and builds cities which finally dominate the planet. Natural space in modern literature reflects this evolutionary pattern, these human options. Man is shown in wild nature, in the field, and entering the urban world. The old vision of the natural paradise is expressed as a kind of stasis of bliss within a limited spatial context. What science, prehistory, and history suggest as a rhythm in the whole adventure of man is experienced in the microcosm of western history from the early nineteenth century to the present. The last wild spaces are encountered and the field becomes the center of human concern, only to yield to the burgeoning cities. Or escape is sought in another dimension of experience. To apply the cycle to a different frame of reference, certain writers, D.H. Lawrence, for example, sum up the same stages in their total work: we begin in a specific region, often linked to the field, move inexorably toward the city, sometimes to be carried onward into new dimensions of wild nature, where space is sought in time, and myth invoked to counter the limitations of the urban end-point. Writers of the period of about 1870 to 1940 who concern themselves with the image of natural space are certainly influenced by the actual historical trans-formations, and by the story anthropology and prehistory were even then coining about man's past.

The Romantic poets, however, were already framing some characteristic modern versions of man in natural space, based on previous literary developments and on their own experiences, and while these would be given a new emphasis after Darwin, they cannot be left out in considering the later coinages of realistic fiction. The Romantic image of natural space, as Whitehead long ago suggested, was partially a reaction to the abstractionism of the scientific revolution and the Enlightenment, and had the function of providing an "existential" basis for man in an active, creative world into which God or the principle of value had descended.[11] This study does not go into the philosophical background of such complex matters, but assumes that this Romantic value-seeking is part of a struggle against the long drift toward abstraction and mechanism in western society itself.

6

If the Romantic confidence in the rendering of the environment declined as science put forth its massive claims in that sphere, Realism and Naturalism (in fact, if not in theory) can be understood as battlegrounds for a poetic vision of natural space that was lost in the aesthetically-derived novels which are taken to be the central texts of literary modernism. Darwinism, which seemed to push literature either into the arms of science or into the ivory tower, can be viewed in retrospect as an enrichment of the writer's vision, while the drive for descriptive realism can be construed as a continuous force from the Romantics nearly to the present.

To take such realism seriously, to explore the domain of what Frye calls "the art of implicit simile" is not necessarily to accept a naive version of the relationship between language on the one hand and environment on the other. Nor need the contextual purity of the literary act be damaged by the assumption that the image of nature in literature is in some sense a truthful rendering of that very environment which is known in another way in the language of science. This position is of course thoroughly compatible with some aspects of the Romantic aesthetic, e.g. with Wordsworth's theory of poetry. Taking account of language and environment in terms of that original tension or dialectic between mind and world proposed by Wordsworth, the critic can accept both the Romantic and Darwinian images of natural space as reflections of the "real" world as literature allows us to know that world.[12] It is not merely as a collection of subjective impressions, or as a manifestation of archetypal patterns, that the literature reflecting nature reveals itself. Rather, we have at issue a great many related yet individual testimonies to the importance of the "biosphere", that "web of life" girdling the earth that we learn of from science.

2. The Idea of Nature in Western Civilization

Ancient man was closely enmeshed in nature until his increasing cultural skills began to enable him to shape the specifics of his own evolution. For a long time the various flowerings of mythopoeic thought enabled him to relate back meaningfully to the matrix from which he had partially released himself. In western society, however, particular historical circumstances led to the articulation of science, which turned the non-emotive language of mathematics to the exploration of reality in a particular way. When the Greek Pre-Socratics broke with the mythopoeic thought of the older civilizations and came to discuss the world in terms of causes, their philosophical leap uncovered a "physical cosmos governed by law as binding as that of human society".[13] "*Physis*", the intrinsic and permanent qualitative constitution of things", evolved slowly from such meanings as "the specific character of a thing, as of a

7

plant" until it could sum up the underlying reality "inhering in these things which made them behave as they did".[14] There seems to be general agreement that *physis* came to mean "the all", that disparate facts were at last subsumed in a totality which could be conceived of in relatively abstract terms. Furthermore, by the fifth century B.C. the word *physis* had been taken up by the Sophists and set in opposition to another word-concept, *nomos*, which had come to mean "not only ancient rules, established custom, accepted moral standards, and positive law, but also 'prevalent but erroneous opinion' and 'merely subjective appearance' ".[15] For the first time in history, perhaps, a detailed and complex dialectic took place between what was innately right and justified, "the natural", and what was prescribed by law and custom, the socially specified. "*Physis*" became that which sprang from the real order of things: it was good or right or just, "by nature", to do thus and thus. And as an understandable concomitant of such arguments, men looked back: *before* society, before the social contract had made actions rigid, there was a spontaneous rightness to men's conduct: it was "natural".[16] That the particular word "*physis*" should have come to designate what is original, primal, and pure, is basically a historical accident, but it was inevitable that man the tool-maker should articulate eventually such a distinction.

The growing contrast between "nature", the universe in space-time, and other realities of the various dualistic systems led to the sense of what C.S. Lewis calls a "demoted" *physis*.[17] There was something else besides *physis*, it came to be believed, and this something else might be Platonic forms, the Aristotelean unmoved mover, or the Christian spiritual order. Christianity, however, had not only demoted *physis*, but related it to God as artifact to artificer. Nature, though retaining for the Christian medieval mind a great deal of the awesome, was something less than the final sphere of mystery. In the middle ages, "nature's realm was supposed to extend only upward as far as the moon".[18] The upper air was relegated from earliest times to the daimons, who later descended, in many senses, and became the demons who held power on the "fallen" earth. It would be over-simple to say that Christian medieval philosophy rejected nature, of course. It is true that the world was the realm of Satan, but, on another plane of thought (with St. Thomas Aquinas, for example), nature could be the "realization of God's creative activity in forms and patterns".[19] Man's nature was to be a rational animal, and he was therefore acting naturally when he follwed reason. In any dualistic system there is a point of contact between one meaningful realm and the other, between "higher" and "lower" levels; to Scholastic philosophy the point of contact was the soul or intelligence, which could discern how to shape the lower nature toward the higher. In such a system, however, the very duality of things allows the "lower" to develop its own strong and forbidden life. As Lewis puts it: " . . . the 'rest of *Nature*' could easily, in opposition to man, be called simply nature. It could therefore be felt that what man shares with (the rest of) *nature*, what he has only because he is a creature and not because he is a special creature, is *natural* in contradistinction to his specific, specially created, differentia".[20] The conclusion is that "man could be most *natural* (most united with the rest of *nature*) in those states and activities which are least rational". If nature, to the medieval man, was, in everyday language, "everything under the sky", it was far from everything that mattered. In so far as it was created by God it was good; in so far as it was equated with the instincts of the flesh, with that which was untouched by grace, fallen or satanic, it was evil and dangerous. At the same time, as E.R. Curtius has shown, there was a medieval literary tradition in which nature was personified and deified as the "Goddess Natura".[21] The rhetorical tradition was connected with the conception of nature as the great mother, which carried on the Stoic idea of nature as itself a deity. Such elements, rich in possibilities as they are, made up only part of the medieval understanding of "nature".

Yet medieval thought inherited above all the specifying habits of the Greeks, the tendency to divide reality up into sharply definable categories or verbal structures. These Hebrew and Greek elements were supplemented by the classifying inheritance of Roman Law, while Christianity's rejection of slavery would spur a technical inventiveness that could provide an everyday realm from which the principle of the machine-universe could be further deduced much later. The Christian middle ages, Whitehead suggests, helped create the modern attitude which consists of "the inexpugnable belief that every detailed occurrence can be correlated with its antecedents in a perfectly definite manner, exemplifying general principles".[22] Without this belief, Whitehead adds, "the incredible labours of scientists would be without hope". This belief was possible because of "the medieval insistence on the rationality of God conceived as with the personal energy of Jehovah and with the rationality of a Greek philosopher. Every detail was supervised and ordered: the search into nature could only result in the vindication of the faith in rationality". Thus, though medieval Christianity retained on the one hand the typical respect for nature of the non-technological mythopoeically active civilization, it contained elements that made the transition to modern technological society possible. The "Renaissance" view of nature, as described, for example, by R.G. Collingwood, is really precisely this single historically eventful aspect of the Christian tradition, one which turns the natural world into a machine (that is, an arrangement of parts designed and put together for a purpose by an outside intelligence).[23] This was the view that finally superseded the Greek view of nature's innate intelligence. With its attainment, the Biblical injunction that man have "dominion" over nature could be realized with a vengeance.[24]

9

During the sixteenth and seventeenth centuries, a newly potent idea of nature developed very strongly: nature as the material world.[25] This at first leads to a specific distinction between "natural" and "supernatural". As the Copernican and the other scientific discoveries made their way across Europe, the term naturalist came to mean not only a philosopher who invokes physical causes, but also one who studies nature *per se*. The first nature studied, however, would be the physical nature of the physicist, since it was there that the scientific revolution initially took hold; later, the nature studied was even more specifically the concrete local world of the biosphere, the surrounding environment of animals and plants with which man's attention was increasingly taken. By the eighteenth century, nature could be the physical order, but also the growing world, and a naturalist could be one who accepted only the physical order, or one who studied the growing world.

Newton's grand synthesis summed up more than a century of famous achievements. The heliocentric theory of Copernicus, Kepler's laws of planetary motion, and Galileo's work on the laws of falling bodies in gravitational fields were all aspects of the shift from the conception of the universe as a hierarchy of being to the understanding of it in terms of matter in motion.[26] Yet Whitehead makes clear the limited character of the "realism" that assumed scientific concepts to be literal representations of nature as it is. He questions the act of faith involved in the necessary assumption of the connection of mind and matter that underlies the mechanistic view. He enables us to understand why such a view must eventually evoke the protest of the poets. From such a universe man stands at a distance, analyzing and calculating phenomena, noting those general truths all too readily derived from simple experience. In this situation, the mythopoeic sense is diminished, while it is only a step to considering nature in terms of the raw materials it offers for human exploitation. It was, however, precisely the tenuous rational synthesis of the eighteenth century, of which the correspondence between universal "nature" and human "wit" may be taken as a typical sample, that was soon to give way before the sense of the organic that the Romantics were hatching. The very development of the word itself shows that the eighteenth century had (so to speak) local nature in its grasp; but it remained for the Romantics to achieve the aesthetic revolution that would sanction a true poetry of the specific by relating local nature to general cosmic energies through the power of the unconscious and the imagination.

As post-Renaissance science began to penetrate to the minute and to expand its vision outward to the distant galaxies, literature took up the challenge of rendering the physical world that "nature" had become. Spirit and nature grow more opposed, but the poets find the spiritual in the natural, and face the prospect of alienation by establishing a literature which depends upon specific natural settings for its existential rootings.[27]

By exploring even the most narrowly local "nature" the Romantic poet turns the vision of man in environment against the tendency of the new science to foster abstractions that would endanger the ideal of a concrete knowledge with its own valid emotional and expressive resonance. Just because of its occasionally radical delimitations, certainly thanks to its new richness, the word "nature" is more than ever potent in the literature of the nineteenth and twentieth centuries, when the concrete and the local, for both literature and science, become necessary adjuncts to the pursuit of the boundless.

11

CHAPTER TWO
Romantic Nature and The
"Exact, Concrete Imagination"

The Romantics had a real interest in nature, in the outer world, and the rendering of that world is an important part of their descriptive intention. Recent critics, attempting to define and explore the operations of the self-sufficient aesthetic imagination, have tended to play down this realism, and to treat the Romantic image of nature in the context of their own preoccupation with literature as a self-contained universe of discourse.[1] The incidental justification for this attitude — that modern literature has inherited such preoccupations from the Romantics — is also and ironically the best justification for going beyond it, since, as now seems evident, the cataclysmic split between "imagination" and "nature" underlies so many of the problems of modern culture — and perhaps need not. Clearly, the strategy of many critics is to try to rescue Romantic poetry from the narrowness of having rendered only "pretty scenery" by interpreting it in terms of its archetypal and mythical connotations. But such a strategy, carried to extremes, distorts two important facts, first, that "scenery" is literature's tacit way of rendering man's place in the living world; and, secondly, that Romantic scenery in particular is, as W.K. Wimsatt points out, the medium through which meanings emerge.[2] Romantic nature description, like all description of nature in all literatures, should be examined for its reflection of man's relation to the whole natural world, or biosphere, in which he is always embedded. We ought to recover the sense in which the Romantics shaped an image of a concrete world, one that may have served them in regard to a specific metaphysics, but which we may see as a significant exploration of a total process in which it is absurd to separate within and without. Not merely recording psychic configurations, the Romantics explored and defined what we have come to call the biosphere in terms of its emotional and aesthetic coherence.

Whitehead suggests of Wordsworth, for example, that "he always grasps the whole of nature as involved in the tonality of the particular instance".[3] Romantic poetry, he argues, was a "protest on behalf of the

13

organic view of nature, and also a protest against the exclusion of value from the essence of matter of fact''. Whitehead asks us to consider perception itself:

> You are in a certain place perceiving things. Your perception takes place where you are, and is entirely dependent upon how your body is functioning. But this functioning of the body in one place, exhibits for your cognisance an aspect of the distant environment, fading away into the general knowledge that there are things beyond. If this cognisance conveys knowledge of a transcendent world, it must be because the event which is the bodily life unifies in itself aspects of the universe.[4]

Whitehead finds this doctrine ''extremely consonant with the vivid expression of personal experience, which we find in the nature-poetry of imaginative writers such as Wordsworth or Shelley''. ''Events'', which are ''the emergence into actuality of something'' are characterized by limitation, and carry ''value'' as their intrinsic reality. ''Value is an element which permeates through and through the poetic view of nature'', and ''value is the outcome of limitation''.[5] Whitehead concludes that ''Wordsworth, to the height of genius, expresses the concrete facts of our apprehension, facts which are distorted in the scientific analysis''.[6]

The mind of the Romantic poet interlocks with those ''obstinate, irreducible, limited facts''. In the much-quoted words of Wordsworth from *The Recluse* (1798).

> . . . my voice proclaims
> How exquisitely the individual Mind
> (And the progressive powers perhaps no less
> Of the whole species) to the external World
> Is fitted: — and how exquisitely too —
> Theme this but little heard of among men —
> The external world is fitted to the Mind
> And creation (by no lower name
> Can it be called) which they with blended might
> Accomplish . . .[7]

Abrams points out that the wavering of eighteenth century theory over the projective primacy of mind or object is resolved here in the Wordsworthian metaphor of marriage, that ''passion and life'' transform the ''inert world''.[8] Yet he also writes that ''what is distinctive in the poetry of Wordsworth and Coleridge is not the attribution of a life and soul to nature, but the repeated formulation of this outer life as a contribution of, or else as in constant reciprocation with, the life and soul of man the observer''.[9] The exchange, the tension, the sense of a real counterpart in nature to the ''life and soul of man the observer'' should not be lost sight of. If, as Emerson later will frame it, the laws of nature are the laws of mind, still ''nature is the opposite of the soul, answering to it part for part''.[10]

A brief glance at "Tintern Abbey" (1798) should help us clarify the relationship between environment and consciousness in one significant and representative Romantic art-work. J.W. Beach's study of Wordsworth's image of nature argues that nature lost her hold on the imagination the moment she ceased to be the exponent of science, of metaphysics, or of religion.[11] The nature to which Wordsworth appealed against the false conclusions of science, Beach suggests, was an ideal construction based on scientific theories. This kind of criticism is perhaps more symptomatic than instructive. Beach is so anxious to make sure that we do not think Wordsworth is inviting us to ecstasy over mere pretty scenery that he plays down the fact of the natural scene too much. He quotes Fairchild to the effect that, for Wordsworth among others, scenery provides the best evidence of what the universe fundamentally is. And what it is to Wordsworth depends upon his heritage of the English Natural Theology of the seventeenth and eighteenth centuries, with its controversy over the "active principle", though links are made also to Shaftesbury's "Characteristics", to Newton, Joseph Priestley, and Schelling. Wordsworth, Beach tells us, puts forth the idea of "universal spirit", together with the idea that each part of the manifold world is interfused with spirit, or independent spiritual entities. But Beach seems to be misled by his own analysis, which takes the poems apart and then attributes the *thought* in them — his own phantom — to Wordsworth. Wordsworth's poems are not thought based on the philosophers but are evidential findings reflecting actual experience of the concrete (see his own theory). Beach assumes that poetic meaning refers to abstractions and leads us away from the very tension between inner and outer that marks Wordsworth's greatest poetry. Because he is sure Wordsworth's nature cannot merely be pretty scenery, Beach discounts its representational side altogether; suggesting its dependence on the past, he doubts its significance for the future.

From another point of view, however, such a poem as "Tintern Abbey" represents rather a testimonial to an occasion, a report summing up an experience whose density is by no means served by a separation of elements.[12]

If "Tintern Abbey" is a poem about time and the meditative consciousness, it depends upon an encounter in the "now" with the specific environment of the rural Wye. "These pastoral farms, green to the very door" make up a spatial component in which the poetic "I" explores the contours of an experience that reverberates beyond the moment. The hermit image reminds us that a "more deep seclusion" feeds possibilities of meaningfulness denied by "the din of towns and cities". Lines twenty-three to forty-nine build to a crescendo of revelation in which the harvest of previous direct contact with rural life is seen as central. From pleasant "sensations sweet" to moral benefits, we are taken forward to the crowning glory of an "aspect more sublime", first defined as a revelation, some new cognition which delivers us from the *weight* of what is unintelligible in things, a mood in which our striving gives way to affections which lead us on until strain itself vanishes. A wholeness is achieved, the body is not cancelled out, but functions spontaneously (is "laid asleep"); we become "a living soul". Harmony and joy combine to enable the hitherto strained and isolated ego to "see into the life of things". This process, though it does not necessarily take place in a natural setting, depends upon the experience of such, and whatever its status as "belief" can be confirmed in the act of renewed meditation. The five years having been reviewed, we return to the present in line fifty-eight, and watch it expand toward the future it must be feeding. The conviction of continuity is strengthened by the image of the child-self instantly one with nature, for though this self has given way to the buoyant youth and the more sober adult, the latter (profiting from a deeper view of nature that reveals his kinship with time-bound humanity) takes comfort from the possibility of identity already suggested in the earlier crescendo, but which is here raised to the level of a universal. The spiritual principle is the "within" of things. Our senses "half create" and half perceive reality, which is a process bridging subjective and objective facts.

In "Tintern Abbey", as in much Romantic literature of nature, the natural description is specific and creates an environment which is not merely the product of human consciousness. Consciousness, through the unified mind-body, may escape from the pressure of time in meditation. The within of self and the within of nature are capable of being brought together. The movement is through specific detail to a more general conviction. A vast world is suggested but is held in check by meditation and scaled to the needs of human order. "Being" is apprehended, if at all, through the particulars, which *precede* the sense of joy. To claim that the natural description itself is irrelevant is therefore a gross misconception of the direction of the encounter. There is in the poem, too, a strong (though mostly latent) distinction between the artificial habitat, the city, where overcrowding substitutes the "din" for the "still, sad music of humanity", and the country, nature itself. Furthermore, the physical emphasis is strong, with "the blood" feeling sensations that subsequently pass into the "purer mind". Both the world and the soul are "living", and that which is man's fate (to be part of a terminating process) is also his joy, for he can sense, feel, and perceive the unity beyond him, of which he is part.

As Henri Ellenberger has shown, Romantic psychology and philosophy had, by mid-century, lost out everywhere to renewed and experimentally active behaviorism.[13] The vast increase in knowledge of nature crystallizes to suggest a time-extension equal to the space-confusion created by the Renaissance. In England, geology becomes a particular focus of crisis, as *In Memoriam* amply demonstrates. In England too, urbanization is swift, ruthless, and pervasive. Positivism in philosophy seemed to reduce Romantic faith in nature to a relic of the "theological" stage of human development. Mill's confident inductionism reaffirms the Enlightenment tradition of rationalism as the sole appropriate method of understanding both the world about us and ourselves. In his famous essay on "Nature" published (though not written) in 1850, he not only denies the beneficence of nature, but laments "that vein of sentiment" that "exalts instinct at the expense of reason; an aberration rendered still more mischievous by the opinion commonly held in conjunction with it, that every, or almost every, feeling or impulse which acts promptly without waiting to ask questions, is an instinct."

"Nature never did betray the heart that loved her", yet Shelley's "Mont Blanc" (1816), predicts what we might call the "ice vision" of Darwinism by evoking the threatening and destructive aspects of the great glacier, avoiding a negative conclusion only by its (perhaps less convincing) assertion of the power of the human imagination to create order. By mid-century Arnold's "Empedocles on Etna" registers the new division between feeling and knowledge, between mind and nature, that is perhaps more hauntingly expressed by Tennyson's figurative "sorrow":

> "The stars", she whispers, "blindly run;
>   A web is woven across the sky;
>   From out waste places comes a cry,
> And murmurs from the dying sun;
>
> And all the phantom, Nature, stands —
>   With all the music of her tone,
>   A hollow echo of my own —
> A hollow form with empty hands."[14]

We might conclude that the imagination, the all-too-human creative power, was too easily transformed into a kind of idol, leading man ultimately away from the very nature it began by grounding itself in. Science meanwhile went on claiming its own territory, and with marvelous efficiency.

Clearly, widely differing judgements about the relationship between nature and imagination in Romantic poetry have produced a variety of critical perspectives. One kind of analysis, a Christian or Platonic one, often sees the critical problem as the pinpointing of the Romantic elucidation of meaning in terms of a return through the word to some factor beyond the purely natural. Romantic poetry is significant in this view in so far as it leads beyond the image that is purely an idolatry of self, toward some complex reflection of the assumed absolute beyond the process. This view of course can be related to Coleridge's metaphysics, and to many other aspects of the writings of the Romantics themselves.[15] Another kind of criticism would, in effect, accept the idolatry of self, but see a compensation in the Romantic power to bring the isolated con-

17

sciousness to terms with the meaningless flux.[16] This view too has support in the actual views of the Romantics themselves.

The difficult alternatives help explain why Erich Heller, in a famous essay, could return to Goethe as an exemplar of unity in a way which goes beyond that of Romantic thought.[17] Heller tells us that, unlike the Romantics, Goethe does not accept that it is "the artist's business to melt away the solid reality of symbolic living forms in the hot paroxysms of the inner life".[18] Heller's essay makes the usual contrast between the power of art, as conceived by Goethe in the age of Romanticism, and the power of science, and strongly upholds the truth of art to penetrate reality in a dimension that reduces "fact" to the limited quotient it is. Unlike the more enthusiastic archetypalists, however, Heller does not gladly accept the artists' flight to the interior. Goethe he sees as significant precisely because that great poet maintained a "faith in the perfect correspondence between the inner nature of man and the structure of external reality, between the soul and the world".[19] Goethe stands, in Heller's view, against both the scientist who puts "nature on the rack", and the Romanticism which puts it out of court. Goethe's definition of truth, though it went beyond "fact", was not limited to subjectivist criteria; Heller quotes the Eckermann conversations to the effect that truth must be a "revelation emerging at the point where the inner world of man meets external reality . . . It is a synthesis of world and mind, yielding the happiest assurance of the eternal harmony of existence".[20] The Goethean test for truth becomes one of the possibility of assimilation, and brings us back to actual experience and out of the thickening jungle of subjective fantasy.

Clearly, neither of the typical modern critical attitudes to Romanticism fully meets Heller's implicit challenge that we reinterpret Romantic literature so that neither the idealistic nor the positivistic sense is allowed to carry all before it. If I may elaborate from Heller's position, I would say that the drift of his remarks is toward a recovery of cultural wholeness through a recognition of the non-absolute character of both the scientific and the literary symbol. Heller, if I understand him correctly, is doing what few modern literary critics have dared to do; he is admitting that the Romantic-Symbolist assertion of the absolutely dominant "inner life" has proved to be a cultural disaster; and he is doing this without for a moment giving up the vision of the power of literature to express meaningfulness in terms that demand a "within".

Heller's demand that the poet too put his trust in the power of the "exact concrete imagination" to render reality, not in the name of the "within" merely, but in terms of a "without" transfigured, but one which not only the poet can recognize, is a legitimate one to the critic who is concerned with the power of nineteenth and twentieth century literature to reflect a reality larger than that of the personal consciousness.[21] Against what has become the "subjectivity" of both modern physics and modern poetry, such a view demands a certain confidence in the reality of the world, but it does not involve the assumption that this reality exists in an exact correspondence with the symbols either of mathematics or of poetry.[22] Man is defined as a symbol-making creature whose symbols enable him to do different things in the world. He is not an idolator because he accepts every definition of himself as provisional, and assumes that no definition which excludes the sense of beauty and harmony is adequate to the total culture, however useful it may be in certain limited areas.

If the language structures which we classify as Romantic poems are read for the real insight they give into the "value" (in Whitehead's sense) of man's perennial experience of certain environments, no scientific demolishment of Romantic assumptions about what nature is need be disconcerting. For it is not the assumptions about imagination as a metaphysical principle or the covert dualism that are important, but the power of the Romantic Word to depict a concretely significant world.[23] In the perspective of modern theories about the limitations of scientific truth, we can see Romantic nature as a "nature" such as only poetry can make, and one that is specifically at its strongest in its testimony to the degree to which environment can be understood as "meaningful space".

The Romantic imagination can be seen in retrospect as an instrument of genuine knowledge of the concrete world, a knowledge which does not exclude value, though it may give small comfort to Idealist metaphysics. Defending Romantic poetry's image of nature, in fact, does not require that we take the position of either the idealist or the aesthete. For we can now affirm with a new confidence what Goethe from his earlier perspective had affirmed, namely, that science is not in possession of an objective world, from which the poet must fly in order to make his own kind of truth; science is merely making what truth it can of the world which is open to poetic exploration as well. This would only become clear, however, after literature had gone through the confusions of attempting to model itself upon a science which claimed a special and simple access to "nature". The confused undergrowth of Literary Naturalism was to bear a rich fruit, and this efflorescence was clearly not limited to the hothouse plants of the tradition of archetypal consciousness; tougher strains of fiction emerged, novels with a more tenacious rooting in common reality. This calls for a revised view of Literary Naturalism, one that does justice to the tension between the theory of the Naturalists themselves and their actual accomplishment, which was to create the basis for an image of nature more consonant with modern science and philosophy than pure Romanticism would allow.

CHAPTER THREE

The Nature of Literary Naturalism: New Values out of Struggle

The new imagination of nineteenth century "Realism" at first pro-claimed its goals in terms that seemed to mimic the "objectivity" of science.[1] Stendhal's image of the mirror in the roadway, Tolstoy's assertion that his hero was simply "truth", remind us that for the Realists the drive toward detailed representation of contemporary life over-shadowed questions of the nature of poetic knowledge.[2] In theory, Realism was getting rid of the fantastic and the eccentric in art, and simply recording the truth of the everyday bourgeois world the writers lived in. Naturalism, of course, chose a more specifically "scientific" orientation, but, even here, analysis of the texts fails to establish anything like "induction" as a truly comprehensive description of what actually goes on in a given work. In practice, various kinds of ordering factors operate in both Realism and Naturalism, and the principle of "reporting the truth" will simply not do as a critical focus, despite the slogans. In practice, certain Realistic and even Naturalistic works retain in some passages an almost Romantic fusion of self and nature as an observable instance, though never in terms of the integrating imagination; while the underlying sense of beneficence in nature yields to a spectrum of values which includes other, and harsher, tones.

It is not a turning to "outer reality" that seems to be significant in the thirties and forties of the last century, but the loss of a key ordering principle that occurred with the disappearance of the Romantic imagina-tion. The physical and social sciences, with their exploration in labora-tory or in the field, were transforming the European pool of knowledge, so that within fifty years or so (to take one example) the science of chemistry could be changed from what were virtually alchemical in-vestigations, to the complex of theory and research that makes up the modern science. The new Realism that accompanied the triumph of the middle classes seemed to be content to accept the definition of reality as everyday ordinary experience. The Realists were cautious, exploratory, diverse. Nature was to be described, examined, and the experience of

21

nature recorded in various ways. This was not only part of the increasing trust in straightforward investigation of the outer world, fed by science, but was also a drive for social, political and sexual freedom in art. The brave new world of Zola's Naturalistic novel has a healthy anti-Establishment flavour to go along with its rampant scientism.[3] Yet the very expression of a theory modeled, on science seemed to cause a reaction. Possibly its inadequacies were only too clear. The defection of J.K. Huysmans from the Zola school is one example of how Naturalism, carried to extremes, could drive a writer into almost the opposite camp. The Naturalistic novel itself was really seeking a center.

The Naturalists had no real basis for a novel of integrated mind and nature. The scientism of their theory called for a mechanistic materialism which their fiction fails to exhibit. Writers as diverse as Zola, Hardy and Jack London create novels which, to be fully understood, must be taken far beyond the theory which supposedly contains them.[4] This situation is corrected in two ways. On the one hand, theory of the novel itself moves away from the will-o'-the-wisp of science and toward a more credible view of what the artist does. On the other hand, the science that inspires literature no longer appears to dictate such narrow terms. What emerges is both a novel of newly coherent theoretical purpose, and a freer more flexible version of the novel of environmental realism, one that takes for granted a psychological dimension. Every novel is a battleground, an attempt at an order, and it is not surprising that a more precise aesthetic at last provided a center for the novelist's art, one that was not merely part of a vague intention. This came about through an interaction with poetry, and it is easy to understand this turn of the novel in the direction of artist-centered aestheticism and Symbolism. Here at last, one would think, was an escape from Naturalism's dilemma. The "methods of science" had been tried and found wanting; now, inner and outer could be related by placing a new emphasis on the inner. Nature would be excluded in the name of a poetry of correspondences, through which the "higher" nature could be evoked.[5] Romanticism's faith in the poet — its confident theorizing — could be retained, though not its drive toward the outer world. Of course there were difficulties. While such a revolution might have its way with poetry, the novel, wedded intrinsically to formal realism, only gradually rid itself of the spectre of scientism. From 1880 to 1920, however, in what might be called the late period of the traditional novel, a new unity is in the making. An emphasis on artistic form derived from Symbolism, and the new exploration of the unconscious from psychoanalysis, helped the novel to define its intentions beyond vague programs of "reproducing reality". From the peak period of Naturalism, when science seems to dictate what the novel should be, we are carried to a new affirmation of what the artist can do. One way of controlling the mechanistic material universe of Darwinism is to reaffirm the shape and power of the artist-creator. Jamesian point-of-view provided a center from which many of the "realistic" forays of the Victorians looked like "fluid puddings". Virginia Woolf could see the realism of Arnold Bennett as inadequate and lacking in human significance just because it left out the "inside"realism of the new psychology.[6] The passage of James Joyce from Naturalism to self-conscious myth and interior monologue is even more significant. In such writers, theory and practice of the novel are much closer together than in the preceding Realism and Naturalism, because the imagination has been affirmed as the center of each work, and form derived from a conscious effort to "shape" reality, not to succumb to it.

Discussion of the "modernist movement" of the twentieth century novel has sometimes passed over the fact that the triumph of the new aesthetic in the novels of Virginia Woolf, James Joyce, Ford Madox Ford and others was only *one* result of the historical situation we have been charting. It has been necessary to point to traditions outside of that one to regain a sense of the richness of the novel as we inherit it from the eighteenth and nineteenth centuries.[7] One of these traditions might include novels in which environment continues to be a dominant factor, and in which the unity sought is not precisely the one we know in the novels of Joyce and Virginia Woolf. The novels I refer to (by Hardy, D.H. Lawrence, Wells, Knut Hamsun, Ignazio Silone, Hemingway, Faulkner and Solzhenitsyn, to name a few) are not so wedded to consciousness, to approaches derived from Symbolism, and to a depiction of social and psychological minutiae in an urban context. These novels, loosely speaking, can be said to assume a roughly Naturalistic view of things, but they do not exhibit any kind of programmatic Naturalism. In these novels a battle is being waged for human values and artistic credibility in a context in which outer nature is given far more emphasis than in the main tradition mentioned above. Clearly, the tradition of Naturalism is a much more complex one in fact than its slogans would lead us to believe. To understand why this is so, a closer look at Darwinism itself is necessary.

While the historical situation explains a great deal, the manifold interaction between Darwinism and social and literary thought seems to depend upon the particular form of the Darwinian presentation, its status as an expression of language.[8] Darwinism was somewhat different from many other major scientific theories in offering its own characteristic metaphors as part of its explanatory function. There is nothing intrinsically poetic in Newton's expression of his theory of gravitation, nothing that strikes the senses with immediate impact in Einstein's $E = MC^2$. But Darwin's theory is science expressing itself initially through words alone, and though these words are straining for an exactness, a precision that would convey the most coherent and limited sense of fact, such a goal can never be reached. Though it ultimately might attain mathematical or modular expression, Darwinism started out in language that was not

23

consistently separable from the metaphorical language of literature. Thus, apart from the question as to the relative symbolic functions of literature and science, Darwinism is a special case. The terminology of "the struggle for existence", "the war of nature", Darwin himself was aware, was rather loaded, yet he could not altogether get around their potential expansiveness.[9] No wonder these images found their way into literature; they are "literature" already. It was the direct use of language in Darwin's theory that caused the influence of Darwinism to be immediate on both literature and the social sciences. The process of translation was easy because so little translation was needed. Literature, however, uses the language of Darwinism not to analyse abstract relations, but to express a human situation. Literature both assimilates and evaluates the key ideas of Darwinism by putting the Darwinian language in a new context of intention. This can be illustrated by a brief comparison of texts.

First, Darwin's own language. Even in discussing a relatively abstract idea — the difference between selection effected by man and the natural selection of his theory — Darwin is capable of a language of suggestive breadth, as the following example from *The Origin of Species* shows:

As man can produce and certainly has produced a great result by his methodical and unconscious means of selection, what may not nature effect? Man can act only on external and visible characters: nature cares nothing for appearances, except in so far as they may be useful to any being. She can act on every internal organ, on every shade of constitutional difference, on the whole machinery of life. Man selects only for his own good; Nature only for that of the being which she tends. Every selected character is fully exercised by her; and the being is placed under well-suited conditions of life. Man keeps the natives of many climates in the same country; he seldom exercises each selected character in some peculiar and fitting manner; he feeds a long and short beaked pigeon on the same food; he does not exercise a long-backed or long-legged quadruped in any peculiar manner; he exposes sheep with long and short wool to the same climate. He does not allow the most vigorous males to struggle for the females. He does not rigidly destroy all inferior animals, but protects during each varying season, as far as lies in his power, all his productions. He often begins his selections by some half-monstrous form; or at least by some modification prominent enough to catch his eye, or to be plainly useful to him. Under nature, the slightest difference of structure or constitution may well turn the nicely-balanced scale in the struggle for life, and so be preserved. How fleeting are the wishes and efforts of man! how short his time! and consequently how poor will his products be, compared with those accumulated by nature during whole geological periods. Can we wonder, then, that nature's productions should be far "truer" in character than man's productions; that they should be infinitely better adapted to the most complex conditions of life, and should plainly bear the stamp of far higher workmanship?[10]

Here, Darwin's language describes the automatic selection process in such a way as virtually to give "nature" the force of a mythopoeic presence, while his incidental examples evoke a vivid physical competitiveness, carried on over vast periods of time. Such a passage has a built-in poetic force which is easily grasped if we compare it with a few sentences from a self-conscious literary work by someone who had read *The Origin*, and who was grappling with the problems of change it raised, also in terms of man and the environment beyond:

> Let us begin with that which is without — our physical life. Fix upon it in one of its more exquisite intervals, the moment, for instance, of delicious recoil from the flood of water in summer heat. What is the whole physical life in that moment but a combination of natural elements to which science gives their names? But these elements, phosphorous and lime, and delicate fibres, are present not in the human body alone; we detect them in places most remote from it. Our physical life is a perpetual motion of them — the passage of the blood, the wasting and repairing of the lenses of the eye, the modification of the tissues of the brain by every ray of light and sound — processes which science reduces to simpler and more elementary forces. Like the elements of which we are composed, the action of these forces extends beyond us; it rusts iron and ripens corn.

Comparing the language of Darwin in 1859 and the language of Pater's "Conclusion" to *The Renaissance*, in 1869, there is no point at which we can say this is "science" while this, on the other hand, is "literature". Darwin's rhetoric has a logic and a direction not so evident in the Pater selection, which for its part is more sensuous and vaguely suggestive, but both passages, in evoking complex processes, invite our perception of and our emotional response to man's place *vis à vis* the natural world. In such passages we see how a common language itself blurs the sharp edges of distinctions otherwise definable, a fact that can be driven home even more strongly if we recall one of Darwin's more overtly metaphorical sallies:

> It is interesting to contemplate an entangled bank, clothed with many plants of many kinds, with birds singing on the bushes, with various insects flitting about, and with worms crawling through the damp earth, and to reflect that these elaborately constructed forms, so different from each other, and dependent upon each other in so complex a manner, have all been produced by laws acting around us. These laws, taken in the largest sense, being Growth with Reproduction; Inheritance which is almost implied by reproduction, Variability from the indirect and direct action of the external conditions of life, and from use and disuse; a Ratio of Increase so high as to lead to a Struggle for Life, and as a consequence of Natural Selection, entailing Divergence of Character, and the Extinction of less-improved forms. Thus, from the war of nature, from famine and death, the most exalted object which we are capable of conceiving, namely, the production of the higher animals, directly follows. There is grandeur in this view of life, with its several powers, having been originally breathed into a few forms or into one; and that, whilst this planet has gone cycling on according to the fixed law of gravity, from so simple a beginning endless forms most beautiful and most wonderful have been, and are being, evolved.[11]

25

Such a passage makes clear the power of Darwin's word to open imaginative vistas, to turn the reader's attention to nature and its minute particulars, and to draw him into a contemplation of order and process. The shock of Darwinism, its upsetting of old complacencies, its picture of a universe in which the "automatic" evolutionary mechanism reigns, must be seen in the context of a language transmission which creates immediate possibilities for that evaluation of experience that literature makes its own. If Darwin's above-mentioned laws are abstractions hemming us in, and reducing us to "factors" in operation that is relentless, the grandeur of the perspective that leads from that "entangled bank" to the "endless forms" that preceded us offers a certain redemption. The beauty of order, the mystery of life, the richness of the human power of contemplation are all in Darwin's words and ready for literature to make more explicit. Such a theory, though it may chasten the mind and expectations, invites literature to a new grappling with man's place, and may lead to a new affirmation of human significance.

This is why so many of the theorists of Naturalism have come to grief, for in taking the theory of Naturalism too much at face value, and positing a literature naively reflective of "mechanistic materialism", they forget both the intrinsic poetry of Darwinism, and the necessity of literature in general to reaffirm the significance of man.[12] Their view is that Naturalism attempted to program itself after the revelations of Darwinism, that it was Realism made more "scientific" and more ruthlessly coherent. One such definition of Naturalism, for example, states that:

Naturalism appears in a novel when the philosophy of materialistic monism is somehow applied to its conception or execution. The perfectly naturalistic novel would be one in which the action is completely determined by material forces — economic, social, physiological. For this condition to exist a corollary requirement with respect to the characters of the novel must be fulfilled: they too must be explained in these terms that impressions of free will and ethical responsibility do not intrude to disrupt the relentless operation of this material causation.[13]

Several things come to mind when one reads such a definition. First, that such a philosophy, rigorously applied, would lead to the destruction of literature and not its creation. It is difficult to imagine such a work being produced; certainly, none has ever been written. The intrinsic character of literature seems to defy such an expression. What then, is Naturalism? We can perhaps clarify the situation by looking somewhat closely at a fairly typical Naturalistic work. On the basis of this, and from an extensive knowledge of a great many other productions of the same kind, we can confidently pinpoint some of the limitations and possibilities inherent in Naturalism.

Reading Jack London's story of 1908, "To Build a Fire", one engages a work which is straightforward and almost naive, in the vein of popular literature, and at the same time, a narrative that is being controlled and shaped toward an artistic effect. It is the story of a man on the trail with his

26

dog in unusually severe temperatures. The man fails to build a fire and freezes to death, and his dog trots off to find other "food-providers and fire-providers". The setting is a wasteland of Yukon ice, and the description creates both the magnificence and the monotony of an alien landscape. The man is not named; we are shown a representative of the species rather than an individual developed in an explicit social-psychological dimension. We do get something of the man's character, however. We are told that he is "without imagination", though it is not the Romantic imagination that he lacks, that "conjectural field of man's immortality and man's place in the universe", but rather the practical imagination that takes in the import of circumstances and draws large conclusions. This man, failing to "meditate upon his frailty as a creature of temperature, and upon man's frailty in general, able only to live within certain narrow limits of heat and cold", is not in a good position to meet the challenge of the environment in which he is placed. For natural space is here rendered precisely as *environment*, as a physical enclosure in which homo sapiens must do certain things to survive. "The cold of space smote the unprotected tip of the planet, and he, being on that unprotected tip, received the full force of the blow". This man has disregarded the wisdom of the tribe, summed up in the figure of an "old-timer" from Sulphur Creek; he has ventured alone into the bush when the temperature is at an extreme low. "No man must travel alone in the Klondike after fifty below", the old-timer has warned, and when Jack London's traveler fancies himself to be surviving the experience, he exults to the point of a dangerous hubris. "Any man who was a man could travel alone". What gives him confidence is his keen observation, and his possession of food and the wherewithal to build a fire. He has matches in his pocket and there is wood on the trail. Yet the extreme cold surprises him, and he must concentrate to keep his morale up. Finally, he meets with a misadventure; after stopping for lunch and building one fire, he falls through the thin ice above an unfrozen stream and wets his feet. He must build another fire and dry out, or his feet will freeze. Now he makes a mistake. He builds the fire under a snow-laden spruce tree, and in trying to get wood from the tree to feed it, he causes the snow on the upper branches to fall and put out the fire. He tries to re-light it, but so quickly has the extreme temperature been working that he is unable to do this. Here London's story delivers its strongest metaphorical cargo. From the first, we have been made aware of the man's physical condition and of his confidence in his own power of survival. Throughout the story, however, we have been made to feel the relentless cold pressing upon him. At this point, his limbs begin to freeze, and the process continues until he is at last immobile. Meanwhile, he goes from a desperate attempt to reassert his mastery of the environment by using the matches, through a stage of animal panic, to the achievement finally of a stoical calm involving a form of reconciliation with death. At the same time, his relationship with

27

the dog has taken several turns. The man is superior to the dog so long as he is a potentially effective fire-provider, so long as he uses his practical imagination to read the total situation; but when his wit and skill fail, the dog's instinct emerges as a superior factor. The man is reduced to crawling on all fours; he becomes a creature of instinct trying to outwit another creature of instinct, unsuccessfully. The dog senses something is wrong and backs away; the man's plan to kill the dog and warm his hands in its carcass fails. London is not affirming the absolute value of instinct, but suggesting that a developed instinct is better than a failed intelligence. The man's intelligence allows him to rely on his tools, but in an emergency situation a finer and more aptly applied intelligence is necessary to prevent the tools from being rendered useless. Thrown back on his cunning, the man is no match for either the dog or the environment. He runs wildly, trying to get his circulation going, but falls at last into a sleep in which the body gradually disappears as a factor in his experience. Conquering his fear, he faces death calmly: "Well he was bound to freeze anyway, and he might as well take it decently", as London puts it. In his imagination he now rejoins the tribe, picturing "the boys" finding his body the next day, picturing the old-timer smoking his pipe. He acknowledges that the old-timer was right. The group wisdom, the tribal experience, should not have been ignored.

Such a story enables us to measure the transformation of the image of nature in literature between Wordsworth's "Tintern Abbey", for example, and the end of the century. This tranformation is poorly captured by comparing abstractions derived from an analysis of philosophical positions. Jack London's story, like most Naturalistic works, suggests a nature of struggle. This is a nature in which work is more important than leisure, and action more important than passivity, or meditation. It is a nature in which man and the other animals are closely related, both sharing, for good and ill, the lower depths of instinct. At the same time, man is understood as superior to the other animals because his intelligence has created culture, specifically technology, and this technology enables him to be successful in a variety of situations in which a mere animal would fail. Mind is thus demoted, without being entirely rejected. The collective and the physical energies of man are valued over interiority, but cunning is emphasized. Man as a member of the human species is the focus and not man as an individual psyche, and the tribal achievement is central. Though it is not so evident in this story, a time-consciousness is created in which the individual in the present is linked to remote ancestors. Life itself is held up as a value, and the individual achieves significance when he links himself to this chain of life, which he does sometimes through a physical ecstasy, a kind of pseudo self-transcendence involving a keen sense of animal vitality.

Formal kinesis is the major mode of the work inspired by Darwinism. Change, movement, conflict, produce the linking to life. Man's potential for inner harmony is diminished, and he is dwarfed by and caught up in the natural scene, where he is pressed upon by forces both from within and without. From without comes the challenge of the environment itself — climate, enemies, the accidents of a nature which is quite capable of betraying the heart that loves her; from within comes the pressure of his own nature, the primordial drives, the tendency to revert, which means losing sight of the cultural superiority he holds over the animals, though it may mean too the experience of an ecstasy which is otherwise denied. When cultural superiority is celebrated, it is often summed up in the simple technology of club, whip or knife, through which man asserts his "mastery". The environmental bases of myth are revealed, without the specific religious dimension being necessarily re-created. A man on the trail lighting a fire becomes Prometheus, though the gods he challenges are Darwin's "forces" and not the rulers of heaven.

This profile of Darwinian nature, the nature we find in the works of the Naturalistic novelists, cannot be expected to do at every point for every writer, but I would argue its relevance in general. It presents a far more accurate synopsis of what Naturalism is than we can gain from any generalization about "mechanistic materialism" as a narrative control.

It is now possible to understand more clearly both the dilemma of Naturalism and its relevance for the future. Let us return for a moment to the Jack London story. "To Build a Fire" shows us a world in which nature is indifferent to man, and in which man must struggle to survive. Even the accident of the falling snow, however, fails to convince us of any actual determinism. Jack London is careful to emphasize the man's freedom and his limitations. It is clearly the man's own fault that the fire goes out; and his death is his own responsibility. Furthermore, Jack London is seeking by various means to give value to the man's experience; he shows him as hubris-ridden, and careless, but also as capable of a courageous facing of death. In his dream, the man is reunited to the group from which he had foolishly separated himself, and he reaches a kind of reconciliation with the figure of the old-timer. Fear being overcome, the traveler dies like a man, and not "like a dog".

Neither the story, however, nor the Naturalistic image of nature is without inner tension and contradictions. We have suggested that Naturalism borrowed from Darwinism a set of ready-made metaphors, a language that could begin to suggest values. The Darwinian language, however, is not striving toward values; and Darwin's theory, *presented abstractly*, lends little comfort to man. Literature thought it was borrowing the world-view of Darwinism, the apparently mechanistic and material view of things, but it borrowed a language rich in possibilities and problems. That language, meaning the whole Darwinian apparatus of metaphor, offers in some ways a vastly more satisfying picture of the universe than we find in the relatively beneficent nature of the Romantics, but it is an incomplete picture *for literature*, because it offers man no

29

real justification for his inner life. The physical ecstasy that Naturalism sometimes asserts is a severely limited, because it is a morally diffuse, experience. Literary Darwinism's demotion of mind to the cunning that creates and manipulates technology, narrows experience too much, and undercuts the achievement of that unity demanded by the Romantic visionary assertion. This may be understood better if we turn for one last time to the Jack London story. Jack London wants to convey the value of the death of the man on the trail, his very human death. To do so he can suggest a certain dream-affiliation of the man with the comrades he leaves behind. But the underlying motive of the man's bravery is quite clearly stated: "Well he was bound to freeze anyway, and he might as well take it decently". In short, the man dies well because he wants to be a good sport, because it would not be gentlemanly to die any other way. This is a value of sorts, but it is a very shaky one. Such a limited assertion diminishes our impression of the man's bravery and mocks his quite magnificent fights against the hostile elements. That there is a certain irony in his dream-vision is also quite clear; a "spiritual" vision emerges only from the body that no longer feels. Though the story exhibits a consistency of setting, and suggests a coherent "world", the attempt to represent the inner dimension of human experience is extremely tentative. This Naturalistic tale like Naturalism in general, may be seen as seeking values. It is partially assisted in this search (which marks all the literature we know) by the richness of the Darwinian metaphor; but it is hindered by what is lacking in Darwinism. The danger that literature faces in borrowing from science is that it will be content with the narrow range of evaluation that science rightly accepts for itself. Naturalism manifests a struggle toward a more comprehensive view of reality, one that will include an inner dimension, and it cannot transcend its limitations without help from values beyond those of "science" in the narrowest sense.

When science begins to give up its version of its own activity as simple inductive investigation of reality, and conceives of itself as a certain kind of imaginative process, the way is clear for literature to understand its own validity in relation to science. Darwinism is seen to be a scientific change of paradigm, not an absolute rendering of reality "as it is", but a comprehensive and useful theory bringing order to chaos, and offering practical results that justify its existence. Literature slowly frees itself from the metaphorical spell of Darwinism, having broadened its sense of the natural world too narrowly conceived by Romanticism. Man's sense of his placing is immeasurably enriched, but the evaluative disciplines, including literature, no longer assume that the triumph of science automatically commits them to its meagre interest in rendering the human meaning of a newly-mapped situation. In retrospect, it can be seen that literature was all the while struggling to evoke meaning, despite its acceptance of slogans.

Toward the end of the century, though the Joycean novel moved away from a real interest in outer nature, other novelists retained the image of nature, and sought values that would allow the Darwinian vision to be rendered in a new human perspective. A struggle toward this end goes on in the novels of Hardy, Conrad, Wells, E.M. Forster, Jack London, Willa Cather, and in many minor writers, for whom environment remains a central focus. Unquestionably the most comprehensive engagement of all issues, however, is found in the novels of D.H. Lawrence, who is Naturalism's great inheritor in the tradition of environmental realism.

We must now look at this process in detail, first through some major texts exhibiting the various perceptions of natural space in modern literature, then in the work of three great modern novelists, in whose work the image of nature as environment plays a central role.

PART TWO

Forms of Natural Space in Modern Literature

CHAPTER ONE

Wild Nature or the Natural Sublime: from Romantic Ecstasy to Darwinian Struggle

The landscape described in a given work may be "wild" or shaped by man. Wild nature includes desert, river, sea, island, mountain, plain. Though all of these may be shaped by man, to the hypothetical first man in the landscape they are "nature" and not yet artifact. To a man looking up, the sky is another open territory. By "open" here I mean usually a long visual perspective extending to "infinity", to the horizon, or the edge of the seeable world. In a given case the view may be blocked by close-up obstacles, a forest or range of mountains, for example, but the wild territory is nonetheless understood as stretching out beyond the observer, real or implied. Wild nature might well be referred to as the "natural sublime", a term borrowed from one of Marjorie Hope Nicolson's studies of eighteenth century literature.[1] There is the evidence of a few texts to suggest that the image of wild nature, or natural sublime, pre-exists the English eighteenth century; in fact, it might be fruitful to assume as a working hypothesis that every culture could potentially produce an image of wild nature in its literature, since every culture has boundaries contiguous with it, and in some sense therefore has to "face" it. How are we to take, for example, the late Australian tribal song, of which I here quote part, if not as conveying a sense of natural distance and the mystery of space?

The great beam of the Milky Way
Sends out flashes of lightning incessantly.
The great beam of the Milky Way
Casts a flickering fire glow over the sky forever.
The great beam of the Milky Way
Gleams and shines forever.
The great beam of the Milky Way
Burns bright crimson forever.[2]

This song apparently accompanies a ritual act. It is unusual among primitive chants in that it seems to express a direct awareness of the space

35

of wild nature, rather than that mythopoeic consciousness in which man is so embedded in a world of presences that he never stands back to describe the shape of an actual environment.

Because man is a mobile creature he has gradually advanced upon distant spatial realms; his curiosity, intelligence, and energy, as well as necessity, have driven him from place to place. Through the insights of modern literature and science we imagine man across the ages standing on the edge of some wild land, working out the complex movements of the stars, possessed by a sense of wonder, and yet destined to transform the chaos of the wilderness into the cosmos of a new social order. There is no doubt that our way of seeing this encounter is our own in so far as we ourselves are the heirs of certain traditions, yet it is hard to believe that this "myth" of man meeting the wilderness with these feelings is not sometimes relevant to situations (both in fact and in literature) that predate by far the "fashion" discerned by Professor Nicolson. Like the tribes described in Mircea Eliade's *The Sacred and the Profane*, the first real men in a new landscape must have often sought a center for their world, and, when their environment and their traditions encouraged it, must have looked out with awe and excitement on the distances beyond.[3]

Natural sublime in modern literature, at any rate, is an image of man's perception of open space, a perception which involves a particular emotional response, an inner reaction. In the face of the wild landscape man may feel himself diminished, and the scale may become radically inhuman. The psyche is pressed upon by the immensity and a kind of agoraphobia of the spirit occurs. The inner is not equal to the outer dimension; or else, magnificently equal — for the psyche may in fact be depicted as adequately in balance with the outer landscape. Or ecstatic contemplation may suggest an expansion of consciousness to meet the challenge of spatial vastness.[4] In short, literature shows various possibilities of relation between the natural sublime and the inner life of the figure in the landscape.

As Majorie Hope Nicolson has shown, centuries of traditional suspicion of the post-Edenic "cursed" earth, and especially of the "warts" and "wens" of mountains which covered it, gives way in the seventeenth and eighteenth centuries to a new appreciation of the sublime irregularity of mountain landscape.[5] Through the writings of Thomas Burnet and others and especially through the Miltonic epics, the infinity found pleasing in the astronomical vistas came to be related to the earth's surface. The descriptive poetry of the eighteenth century, typified by the poetic "excursion", and demonstrating a new conviction in the power of sight, could sustain a tradition of rendering of nature because the historical conditions conspired to encourage such a development.

It remains to be pointed out, however, that Thomson, Young and the other pre-Romantic nature poets occupied a particular relation to their tradition, one that leads almost all critics to make a sharp distinction between them and the later, great Romantics. The pre-Romantic nature poets combine a vision of the natural world with a vision of a certain metaphysical order, but the two remain in a rather uneasy balance, because a principle of interiority is still to be found. Newton's synthesis had resolved for a time the sense of vertigo about space made famous in Pascal's well-known assertion of terror, and had sustained the confident generalizations about the God of Nature that were at the heart of so much eighteenth century theorizing. The pre-Romantic descriptive poets produce an image of nature which they constantly link to the generalized visions of the God of Nature familiar in the thought of the period; a sense of majesty and awe is produced, but the resolution is always found in a praise that harks back to the God of the new synthesis. This is "scientific" poetry indeed, a poetry of surfaces and generalities, a rhetoric of accepted ideas. But when a comprehensive vision of the human self appears, and when the Enlightenment synthesis no longer seems reassuring on the level that matters, nature takes on quite a different cast. And it is precisely such a cast that we discover in the tension-ridden great Romantic poetry, in "Tintern Abbey" or the "Ode to a Nightingale." It is not so much that the eighteenth century vision has been assimilated; it is that it has been superseded by the necessity of the self to confront a world of time and change that can no longer be resolved in the consolations of generalized religious rhetoric. This is precisely the point at which earlier the work of Blake had stood against the exteriorized raptures of the new nature poets and had suggested the solution of the imagination against the pseudo-interiority of the eighteenth century. It is precisely this historical role of the great Romantics that Whitehead insists on in his *Science and the Modern World*; by comparison, Professor Nicolson's eighteenth century tradition offers us a poetry of "misplaced concreteness". It is not until the advent of Blake and the great Romantics that the new science is encountered by literature in terms of literature's true role; it is only with Blake and the great Romantics that literature becomes a battleground for the assertion of specific values *against* the generalities of science. Space must be experienced through the mode of poetry, as a concrete fact, and not rendered in a rhetorical apostrophe.

If we take Edmund Burke's *Enquiry into the Sublime and the Beautiful* of 1757 as a convenient reference point among many, we can see how conceptions of rhetorical and natural sublime come together in a work which explores the shock of distance in terms of a literary effect which provides the "strongest emotion which the mind is capable of feeling".[6] Burke's treatise pushes the rational categories of the age to the limit, without producing a version of the imagination as such. Yet, as J.T. Boulton points out, "a growing reliance on feeling as a means of insight, allied to the current belief that the best poet was the one with the widest experience, led to the development of sympathetic imagination as an aesthetic idea".[7] Burke was the first to convert the link between sub-

37

limity and terror into a system. What was previously considered as a style of writing is transformed by Burke almost into what we should call in today's language an existential position; here Burke's emphasis on "self-preservation" is significant. The sublime is characterized by a sense of danger which threatens the self-preservation of the single individual, though not too closely. A distanced threat toward the individual can be *enjoyed*; this is the sublime. Translated into spatial terms, such a feeling occurs where man sees himself as an isolated individual threatened by the vastness of the natural environment. The real world of craggy mountains and rugged seascapes activated those feelings of terror and delight noted by Burke; such a landscape could not be assimilated in terms of quantities to be formulated in the abstract terms of science or religion. The contemporary natural philosophers might carry on their rarefied disputes about the God of Nature, but the poets were being provided with an aesthetic which would involve a renunciation of abstractions in favour of a confrontation between the isolated sensibility and the specifically disturbing aspects of the natural scene. Blake might dislike Burke's treatise on the grounds that it smacked of Newton and Locke, but the later Romantics, who chose to encounter natural space more directly than Blake, are its heirs where they predicate a *meaningful* exchange between the psyche and the vastness which threatens to engulf it. Far from anticipating such an encounter, the pre-Romantic poets discussed by Professor Nicolson rather evade it, given as they are to the assertion of modes of relationship between man and nature that stop far short of concrete and specific interpenetration.

The natural sublime as a significant fact of major poetry in the modern era appears only with the Romantics proper. As Poggioli points out: "The coming of Romanticism introduced a novel imagination, equally hostile to the conventional and the fanciful".[8] He goes on to declare that the Romantic imagination "expanded nature into a boundless realm, which replaced the meadows and groves, as well as the orchards and gardens of traditional poetry.[9] In order to understand the strategy of Romantic poetry in relation to "infinite" space, we must look at some familiar texts in a new way.

Wordsworth's great vision of the "types and symbols of Eternity" in *The Prelude* (1799-1805) illustrates the ordering of wild nature by imagination and language. The Alpine scene is described in detail from the point of view of the traveller on the road through the "narrow chasm". The main visual extension is upward, along the line of the woods, between rock fissures, and toward the open sky. There is a sense of being hemmed in (by "the rocks that muttered close"), and even threatened, but the ultimate evaluation is favourable.

> The immeasurable height
> Of woods decaying, never to be decayed,
> The stationary blasts of waterfalls,

38

And everywhere along the hollow rent
Winds thwarting winds, bewildered and forlorn,
The torrents shooting from the clear blue sky,
The rocks that muttered close upon our ears —
Black drizzling crags that spake by the wayside
As if a voice were in them — the sick sight
And giddy prospect of the raving stream,
The unfettered clouds and region of the Heavens,
Tumult and peace, the darkness and the light —
Were all like workings of one mind, the features
Of the same face, blossoms upon one tree;
Characters of the great apocalypse,
The types and symbols of eternity,
Of first and last, and midst, and without end.[10]

The description captures a sense of struggle that might lead toward the actual alienation of consciousness from nature; but instead, the imagination holds the opposites in balance and implicates language itself in the natural process, so that the "speech" of the wild landscape is eventually heard, though not in subject and predicate order, but via what are almost pictographic symbols. In the apocalyptic Now, all the disparate elements function together and suggest mind in general, human presence, and the blossoms of a tree. The elements within a system that seem to clash may be harmonized, as systems themselves may be linked, making for a visionary unity which the poet embodies in language. What we witness here is Wordsworth's struggle to integrate an honestly recorded alien vastness into some *humanly readable* context, which he does without losing the sense of tension implicit in the encounter.

Shelley's "Mont Blanc" (1816), in its more complex vagueness, defies brief interpretation. Yet the massive descriptive apparatus, particularly in section four, suggests Alpine nature as the epitome of threatening chaos — to such an extent, in fact, that we may be reminded of the Darwinian "ice vision" of the century's end. Shelley's emphasis on the "unseen" sources of the glacier's thrust are directed toward a characterization of nature without man as a merely blank power-process. There is no doubt that the poem attempts to suggest the positive force of the imagination of the "wise, the great, and good" acting against a tendency in life and nature to dissolve everything to a nothingness. The ambiguous final lines of the poem might be read as asking what nature would be if the mind could not grasp its essential silence and emptiness as also important, and see them not as vacancy but significant. The implied answer is: chaos.

The influence of Shelley has been detected in some of Byron's renderings of sublime nature, particularly in the stanzas in "Childe Harold's Pilgrimage" (1816) which exhibit a rhapsodically transformed Lake of Geneva.[11] The agitated sensibility of the Genevan cantos of "Childe Harold" offers us an example of the spatial rapture that is so "high" and uncontrolled that it threatens finally to plunge the hero into self-destruction. In flight from physical reality, and without a coherent inner vision, the psyche seems to dissolve in space. One may recall many poetic variations on this crisis of inadequate balance rendered in terms of threatening space, among them Goethe's *"Grenzen der Menschheit"* and Shelley's "Alastor". Byron's ocean may be seen to possess the same kind of duality of threat and beneficence as his Lake Leman, but here physicality is not evaded. Childe Harold sports in the sea and rhapsodizes on its powers of destruction. Nature becomes for the poet a medium of "immersion" in a kind of sensual beatitude, which counters to some extent, with a specifically human closeness, the threatening "alien" aspects of the environment. The "pleasing fear" felt is that of one who in his daring implicitly challenges the gods, but who does so in this case by exposing himself, child-like, to their elemental power. Byron's swimmer becomes an image of not-too-calculated risk; he is one who by letting go in the moment's physical self-indulgence, remains in touch with the creative-destructive forces in nature. The strategy here almost anticipates what we shall notice later in D.H. Lawrence in paricular — the countering of "wild" nature with a "paradisal" affirmation — one spatial form juxtaposed against another. [12]

Implicit then in the Romantic apprehension of wild nature is a drive toward the primitive and the physically fulfilling, away from the social restraints of the *nomos*, away from mind and spirit as disembodied factors, but toward a meaningful knowledge which includes many kinds of value. A.O. Lovejoy's well-known distinction between "Romantic primitivism" and "Romantic dualism" reminds us that the concrete renderings of much of Romantic literature may carry us directly to the body itself, literally "alive" with meaning; or else we may take a step further back, from where we see the physical element dissolve in a kind of spiritual essence. [13] Such drifts are usually only irreconcilable at the strictest analytic level, from a point of view quite removed from the work; and such irreconcilability is irrelevant unless the experience of the work is taken to be the measure of its abstractions. Yet Lovejoy has a valid point, which can be extended to suggest that the later, diverging perspectives of Symbolism and Naturalism signalled a final splitting up of the great synthesis found in the most comprehensive Romantic poetry. While in such poetry the imagination works to render vast nature meaningful, and assertions of unity do not usually exclude an awareness of the body, in the generalized religiosity *cum* sensuality of many lesser poems, we see the beginnings of a dissociation in which "higher" values do not seem to flow from a concretely rendered center with energies radiating out to suggest what lies beyond.

Byron, for example, is significant because his lack of faith in the imagination could lead him to display the gestures of Romantic redemption of space, without always controlling the sweep of his ecstatic apostrophes. Childe Harold caught up in nature seems often as helpless as some hero of Naturalism, under the sway of abstract physical "Forces". The gestures of confusion, from a distance, may look like the gestures of despair. Yet when, as in Childe Harold's apostrophe to the ocean, body, psyche and environment are nearly reconciled in the moment, a many-dimensioned meaning, not summed up by being tagged as "anti-nomian", replaces the confusion, and we feel Byron's sincerity and the coherence of his vision. Even so, such an emphasis reminds us not so much of Wordsworth or Keats, with their more complex sense of "process", as of Chateaubriand and Balzac.

Chateaubriand, whom Humboldt in *Cosmos* (1845 and f.) singled out as the only living representative of the art of poetic landscape he cared to name, we know as a master of a new kind of objective description. Inheritor of the tradition of Bernadin de Saint-Pierre (whom Humboldt and his travelling companion Bonpland read constantly in the tropics), and of Rousseau, Chateaubriand tried to exclude the classical mythology that he felt would blur the effect he aimed at. "*La mythologie si vantée, loin d'embellir la nature, en detruit les véritables charmes...*" he wrote.[14] To imbue the landscape with sentiment, and to sustain a certain level of precision were Chateaubriand's aims. T.C. Walker, who has made a close study of Chateaubriand's descriptive art, points to his emphasis on the forces outside of the characters, to his escape from psychology and a certain kind of myth, as a foreshadowing of French Realism.[15] Chateaubriand is interesting in another respect, however, for his spiritual energizing of landscape is sustained by his Christianity, which serves "officially" as the "inner" principle here as it could not for Byron; while his faith in the body, in antimonian delight, is often as vividly expressed as Byron's. A.O. Lovejoy, writing of *Atala* (1801) points to the distinct conflict or at least tension between these elements.[16] In *Atala*, the primitive wilderness is at once an environment conducive to "exotic" and dangerous passions and the living manifestation of the God of Reason, as interpreted by Father Aubry. The hermit's ideal is not identifiable with the extreme chastity we witness in Atala's vow, nor does it embrace the hardly bridled lust of the young Chactas. The hermit affirms the natural law as interpreted by rational insight over primitive energies, yet the narrative as a whole seems suspended between alterna-tives which can only be reconciled at a certain level of generalized exaltation.

Chateaubriand and Byron are alike in evading the sense of sin be-queathed to them with their conventional metaphysical assumptions by a visionary assertion which overrides but does not conceal a lack of inner coherence. Because they fail to find a consistent principle of transforma-tion, they force upon us an abiding sense of physical and spiritual dissociation. Their uneasy reconciliation of discordant elements con-trasts with the more radical solution of many of their contemporaries and

41

foreshadows the fracturing of the Romantic vision of unity between self and cosmos under the new thrust of nineteenth century science. Chateaubriand and Byron dramatize heroic gestures in which the individual self projects a mood of benevolence upon sublime nature; but such a mood may be reversed in a moment, as "The Ancient Mariner" and many another great Romantic poem shows. An imaginative principle of coherence must embody the power to endure negativity, and the poet must be prepared to affirm the larger reality that includes time and change. It is not a pulse of feeling, but a vision that is called for, a sustained inner power to see beyond the contraries of the moment. At the nadir of feeling vast spaces may become an abyss of threat; Chateaubriand and Byron, free with their ecstasies, are often perilously close to evoking the vastness of the Void.

Balzac's famous story "A Passion in the Desert" (1832) by contrast, shows a triumph over the Void through an acceptance of the flesh which engenders its own spiritual values.Here, the desert is not merely a traditional symbol but an environment rendered credible through the energy of a newly confident realism. The story tells of a Provençal soldier who is separated from his comrades and familiar terrain and brought face to face with the power of vast nature, the desert of North Africa. The landscape is an occasion of terror for him, but Balzac's description by no means divests it of positive qualities. It is a landscape of power and naked beauty, but on an inhuman scale. The hardness and clarity are emphasized in imagery which suggests a world far distant from flesh and blood; and that this is a kind of universal sublime is conveyed by the sustained comparison with the sea. If vast nature, here in the form of the steely desert, is a mirror, man is not what it reflects.

The soldier's first recovery is marked by a seizing upon of familiar elements: the remains of human habitation, the more comfortable scale of distance provided by the trees of an oasis. At this point, a threatening panther appears, the very symbol of the unassimilated instinct of primitive nature. Balzac dramatizes the affiliation between the soldier and the deeps of nature in terms of a sexual metaphor: the panther is female — dangerous, magnificent, and by turns frightening and beneficent. The soldier literally makes contact with the inhuman distances through his new fleshly life, through his "animal passion". "The solitude revealed to him all of its secrets, and enveloped him in its charms. He discovered, in the rising and setting of the sun, sights unknown on earth. He knew what it was to tremble when he heard over his head the soft beat of the wing of a bird — rare visitors — and watched the travelling clouds melting and changing, colour upon colour." What the soldier gains is a kind of visionary power, one which does not omit perception of the destructive side of nature, but which represents all the more a newly valid and intense kind of knowing, one which lifts the soldier beyond the conventionality of his past life. He is immersed in a new time-flow,

42

integrated in the rhythm of his environment, open to a pulse of knowledge in which the vast energies of nature are transformed into a humanly graspable fact. The recognition of the "soul" in the beast occurs in the golden magic of a sunset which enshrines neither ordinary rationality nor the effusiveness of a conventional religious vision; abandonment of the flesh, here not hedged in by lingering moral scruples, humanizes the wilderness. Interiority and integration emerge through the quickened sensual life; spirituality and fleshly knowledge are inseparable. When the soldier murders the panther and breaks the contact with his environment, he manifests the unpredictable perversity of many Romantic heroes. In one sense we are shown how man kills his deepest relationship to nature through lack of faith in instinct; yet, in another sense, the relationship between man and beast can be seen as necessarily limited. When the link is broken, the soldier returns to ordinary life, but he carries with him the mark of his transformation; to him the desert has become beautiful; it is, in fact, "God without mankind", the enclosing spatial magnificence which is meaningful beyond human definition, but which, given the appropriate conditions, can become a medium of human *redefinition*.

French culture, from Chateaubriand to Gauguin and Gide, delivers itself from the curse of bourgeois "fact" by a search for the exoticism that sometimes releases buried artistic and spiritual energies, while American literature reveals vistas of prairie and ocean framed by the questing imagination. Poe's "A Descent into the Maelstrom" (1841) leads us back to the problem of the psyche threatened by the blank phenomena of nature. Not the glacier world of "Mont Blanc", but the coiling, destructive sea, is the central image, though the story opens on the edge of a towering precipice:

A panorama more deplorably desolate no human imagination can conceive. To the right and left, as far as the eye could reach, there lay outstretched, like ramparts of the world, lines of horridly black and beetling cliff, whose character of gloom was but the more forcibly illustrated by the surf which reared high up against it its white and ghastly crest, howling and shrieking forever . . .

Poe's elaborate narrative framework establishes a receptive listener in the opening scene of the tale. We are shown the fisherman after his encounter with the maelstrom, in a state of nerves and with prematurely whitened hair. The narrator unfolds an elaborate "scientific" description which the succeeding story shows to be merely a surface rendering of the *experience* of the maelstrom itself. We are to be brought face to face with the desolating challenge of the epigraph, ostensibly from Glanvill, but modified by Poe for his own purposes:

The ways of God in Nature, as in Providence, are not as *our* ways; nor are the models that we frame any way commensurate to the vastness, profundity, and unsearchableness of his works, *which have a depth in them greater than the well of Democritus.*

It is precisely the skill with which this metaphysical challenge is embodied in the very imagery of the story itself that enables us to measure the range of Poe's demonic wit. The well of Democritus, however deep, should hold the truth, but what "truth" can structure, what model can be adequate to, the vast reaches of sublime nature? Certainly, the "documentation" of science seems ludicrously irrelevant after we have actually been taken inside the maelstrom through the fisherman's narrative.

> The rays of the moon seemed to search the very bottom of the profound gulf; but still I could make out nothing distinctly, on account of a thick mist in which everything there was enveloped, and over which there hung a magnificent rainbow, like that narrow and tottering bridge which Musselmen say is the only pathway between Time and Eternity . . .

Here Poe captures the shock of the destructive element; sublime nature is envisaged as a vortex in which humanity and human invention are swallowed up. The nature which expresses itself in such a phenomenon may or may not be ultimately measurable in a human frame of reference; what is certain here is its inhuman majesty, its connection with some power that links time and eternity. Poe's solution, the solution of one who in an early sonnet had already lamented the demythologizing effect of science, is remarkable. The fisherman avoids the "profound gulf" by calling upon his observation, and by making use of the law of buoyancy, to float himself free. His escape is a product of his ability to control those feelings of terror that first seize him, so that he *analyzes* the action of the whirlpool, and reaches the calm sea. Is reason then the path out of the storm? Poe's story points up the growing dichotomy between mind and feeling that nineteenth century science forces upon the inheritors of the Romantic tradition. Poe's fisherman saves himself from destruction by exercising that "ratiocination" that Poe fell back on when the maelstrom of vast nature seemed otherwise unfathomable. Although, unlike Arnold's Empedocles, he escapes the gulf, he pays a price: nor is his triumph more than a minimal achievement against the memory of the disturbing vistas of moonlight and water, of that perspective "downward" where human vision fails to reach. Poe's story reveals the imagination groping to order and humanize the vast nature of brute power and mechanics, behind which may or may not lurk some ultimate metaphysical darkness — but here the resolution fails to involve new knowledge (as in the Balzac story) — here the question has become one of survival.

By mid-century the Romantic drive to humanize vast nature had spent itself and the latest great paradigmatic shift in scientific thinking began to force literature to new perceptions of man's place in the world. To the sense of sublime space or of Newtonian mechanics without, Darwinism would add a conviction of mechanism which includes the human subject. The integrative power of the imagination threatened to dissolve; the body seemed trapped by its own incorrigibly bestial impulses, while the alienated mind could only contemplate forlorn unities. Though this may

44

be a fair generalization, one must not oversimplify developments. Realism itself is only a first response to the impact of the new scientific vision; literature struggles to reassert the human scale, but an integrating principle is slow to emerge. Almost every work can be seen as a battleground in which the writer fights to relocate values in a vast nature increasingly bereft of them, and searches for a language which would do justice to the scientific vision while restoring man to a meaningful scale in the space that calls his values into question. The key is a shift in the relationship between mind and body, and an assimilation of the Darwinian sense of struggle into a vision of spiritual order.

Tennyson and Arnold, those representative Victorians, evoked for their age the sense of space and time as awesome realities and are not far removed from Naturalism, in which man is so often dwarfed and humbled by nature's vastness. Arnold's humanism fails to develop an answer much beyond stoical resolution, while Tennyson's *In Memoriam* dramatizes fully a sense of the mechanical flux which shatters what Wordsworth had assumed to be the human unity. Brute nature is rejected but may be redeemed in evolutionary time by Christ, the spiritual principle who is affirmed in a love which verges on both mysticism and nostalgia. Such a novel vision may be compared with the tensioned but disciplined restatement of the Christian synthesis by Hopkins. In such a poem as "That Nature is a Heraclitean Fire and of the Comfort of the Resurrection" (1888), Hopkins assures us that though "vastness blurs and time beats level" the immortal transformation of our "mortal trash" is the very substance of the overall cosmic progress.

While Tennyson and Hopkins struggle to express a new human confidence *vis à vis* vast nature, Walt Whitman's many evocations of sublime nature are marked by a sense of exhilaration based on other sources. To Whitman, whether "inhuman" in its implications, or directly serving man, nature can only be encountered with the deepest levels of the self. Eastern mysticism *via* Transcendentalism, and an inheritance of Fichtean Romanticism, do not dilute Whitman's massive acceptance of the concrete physicality, but rather serve to provide a principle of integration for "the ten thousand things", whether these are encountered in a vision of the maelstrom, or in a view of the azure heavens. In such poems as "The World Below the Brine" (1860) Whitman sustains positives and negatives within a totality of vision, that in its scope, takes us back to the great Romantics. But his almost unfailing confidence in the power of the ego and the liberated flesh is one line of development against the threat of inhuman distance hatched by the pure intellectualism of nineteenth century science. In Lawrencian terms, only the "disembodied mind" can be at the mercy of sublime space; Whitman's spatial realm, vast as it is, and as full of "wars, pursuits, tribes" as it is, is never an occasion of terror. "The World Below the Brine" leads us from the maelstrom of leviathan to the spheres where as

45

Lawrence would put it, one not only *moves*, but where one can *be*. With Whitman, as with the Naturalists, life itself becomes the key value, but whereas Naturalism presses space *down* upon the individual, Whitman's poetry sweeps him up into it: in becoming truly himself, in realizing himself as integrated flesh-spirit, Whitman's solitary becomes a new kind of cosmic man — and the measure of his strength is the measure of the courage required to break through all the deep shadows of guilt and doubt telling against his self-annunciation.

Darwinism expressed itself as a development of forms in space through time, scaled to a vastness that could daunt poetic confidence in man's potential for realizing his inner space. What emerged in Naturalism was a sense of the species as a whole, carried along by the mysterious energies of life, toward unknown destinies. The individual was often placed in a landscape that threatened to overwhelm him, a landscape given the tone of a "primordial" world, rendered in terms of the "inorganic" forces of great masses of rock, in terms of glacier or desert, or of the "empty" vastness of outer space. Yet various strategies were at work to redeem the bleakness, and to understand Darwinism's transformation of man's sense of sublime nature, it is necessary to examine more closely one or two of the great modern works in which this image predominates.

Joseph Conrad's massive devotion to the rendering of the visible aspects of the material universe was an integral part of his central aesthetic and moral concern. In *A Personal Record* (1912), he suggests:

> And the unwearied self-forgetful attention to every phase of the living universe reflected in our consciousness may be our appointed task on this earth — a task in which fate has perhaps engaged nothing of us except our conscience, gifted with a voice in order to bear true testimony to the visible wonder, the haunting terror, the infinite passion, and the illimitable serenity; to the supreme law and the abiding mystery of the sublime spectacle.
>
> (Chapter Five)

Conrad's versions of natural sublime sum up not only an actual experience of consciousness encountering the untamed in sea or tropical jungle, but also a specific metaphysical and moral configuration that derives from a particular world in which "all is seared with trade; bleared, smeared with toil". Conrad writes as an exile and agnostic, finding nature to be a panorama of effects offering no intrinsically meaningful pattern. "The immense indifference of things", however, is the product of not merely a philosophical pessimism, but of the experience of a world in which the moral darkness of exploitation seemed to dominate man's encounter with nature. Conrad's nature is a sphere of challenge in which the kind of moral complacency encouraged by civilized life will be tested to the utmost. Conrad's Darwinism is real and central but not because it suggests a redemption in any primordial ecstasy. To Conrad, Darwinian adaptation is refined to a point of moral coherence; the fittest who survive are those who have won through to an inner life that is strong enough to resist the temptations of the bestial.

46

Nearly all of Conrad's characters share part of the guilt of western man and face a nature which is a dark reflection of human evil.

Wild nature in Conrad functions as a central environment dramatizing man's sense of alienation — a natural world in which primitive struggle is the ultimate reality becomes the testing ground for the individual's power of survival as a moral entity. The illusions that may be momentarily sustained in what Conrad sees as the shared guilt of modern civilization are inevitably lost by the individual in the environment of primitive nature, where he will be thrown back upon his own intrinsic stuff. Conrad's nature is one of the touchstones of modern existential humanism, and as such could not fail to arouse the resistance of Lawrence, who was to push Darwinism much farther toward a recovery of meaningful integration between man and cosmos. In *Women in Love*, however, Lawrence's own vision of nature reproduces the bleak contours of Conrad's world, precisely because at that point Lawrence is most fully engaged with the negative exploitative drives of western industrial man.

To pinpoint Conrad's image of wild nature it is necessary to concentrate on some of the passages from well-known works of his maturity, ignoring the very earliest writings with their lush tropical atmospheres and also the later more urban-centered novels. "Before the Congo I was a simple animal", Conrad confessed, and *Heart of Darkness* (1898-9), from every angle of critical judgment, testifies to a sense of moral shock that encompasses the horror of what "man has made of man". Notable in the story are the links perceived between the civilized sources of the darkness and the jungle outposts where rationality itself seems to fail. The connection between Thames and Congo is one obvious example of Conrad's historical vision of the progress of conquest and imperialist transformation of the wilderness. Nature is alien partially because man has alienated himself from it, but Conrad sees no possibility of a reversal of western "progress" in any break with the process of historical development of civilization. In such a situation, what is important is the way in which the individual faces the necessary guilt of his participation in the seemingly inevitable development of industrial civilization, a development apparently inseparable from exploitation and injustice. Marlow survives due to his devotion to the work ethic of the seaman; he pulls the steamer's whistle at the critical point when contact with the darkness has served its purpose of awakening him to the fact of his own unhealthy fascination with Kurtz. Kurtz, it is implied, has gone mad — his noble idealism masks obsession and a kind of savagery. Participation in some hideous form of primitive ritual is suggested. But wild nature offers a mystery to which there is no initiation. Conrad pictures it as resistant to the penetration of enterprise and "development", but this is not the central issue. What is central is the vulnerability of the individual psyche and its dangerous temptations in a world deprived of clear moral imperatives.

47

Despite some touches in the famous jungle descriptions that suggest a vengeful nature, we are meant to see through Marlow not God's wrath but man's encounter with the darkness of his own projecting. Conrad's nature remains morally neutral; it is not an actual sphere of evil, though it is a poor model for human morality, as Mill argued. Man's kinship with savagery is real, and can only be met with discipline not with principles. An implicit distinction suggests itself here between the Africans, who have worked out rituals to control the dark impulses and the European cut adrift from his own social order, to whom the plunge into the primitive world would mean destruction. Conrad writes as one who refuses to blur the distinctive levels of civilization, who offers no alternative to the western drive toward control of nature, yet who criticizes it as a doom-ridden journey in which man can never be free from the evil that accompanies all his ostensibly noble enterprises. Like Wells, Conrad sees primordialism largely in terms of brutalizing instincts, and society as a tenuous and inadequate structure that cannot always protect us from our own worst impulses. Unlike Wells at some moments, and unlike Lawrence throughout, Conrad rejects any notion that the power of instinct can retrieve what is lost in the action of misguided idealism. Conrad's nature is a fallen world, but redemption involves neither metaphysical extension, nor an antinomian descent into the wisdom of the body: redemption occurs when the power of action is sustained in a moment which is a precarious balance of the ideal and the animal drives, when positive habit and specific perception combine to carry a human being forward to some real goal.

The most effective rendering of the encounter between man and sublime nature in Conrad occurs perhaps in *Typhoon* (1902), where the language is clarified to a degree not always characteristic of this writer, and where the themes emerge directly and strikingly from the form. Captain MacWhirr's engagement with the typhoon is presented in the imagery of contest. Nature may not always challenge in such a direct manner, but against MacWhirr she vents her force in a terrific storm that is matched by his determined voice — the power of the "within" against the force "without". MacWhirr's culminating cry of "all right" is more eloquent than any laboured rhetoric, and it outsounds the storm. The ship, product of man's technology and greed as well as of his noble enterprise, is "looted", and the hoardings of the coolies hopelessly mixed up. MacWhirr, having been tested in the actualities of experience, intervenes with a renewed energy to settle the "economics" of the situation. Discipline in duty and clarity of vision enable a man to operate with probity in a questionable overall system. Experience is more important than theories; one does not navigate around typhoons by means of abstract readings. It is not a question of intelligence, or of "instinct", but of perception, and courage. In summary, it is clear that Conrad's rendering of man's relation to sublime nature turns on the creation of a moral environment: he meets Darwinism with an option which takes him away in the end from any attempt to restore values to man by invoking the physical system itself as a constituent of the "within". As we have seen, literature is quite capable of engaging Darwinism in this latter, more complex fashion. Let us now examine one such engagement, perhaps the most notable attempt of modern fiction to transform the bleak vastness of Darwinian nature into a vision of spiritual order.

Johannes V. Jensen's *The Long Journey* (1924), a set of novels which brought him the Nobel Prize, is a prose epic of evolution; human history is recounted as a passage from nature to culture to spirit. Through a succession of rebellions of the individual against the group, the human mass is raised from savagery. Sublime nature is depicted as the permanent background to the activities of man; he breaks through the limitations of each relationship he forms with it only to find himself encountering a new challenge. Thus, human perspective constantly shifts to wider and wider horizons, though Jensen builds toward this sense of universal human consciousness from the most limited regional setting in Denmark's Jutland. Jensen's vision is one of biological struggle resulting in adaption to a specific environmental situation. The adaptation leads to stability and the stability is challenged by the discontent of the born leader or visionary. Jensen's imagery is transformational; human cultural development is suggested by a continuous series of operations in which natural materials are remoulded into objects that become symbols of various stages of progress; one invention leads to the next until we have the whole complex of modern technology. The Darwinian vision of man the toolmaker is retained in a quest narrative that has other affiliations. Physical motion in space-time, and the growth of the human cultural apparatus are depicted so as to suggest the widening of human awareness, manifested in various myths, which Jensen relates at every point to a specific interaction of man and nature. The time-sequence is speeded up as we move toward the present, and clashes between various offshoots of human culture provide a wider dynamic. There is a certain insistence on violence, curious linkings of persons and factors historically separate and a strong sense of the value of the blood-consciousness. The several books of the novel are structured as dramatic contrasts between the temptations of the Edenic and the challenge of the sublime. While Eden may be consolatory for a while, and is an enduring myth or race memory, escape from Eden is the precondition of advancement. Jensen's Eden, or the "Lost Land" is the warm forest of prehistoric Europe; when this vanishes with the coming of the Ice Ages, most men flee southward, even though fire has been invented, and one cycle of human ingenuity is complete. The hero of the second part of the epic, Carl, remains to face the challenge of the ice, and eventually rediscovers fire. Carl's shadow dominates the primeval sea, forecasting the emergence of humanity from the swarm of life to dominance. Become an amphibian, and in the

Cambrian swamp, he first sees the milky sun among the lush vegetation that millions of years later will be transformed into coal, providing man with a remote form of solar energy. His vision of the salamander, projected as his soul, reminds us again of man's association with fire: for the salamander lives in fire, and is the symbol of the element fire. The next vision carries Carl to the streets of modern Chicago, where warmth and light are the product of the fern forests, and a great flywheel sums up the centuries of man's invention. Jensen's poetic linkings miraculously expand the reader's imagination, but all is rooted in Darwinism. The spiritual consolations derive from an acceptance of the apparently brutal "facts" of science. The pattern, however, enables us to see the facts as transformed. At the next stage of Carl's vision we are brought face to face with eternity through the poetic rendering of sublime space. Carl has died but once again restrikes the fire-stone:

> A flood of unearthly light about him! He is in the midst of the Forest of the Living. The soil is of skin with coarse pores, here and there overgrown with hair and in places hardened to black-and-white striped horn. Hills and the long folds of valleys show where the earth's bones protrude and where miles of ribs run, and the plains are strewed with blocks of old blanced bone . . . .
>
> The forest extends, flesh-coloured and boundless, as far as the eye can see, and the air is so clear that it ranges for hundeds of leagues. In some places, far and near, it is flecked by shadows, and these shadows seem to be of a definite oval form and to move slowly over the landscape . . . . The vast size of these flying ovals makes the forest and everything on earth seem low and small. But the red light in the sky above the flying things draws the eye higher, and soon even they are forgotten like motes in the air, for the vault of heaven ranges away into infinite space.
>
> The universe is of a glorious colour like the flush of dawn, the very source from which all feeble myths of the joy of life are derived. A sun lies quite near but does not dazzle the eye, so that he can see the wonderful gaseous body resting in its prolific spherical being, expanding and contracting, rarer than air and yet tense, like a swarm of bees in the free summer air; round about it hang many planets in their happy orbits, and in the background a host of constellations proclaim that untold suns are circling each for itself, solitary but in freedom after the same blest laws of flight. Blue and yellow spheres hang quite near, so that the lines of their continents can be described. Milky ways lying billions of miles away swim like fine clouds in the universe.[17]

(Fire and Ice, Chapter Ten)

Man and nature are imagined together in the forest of the living. The forest is collective, yet each individual counts as part of the immortal species, which stretches from the past to the future. Jensen records the achievement of flight in the description of the dirigible balloons, which, like all of man's inventions, reiterate organic shapes. The whole universe extends in fiery grandeur through infinite space, taking the shape of a wheel. We have moved from microcosm to macrocosm, from time to eternity, from flesh to spirit. This passage, like almost every climactic point in these novels, looks forward to the grand conclusion, which sums

50

up Jensen's transformative vision. This conclusion, entitled "Ave Stella", shifts the emphasis from the consistent Promethean challenge. The earth itself has become "spaceship earth" (the concept belongs to Jensen) and is dominated now by man's cultural activities, an earth which consciousness has engirdled, and which faces the stars. The cosmic woman who hovers over the earth, the feminine spirit, composed of light upon light, is in one sense Venus, the morning star; in another:

... Life, the stem of Life beyond the aether, from which the germs have come to earth; true Life the source of Love, of which we can know no more than longing teaches us.

Have the creatures of Earth, through a long process of life and change — approximate, faulty, abandoned and taken up again — been seeking a form for an eternal, intrinsic, unknown type existing on other stars?

Ave Stella!

(*Christopher Columbus*, Book III, Chapter Four)

The "masculine" striving into sublime nature has raised man to a state of consciousness in which he perceives the "feminine" opposite leading onward from struggle and fleshly existence toward a spiritual dimension. Life, perhaps itself from beyond the stars, must return, ennobled, to the stars. It is an old vision, one buried deep in the Gnostic sources of western tradition, but stated in new terms by Jensen so as to carry us from the physical, measured world of science to a realm of value that science sometimes seemed to deny.

What conclusions can we draw from these brief references to some of the great nineteenth and twentieth century texts which offer an image of boundless nature? Arguably, the Romantics succeeded to a remarkable degree in their various attempts to render meaningful the vast spaces of nature opened up by the earlier scientific revolution. In the greatest Romantic landscapes consciousness interlocks with physical and natural energies to yield a spiritual order that is the product of experience of the specific but which reaches out to embrace the universal scene. As belief in the power of the Romantic imagination faded under the assault of the new utilitarianism and science-inspired mechanism, however, fresh strategies had to be found to deal with the nature of struggle and blind impulse from which man seemed more than ever alienated. The writers following closely after Darwin had to face the challenge of a new vastness which seemed to diminish the scope of conscious values, while reducing the human body itself to a battleground of primordial impulses. A new sense of the within, a new interiority was sought, at first quite crudely, through the values of the body and in the name of a vague life energy, but ultimately through a natural piety associated with the more balanced perspectives of a universal ecology in which man had a valid place. The problem was complicated, however, by the fact that the vastness of pure space apprehended by the Romantics had become, with the discoveries of geology, a vastness of space and time, and that the end of time was sometimes seen as a doomsday of negative entropy, while the supposed

51

mechanisms of life and mind had their brutal coordinates in the cultural sphere, in what Lewis Mumford has ironically called the nineteenth century "paleo-technic paradise" — thus making humanistic affirmation difficult on every level.

The widening of human perspectives fostered by science in the modern era has had fruitful issue in the post-Darwinian or ecological period that comprises the present and the recent past. If, in much recent literature, the sense of vast nature as a threat, that sense of the "malady of space-time" defined by Teilhard de Chardin and others, has been less acute, it may be partially attributed to the fact that the kind of realism we are discussing here has itself been less central. As Gaston Bachelard and others have shown, images of vastness often become part of a complex spatial rendering that takes us far beyond the primary act of mimesis. Yet there is also a new realism which strikes a balance between the positive and negative apprehension of nature's sublime distances.[18] In one of the liveliest veins of this new realism, in science fiction, for example, man's encounter with infinity is often depicted with great steadiness, and in ways far removed from, but intimately connected with, the visions of those who, like Galileo, pushed out human imaginative frontiers by means of the simple technology of the very first telescope.

CHAPTER TWO
The Image of the Field

The image of the field suggests the cooperation of man and nature. It is through agriculture that man has usually tamed the wilderness and built his civilizations, and the field may be seen as a median point between the primal world of nature and the advanced world of urban technology. In the image of the field we are aware of social and collective factors not present with the same explicitness in the images of sublime or paradisal nature, and any analysis of the literature of the field must include a definite social reference. For this reason, it seems proper to keep in mind the agricultural variants actually visible in nineteeth century history — the activities of both "pleasant" and "pioneer" — though in what follows I shall deal only with the former.

Peasant and pioneer works demonstrating a significant descriptive element share a common ecological frame of reference. Pioneers are those who are depicted as settling a wilderness, transforming wild nature into a new social order; and whereas the peasant consciousness suggests place-rootedness, timelessness, a sense of stability and harmony within a hierarchic order, the pioneer consciousness evokes a sense of mobility, egalitarianism, the profit-motive, telescoped time-sequences, and a sub-urban end-point. Consider, for example, what Frank Norris had to do in order to adapt Zola's soil Naturalism to the American scene. Or compare the consolation Tolstoy's Levin takes from his peasants with what Willa Cather's Jim Burden (in *My Antonia*) takes from the pioneer Shimerdas clan. The pioneer novel often focuses on the future, the archetype of the child, or laments the lost energy of the heroic settlers, whereas the peasant novel often centers on the archetype of the old man, and cel-ebrates the recovery of ancient wisdom, or the tragic suffering of the worker in the field. The ecological reality underlying both kinds of literature is "the field". The image of the field always suggests con-nection with the soil, place-stability, dependence on the seasons, certain rhythms of planting and harvest, and so on. And in both cases we observe the human figure in a landscape involving horizontal perspectives toward man-made boundaries, a generally middle-distance view of men and women at work transforming nature into nurture.

Though we may be inclined to think of the literature of the peasant as part of the history of nineteenth century Realism, to understand the image of the field *per se*, we must turn to the Romantics. Romantic literature contained within itself the early fruition of that complex idolization of the peasant which had its roots in the eighteenth century.[1] For one thing, Romanticism coincided with the initial polarization of city and country that was taking place as the Industrial Revolution manifested itself in its first faint stirrings. Furthermore, the "nature" that the new science had examined in the broad dimensions of physics and astronomy had by this time come to include also the local rural scene, which could increasingly be affiliated to larger conceptions, as part of a newly perceived set of objective relations. We can understand, too, how the blow to the principles of the *ancien régime* dealt in the French Revolution could destroy further possibilities of envisaging country life in the old pastoral terms: the new version was to be embodied in the figure of the working peasant, and was no longer framed as an imaginative masquerade of shepherds and shepherdesses, to be played out in court and castle. What is more, the nationalism that grew up in the wake of Napoleon caused a turning toward the rural world as a source of the strength of "*Das Volk*". While Herder, for example, had emphasized the sharing of a common culture as the foundation of a common political identity, and had stressed the cosmopolitan aspect of folk-song, the German Romantics (Arnim and Brentano, e.g.) promoted the goal of the literary expression of the common life of the people, which meant specifically the German people, and their agricultural life, since there was little urbanization.[2] The sense of an organic link through the people to the past brought together medievalism and the interest in the peasant, for the peasant was a connection with the past, a living embodiment of the medieval world.

Recalling the encroachments of urban on rural life in the nineteenth and twentieth centuries, we can see, then, a conflict of two forms of consciousness, with the creative literature of the period anticipating the later insights of the social theorists in its generally sympathetic rendering of the peasant life-order. This life-order is first of all based on an ancient relation to the land, and secondly, on the specific conditions of the European Christian tradition, in which the stable "estate" of the peasantry with its medieval foundations, was subjected everywhere ultimately to the pressures of a rapidly developing urban technological base.[3]

Taking into account principally the writer's measure of identification with the peasant life depicted, considering his angle of approach, perspective, and the degree of ironical detachment, it is possible to divide the modern writing of this kind into two streams. In the first of these, the writer seeks to dramatize the integral peasant life, usually in the name of a conservative or communal moral sense. The goal here is often identification with the peasant consciousness in all its strength of endurance and in the place-relation we have already commented upon. The Christian or pagan matrix with its darkness, unconsciousness, and sense of suffering is presented as an integral "world"; and we are led to view it either as a battleground of spiritual powers, or as a closeknit realm dominated by the experience of the senses in relation to the soil and its cultural offshoots.

The second kind of story, which can be termed the novel of "double consciousness", sees the narrator's emphasis divided between the concrete qualities of the surviving rural life and the triumphant reality of the city. It may take the form of an attempt by a sophisticated outsider to reach some kind of identification with the peasant world, or it may make use of the "return of the native" structure. In any case, ironies abound, and in some late versions of this second kind of peasant novel the narratives may become retrospective or outrightly nostalgic, or else the peasant's life in the field may be seen as a fossilized order, doomed by the encroachments of urban life.

There is no simple chronological relation between these two kinds of fiction. While the "integral" novels tend to be the earlier ones, it was still possible for the French novelist Jean Giono, for example, to write such a novel in the nineteen thirties (Cf. his *Regain*, 1930). Furthermore, within the larger framework of these narrative strategies, many specific kinds of novelistic tactic may be evident. The novel of double consciousness may be a *Bildungsroman* or a picaresque tale, and the specific tone of the narrative in relation to the material still remains to be explicated by the critic. In what follows, we shall look more closely at both types of story, as they emerge from the Romantic preoccupation with rural and agricultural themes.

Wordsworth's theory and practice mark a decisive phase in the rendering of the image of the field. The "Preface to Lyrical Ballads" (1800), though the outcome of a long preparatory theorizing by various eighteenth century aestheticians, crystallizes notions of the value of rural life in the famous phrases which themselves sometimes expand into demonstrative metaphors: "Humble and rustic life was generally chosen, because in that condition the essential passions of the heart *find a better soil* in which they can attain their maturity . . ."; and also, " . . . the manners or rural life *germinate* from those elementary feelings . . ." and so on. We know that Wordsworth's theory involves certain assumptions about the emotional origin of language, that it implies a uniformitarian view of human nature, and that the shift to "low" subjects is made possible by his faith in the reservoir of feelings common to mankind. Clearly, Wordsworth's standard of "nature" is complex, and revives the apparently inexhaustible dichotomy of *physis* and *nomos* in favour of a poetry that will circumvent the artificial so as to arrive at the universal expression of the human essence in a given situation. Yet it is clear too that the mission of the individual poet is in no way derogated, but rather framed as the application of a spontaneity which is the product of intellectual discipline. Thus we get the characteristic Wordworthian tension between the

55

ordinariness of the life in some cases to be treated, and the relatively "high" role of the poet who, from an experience felt in the real world, and subsequently meditated upon, must shape that "new emotion" of the poem, losing nothing of universality in the process, and giving pleasure in the product, though the subject be painful. In this situation "the real world" is usually the essential world of rural life, characterized by artless speech and elementary feelings, the life that shows the "passions of men" incorporated with "the beautiful and permanent forms of nature". Wordsworth offers us the image of the poet moving through the locale, through the agricultural world which remains partially "natural", to find his way to the larger nature which is meaningful beyond the chaos of passing time. This is not merely to put grandiosely Wordsworth's perception of what Abrams sums up as "the subject matter of the ways and speech of men living close to the soil, comparatively insulated from the rapid changes of life and manners in the urban world."[4] If Wordsworth, "by doctrine and example, brought into the literary province the store of materials which has since been richly exploited by writers from Thomas Hardy to William Faulkner", it remains to be seen exactly how such a "store of materials" functions in relation to the poet's specific mission, and what connections it enables us to establish between him and his successors.

That Wordsworth is most often a poet of double consciousness, that his image of the field involves a perspective of the sophisticated on the simple, is a fact that cannot be divorced either from his poetic theory, or from his position in English society at a time when the polarity of city and country was beginning to mean more than a choice of residences for the gentleman. The civilized man, of whom the poet is a representative, is aware of the fact of death and change, yet hemmed in by encroaching trivialities. He meets this by the power of the imagination to challenge time, by cultivating an ability to recapture the past (which includes a childhood of more immediate relation to nature), and by the ability to move directly from the concrete experience to the larger process. But it is not only "vision" in the sense of the individual psyche's penetration of non-human reality that is relevant, but also the poet's power to evoke human examplars. Wordworth's ideal poet characteristically seeks a link with the almost preverbal level of the rustic. One aspect of this would-be simplification of language is the striving for an image of what such "silent speech" should sound like. The achievement of the outsider, of the self-conscious man, is incomplete without this link to what is falsified in being expressed in sophisticated terms. Wordsworth's interest in the "peasant consciousness" is a result of his grasp of its relative wholeness and stability. In "The Solitary Reaper" (1805), for example, we are made aware of the power of the human figure to fill out the environment; the voice of the highland girl breathes signigicance into the landscape. She is the anonymous, tireless worker in the field, whose song must go on forever. The outsider, the poetic consciousness, carries away the *music* of her song; assimilates its inner significance, its message of endurance, but does not "translate" it. The distance is maintained.

If the Wordsworthian solitaries speak their own wordless language, it is no theological or mystagogic message that they imply. What they have achieved is a calm living with death and hardship; the key fact is their power of inter-relationship with the environment. Like the Leech-gatherer, or the old soldier, they endure. The sophisticated narrative consciousness carries away that fact above all, a precious knowledge of the possibility of survival, and not merely one achieved at the price of an aristocratic stoicism. For the survival is in joy. This we learn, for example, in the narrative of "The Ruined Cottage" (1797-99), which places us at double remove from the suffering Margaret. In one of the versions Wordsworth completed before yielding to the temptations of piety, we are given (through the old peddler Armytage) the natural fact in all its density as something to be loved despite its killing power.

"I well remember that those very plumes,
Those weeds, and the high spear grass on that wall,
By mist and silent raindrops silvered o'er,
As once I passed, did to my mind convey
So still an image of tranquillity,
So calm and still, and looked so beautiful
Amid the uneasy thoughts which filled my mind,
That what we feel of sorrow and despair
From ruin and from change, and all the grief
The passing shews of being leave behind,
Appeared an idle dream that could not live
Where meditation was. I turned away,
And walked along my road in happiness."[5]

The poet carries away from Armytage or Matthew, no formula of wisdom, but the power of conceiving in fact a process of inter-relationship between man and environment, the inward sense of a connection so concrete and at the same time so transparent, that it defies despair. From a positioning within the man-nature relationship of the rural order, the poet could imagine something beyond the wasting of time. Yet he himself as the shaper of the "new emotion" of poetry cannot simply abdicate the responsibility of the word; he must somehow find that perspective available to the non-literate, and dramatize it, giving voice to the inarticulate. This means affiliation with a set of intermediary figures; it means the narrative of double consciousness turned to a specific end.

In "Michael" (1800), therefore, the reader will note the elaborate preamble, the adoption of a certain distance from the tale that unfolds. The tale is specifically "for the delight of natural hearts," and "for the sake of youthful poets" who will be the poet's second self when he is gone. The poet tells us that even before hearing it he had already grasped something of the situation implicit in the tale through his own experience of "the power of nature," but that this story itself enabled him to bridge the gap between natural and human life in a new, though still imperfect way. Perhaps his retelling of it will make the most important connections between man and nature clearer still for that posterity of sophisticated but sympathetic outsiders who are the projected audience. The narrative proper therefore concerns itself with the creation of the figure of the shepherd Michael, whose survival of his son's defection is attributable to his rootedness and his sense of relation to a sustaining environment. This is something the sophisticated narrative consciousness can feed upon, an image of the power of the human heart fixed on the eternal. Although in the case of Luke, the dissolute son, what we have is not a depth study, the reader is led to share the narrator's admiration for the steadfast qualities of Michael himself who emerges as a fully human figure of dignity, though the long chain of connections between him and his ancestors is about to break. What drives home the meaning is the shift of the narrative that invokes community testimony at the end. The reader is made to witness the power of the coherent community to give point and context to the vicissitudes of the individual. Although it is Michael who suffers his own destiny and must live it out, the relationship to nature underlying the experience encompasses more than subjective fact.

> Among the rocks
> He went, and still looked up to sun and cloud,
> And listened to the wind; and, as before,
> Performed all kinds of labour for his sheep,
> And for the land, his small inheritance.
> And to that hollow dell from time to time
> Did he repair, to build the Fold of which
> His flock had need. 'Tis not forgotten yet
> The pity which was then in every heart
> For the old Man — and 'tis believed by all
> That many and many a day he thither went,
> And never lifted up a single stone.

The poet becomes the transmitter of the wisdom of the traditional community which has a well-tested perspective on man's place in nature as a result of its actual integration with the living world through ritual and custom. It is the rural community that enshrines more than other existing societies the "power of nature" as tuned to the essential needs of the human heart. The collective wisdom of such a community will have an elemental quality, the power of simplification so badly needed by the sophisticated consciousness haunted by trivia. The retelling of the story of "Michael" is the necessary refraction of the wisdom of the community through the articulate presence of the narrator. Both narrator and community are essential for the final effect, which is that of the expression of the attested wisdom of endurance for those who would know more fully what man is. That there is a questionable social and political dimension to Wordsworth's vision is clear. What we must not lose sight of, however, is the essential truth of his rural poetry, his rendering of the peasant consciousness in all its manifold strengths, and the extent to which that rendering is bound up with a strong perspective on society and nature that might be unavailable to a writer with a more liberal ideology.[6]

In the narratives of the integral community of Christian Europe, there will often be a similar difficulty in disentangling the elements at hand. As we pass from Romanticism to Realism and Naturalism, the emphasis shifts, as the attempt is made to establish the validity of the experience depicted, without the writer's intellectual assent being given to the old order from which the experience derives. The objective rendering of process that Keats could sustain in his ode "To Autumn" (by minimizing the social aspect and writing of the biological process underlying the field) points in one direction. Others, wishing to render the social and political dimension, could resort to devices of irony, widely varying perspectives, and narrative figures from the outside who converge meaningfully upon the matrix material. This is one aspect of the growth of the modern relativistic and secular consciousness, which may value the natural and social coherence of the traditional world, without crediting the particular religious dogmas or social assumptions of that world. The point will be clear if we call to mind the position of Tolstoy, Hardy and Lawrence, who, as we shall see, may be viewed as engaged in projecting a vision of the experience of rural man beyond the limits of a particular and limited historical context.

Many works of European literature reflect the integral peasant order, creating the sense of a coherent social and natural space while drawing the reader backward through time to the immemorial past of communal experience. One of the most famous is "The Black Spider" (1842), a short novel of the Swiss master, Jeremias Gotthelf. Images of plenty proliferate in the prosperous Bernese valley of Gotthelf's opening pages, set in a nineteenth century daylight world, where the relations among the orders of man, nature and spirit seem happily established. The black window-post, however, serves to introduce the dark past of communal memory, when the terrible plague of spiders appeared in chastisement of the peasants, who had abandoned traditional pieties for evil ways. The origin of the evil is seen in the breaking of the feudal pact by the Teutonic knight von Stoffeln, who exploits the peasants and forces them to participate in a violation of the organic order. To uproot a beechwood grove the peasants enter into a bargain with the Green Huntsman, the devil in disguise, and when they fail to fulfill their part, they are visited by a plague of spiders, representing the "revenge" of the organic in the shape of the Black Death, an evil which their physical-moral lapse invited, and which destroys the coherence of the community, beginning with the farm stock itself. This "visitation" and the second plague which occurs a few generations later when complacency again settles upon the valley, are ended only by Christian acts of self-sacrifice. The grandfather who tells the tale is aware of himself as the bearer of a tradition which has moral point for the present generation, a belief reinforced by Gotthelf's narrative tone, which itself achieves identification with the Christian community. Folklore and the Christian popular imagination (with its opinion of the connection between women and temptation, for example) are enlisted in a coherent drama of good and evil, which ends with the sun shining again over the prosperous valley. But we have been carried to the darkest recesses of moral defection, and learned that the relations of the various members of earthly society are part of an integral order extending through nature to spirit. Violation anywhere in this order means chaos everywhere until the seamless unity is restored by Christ-like moral heroism.

When we turn to stories such as Stifter's "Rock Crystal" (1841) or to Turgenev's "Byezhin Meadow" (1851), on the other hand, we are confronted by a portrayal of the integral community from a cooler and more objective angle, yet one that hardly suggests the tensions and dichotomies of the full narrative of double consciousness, which will become almost mandatory at the century's end. The hunter of Turgenev's "Sketches" might have been created as figure of sophistication encountering the great dormant mass of the Russian peasantry, but he is used more as a purely exploratory device than as a thematic entity. The hunter is a clear glass through which the reader sees the panorama of estate-life and not as a consciousness who interferes in that perception. The hunter's version can be trusted because he has no opinions; he is the spy for whom the reader may frame what ideology he wishes — though this could only with difficulty be a reactionary one. "Byezhin Meadow" opens with a description of a clear and sunny day in contrast with the main part of the story which is about night and a journey into the dark recesses of the primitive peasant world of folk-belief and superstition. The ordinariness of the beginning, the hunter's casual and leisurely ramble, are transformed by the sudden opening of the great chasm of the plain into something strange and wonderful. Submitting himself to chance, like the hero of a *Märchen*, the hunter literally stumbles on the secret world of the boys on the plain. The fire in the darkness creates a sense of magic, and the conversation gradually leads hunter and reader into the dark past of traditional lore, ghosts, and water-sprites. The fertile creativity of the peasant imagination is displayed in the fireside exchanges. Traditional belief newly embroidered is set in an atmosphere in which it seems living and relevant. We feel the earth as a real presence, turning in its primeval rhythms from day to night and back to day. A subtle narrative art, making striking use of a particular spatial ordering, has enabled us to experience the primary unity between man and cosmos as expressed in the mythopoeic language of the peasant. The hunter has served his purpose as our guide to the integral world that is stagnant, fatalistic, tragic, but also rich in emotional relation to the environment, and therefore peculiarly human.

The agricultural base obliterated and superseded, the discovery of the biosphere initiated — modern literature reflects the uneasy transition from local to planetary culture. This takes form in a number of versions of the novel of double consciousness, which we must look at in the context of fully developed Realism and Naturalism. The novel of integral community life, of course, does not altogether disappear, even with the growth of a predominantly urban culture, nor is it strictly limited to excursions tinged with nostalgia. Writers as various as Giovanni Verga, Zola, the early Hardy, W.H. Hudson, Jean Giono, Wladyslaw Reymont and C.F. Ramuz can be understood as occasionally dramatizing the peasant consciousness apart from a strong sense of the polarities that characterize the true novel of double consciousness. Yet during the last thirty years of the nineteenth century, with an accelerating growth of urban populations nearly everywhere, the image of the field becomes polarized with that of the city. Increasingly commonly, the writer explores the rural man and his environment through the medium of a sophisticated protagonist. Tolstoy's Olenin and Levin, Strindberg's comic figure Carlsson, and various of Hardy's heroes, form part of a long line of characters that stretches all the way to Silone's Pietro Spina. Many variations are possible in terms of the basic dichotomy. The theme of the attempted "return" of the native son is common, as is that of the frustrated city-dweller in search of a new life. Sometimes the aim is transformation of the fossilized society, often shown to be resistant to such "crusades", rich in its own relation to the environment, enduring. Usually, the writer wishes to circumvent the dubious social and political ideologies of the rural order and to penetrate to the elusive values of a world still in touch with the natural matrix. The urban order is to be challenged by the weight of a countering element that is seen to have its own particular, though sometimes perverse, strength.

In Tolstoy, we find a major attempt to define individual moral possibility indepently of the conventional "feudal" aspects of a rural life whose roots are ancient. *Anna Karenina* (1878), its immense range encompassing most significant aspects of nineteenth century life, deals significantly with the relationship between the individual consciousness and the rural life-order. Levin's contacts with the peasants and the country are manifold: at different times he may be seen as landowner, amateur economist, technological innovator, and self-conscious seeker after encompassing spiritual wisdom. Much earlier, in *Cossacks* (1862), Tolstoy had shown the predicament of the jaded hero in search of the natural life. Olenin is brought face to face with the impossibility of ever casting off his civilized skin in the name of pagan and natural virtues, but Tolstoy resolves the question more in terms of narrative device than by the dramatization of a real inner conflict. Levin is of course a far more complexly rendered character and exists within a context of exploration of aspects of instinct and intelligence that forms one of the main thematic

61

centers of the novel. One of the great scenes in nineteenth century literature finds Levin joining his peasants in the mowing of the fields. Here, the sophisticated consciousness submerges itself in the reality of a work which binds man to nature and breaks down social and economic barriers to create an image of universal humanity. Levin's mowing is not motivated by spurious "idealism". He is simply disgusted with the vanities of intellectual exchange and decides to exercise himself physically; fantasies about "becoming a peasant" occur to him only later, to be soon banished by the vision of the "chic" Kitty. During the mowing, Levin sinks into the pure physicality of work, and we are not led to believe that this is easy.

> They did another, and still another row. They went on mowing — long rows and short rows, with good grass and bad. Levin lost all awareness of time; he had absolutely no idea whether it was late now or early. A change had begun to take place in his work now that gave him an enormous amount of pleasure. In the midst of his work moments would come over him when he would forget what he was doing; it became easy for him, and during these same moments his row would come out almost as even and as good as Titus's. But the instant he would recall what he was doing he would feel the full burdensomeness of toil, and the swath would come out badly.[7]

(Part III, Chapter 4)

Levin's difficulty in terms of sheer strength and physical energy is not minimized, nor is the counteracting pressure of mind on body forgotten. Learning that work may be a vehicle of encounter with the universal, he feels himself swept up by some "external force" as his mental resistance ceases to interrupt the free flow of his bodily rhythm. The scene becomes a reference point for Levin's later realization of the importance of living out each minute "naturally" in its existential fulness. The relationship between the environment of the peasant and his steadfastness and moral energy, as perceived by Levin, is established. In a world which so retains its roots, however corrupted it is by its burden of social ills, there is the possibility of renewal, for contact with nature through work can transform the simplest necessity into a unique pleasure. Levin has "never had a better drink than this warm water with green stuff floating in it and the rusty taste of the tin box".

In the light of this scene, then, the long process of self-examination that concludes the novel takes on a special significance. There Levin feels the scientific world-view press upon his settled conviction that the world must have meaning, that his life must have a purpose. He cannot solve the problem intellectually by carrying further the scientific concept that "in time that is infinite, in matter that is infinite, in space that is infinite" he is no more than a cell that must dwindle into nothingness. Such a narrowing concept seems to be a falsehood from which he can only free himself (ironically) by suicide. At this point, a talk with a peasant shocks him into an awareness of the power of commitment through living for the soul. Reason could not by itself have discovered the altruism without which life becomes meaningless. Levin cannot simply become an untutored peasant, but he can live at his own level in the texture of the moment, and not allow himself to be split off from his own impulses by the necessity of thought. Levin in no sense opts for primordialism, because his choice involves not simply a plunge into instinct, but an affirmation of the power of feeling in a broadly moral context: '' . . . from now on my life, my whole life, no matter what happens to me, every second of it, is not only not meaningless as it was before, but it has the incontestable meaning of the goodness I have the power to put into it!''

If we consider Levin's experience of the mowing with his final conclusions about the necessary mode of his everyday existence, the exact character of Tolstoy's mediation between the sophisticated consciousness and the rural world becomes visible. We know to what extent work itself in the nineteenth century replaces the old metaphysical guarantees and becomes a center of meaning, a focus of certainty. However, in most cases such work represented a false god. It was in fact a kind of idolatry, arising within an exploitative capitalistic system, and carried out in atmospheres divorced from the traditional environment and in a context devoid of charity. Levin learns that work can indeed be a centering experience, but only when it occurs in an environment which allows room for reverberations back into nature, and toward one's fellow workers. This can take place in the field, but only because Levin is not actually and socially bound to the work, and engages upon it in the name of self-development and balance. Tolstoy does not suggest an unqualified celebration of the whole order of the peasant life, but shows Levin attaching himself to it to recover an experience lost in the foppery and intellectualism of his own class. This core experience puts the analytical conundrums of science in a new perspective; the actual physical universe is no longer a problem but a felt reality, a rhythm extending through the swing of the scythe to the distant stars. The "ideology" of the peasant world may be superseded, its social structure may cry out for reform, but its function as a mode of re-entry into the primal and still valid experience of the physical texture of life endures. In the rediscovery of the physical, Levin finds an alternative to the mechanized consciousness dominating the century; he recognizes the possibility of spontaneous action out of which a sense of brotherhood may grow. Levin remains a separated and sophisticated consciousness, quite removed from the peasant in his individual and social being, but capable of being assimilated by the same rhythms of toil and so of joining him in the human order in nature.

The narrative of double consciousness which in Wordsworth is embodied in the sensibility of the poet attendant upon peasant life is in Tolstoy centered in the questing narrative figure caught between two realities. The vision of each writer at its profoundest touches the ecological roots where the peasant tradition functions as a valid mode of knowledge apart from specific social or political structures, though

63

Wordsworth's poet-observer remains removed from the actual experience of toil and joins the community chiefly by invoking its testimony. In both cases environment and moral perceptions are closely connected; Wordsworth's "natural heart" is one that has not lost the ability to understand the value of suffering and endurance; Tolstoy shows Levin regaining sensitivity to the power of goodness through the experience of the value of concrete action that unifies mind and body and banishes the abstractionism of thought divorced from its context. Like Hardy and Lawrence, Tolstoy the artist seizes upon the aspects of the peasant consciousness which he can bring to bear against the impersonal and antihuman texture of modern life. At this critical juncture, Tolstoy's own sharp sense of tension between the polarities of instinct and intelligence, feeling and thinking, experience and abstraction, issues forth in the tortured balance of *Anna Karenina*. We may ask whether Levin's "resolution" is really a resolution; whether the power of concrete action in the moment inspired by a vision of one aspect of an integral culture can be sustained in a society that has sacrificed a closed phase for an open one, and in which the domination of science makes the analytical mode predominant. Tolstoy's note of implicit pessimism sounds as cruelly as Hardy's and his sense of urgency is often as desperate as Lawrence's. In discussing their work in detail we shall be returning to the larger questions raised by Levin's option.

It remains to examine a few of the "climax" versions of the image of the field, works that capture some aspect of this literary reflection of the biosphere at the particular moment in human culture when the city is beginning to dominate the whole planet. If the literature of the field suggests manifold links beteen the social and natural order, it is capable too, not only of celebrating fruition, but of expressing in a pure form certain repressed feelings about the environment itself. Toward the end of the century, a marked sense of weariness seems sometimes to afflict the literary mind. In many passages Hardy describes the consciousness of doom that forces itself upon the contemporary writer. This seems to be not merely a product of social despair, but part of an increasing awareness of the ravages wrought upon the natural order by the whole exploitative mechanism of the century. As we have seen, sublime nature becomes threatening, a glacial image of icy inhumanity, or a jungle thick with the evil that man suffers in his darkest heart.

The question of biological process and the social order haunts Naturalism, and in Zola's *La Terre* (1886) it is possible to see some of the elemental facts that give validity to the work of the minor Naturalists harnessed to a vision of man in society that is strong in both documentation and poetry. *La Terre* comes close to being a novel of the integral community, but, as we might expect, there is a strong undercurrent of reference to the "outside" world of the city, both in the conversation of the peasants, and in the figure of the rather pallid hero, Jean Macquart, who attempts to find peace in the country after his years in the army. Macquart, though he hardly qualifies as a sophisticated consciousness, even in relation to the peasants of La Beauce, does serve the purpose of providing us with a notable example of someone who, in Zola's rural context, is ironically weakened by such sensitivity as he possesses. In this novel, Zola demonstrates an active historical sense. His version of the agricultural community gains in depth thanks to a certain alertness to specific factors operative in the French situation. The problems of land-division that the novel explores may be exaggerated, but they are related to the actual French post-Revolutionary tradition. What's more, the novel raises the question of the competition of North American wheat, the value of protectionist policies, the prospects of peasant versus urban worker, and even goes into the comparative merit of traditional and "scientific" farming. Such historical anchoring is one level of Zola's attempted penetration of reality.

If he writes of the traditional order, however, Zola's abiding interest is in destroying all our sentimental conceptions of the ideal peasant. Perhaps, in his obvious enthusiasm, he oversteps the mark in the other direction: we are confronted with an almost incredible panorama of country brutality and peasant acquisitiveness. In this novel the sense of wholeness discoverable in the peasant consciousness is overlooked in favour of the Naturalistic metaphor of aggression. Struggle is the pervasive reality, struggle that is often carried out in the most brutal physical terms. What Zola calls *"le ferment du tien et du mien"* is everywhere active at the center of the characters' concerns. One great scene depicts the reading of a government propaganda pamphlet which is full of the joys of country life to the illiterate baffled peasants, whose only thought is how they can make more money. Their passion for money leads to the primary aggression sequence in the story: the rape of the land. In Zola's terms this does not mean a failure of conservation, but rather lust for possession that is equivalent to a sexual frenzy. Zola emphasizes that such a man as Buteau will stop at nothing to achieve possession. Possession means money, but it is significant for its own sake too. Sexual aggression and land aggression are connected in a manner distantly related to Lawrence's more subtle equations to come; but Zola is not a severe judge. In a scene that is the ironical center of the story Buteau rapes his pregnant young sister-in-law Françoise with the help of his wife, ostensibly to try to get her to have a miscarriage so that her land will revert to them. Buteau, however, is too excited by the encounter to remember his purpose, and Françoise for the first time in her life realizes that she loves the man who has so callously attacked her. She has her pleasure and a moment later is fatally wounded by a scythe wielded by her sister. Yet she refuses to sign the document that will enable Jean Macquart, her husband, to inherit the land they possess together. Earlier, we see social realism, symbolism and psychology merge when Jean

65

withdraws in the act of first making love to Françoise. "The human seed, diverted and lost, spurted into the ripe corn, onto the earth which never denies herself, opening her flanks to every seed, eternally fecund."[8] Unmarried, Françoise does not want the burden of a child, but she also thinks, even then, of Buteau. Jean, for his part, is seen as rather futile and inconsequent. Behind the play of human emotions Zola discerns the biological process, the enduring environment. Buteau's rape of Françoise effectively regains him the land; it destroys Jean Macquart's future, and makes inevitable his defeat at the hands of the family, who move closer together as he loses ground. Jean is driven from the community as a fugitive, as the loser in the brutal struggle for possession of the land.

Zola's sympathies are with Buteau, murderer though he be. He renders the ecstasies of this coarse peasant with a vivid touch:

> "A year went by and this first year of possession was for Buteau sheer ecstasy. In those days when he had worked as a labourer like the others, he had never ploughed the earth with so profound an effort, but she was his now and he wanted to penetrate her, to fertilize her all the way to the bottom. Each evening he came home exhausted, with the ploughshare gleaming silver. In March he harrowed his wheat, in April, his oats, unstinting in his care and giving every ounce of his strength. When the strips had no need of more work, he still went to look at them like a lover. He walked round, bent down, and with his habitual gesture took up as fistful of earth, a rich clod which he loved to crumble and let run through his fingers, supremely happy when he felt it neither too dry nor too humid and smelt in it the good smell of growing bread."
>
> (Part III, Chapter 1)

The sexual imagery here is obvious and inescapable. Zola does not stop there, however; his vision of the roots of things includes, as it were, the poetry of excrement. Hordequin, a relatively educated farmer, at one point unfolds his fantasy of a new fertilizer:

> "With a sweeping gesture he embraced the whole flat and immense expanse of La Beauce. In his enthusiasm he saw Paris, all Paris, opening the flood-gates of its sewers and loosing the fertilizing river of human manure. Streams went winding in all directions, every field was richly spread, as the sea of sewage mounted higher under the cloudless sun, under the great winds which wafted the odour far and wide. The great town was giving back to the fields the life she had drawn from them. Slowly the earth drank in the fertilizing tide; and out of the gorged, enriched soil the wheat for the white bread would grow until it burst forth in giant harvests."
>
> (Part V, Chapter 1)

This "pure gold", the excrement that is another form of money Zola describes with all the power of an instinctive and pre-Freudian genius who is aware of the secret connection between feces and acquisitiveness. Breaking through the barriers of convention, Zola delivers his treasure in a novel that is anything but constipated. Significantly, the character

66

whose ability to break wind is monumental, Jésus-Christ, is rather happy-go-lucky and distinctly careless in his campaign for plunder. Though there is no consistent relation between the excremental imagery and the dramatization of the instinct for acquisition, Zola's use of the two factors in such measure takes the reader to a level beyond the mere recording of the "earthy" customs of the country. Seizing upon the natural setting directly as he does in this novel, however, Zola is able to render in a specific way the kind of value he finds in man "following nature". His characters in fact "follow nature" by indulging to the full in every impulse of hunger, lust or violence. They become primordial beasts, whose instincts are moderated by cunning alone, because it is precisely in this way that they make their survival more likely. The imagery of this novel suggests the release of the body from constraint into primordial impulse in the name of life itself. This is what Jean Macquart glimpses at the end, as he goes off to war, hoping that by killing Prussians he can recover some of his lost pride and exorcise some of the misery of his defeat at the hands of the more aggressive Buteau.

Zola's brutal peasant is therefore only in a muddled way an effort in the direction of what we might call "higher" values. The furthest he can get toward redeeming the "scientific" vision of brute nature is to idolize the life-impulse itself. Unlike Johannes Jensen, however, Zola is not quite ready to grant the life impulse more than a vague hope of achieving something that will confer permanent value on man's efforts. He lumps together suffering and active evil as simply "factors" in what must be seen as a chaos rather than a process. His vision of the field is therefore radically divergent from Tolstoy's, though both involve an emphasis on the connection between rural life and physical energy itself. Tolstoy seeks physical energy as a way of circumventing the "bind" of thought directed at a universe which must be lived in order to be understood. The trigger for Levin's vision, we have seen, is an "irrational" assent to the altruism he sees in the peasant's attitude, which he feels may be able to stand against the threat of the space-time terror hatched by science. Zola, on the other hand, points to the insignificance of suffering in the space-time universe, and sugests a cosmos whose amorality encircles the good wishes of man. Perhaps in the long run a scoundrel like Buteau is more moral than the hesitant Jean Macquart; until we can read life's "hidden ends" we cannot be sure. Such a reading can only appear when a true interiority is present and this is what Naturalism cannot often admit to its nature of impulse and struggle. Despite his narrowness, however, Zola shows great strength in his vision of the physicality of things; it is precisely this physicality that must be secured against the spectre of absolute consciousness divorced from the body that narrows modern literature and has perhaps narrowed modern life. Zola's image of the field is a vision of the release of the body; he celebrates the connection of man with the earth in a process that is creative as well as destructive. What remains, however, is the task of discovering a higher form of discrimination, so that confusion will not equate the positive with the negative and allow life itself to dissolve in a shower of violence. Such a power of discrimination is what is being sought in the later novels of environmental realism.

One of the greatest of these is Knut Hamsun's *Growth of the Soil* (1917), in which pioneer and peasant elements blend, and the inarticulate consciousness receives one of its fullest literary presentations. Isak the peasant and worker goes north to the frontier of the unsettled land in Norway. With the help of his wife Inger and an outsider named Geissler, who appears at certain critical junctures, Isak builds up a new settlement in the wilderness. Without losing anything in the presentation of concrete physical reality, Hamsun goes beyond Naturalism to emphasize the human significance of the artifact of the field, seeing in its creation the power of man to raise himself from loneliness and savagery to the level at which he can become reconciled to his existence in a universe that guarantees nothing. Hamsun makes use of the narrative of double consciousness. The peasant world meets the articulate world in Geissler, who fades away as Isak rises in stature and wealth. Geissler is simultaneously a figure of contact and of inadequacy. His moral validity is achieved indirectly, and he lives vicariously in Isak's reality. Hamsun's vision embraces both Isak the peasant, and Geissler, the educated man. Articulate culture, summed up in the writer, can fasten itself to the peasant world by an act of sympathetic imagination, but this imagination in truth must embody the tenuous quality of the contact. This is what Geissler stands for, and when he sums up the wholeness of the integral agricultural order in his fine speech to Sivert at the end, we are both impressed, and at the same time cautious. The man who can settle nowhere is seeing Isak's world from a certain distance, and we must not take him quite literally; we must go back to Hamsun's story of Isak's struggle; we must go from there, for ourselves, into the experience that has inspired all this.

It is true, of course, that Hamsun's novel is nostalgic in its celebration of the life of a valley isolated from the benefits as well as the follies of modern life; and one feels a certain deficiency in the unresolved ironies of its picture of gradual mechanization. how can Sellenraa, the new community, remain vital if it ceases to grow? And if it continues to grow, how can it retain its rural virtues? Hamsun arrests the sequence of country and city at a moment of balance, creating an ideal of harmony, articulated by Geissler in terms that may be too simple. Hamsun wants to detach the traditional peasant world from its political and social limitations, and re-creates it as frontier, but by doing so he unwittingly evokes the spectre of progress that accompanies frontier development. How long will Isak hold out against the mines and merchants?

The novel polarizes city and country and exalts patriarchal ways; Inger goes to the city and gets a bit spoiled and Isak has to give her a good shaking. There is a great difference, we are told, between happiness and foolishness. The eldest son Eleseus takes the role of Luke in this variation of Wordsworth's "Michael". He goes to America, and never comes back; it is clear that he is condemned to the life of the uprooted. None of these elements represent the strength of the novel; they are simplifications on the level of Zola's simplifications though in the opposite direction. The easy contrasts invite us to share the preconceptions of the novelist, and we may find it necessary to decline this option.

The strength of the book lies in its rendering of Isak and Inger in terms that comprehend the human fullness of their existence, though for much of the time that existence is not rich in "linear" modulations. Hamsun's narrative tone is both distanced and full of understanding; it is that of a man who, while not blinding himself to incidental follies, nor concealing outright brutalities, is able to see the essential value in Isak's creative transformation of the land. *Growth of the Soil* takes us beyond the physical surface of rural life without landing us in the primordial deeps. Isak and Inger live in a world with particular sensory richness; their minds register the concrete facts of their environment, but not mechanically. There is a great deal of subtlety in their perceptions, and their judgments and decisions are the products of complex circumstances. Isak is both an individual and a participant in a universal working order; as an individual he is capable of achieving his own selfhood, his unique inner coherence in the face of time and change. As a sower in the field, he shares in a total human effort, becoming a symbol of the human energy that transforms necessity into beauty:

Isak walked bareheaded, in Jesu name, a sower. Like a tree-stump with hands to look at, but in his heart like a child. Every cast was made with care, in a spirit of kindly resignation. Look! the tiny grains that are to take life and grow, shoot up into ears, and give more corn again; so it is throughout all the earth where corn is grown. Palestine, America, the valleys of Norway itself — a great wide world, and here is Isak, a tiny speck in the midst of it all, a sower. Little showers of corn flung out fanwise from his hand; a kindly clouded sky, with a promise of the faintest little misty rain.[9]

(Part I, Chapter Three)

The corruptions of the city slowly encircle the settlement, but Isak moves toward personal fulfillment. His family grows and he thinks of building a separate house for himself and Inger, for their old age, a house to die in. Clearing space for it he comes upon a stone he cannot move, and is depressed at his now failing strength. But, in one of the novel's greatest scenes, Hamsun shows Isak accepting his wife's help — together they are able to move the stone, which turns out to be a very special one, "mightily broad, finely cut, smooth and even as a floor." It is a door-slab for the new house, a symbol of domestic integration, of the unity their life is growing toward. With the strength of a human wholeness, Isak will step into death, secure in relation to the land and in mastery of self.

69

The image of the field gives us nature composed and bounded, and related to the productive effort of men. In the European literature of the nineteenth and twentieth centuries, such a configuration takes shape from the peasant world, and the man or woman in the field is seen as part of a coherent life-order emphasizing values of endurance, stability, and earth-rootedness — which in the negative or satirical vein may turn into acquisitiveness, brutality or immobility. Sensing the unique and usually positive qualities of the peasant order in nature, however, the writer works through one of two basic strategies to bring it into relation to his own "outside", sophisticated, or increasingly urbanized context. In the integral novel we glimpse the "dark backward" of human experience of the land, played out *in illo tempore*, within a closed community, and in terms of the oldest rituals. In the novel of double-consciousness, field is polarized with city, and the mediation between sophisticated and simple, urban and rural, becomes overt. While the "negative" or satirical versions of such encounters show the country bogged down in backwardness, comically secure in its incorrigible traditions, the more positive versions dramatize values that seem to be directed at the often alienated and over-intellectualized man of the encroaching world-city. yet in almost all cases the reader is invited to recall the significance of the root-processes on which higher civilization is based; he is made aware of immemorial energies, which are not necessarily circumscribed by the narrow political and social order which gave them birth. The adaptation to the natural setting fashioned by peasant culture turns out to be rich in sensory experience and sensitive to communal relations; it is these elements, above all, which are visible in the image of the field as projected by many of the writers in this tradition from Wordsworth to D.H. Lawrence.

CHAPTER THREE
The Natural Paradise in Modern Literature

A sheltering, beautiful enclosure in which struggle seems to have been banished and bliss discovered, in an environment transformed out of the reach of "everyday" disappointment, a nearby lake or patch of wood, a tropical island, a landscape in past or future time — these may suddenly blossom as occasions for the magical experience of a nature in which man is suddenly and miraculously at home.[1]

Historically, the paradisal mood has often been expressed in the image of the garden, but during the nineteenth and twentieth centuries, writers captured the characteristic feeling of the "*locus amoenus*" in various forms of natural space.[2] All such spatial forms, however, have in common a sense of sheltering from challenge, a feeling of easy bliss and momentary peace. The survival of the paradisal image in the context of a relatively realistic literature may be attributed to its function of reminding us of the value of our relationship to environment, which is not only to be used and exploited, but which offers us the possibility of an awareness expanded in many directions. Womb-bliss and sexual bliss translating themselves into an image of environmental euphoria: momentary escape from the constant tension and aggressiveness of the species serving the tonic function of release and relaxation in pleasure — this is the state of paradisal nature.[3]

Although there are elements of the nature of the countryside at least implicit in many of the classical versions of the Golden Age, the paradisal myth of specifically eastern coinage affords an even more definite picture of the natural scene. Eden means "delight" and "paradise", a Persian word adapted into Greek, means "magnificent garden". The fusion of ideas of the Golden Age with the Edenic myths of the Near East gave full shape to the paradisal image in western thought and literature.[4] While it was accepted by Christian thought as early as Origen that an earthly paradise existed somewhere in the present, real world, so long as aggressive encounters with alien cultures dominated Europe's attempts to shape itself, it was difficult to formulate an ideal, or even a positive image, drawn from the extra-European world.[5] According to Henri Baudet, it was the special character of the Crusades that changed this perspective.[6]

71

Thereafter, the picture emerges of a technologically advanced Europe creating a series of counter-images, sustaining the myth of Eden or the Golden Age, first in the lost past, then in the present, both in the form of an imagined "real" place, and in the figure of the noble savage, the naturally good man, the man untouched by the vices of the advanced civilization.[7] In the literature of the nineteenth and twentieth centuries, the vision of the natural paradise is an ambiguous testimony to the increasing commitment of western society to technology and urbanization.

According to C.L. Sanford, the myth of paradise grows as a dream among actual social conditions regarded as restrictive and oppressive, and it has the dual character of being a drive toward cessation of struggle, while at the same time being an ideal of change, that is, one directed against the confining social conditions. It thus becomes, as it were, "a long way round to nirvana", as Santayana puts it.[8] One could argue that though the creation of an image of a natural paradise is in a sense an escapist gesture leading the writer away from industrial society, it is also a specific revolutionary act, and remains so, even though it ends in quietude and passive resistance. The historical irony that myths of paradise have affected social revolutions becomes more understandable when we remember the character of the paradisal affirmation, and it should not surprise us to find paradisal conceptions throughout the work of nineteenth and twentieth century writers who make a determined resistance to a specific social order — Shelley, Thoreau, and D.H. Lawrence being obvious examples. In such cases, there may be a strong tension between wish-fulfillment and engagement with social reality, and to avoid the charge of escapism a writer must place his paradisal vision within a strong context of time and change and suggest other, less passive, aspects of the world-order in which he lives and creates.

In an age of burgeoning technology, in the era of the triumphant work-ethic, the paradisal moment is an expression of the pause that is leisure, the dream of man on nature that energizes love, poetry, or a new vision of the cosmos. Sebastian de Grazia has pointed out the connection between leisure and awareness, contemplation, and happiness. The very root of the Latin word *schole*, from which we derive our word for school, is linked with the idea of a halt or a cessation. Leisure is freedom from the necessity to labour, in short, a momentary freedom from the struggle for existence, a halt — the very *otium* that the image of the Golden Age holds up against the *negotium* of the everyday world, Adam's freedom before he had to earn his living by the sweat of his brow. In the state of leisure "the contemplator looks upon the world and man with the calm eye of one who has no design on them. In one sense he feels himself to be close to all nature. He has not the aggressive detachment or unfeeling isolation that comes from scrutinizing men and objects with a will to exploiting them". In the time-ridden world of modern man, leisure confers the freedom of a moment expanding forever, but it is not merely a loose state of being unemployed; it contradicts the divisiveness and strain of the working round by suggesting a wholeness of feeling, the activity of a passivity that is creative and relaxed. "If you look on the world with intent, you can see little or but partially. You are observing, not contemplating. You are a slice, not the whole". Leisure, de Grazia suggest, is a precondition for man's contemplation of the gods.[9]

In the nineteenth century, then, the paradisal takes the form of rebellion against the work society, encompassing a number of versions of natural bliss in various settings. All these show a marked sense of euphoria creating an enveloping peace that draws space downward until an emotional equivalent of womb or sexual embrace is created, yet rather than being merely escapist this has the positive function of counteracting the dominant working and combative round. While reformulations of a more iconic paradisal occur, e.g. "Kubla Khan", the main development is toward evocations of bliss derived from close observation of a real environment, for the Romantics chiefly the Mediterranean, for later writers, often the tropics. Nor does Darwinian nature simply cancel out such versions of bliss, for one effect of Darwinism was to give credence to a developmental view of society in which the primitive could be seen as a simpler and more directly appealing way of life. While Darwinism tends to favour the "hard" primitivism of struggle, it is capable as well of inspiring the "soft" primitivism of Eden.

Wordsworth himself is perhaps the first to sound a new and realistic note (in "The Recluse", 1814) when he writes as follows about the image in question:

. . . Paradise, and groves
Elysian, Fortunate Fields — like those of old
Sought in the Atlantic Main — why should they be
A history only of departed things,
Or a mere fiction of what never was?
For the discerning intellect of Man,
When wedded to this goodly universe
In love and holy passion, shall find these
A simple produce of the common day.[10]

What is disavowed here is the pastness of the paradisal experience, and its reduction to fantasy. The image of a primal catastrophe is given up, and the assumption of a hierarchic world negated in favour of a sense of the creative consciousness in touch with a nature in which possibilities of meaning can be realized. Real nature in its beneficence and bliss can be conjured up in the marriage of mind and environment, provided that this union is one of true sensual linking. Such a linking, as it were, "grows" pleasure and knowledge in the everyday perceptions, as part of man's existence in the world he otherwise takes for granted.

The forms of the modern vision of the natural paradise are various. The familiar environment, perceived with a new intensity, may become the

73

enclosing center of a pleasure that sustains the individual against the bite of time and change. Or escape into an exotic space may be necessary as the working world impinges all too sharply upon the meditative moment. Or, in a new kind of mythical projection, a fictive world may be distanced in time, or expressed as a coherent fantasy based on a "realistic" perception of a specific environment. What these strategies have in common is the determination to counter the distorting present with a sense of the truth of nature lost in social strangulation, or in the largely unconscious but nonetheless persistent drive to urbanize the earth.

In general, the paradisal seems to be an expression of the timeless moment; it summons up an Eternal Now, which may be rendered in various ways. Clearly, the strong physical emphasis in this configuration, the dynamic knowledge that emerges almost directly from the body itself, tends to negate the kind of abstract time-consciousness associated with an elaborate intellectualism. The paradisal image in fact shows man in flight from the highly artificial experience of time that occurs in thinking itself, in self-consciousness, or within the context of the rigidly imposed clock-time of the working world. Our three kinds of paradisal moment, however, exhibit this static time-awareness from slightly varying angles. In the paradise of the common day, we are usually invited simply to step out of the urban work-society for an experience of the nature that is available as a perennially existing, forgotten matrix. In the exotic paradise, on the other hand, there is a flight in space. This, however, often ends up as an immersion in a mythopoeic world, in a culture which has not moved forward with the world-drift toward urbanization, so that here too, we are being invited to experience something other than the complex time of our own culture: we are being brought back to a landscape saturated with that Mircea Eliade calls "archaic" time; the "terror of history" being cancelled out in the bliss of the body in nature.[11] This kind of experience takes on a slightly more complex form in some of the mythically structured paradisal moments we have referred to. Here, the mythical pattern itself involves a distancing effect; the surprise comes when we see a contemporary problem or existential situation replayed in an imagined medium: we may begin then to sense continuities in historical or evolutionary experience that we had scarcely dreamt of before. This has the effect of softening the bite of time, of linking meaningful experience across historical gaps, or at least of setting our present limitations in a new light. In such terms, the paradisal moment can become a model designed to influence our present sense of what experience can offer. Obsessed with change, we may be given a vision of the value of the arrested moment. In terms of the specifically evolutionary pattern, we may be called upon to re-evaluate the Promethean act of transformation, to begin to make room for a new perspective of values, so that within the flux, and in the face of radical changes in technology, we are recalled to the value of the dreaming pause.

74

This, of course, need not mean that the challenge of sublime nature is rejected, or that the essential thrust of evolution is turned aside. As we shall see in considering the paradisal image in the novels of D.H. Lawrence, such moments of enclosing bliss may exist within the context of an overall recognition of change.

Thus, any simple equation of the modern paradisal image with a lack of social responsibility seems facile. The identification between the secular revolution and the millenial hopes that lay burried in the Protestant Christianity of the eighteenth century may have led the English Romantics to a certain despair when the promised revolution failed, but it did not ensure a literature of escapism. On the one hand, the conservatism of Wordsworth's late poetry is not the whole story; on the other, "Kubla Khan" (despite the high artifice that anticipates Symbolist "correspondences") is not altogether unmoored from that landscape of the body which underlies, for example, the more "realistic" paradise of Shelley's "Epipsychidion" (1821). Certainly Shelley's vision in this instance is by no means adequately accounted for by references to traditional archetypes of the islands of bliss — a procedure adopted by even so literal a critic as Desmond King-Hele.[12] Shelley may rather be seen as anticipating a trend of the whole century by turning to an exotic landscape (in this case one strongly based on that of the Mediterranean littoral). Here, the unresolved conflict between ideal love and its social embodiments dissolves in an atmosphere of sustained euphoria. The validity of this procedure, however, depends upon the concrete realization of the natural space itself. The fantasy is precisely anchored to a setting which encourages us to take seriously the implied criticism of the existing world. Nor argument could match the power of Shelley's description in conjuring up the virtues of a human-scaled and physically apprehended world, where nature and art are harmoniously blended:

> For all the antique and learned imagery
> Has been erased, and in the place of it
> The ivy and the wild-vine interknit
> Thè volumes of their many twining stems;
> Parasite flowers illume with dewy gems
> The lampless halls, and when they fade, the sky
> Peeps through their winter-woof of tracery . . .[13]

In this poem, eroticism and leisure cancel out the prohibitions we have placed on delight, and spiritual knowledge emerges out of the physically-based experience of a specifically possible place. This is precisely the kind of blissful reassurance and renewal that the Romantics (not to mention generations of sensitive tourists) sought and sometimes found in the real havens of the Mediterranean shores. Clearly, the north-south polarity in English literature, from Shelley to E.M. Forster, has something to do with real differences of environment and cultural emphasis, and with the power of the writer to suggest the concrete facts of his encounter with the alternative locale. Exoticism, or the "escape into space" is, of course, a very comprehensive phenomenon. As Western Europe and North America moved toward a total work-society, the writer often sought first the Mediterranean, and thereafter the remote and undeveloped areas of the earth, in order to capture a complete "counter-world", rooted in reality. French culture from Chateaubriand and Balzac to Gauguin and Gide expresses some memorable images of the paradisal enclosure, while in American literature Melville's south seas and Lafcadio Hearn's orient offer similar glimpses of the possibilities open to a fugitive from a burdensome social order. Often, it is in the form of a travel narrative that the Edenic world emerges. Once again, these exhibitions of a certain relation to nature need not imply the choice of a dream-world, divorced from all challenge. For in many such works, the paradisal functions as part of a struggle of the corrupted world to recover its matrix knowledge, or else it represents a glimpse of the necessary stasis almost lost in the helter-skelter of the everyday modern life. ("Epipsychidion" shows that the social restraint which imprisons Emilia may be corrected by a natural impulse creating a world suitable for human habitation). Except in the completely naive vein of popular literature, the all-encompassing "escapism" often attributed to this configuration is seldom visible.

If the importance of a full sensory knowledge, emphasized in certain exotic landscapes, saves these from being mere wish-fulfillments, it does not make them any the less exotic, and leaves open the question of the re-establishment of such knowledge in everyday life. This problem is not so acute in the case of those paradisal visions occurring within the terms of that "common day" referred to in Wordsworth's poem. As we move toward the Realism of the mid-nineteenth century, certain moments become frequent in literature; in these, there is no real flight, but simply a stepping out of the boundaries of the impinging social reference, and into a natural world where a renewed physicality becomes the basis for a joy that may rise to the height of spiritual insight. In Thoreau's Journals, in some of the recollections of Turgenev's hunter, or in Mark Twain's description of Huck and Jim on their island, we have snapshots of a bliss that does not have to be searched out in an alien culture. And even in J. Henri Fabre's recollection of how as a child he discovered the intimate life of the local pond, we see the future scientist enclosed in a magic circle born of his own wonder. Childhood, wrote Novalis, is where one finds the golden age, and childhood is in fact free from things that deny leisure, if not always ready for its manifestation. Huck and Jim on their raft form a striking contrast, not only to the evil of the towns they float past, but to those pathetically victimized children of Dickens and Dostoevsky, already crushed by the machinery of urban life. Not only childhood, however, but extreme old age, is capable of reflecting the landscape of the natural paradise. Whitman's *Specimen Days* (1882) provides an example:

76

As I walk'd slowly over the grass, the sun shone out enough to show the shadow moving with me. Somehow I seem'd to get identity with each and everything around me, in its condition. Nature was naked, and I was also. It was too lazy, soothing, and joyous-equable to speculate about. Yet I might have thought somehow in this vein: Perhaps the inner never lost rapport we hold with earth, light, air, trees, etc., is not to be realized through eyes and mind only, but through the whole corporeal body, which I will not have blinded or bandaged any more than the eyes. Sweet, sane, still Nakedness in Nature! — ah if poor, sick, prurient humanity in cities might really know you once more!

("A Sun Bath — Nakedness")

Whitman's "Adamic" self is awakened to the possibility of a full physical knowledge linked to the inner life, and a wholeness frustrated by the city emerges in the blissful natural setting. The obvious eroticism is not at odds with the ecstatic certainty of the value of the experience beyond that; we see rather the interconnectedness of bodily and spiritual beneficence in such naked and secular baptisms. And it is precisely such a secular and yet spiritual joy that is reflected in so many modern versions of the paradise of the common day, in writers as diverse as W.H. Hudson, John Cowper Powys, Jack Kerouac, and Malcolm Lowry.

Two further examples of this kind of paradisal experience are worth closer examination —, the first, from Hemingway, remains within a context of fairly stringent realism, while the second, from a short story by Giuseppe de Lampedusa, leads us to the question of the mythical transformation of the core experience.

Hemingway's image of nature suggests a classic preserve, opened at last to the wider, weathering reality. In the "Big Two-Hearted River" stories (1924), Nick Adams escapes the burned-out town, the black locusts, and feels "the old feeling"; war is temporarily effaced, as is the *nada* of suffering consciousness. The stream flows eternally, trout swim, a kingfisher rises. Nick makes his camp, it has been suggested, with compulsive care: the ritual of order shuts out the demons. There is no real communion, no meditation; nature is a kind of coloured film stretched thinly over a nightmare. Though the description is clipped and straight-forward it would be a mistake to emphasize the "objectivity" of the scene rendered; in fact, it is an extremely subjective landscape, because it is one tuned point by point to the needs of the experiencing psyche. The two suggestions just made are connected: because the apprehension is so tense, the rendering of nature so selective and therapeutic, the reader is given no sense of its being something divorced from Nick's conscious-ness. Because everything is pinpointed from within, there is nothing to meditate on, nothing to exist inside. The reader feels the presence of nature, but it is Nick's vision of nature he is in touch with, not with something larger, something that might exist outside of Nick's ex-perience.

In *The Sun Also Rises* (1926) the true paradisal emerges in a perception held just as sharply on the object, but without the presence of threat that forces the emotion to a vice-like grip at every point. Jake Barnes, the impotent man of passion, is swept from the Paris wasteland, the urban over-civilized sphere of bitch-women and bought love, to Burguete, a high point before the plunge into the moral ambiguity of Pamplona. At first the description is from a largely visual perspective, the effective, "distanced" description of the Hemingway of many of the stories (and a "painterly" layout) is suggested, but with the actual entry into the fishing ritual later, there is a subtle change. A sense of peace suffuses Hemingway's famous description of the actual walk to the river. Here, the landscape is not quite like the one observed earlier from the bus, for the scale is different, and so is the quality of reception. Human beings fit well into this landscape and can enjoy it through a variety of sensory points — it is not just observed from the outside, it is experienced. A number of details contribute to the sense of ease, of comfort, of reassurance. We are at first high up, raised above the surrounding land, but pleasantly, not dangerously, then gradually we enter the valley, where the paths are well-worn and attest to the continuous human presence. The wood itself is light, spacious and without any threatening or hidden under-brush. It is park-like, as if produced by human effort, for human enjoyment. For once, the narrow personal feelings of Jake are effaced, and there is no nervous eagerness to enjoy: the landscape is taken for what it is, and seen simply, and we feel, truly. The effect of this is remarkable. It creates a sense of the natural world enduring just that way and regardless of the uses of men, yet this sense does not operate to make men seem puny, because the scale is held to perfection. What we feel is the ability of man to find an objective nature, rich in beauty and simplicity and nobly suited to his capacity for true leisure and ease. Such a landscape represents the finest essence of what man has won from chaos; it is not at all the sublime landscape of exaltation, but a landscape of pleasure, something lacking in the strained, fun-seeking tinged with desperation that marks the rest of the book. And by the end, after further experience at San Sebastian, Jake has learned that life involves necessary suffering, that pleasure when it comes must not be related to the forcing will, that submission to the destructive element may in itself yield something unexpected. His impotence, cutting him off from the fulness of life, does not cut off his feelings, but it gives him a special insight into the moral and spiritual effectiveness of passivity. His letting-go in the natural setting puts him in touch with nature, his self-sacrifice in the personal sphere puts him in touch with — what he has instead of God.

Hemingway's novel, remaining within the boundaries of common experience, hints at the exotic in its depiction of fugitives from the workaday world at a *feria*. In "The Professor and the Siren" (1957) by Lampedusa, the Sicilian writer treats his own familiar locale as an exotic refuge from the pressures of achievement, and introduces a mythical transformation that leads us close to the third group of paradisal instances in modern literature. In Lampedusa's story the narrator, a somewhat jaded playboy, meets a world-famous professor of Greek, who relates how as a student he actually lived with a Siren on a beautiful Mediterranean bay beneath Etna. Overcome by the strain of his studies and by the pressures of the town, the would-be professor is visited by "Lighea, daughter of Callipe", who initiates him into the physical knowledge of the ancient culture he is trying to force into his overstrained mind. As he confides to the narrator, this experience unites high and low in a perfect unity: "Suffice to say that in those embraces I enjoyed both the highest forms of spiritual pleasure and that elementary one, quite without any social connotations, felt by our lonely shepherds on the hills when they couple with their own goats; if the comparison disgusts you that is because you are incapable of making the necessary transposition from the bestial to the superhuman plane, in my case superimposed on each other".[14] The Siren invites the student to join her in the sea, but he goes on to his career and ends up an embittered old man, who literally "spits" upon modern culture in all its manifestations. At the end of the story, he disappears on a sea-voyage to Portugal (the Odysseus parallel is invoked) and his books and art treasures are looted and largely destroyed in the war.

The story is an Italian and Mediterranean version of Wells's "The Door in the Wall", which is not mentioned, although the professor alludes to another Wells tale and confesses that it "makes me want to spit for a month on end". Lampedusa's sensual paradise may be compared with Wells's prenatal one. "Intercourse" with the Siren communicates to the student of Greek a far deeper knowledge of the classical reality than his books can. The beast who is also an Immortal, Lighea is the natural spirit with which one may commune in the intensity of an unfettered pleasure in nature. In her, the joyous delicacy of the carnal is no escape from understanding. The student who experiences her grows into the old man who longs for her, and who finally seeks her in her own element, the waters which hold life, and death. Like Wells's garden, Lampedusa's paradise offers an ambiguous image that is best defined in terms of the trope worked out in Panofsky's famous essay "*Et in Arcadia ego*".[15] Analyzing the traditional landscape of Arcadia in art, Panofsky finds that the well-known Latin motto should be read to mean that death haunts even the pastoral dream. At the same time, he notes that this wisdom is inextricably bound up with its opposite: even in death may be Arcadia. In other words, a spiritual consolation may be drawn from death associated with beauty and the enjoyment of life at a certain height of sensitivity. In the Wells and Lampedusa stories we are balanced on the fine line between skepticism and belief, but Lampedusa evokes a more telling truth. Acute sensual knowledge links mind and nature, foreshadowing and softening the fact of death. The moment of bliss remains free from tension, though

79

the quotidian world surrounds it with the reality of time and change. The point is that in the naturalistic context commitment to the moment, a passage *through* it, represents the only possible entry into the higher realms of meaningfulness; and even a death experienced in the full awareness of its actual sensual texture renders one superior to the multitude, for whom death is the final triviality in a chain of events only half lived-through. And this is why Lampedusa's paradise is more significant than Wells's — just because the actual experience contained in it is less cerebral and fanciful and more concretely resonant. Lampedusa's Siren, who is the spirit of concrete experience in art and nature, may destroy our complacency about some of the cherished values of the modern world; and if there is a touch of the Romantic death-drive in such a vision, it is balanced and redeemed by its emphasis on the real content of an experience proved on the pulses and not merely conjured up in fantasy.

In such a story, we come close to the kind of tale in which a coherent mythical pattern is linked to a specifically rendered environment, where the paradisal vision is distanced from a real present, yet by no means unrelated to the problems of the common day. The important point here is that such stories conjure up a consistent and credible natural setting; they are not fantasies, nor do they make an obtrusive use of hermetic linkings. While the realistic surface may not be of the low mimetic variety, there is a presumption of a necessary plausibility of detail, undisturbed by any blatantly imposed psychic configurations. This grouping would include such double-visioned, reading-inspired voyage-myths as Tennyson's "The Lotus Eaters" and "Voyage of Maeldune", a realistic novel with strong symbolic patterning such as Alain-Fournier's *Le Grand Meaulnes*, the Darwinian epic world of Johannes Jensen's *The Long Journey*, and a few examples from modern science fiction — in all of which one may find images of the natural paradise rooted in a specific and coherent natural setting that is not merely fanciful. (What is common to these and other works exhibiting the paradisal moment in nature, is, of course, no "archetypal pattern", no image of garden or of another specific local, but rather a common spatial ordering, a meaningfulness based on the projection of human values threatened by the dominant culture.)

In order to suggest the range and variety of the fiction exhibiting the paradisal moment within a mythical context, three wholly diverse examples may be considered. The first of these is Pater's *Marius the Epicurian* (1885). In *Marius*, Pater produced a work in which the interaction of the isolated consciousness with place is the central dramatic fact, one in which the Victorian present is encountered through the distanced and mythical world of the Rome of the Antonines. The book enshrines a quest, and one extremely relevant to its age and ours. Indeed, like the D.H. Lawrence of *The Rainbow*, Pater comes to terms with Darwinism in a narrative which carries us from the immemorial rural world to the profane "world-city". Pater's extensive use of natural space includes several glimpses of the paradisal moment. In one scene, early in the novel, the fever-ridden Marius goes to the temple of Aesculapius for recovery. Pater's description captures the atmosphere of calm around the fountain and garden, and shows us Marius casting off his bad dreams through a specifically bodily restoration. The harmony slowly settling upon Marius's disturbed consciousness is a product of the enclosing beneficence of the human-scaled landscape and buildings; the change of air and the draught of healing water are experienced in a landscape of golden light which recurs at certain key moments throughout the book. Pater was forced by his immersion in evolutionary thought on the one hand, and by his search for the fixed point of meaningfulness on the other, to attempt a reconciliation between change and the power of consciousness to grasp an essential and enduring world. In *Marius*, the drive is to go beyond the visual, but everything begins in the visual, in the specific environment, out of which comes a new meaning for the adventuring consciousness to carry forward to the next stage. Pater creates the paradisal enclave in settings that call to mind a series of pictures washed by the patina of time, yet recognizably related to the Italian landscape that is a palimpsest of impressions and cultures. The vitality of the quest is strong enough to save the book from degenerating into picturesque irrelevance. Social reality and the clash of personalities yield in this fiction to meditation and dreamlike reverie, yet the book grapples with the challenge of Darwinism in its own way, rejecting the morality of the arena through the power of true seeing, and rising finally from awareness to awareness: the isolated consciousness is healed in nature, reads meanings from evidences of human culture, and finally seeks contact with human beings in their suffering reality. Here, the paradisal moment is not a purely "aesthetic" savouring of a certain atmosphere, but the formulation of a vision of the sacred in the face of the profane world and against the erosions of time. Pater's insistence on the power of the senses enables him to rise plausibly from a dramatization of physical to spiritual energy, his grasp of evolution includes a vision of the continuity of values amid change; and at the end the secular golden age becomes merely a glimpse of that higher spiritual order which contemporary man must create in his own way, as "a sort of religious phase possible for the modern mind".

Yet the paradisal enclave which we have designated "mythical" can occur not only in an historically-shaped dream, anchored in a specific landscape, as in Pater, but in terms of animal fantasy, as conceived, for example, by Kenneth Grahame in *The Wind in the Willows* (1908). Here we move at one point *via* the sharpened senses, to a peak of religious experience, which is surprisingly serious and successful. If it is true that as adults we can refuse to be wholly captivated by Grahame's "nineties" paganism, his spell remains nonetheless potent, within certain well-defined limits.

The Wind in the Willows, of course, is an animal story in which the animals are partially recognizable figures in English society — the eccentric squire, the middle-class intellectual, the member of the landed gentry living in "The Hall" — and partially animals with animal senses and "codes". A carefully laid-out scene helps to create the symbolic reference. There is first of all, The River — the well-established, central order of society, where things are always "normal" and one can live a life of Aristotelean mediocrity — the kind that is golden. Beyond is the Open Road, leading to all imaginable adventure, leading to the Wide World, where anything may happen. The Wild Wood, by contrast, is a dangerous "primitive" sphere, where conflict is suggested, if not directly portrayed. When Mole joins Rat on the river, he is the ordinary middle class citizen, interrupting what seems to be his all-important spring cleaning to discover the delights of a picnic. Yet there are discoveries to be made once one takes leave of the workaday attitude, once one departs from the "main stream".

Grahame's book defines a certain relationship between the workaday world and the world of the imagination. It suggests the difficulty of retaining a true visionary sense in the workaday world — Grahame's own problem of course, as banker and poet, but one that has relevance for all of modern society. Grahame suggests that a too impulsive surrender to romantic impulse will lead one astray, yet the obliteration of that impulse hands one over to the workaday world. Badger is too lacking in imagination, untouched by quixotic impulse. It is better to be like Rat and Mole, open to the mystery of life, receptive, without going too far. To go too far is to fall into absurdity. There is a narrow channel, distinct from the broad main stream, where one may sail to the island of Pan.

The experience of Pan is that deeper level of instinct and mystery that human beings may find in nature, if they do not shut themselves up, or fill their heads with nonsense. It is an experience of stillness with just the hint of a sound — like the wind in the willows. It is the final height of the relaxed good-nature, the peaceful ease of being attained by Rat and Mole. Such an experience is numinous, an experience of awe. It is the paradisal reward for patient but unfixed attention, and it cannot be forced, nor can it be conveyed to anyone else or even recalled clearly when it is over. It is just Experience. (Only on second thought do the negative implications of the description strike the reader: the obvious references to death, the funereal quality of the Styx-like river. Banishing eros from his work, Grahame allows thanatos to appear. In its own way, this passage from *The Wind in the Willows* strikes as ambiguous a note as Wells's "The Door in the Wall" and Lampedusa's "The Professor and the Siren".)

Yet after all, Rat and Mole sail away, carrying with them the visionary gleam and the longing. Grahame turns the book over to Toad, which is perhaps a mistake, but characteristic. The island of Pan must be hidden, giving way to the broad comedy. The book ends with the restoration of peace to River Bank society. Order is preserved; even the Wild Wood seems tame and suburban. One wonders whether Grahame has not sacrificed too much, whether Pan will ever appear again.

Grahame's fantasy suggests the difficulty of finding a vision in a society which has cast out too much in the name of order, yet we are not certain that he would really have had it different. One senses in his work the stifling of passionate yearning too early and too easily. His awareness of the social necessities and of the harshness of the natural world from a certain angle, press too closely on his vision. Yet the vision of the golden age, and the smile of Pan remain — for a moment — real. In a world of necessary compromises, Grahame creates an island of bliss, a point of contact with sacral nature. It is through the senses open to the wonder of nature that one discovers the timeless — such seem to be the point of contact between Grahame's vision and the other works we have been discussing here.

But the paradisal option can also be part of a vision strongly affected by ideas of man's evolutionary powers and limitations. We see this in William Golding's study of the clash of two forms of consciousness-in-nature, *The Inheritors* (1956). Golding's novel begins as an ironical commentary upon H.G. Wells's supposedly complacent view of history. Wells's slight piece of journalism, ''The Grisly Folk'', (and his famous *Outline of History*), are taken by Golding as evidence of Wells's naive and all-too-transparent belief in ''progress''. It is as if Wells were to be wholly identified with the character of his 1936 film, John Cabal, the technocratic visionary, for whom all human moral complexities are resolved in a flight into space and time. Certainly, this is a real aspect of Wells, as we shall see, but it is far from being the central one, and the Wells critics have known this for some time. Nonetheless, it was fair enough for Golding to seize upon such a position as a point of departure for his own vision, and to use the Wellsian imagery of ''The Grisly Folk'' in a devastatingly witty reversal of meaning, for the resulting fiction invites us to examine the issues involved with a more alert self-awareness, and with a sense of our own involvement in the shifting perspectives of our culture.

In *The Inheritors* Golding transforms Neanderthal Man from a bogey into what, in the jargon in the sixties, would be called a ''flower-child''. ''The people'' he sees as precisely located at the nexus of suppressed gifts which our writers dealing with Homo Sapiens have framed as a ''paradisal moment'', possible only on certain favoured occasions in the workaday reality of modern life. In fact, it is difficult to pinpoint a perfect instance of the paradisal experience in *The Inheritors*, precisely because the Neanderthals are assumed to be always in it — though the book tells us chiefly of those ''vanishings'' and ''obstinate questionings'' — which, of course, they experience in their own measure and kind. At

83

many points, however, we are given a fleeting sense of the possible bliss of this already disturbed tribe of the meek who will never inherit the earth. Their place in nature is of a special intensity and fulness, and they themselves are capable of sinking into a collective physicality, in which divisive consciousness yields to a wholeness that makes them virtually one with their surroundings. The Neanderthals, non-thinking (in our sense), have an amazing capacity to unify emotionally in a group. Living in an ecologically-balanced world, they possess only a primitive culture, and worship the earth-goddess Oa. Though far from being depicted as in some never-never land, (food is crucially important to them, one notes), they are non-violent, without much sense of time and change, and integrated in the natural setting in a way that seems almost idyllic at its best moments. Their senses, strong and alive, make pleasure independent of these elaborate ego-processes which bless and afflict Homo Sapiens.

Golding's ingenuity in building up contrasts between the Neanderthals and the invading Homo Sapiens group is monumental (and perhaps a great deal too elaborate). Nonetheless, there is a remarkable shift in his perspective, one that makes all easy contrasts dissolve in a final vision of human complexity. For he does not of course stop at the point at which we are beginning to see the limitations of Wells's imagining — which remained outside the consciousness of the Grisly Folk. The first movement of the novel is satiric (the "People" are actually in touch with experience whose fullness Homo Sapiens longs for and would express as a paradisal drive in his higher culture), but the second (apparently added in a revision) is truly ironic: Homo Sapiens is indeed the glory, jest and riddle of the world, precisely because his striving is inseparable from guilt and self-recrimination.

The Neanderthals imagine themselves to be in a stable world, but the world is changing, and challenging them to adapt. The final price of their adaptation would be to become like the New People, but this ultimate stage of "dark" knowledge is never reached. The Neanderthals are wiped out while in a state of innocence, or at least while they are only on the border of truly human experience. The river and the fall are barriers which the Neanderthals find it hard to cross. Golding's image of the golden age or the paradisal state is framed by a sense of the "bite" of Darwinian nature. Homo Sapiens, with his big fires and his ruthless exploitation of his environment, makes the very terms of his own unease and creates the conditions of his ultimately divided consciousness. The Fall is bound up with the act of evolutionary commitment; Promethean man cannot separate striving in a collective sense from individual selfishness and evil. The power to transform nature puts man in the position of having to choose between intolerable alternatives: he must either give up higher culture or learn to live with his guilt. As the ending suggests, this latter alternative may be possible, but only as an act of love and vision. Fear of the unknown can be banished, and the severing of the two natures healed perhaps only in art. Tuami's carving may stand for the very unity which Golding and all the other creators of the modern paradisal vision are perhaps in search of: the creative act that will heal our one-sidedness, not by the acceptance of fantasy, but by the penetration through the clichés of our culture, into a level of deeper truth.

In *The Inheritors* Golding translates the Fall from Christianity into anthropological myth, and frames the paradisal experience as an imagined prehistory which bears directly upon our present situation. The power of innocence in nature is fully measured, but not accepted as in itself a realistic position for modern man. Though the kind of knowledge summed up in the Neanderthals, taken by itself, would lead to our extinction, it must be assimilated in some sense, if only as a measure of our own ambiguous bearings. Golding's position is as finely poised as Wells's (in "The Door in the Wall") and Lampedusa's in "The Professor and the Siren". In Golding's novel, as in those stories, the paradisal moment generates a knowledge which our culture, at times, seems unable either to live with or without. The point is perhaps that something of this knowledge of concrete experience must be brought into our awareness and become part of what we are. And though this indeed may be a specific and real commitment to a certain consciousness and a way of relation to nature that we have abandoned, such transformation cannot involve a simple reversal of our evolutionary commitments. Indeed it may emerge as simply the power of art to recall to us the necessities of a concrete existence, so that Tuami's carving would in the final analysis become a symbol of the reintegration with nature possible in the psychosocial phase of our evolutionary journey: a small reminder of the necessity of both energy and repose, intellectual drive and emotional coherence, and a pinpointing of the power of the art to restore us to a complete sense of those values within which the paradisal experience becomes a significant, though not a total, expression of what we are.

CHAPTER FOUR
Man in the Biosphere:
Toward an Ecological Imagination

Man does not stand alone in environment; he is part of the living world of plants and animals, competing for space with them, using them, seeking identification through them or "above" them. From ancient times this complex ecological positioning has been suggested in totemic structures, animal and vegetative myths, and stories of transformation. It is important at once to distinguish between observation and iconography, though one initially inspires the other and in the fine shadings they will obviously blend together. The literature of man's biomic connections is that in which observation of animal or plant reality has (at least at some point) been sharply objective. Already such an epitome as appears, for example, in *Ecclesiastes*, shows a late stage of man's reflection on his place in the biosphere: "For the lot of man and of beast is one lot; the one does as well as the other. Both have the same life-breath, and man has no advantage over the beast; but all is vanity".[1] Yet man has consciousness which enables him to perceive his necessary death in advance, as Bergson points out, and also culture which survives him and enables his successors to carry on from beyond the beginning.[2] The forms which express his connection with the animals are at the same time the measure of his removal from them, though rooted of course in a common biological reality. Relatively primitive literature is already capable of very subtly embodying a specific observation of plant and animal behaviour, to the end no doubt of achieving specific goals, but without loss of the emotional identity that is yet another specifically literary, or religious, way of relating to the real environment. The great cave paintings of Lascaux are significant because they show an immense capacity to perceive outer reality, and a tender feeling for the actual and specific activities of the animals depicted, whatever the precise "scientific" aim. They are the earliest and remain one of the greatest of images in which art, science and religion come together in a perception that is clear, concerned, and which probably aimed at being practical.

Despite the constant tendency of art to turn such images of animals and

87

plants into static traditions of representation, one can see a renewed sense of awareness of the living character of biomic forms breaking through crusts of formalization. In the case of the animals, man's sense of his own superiority as culture-maker led to the gradual acceptance of lordship, the superiority principle expressed in myth and story, but this sense of positioning failed to obliterate the careful rendering of animal life completely, though it built in too many preconceptions and tendencies to humanize and at the same time denigrate other animal life in terms of human cultural achievement. The relative thinning-out of European wildlife at an early stage removes the possibility of exact observation, and by the Middle Ages the best animal description centers on animals of sport — falcons, e.g., or expends itself in the creation of the half-imagined beasts of the bestiaries, whose shapes were fed by rumour and fancy and made static in iconic tradition.[3] During the Renaissance precise observation again began, and the available domestic and local animals were once again the focus of perceptive description. The real fruit of this in terms of literary significance is the various traditions of amateur descriptive studies of which the English versions of the Gilbert White variety are a well-known example. By the time of the proto-phase of modern biological study, with Goethe and Humboldt, the attention to detail had become part of the artistic pleasure of rendering.

During the eighteenth century, the underlying philosophical theory was that of the Great Chain of Being, within which the new analytic and mechanistic approaches to nature were at first subsumed, without resulting in an abandonment of the sense of a hierarchical harmony in which man has a special place. The philosophical trend of the Enlightenment supported for a while the humanistic vision of a world of mutually related forms, with man as crowning intelligence linking visible and invisible worlds.[4] In a setting enhanced by the development of landscape and garden art, which gave the wealthy at least a rare sense of integration with nature, the philosophers could confirm the universal order simply by taking a walk. In the great age of the amateur naturalist it seemed clear that the view of each species as a relatively static part of the eternal chain could be confirmed by experience. Though specific facts were often sought by "natural philosophers" as part of an effort to "fill out" the missing parts of the linked order, literature in the mainstream retained its neo-classical predilection for "generic" configurations, and its renderings remained at a certain distance from the concrete and specific environment.

The next phase, however, saw the development of a strong counter-tendency, one which involved, so to speak, a "descent" from the Deistic God and the assumed generality, toward an overriding sense of plenitude, summed up by Lovejoy in his idea of the "temporalizing of the chain". Arguments against immutable species appeared and the discovery of microscopic forms began to upset the confident sense of harmony that some had previously assumed.[5] Though the formulation of the "struggle for existence" was not yet consistent, various forms of evolutionary thought were increasingly dominant. Romanticism is itself curiously set at the crisis point of a transitional phase. It is part of a new and increasing attention to the details of the biosphere (inherited perhaps even more from the thought of the eighteenth century that from its literature), but it does not really commit itself to the placing of human and animal life on anything like an equal basis. The Deistic God has descended into "nature", but this is a nature of landscape as *Gestalt* rather than of forms competing in space. When the animals are directly contemplated by the Romantic poets, various viewpoints appear. One of these may be seen in Goethe's "Metamorphosis of the Animals", which, although perhaps not written until 1806, looks back in some ways to the Enlightenment harmony. In Goethe's words: "Every animal is an end in itself, it comes forth perfect from nature's womb and begets young that are perfect. All limbs develop according to eternal laws, and even the rarest of forms mysteriously preserve the archetype". Such Platonizing leads predictably to the assertion of human centrality, as the reader is advised to let his "mind dwell with delight upon this noble concept of power and constraint, of caprice and law, freedom and moderation, movement within order, pre-eminence and deficiency". Man himself is addressed by the poet at the climax. "Rejoice, supreme product of nature, in your ability to rethink her supreme thought, the highest to which, in her creativeness, she has risen". It is "fact" and not "fancy" that the muse guarantees; and as part of such confidence a whole range of rather generalized "observation", such as Goethe musters here, can flower into knowledge, but there is clearly no real equation of man and the animals, indeed, quite the reverse. Goethe's harmonious resolution, however, seems to be more of a retrospective summary than a pointer for the future, when we begin to consider what the Romantic imagination could mean for the English poets in particular. For on the one hand, it could serve to lead them away from nature into the "contemplation of the archetype" in a much more radical sense than Goethe would have allowed, while on the other hand, it could send them groping toward instincts that would take them closer to the animal life whose plenitude increasingly pressed upon their inherited sense of distinctions of species. As the mechanism of science became clear first in the realms of physics and astronomy (despite Descartes' early attempt at turning the animals into machines), it was still possible for the Romantics to take the "living" nature of the animals and plants as something that could be set against the abstracting consciousness implicit in that science. If the eighteenth century usually assumes man's superiority to the forms with which he is connected in the larger order, and Darwinism man's equality as mechanism with the primordial mechanism of nature, then the Romantic vision is set somewhere in between. With the Romantics a plunge into the biosphere begins, but chiefly as a means of preserving a certain kind of human uniqueness.

That the Romantics developed the power of representation of the biosphere can hardly be doubted, but we have to be careful not to distort the character of their interest. The poetic rendering of outer nature that would connect man with the animal and plant life around him was slower to develop just because it lacked a central principle of justification — which Darwinism would provide, though with devastating consequences for man's self-image. One has to see the whole tradition of the amateur naturalist from Sir Thomas Browne to Gilbert White as proceeding from a perspective that encouraged immense confidence in human centrality and man's special destiny, a luxury that western history was about to dispense with. The post-Renaissance rational investigation of nature carried literature along with it, but a divergence began to occur when the findings of natural history could no longer feed the optimism of a safely generaliz-ed Deistic point-of-view. The new crisis about man's place in the order of things is occurring just as the Romantic vision of nature establishes itself — indeed, that vision can be understood as in some ways a response to that crisis. But the overturning of man's central position has not gone far enough for the emphasis to be placed in a relatively objective manner on the animal and plant consciousness itself. The linkings are made through metaphors that leave many areas of plant and animal life unexplored. Keats' ''Ode to a Nightingale'' (1819), for example, is clearly full of the sense of eroding time, and represents no complacent vision of natural harmony; yet the nightingale is promoted as a symbol of immortal song, rather than being brought into the vision of transience because of its intrinsic biological character. In the seventh stanza one sees Keats playing on the idea of the bird as part of a species whose song endures as a fact beyond the death of the individual bird, and contrasting this with the individual human consciousness receiving the song in painful awareness of its own limiting mortality. But the comparison is not made in biolo-gical terms; species-identification is only an empirical basis for the symbolic presentation of the bird as an emblem of poetry itself, and is not used to set up a contrast or comparison between bird-life and human life. It is only when the individual life patterns of human and extra-human forms become indicative of man's overall place in the nature of things that they can be explored in terms of equality and centrality in a signifi-cant total context. The Romantic vision of animal and plant life remains peripheral because animals and plants have not yet been recognized as significant clues to man's fate. They may be illustrations of a certain human condition, or the subjects of moralizing, or emblems of human aspiration — they may even be the objects of an honest transcript of the artist as reporter — but they are not significant sharers of man's fate, and so cannot form the basis of a direct comparative rendering in which their own life-patterns emerge as important.

Yet without associating it exclusively with Romanticism itself, we can date from this period a new sense in literature of the complexity of animal existence. Complacency yields to a sense of inquiry, and the new Realism's sense of fact includes the more objective examination of other life forms. Even in Romanticism, the animals are increasingly linked to man, and man to the animals, in terms of instincts, both "positive" and "negative". (This may or may not include a sharp separation between the social and natural orders). In this situation the erosion of the confident old rationalism includes sometimes a dramatization of what man can gain by a plunge into the depths of a new kind of knowing, often symbolized by the animal's sensory richness. On the other hand, the new rationalism of scientific Darwinism may become in Naturalistic terms a plunge that leads man into the chaos of brutality and "the red rage". With the break-up of the old sense of harmony the sharp separation of man from a total metaphysical order may be emphasized; the depiction of other life forms as completely alien looks to a future existentialism in which man is quite separate from an essentially meaningless nature. On the other hand, reiterations of a kind of traditional holistic pattern are possible; in these the drift toward idealism (and sometimes Christianity) is notable. More significant, and quite pervasive in modern literature, however, is the post-Naturalistic emphasis on some kind of totality that does not imply a lingering Christian idealism, but which dwells on the inextricable connection of man to the other natural forms in terms of some vision of human-inspired values that does without traditional metaphysical guarantees.

To find the direction of a future objectivity in Romantic writings, however, one must turn to the fringes, to Dorothy Wordsworth's journals, or to the minor poets, like John Clare and Leigh Hunt. In the writings of Clare, above all, realism is pervasive, the product of a detailed observation that is rare and striking. Clare's nightingale is as realistically observed as Keats's is symbolically resonant, while "Badger" is perhaps the first real "wild animal" poem in English literature. In such pieces as "The Fens" and "The Meadow Lake", Clare imagines a specific biome, and records the impact of man in exact terms, drawing our attention to the fine tunings of natural relationships within a spatially delimited area. Leigh Hunt's well-known (1835) trio of sonnets about man and fish, on the other hand, raises in a comic vein a problem that begins to haunt the modern imagination: the isolation of all the species from man, who is just beginning to see himself as equally part of nature with them. Man, the "long-useless-finned, haired, upright, unwet, slow" lord of creation had already been taught by Malthus the fact of the competition of forms in space for mere survival. At the dawn of a new awareness of animal reality, we find certain increasing signs of the tension among the linked forms that much of eighteenth century thought had celebrated. Hunt's trio of poems does not dwell on the gap between human consciousness and "life" in the sense that the "Ode to a

91

Nightingale" does. It rather expresses a certain shock at how structure and environment may shape perspective. The old confidence in nature's harmonious order is dutifully expressed in the affirmation of the spirit voice in Hunt's third sonnet, but the real effect of the poems is to suggest the strangeness of a specific *biological* divergence. That the point of view of the fish is taken seriously is what is shocking, and from this angle of vision man seems rather absurd. Quite simply, man's is not necessarily the last word on the order of creation. The sense of the alien life is being born.

The best evidence of this among Romantic writings is perhaps Mary Shelley's *Frankenstein* (1818). The monster pursues Frankenstein because he is a species to himself, alone, and unable to communicate with men. Frankenstein at first agrees to create a mate for him, but then changes his mind when he imagines the possibility of a new race competing with humankind. There are many parallels in the novel with Coleridge's "Ancient Mariner", but significantly, there can be no reconciliation with apparent ugliness because there is no total metaphysical order which guarantees unity among created things. In his search for knowledge Frankenstein temporarily throws over rationality and gives way to an ecstatic hubris of power-seeking. The separation of intellect and feeling are symbolized in the image of the "double", here the monster, who is in the position of an alien species in a unique way, because as a special creation he is linked to his creator. But the relationship between the monster and his master is in some respects like the split between the lower and the higher instincts in man that Darwinism will evoke in comparing man with the other animals. (It is not that either monster or man is always "lower" or "higher", but that they commonly face each in these terms, always on the verge of some purely physical struggle). Though the Frankenstein story is of a special complexity and suggestiveness, one of its effects is to establish the principle of competition of forms of life at the dawn of a new awareness of animal reality. Furthermore, Mary Shelley's emphasis is (in a sense) on man's tool-making powers, and like many of the post-Darwinian writers, she shows that these tool-making powers are not enough in the hands of a being essentially irrational.

In *Frankenstein* the hubris of rationality unleashes an opposite and dark self that threatens to destroy the human creator and even all of mankind. Though the increasingly vivid outpouring of scientific fact toward the mid-nineteenth century was beginning to demolish the older idea of the Great Chain of Being once and for all, the drift toward detailed realism of depiction affects those writers who can still affirm something of the majesty of the whole order of plant and animal life that has man at its center. American Transcendentalism is a strong guiding force in the lingering expression of the moral and physical harmony of the world, soon to be shaken by the Darwinian assertions. As early as 1834, in an address on "The Naturalist", Emerson had set the tone with a confident encouragement to scientific research, which could only confirm the philosopher's vision of humanity's abiding significance:

> When a reasoning man looks upon the Creation around him, he feels that it is most fit as a part of the study of himself that he should inquire into the nature of these related beings. He sees that the same laws that govern their structure govern his own; that his very superiority is yet in strict harmony with their natures. He wishes to comprehend their nature, to have such knowledge as shall place him as it were at the heart of Creation that he may see its tribes and races unfolding themselves in order (as the orbs of our system are seen from the sun), that he may have a Theory of animated nature, understand its Laws, so that his eye may predict the functions and habits of the individual before yet they show themselves. [6]

Joseph Wood Krutch credits Thoreau with being the first writer to treat animal and human life on a basis of absolute equality; but it seems that Thoreau's massive objectivity is really in the spirit of the Transcendentalist vision of harmony affirmed by Emerson. In the famous account of the moose hunt in *The Maine Woods* (1853-8) Thoreau shies away from the destructiveness closely associated with the frontier. It is the violation of the living body of nature in the skinning of the moose that disturbs Thoreau; he is shocked "to see that still warm and palpitating body pierced with a knife", and reflects on "the afternoon's tragedy" in a tone of guilt deriving from his participation in the hunt. He imagines that nature looks sternly upon him as a result of the killing of the moose, and we learn in the grand peroration to this episode that "every creature is better alive than dead, men and moose and pine trees". The poet is the true lover of the wood because it is he who understands the "living spirit of the tree", which is, "as immortal as I am, and perchance will go to as high as a heaven, there to tower above me still".

The equality that Thoreau envisages is ultimately based on an ideal unity achieved through the human perception of values in the traditional sense, a spiritual equality that looks backward to Emerson and Goethe, and forward mostly in terms of its massive factual detail. If we turn to the cosmic visions of Melville and Whitman, we find something of the same blending of spiritual and natural elements, but here the shock of the perception of an alien element, of something monstrously inhuman, obtrudes upon the sense of harmony to produce that "darkness" characteristic of Melville and redeemed and balanced in Whitman only by an equally powerful self-confidence. Melville's image of the leviathan life in the chapter "Brit" from *Moby Dick* (1851) suggests the meeting of visible and invisible forces in a vast setting in which man is an awed spectator. Such passages may be compared with the Whitman poems "Patroling Barnegat" (1880) and "The World Below the Brine" (1860), already referred to in chapter one. In section XXXI of "A Song of Myself", the sense of interpenetration of man with nature is achieved by a rapid shuttling back and forth between macro- and micro-cosm, pos-

93

sible because of the exuberance of the unifying ego-confidence of the visionary poet.

In vain the speeding or shyness,
In vain the plutonic rocks send their old heat against my approach,
In vain the mastodon retreats beneath its own powdered bones,
In vain objects stand leagues off and assume manifold shapes,
In vain the ocean settling in hollows and the great monsters lying low,
In vain the buzzard houses herself with the sky,
In vain the snake slides through the creepers and logs,
In vain the elk takes to the inner passes of the woods,
In vain the razor-billed auk sails far north to Labrador,
I follow quickly, I ascend to the nest of the fissure of the cliff.

If one compares this post-Darwinian confidence with Tennyson's early despair about the power of Paley's "evidences", a significant testimony appears to the steadiness of the Transcendentalist vision. In some of the famous outcries from *In Memoriam* the shock of the new geological investigation overrides the hope of unity inherited from the past:

I found Him not in world or sun,
    Or eagle's wing or insect's eye;

And again, lamenting that lost "splendid purpose" of men now destined to be "seal'd within the iron hills" the poet asks if there is:

No more? A monster then, a dream,
A discord. Dragons of the prime,
That tare each other in their slime
Were mellow music match'd with him.

The vastness that appalls Tennyson is exactly what confirms in Whitman his own sense of significance and, much later, when Tennyson returns rather wistfully to a vision of possible unity, it is the hesitation and the mental standing-back that we notice, not the conviction.

Flower in the crannied wall,
I pluck you out of the crannies,
I hold you here, root and all, in my hand,
Little flower — but *if* I could understand
What you are, root and all, and all in all,
I should know what God and man is.

Metaphysical security *might* be obtained by the creation of an intellectual distance between mind and nature, by an exercise of the narrowest rational tools sanctioned by the old synthesis or the new science. However, the "if" is notably underlined, and the emphasis is on lost possibility rather than achievement. (As has been pointed out, the plucked flower would be in fact split from the "all in all", and the poet's knowledge of nature therefore of a very limited analytic kind).[7]

Insect mechanism, the fish and reptilian life of cold blood, and the supposed rapacity of the carnivore — how these images dominate the post-Darwinian literature of the biosphere, and what a strange angle of reflection they cast upon human self-awareness! Most writers seem determined to explore the limits of apparently "automatic" functioning

94

of organic nature, while at the same time seeking values in the tangle of instinct. Sometimes, however, they can only stop in bafflement (and even horror) before the resulting sense of man's alienation and from the "all in all" that such explorations activate.

> ... a great part, perhaps the whole, of nature and of the universe is distinctly anti-human. The term inhuman does not express my meaning, anti-human is better; outré-human, in the sense of beyond, outside, almost grotesque in its attitude towards, would nearly convey it. Everything is anti-human. How extraordinary, strange, and incomprehensible are the creatures captured out of the depths of the sea! The distorted fishes; the ghastly cuttles; the hideous eel-like shapes; the crawling shell-encrusted things; the centipede-like beings; monstrous forms, to see which gives a shock to the brain. They shock the mind because they exhibit an absence of design. There is no idea in them.

As Richard Jefferies, the author of this passage (from Chapter Four, *The Story of My Heart*) admits, it is really a question of unassimilated sights, of patterns which man has not yet brought into a frame of reference that makes these forms so horrifying. It is precisely the courageous encounter of post-Darwinian literature with such alien life that constitutes one of its achievements. The writer in such a situation is extending the possibilities of human consciousness; man must not be allowed to be shocked into an acceptance of "the chaos" that Jefferies takes note of. Darwinism provides the possibility of an extension of the human world, for our fear of Leviathan is the result of an incomplete vision; but, science itself, though it contributes positively to a steady contemplation of life by its objectively grounded insights cannot register the finally human statement, because a fully human statement requires emotional affiliation. It is for the post-Darwinian writers to play out the drama of newly discovered horrors which are the result of seeing nature through a particular and limited human self, and to lead toward the finer vision that marks a new sense of values in the self, and hence in nature too.

The critics have been too impatient with the *longueurs* of some kinds of Naturalism. A great effort was being made by these writers to re-establish the alienated human consciousness in its natural matrix. Jack London's novel *The Call of the Wild* (1903), for example, is a poem in celebration of instinct, physicality, competition and reversion. The art of the book lies in the skill with which Buck is presented both as dog and as a semi-human character, so that the reader can concentrate on establishing certain connections, without being distracted by the complexities a human-centered tale would demand. (This kind of dramatization of "animal consciousness" is one of the minor triumphs of Naturalism.) A vision of life is evoked in which man is understood as the inhabitant of an environment which includes technology. Man's technology gives him supremacy and enables him to shape nature to a certain extent, but there is a life-quality which he shares with the animals, which is, or should be, the root of his values. The book follows Buck's reversion to the wild, carrying us backward along the line of human development until we recover a sense of the continuity of evolution, are initiated into the pure physicality of existence. (Such knowledge must remain underdeveloped in settings like that of the Judge Miller estate described at the beginning). As the relationship between Buck and John Thornton grows in the wilderness we learn the value of co-operation for survival and come to know the instincts that enable species to bridge gaps in communication. The final reversion activates a sense of the particular that at first seems merely a new range of canine knowledge, but which may also be taken to express what man has lost in the mechanized world left behind. This involves a kind of tactile encounter with the earth itself in which the dog could "thrust his nose into the cool wood moss, or into the black soil where long grasses grew, and snort with joy at the fat earth smells; or he would crouch for hours, as if in concealment, behind fungus covered trunks of fallen trees, wide-eyed and wide-eared to all that moved and sounded about him".

The limitations of London's vision are symptomatic of the Naturalistic dilemma at this stage of development. Mind has been demoted to the level of cunning and manipulation of technology, and the result is an incomplete system of values, given away by the striking celebration of "life itself" as the ultimate determinant:

> All that stirring of old instincts which at stated periods drives men out from the sounding cities to forest and plain to kill things by chemically propelled leaden pellets, the blood lust, the joy to kill — all this was Buck's, only it was infinitely more intimate. He was ranging at the head of the pack, running the wild thing down, the living meat, to kill with his own teeth and wash his muzle to the eyes in warm blood.
>
> There is an ecstasy that marks the summit of life, and beyond which life cannot rise. And such is the paradox of living, this ecstasy comes when one is most alive, and it comes as a complete forgetfulness that one is alive. This ecstasy, this forgetfulness of living comes to the artist, caught up and out of himself in a sheet of flame; it comes to the soldier, war-mad on a stricken field and refusing quarter; and it came to Buck, leading the pack, sounding the old wolf-cry, straining after the food that was alive and that fled swiftly before him through the moonlight. He was sounding the deeps of his nature that were deeper than he, going back into the womb of Time. He was mastered by the sheer surge of life, the tidal wave of being, the perfect joy of each separate muscle, joint, and sinew in that it was everything that was not death, that it was aglow and rampant, expressing itself in movement, flying exultantly under the stars and over the face of dead matter that did not move.
>
> (Chapter Three)

The deep ecstasy of human nature comes about in complete spontaneity, and results in action — *is*, to a great extent, physical action. But the moral scope of the action is unimportant, killing is as good as creating, the "war-mad" soldier is equated with the inspired artist. Physical kinesis of this ecstatic kind divides the living from the non-living; "life" is greater than "matter". Jack London here attempts to carry the "struggle" of Darwinism into a realm of values; to turn the limitations of the new vision of nature to account. Man can rise to the "summit of life" when "nature" triumphs over the civilized self, when he activates the "deeps" he shares with the beasts. A few observations suggest themselves at this point. The passage to the deeps, as the book makes clear, is through violence. Now if we compare what Jack London could take from Darwinism with a contemporary account of animal and human "aggression", we gain an interesting perspective on such "primordial" values. Konrad Lorenz, in *King Solomon's Ring*, discussing the "violent" propensities of wolves, emphasizes in fact the instinctual checks on any struggle to the death. Wolves do not really indulge in the ruthless tactics which Jack London evokes as part of his metaphor of the "wolf nature" in Buck the dog, and in men. When a submission signal is given, the "dominant primordial beast" does not press his advantage for the sake of ecstasy. As Lorenz points out: "When, in the course of evolution, a species of animals develops a weapon which may destroy a fellow-member at one blow, then, in order to survive, it must develop with the weapon, a social inhibition to prevent a usage which could endanger the existence of the species". It is precisely Lorenz's point that man's technology has been developed in the absence of such prohibitions. Contemporary science, looking more closely at animal behaviour, turns Jack London's set of values around, for whereas Jack London envisages man as (fortunately) a beast gifted with technology who retains access through violence to his beast-nature, modern ethology suggests that man should be seen as (unfortunately) a beast gifted with technology who suffers from an insufficiently developed instinctual control apparatus, and who must in consequence develop an ethical system to prevent his own self-destruction. Activating the "deeps" that we supposedly share with the beasts would not be the summit of life; it would more likely be the slope of death, in so far as our own human species is concerned.

Nonetheless, Jack London's vision of ecstasy is at least a positively directed answer to the threatening "mechanism" of Darwinism; it suggests the power of literature to restore meaningfulness, even though in itself it manifests an insufficiency of language and substitutes a false "within" for a true one. If it remained for D.H. Lawrence above all to assimilate the Darwinistic "primordial" vision in the name of human values at a greater level of complexity, many writers of the period up to the present could join in Jack London's portraiture of a newly extended human awareness of links beyond the old narrow rationalism, without necessarily leading man into the murky depths of an instinctive life where all values are reduced to the level of a physical spasm.

Here we may point to the post-Naturalistic emphasis on the ecological totality, largely predicted by such writers as Hardy, D.H. Lawrence, Jensen, and Robinson Jeffers, in spite of the strength of other factors in their work. Scientific ecology derives directly from Darwinism, and is simply the expression of the relationship of animals to one another and to their environment in numerical terms.[8] What is being sought are the laws operating in the world of living things. The "ecological" phase of literature might be said to be characterized by a de-emphasis on the sheer fact of brute struggle in the natural world and by an increased attention to cooperation in evolutionary progress. Awareness is valued over sheer "instinct"; technology is no longer the focus of man's superiority and degradation. The new attitude of man to the animals visible in some important texts of modern literature is neither one of "rational" superiority, nor of self-conscious "bestiality" but one involving a sense of the necessary inter-relationships of man, animals and plants in the total biosphere. Such literature rejects the temptation of a flight to the "pure" imagination and continues to reflect the totality of human experience, the tensions of the within and the without. In this tradition of environmental realism many variations are possible, and the human angle of vision varies, but what is ever-present is the beneficent influence of Naturalism's courageous encounter with the kinetic physical nature of Darwinism.

An examination of two quite different examples of this post-Naturalistic vision may serve to illustrate these developments. William Faulkner's "The Bear", published in 1942, is set in the period of the last quarter of the nineteenth century; it is the only Faulkner story that goes back so far, and Faulkner suggests a period of critical transition from accessible wilderness where the ancient hunting ritual is played out, to a recent period of economic domain, in which mechanism replaces specifically human values. The story therefore recapitulates the perennial antithesis we have already noted between nature as sphere of leisure and experience and nature as sphere of exploitation and use. This significance is built up in a fairly obvious way, in terms of the diverse characters joined in the quest of the bear, organized through the specific consciousness of Ike McCaslin, the boy who is initiated into the quest, and illustrated in the contrast of the shrieking locomotive and such natural images as the bear itself, Lion the dog, and the snake. The sphere of action is essentially the wood itself, though there is a long diversion in which Ike tries ineffectually to act on the code of the religious sense of the evil of ownership derived from his experience of initiation.

Faulkner's wood has characteristics that control the meanings of the story, and we must first examine its specific quality and relevance. To begin with, the wood is not described in much detail at all, nor is it set apart from the surrounding country in terms of descriptive isolation — as is the case for example with the forest in W.H. Hudson's *Green Mansions*. Faulkner's wood is really a set of specific place-experiences that we encounter in Ike McCaslin's consciousness. It is only made visual at moments of specific intensity, when the effect seems to be one of a generally blurred and overarching natural growth suddenly becoming frozen and fixed in a specific and short-range view. We experience therefore no sense of spaciousness, none of the cathedral-like expansiveness of Hudson's wood, but rather a sense of an immense and tangled "bush" of great density and darkness, virtually unbounded, and pressed closely around Ike, who stands still to absorb the specific meaning of each occasion. The wood is therefore best understood as a representative ecological domain, as a symbolic biosphere, and not merely a sphere of Darwinian struggle; it is a place where man must establish himself in relation to a total order, in which he must learn the balance between struggle and restraint that is true maturity.

This wilderness, with its mystery and darkness, is given immemorial significance from the start: "the big woods, bigger and older than any recorded document; of white man fatuous enough to believe he had bought any fragment of it, of Indian ruthless enough to pretend that any fragment of it had been his to convey". It is at once the substance of saga, and accessible only to hunters "not women, not boys not children"; it is they who celebrate it with sacramental whisky, when they are not actually engaged in the ritual encounter with it. And the spirit of the wood is of course Old Ben the bear who melts into its shadows and whose slaying marks the end of the old dominion of participation and the beginning of the new era of exploitation. Ike is initiated into the fellowship of the hunters, slowly growing up in the process. We follow him through a series of encounters in which the wood is suddenly illuminated with a particular relevance. He sees the bear first in his dreams, is aware of being watched by it, then discovers its footprints, but he must strip himself of civilized accoutrements, even gun and compass, in order to see the bear itself. And then, when he knows the wood better than all the others, he cannot himself slay the bear, although he has the opportunity. It is Boon, half-animal, half-man, the Caliban spun from the dark side of southern rhetoric, who kills the bear in hand-to-hand combat, out of a fierce courage in defense of his animal equivalent, the mongrel dog Lion. On this day, with perhaps too neat a symbolic resonance, Sam Fathers, purebred Indian and real master of the wilderness, is mortally stricken. Both Indian and Negro have asserted only a kind of primal relation to the wood, something less and something more than ownership, while the white man, in defiance of the Biblical injunction to be merely overseer and not possessor, has staked out his legal claim to it, "like pygmies about the ankles of a drowsing elephant".

"The Bear" encompasses two falls from grace. One is ancestral, part of the white man's assertion of ownership. This has polluted his past and continues to haunt his present. It is the Puritan sense of sin carried by Ike and which he seeks to exorcise (unsuccessfully) by his good works, giving up his claim to any land and attempting to find the descendants of old Carothers and make them economically independent. The second fall is the specific historical destruction of the wood, carried out inevitably because of the first, because even those who love and serve it, the hunters, have emasculated themselves by their tacit participation in the ancestral fault. The hunters, even Ike, the most sensitive, are themselves shadowed by a sense of doom and inevitable fate, and perform in the final tragedy like men walking in their sleep.

Yet the very rhetoric that enforces this sense of doom, images at the same time, the essential indestructibility of the matrix men have apprehended in a false relation. Even before his meeting with Boon, who sits in futility, — his gun in pieces as he asserts his domination over an empire of squirrels, — Ike has been granted a vision of immortal nature, which has taken its initiatives to itself: Sam, for example —

> not vanished but merely translated into that myriad life which printed the dark mold of these secret and sunless places with delicate fairy tracks, which, breathing and biding and immobile, watched him from beyond every twig and leaf until he moved, moving again, walking on; he had not stopped, he had only paused, quitting the knoll which was no abode of the dead because there was no death, not Lion and not Sam; not yet held fast in earth but free in earth and not in earth but of earth, myriad yet undiffused of every myriad part, leaf and twig and particle, air and sun and rain and dew and night, acorn oak and leaf and acorn again, dark and dawn and dark and dawn again in their immutable progression and, being myriad, one and old Ben too, old Ben too; they would give him his paw back even, certainly they would give him his paw back; then the long challenge and the long chase, no heart to be driven and outraged, no flesh to be mauled and bled —

History has moved from corruption to corruption but beyond the flesh and blood of history is the organic whole, passing into the spiritual, the immortal cycle. Here the symbol is the snake, "evocative of all knowledge and an old weariness and of pariah-hood and death", a being "free of all laws of mass and balance", whom Ike addresses in the Indian tongue as "chief" and "grandfather". The snake slides always towards a mysterious and doubtful future whose only certainty is the repetition of occasions of struggle, fall and recovery, summing up in itself the knowledge beyond those boundaries men artificially prescribe, the shape-shifting organic life. It suggests that the irony of the ending has a specific historical force, rather than one that encompasses all of man's acts, for man, if he renounces his servitude to possession, and renews his relationship with the "myriad life" in ritual participation can work his way out of the traps toward a new stewardship. For this, perhaps, is necessary the sacrifice by the white man who brought the curse on the land, of his perennial greed. At the end of the story, when that greed seems in fact triumphant, the snake slipping away into the bush reminds us of man's persistent relation to the organic; of the temptation to grasp the forbidden, of the serpent wisdom which remembers greater issues of life and death.

Ernest Hemingway's *The Old Man and the Sea* (1952), appearing near the end of the writer's tempestuous life, marks a break with

Hemingway's depiction of a typically protective natural enclosure, and shows his capacity for making the most of a "primitivistic" reduction in a new light. The woods of Burguete, the carefully delimited campsite on the Big-Two-Hearted River, give way to vistas of the immense open sea. The sea clearly represents for Hemingway what the big woods do for Faulkner: the total natural sphere with its challenge and its possibilities for the making or breaking of a man. It is not simply a Darwinian image, in the traditional sense, that we encounter, however, but a unified order in which man has a part, one to which he can establish a meaningful affiliation, if he is willing to commit himself to love and work and self-restraint. Hemingway's assumption of the simple consciousness of Santiago is achieved, by and large, without strain. Santiago confronts all of life's terrors — failure, death — yet he steers straight into the struggle, himself part of the sea which he knows in detail in its reality. The clouds, the fish, the birds, the prismatic colours, the other shores of the same sea — he accepts them as part of his world. This world has its laws and uses; it is a tragic world, but one where a man must live. Darwinian nature is confronted in all its ruthlessness, for, we are told, all things kill one another, yet there are acts of love and courage which balance the killing and the waste. A small bird lands on the line and Santiago welcomes it; he blesses the fish he must kill, and even the shark that comes first to feed on his fish. Santiago does not complain beyond measure at his defeat for he knows that he went out too far and nature has its inevitable laws. Santiago in his equality of acceptance, in his capacity to love and bless, achieves greatness, for he is a man measured against an immense scale. Santiago wears scars that are "as old as erosions in a fishless desert", yet he shows the particular human qualities that rescue meaning from struggle. He is undefeated because his understanding reaches through the illusory divisions of things to grasp life's totality. Santiago's organic sense of life reverses the old Hemingway attitude to the feminine or at least transcends it; the sea is a bitch by universal law, and must be loved. And how deeply Santiago knows the sea is registered again and again in description which suggests the biological environment touched with love that comes through long experience.

> The clouds over the land now rose like mountains and the coast was only a long green line with the gray blue hills behind it. The water was a dark blue now, so dark that it was almost purple. As he looked down into it he saw the red sifting of the plankton in the dark water and the strange light the sun made now. He watched his lines to see them so straight down out of sight into the water and he was happy to see so much plankton because it meant fish. The strange light the sun made in the water, now that the sun was higher, meant good weather and so did the shape of the clouds over the land.

Point by point the sense of being at home, the sense that "no man is ever alone on the sea" is created. The great struggle with the marlin is fought and the fish taken in a manner which shows Santiago's deep aesthetic concern. For Santiago, like the writer, is a craftsman whose material is

101

nature, and his occupation is also his pleasure. Unlike the matadors who move with split-second decisiveness across the horns of death, the fisherman meditates his confrontation. His experience is timeless, measured only by the sun and moon, and he is slowly taken beyond all familiar landmarks into the open sea, bound by ties of necessity, but ordering and shaping experience by his long-learned craft. When he goes too far, the law of balance decrees that he must lose what his courage earned, but nothing can destroy the inner cargo. In his fisherman Hemingway finds for once a man in whom morality is not divorced from action, in whom contemplation and action are united. And when there is nothing more for the sharks to eat, his victory is secure:

> The old man could hardly breathe now and he felt a strange taste in his mouth. It was coppery and sweet and he was afraid of it for a moment. But there was not much of it.
>
> He spat into the ocean and said, "Eat that Galanos. And make a dream you've killed a man".

After that, he sails in "well" and "intelligently", noticing the lightened skiff and thinking of the "great sea with our friends and enemies".

Haunted by the sense of emptiness that the American midwest seems to bestow on its products, Hemingway consistently invoked the primitive as a mode of encounter with the raw forces of nature, as a dramatic *form* of confrontation with his deepest fears. The primitive was capable of providing a ritual with which to meet death, an aesthetic that was also a morality. Nature was struggle; very well, then — it must be engaged as ritual struggle, under the emblems of lion, bull or fish. Personal will doomed to failure could be rescued by form. For Hemingway there were many failures, fallings off into mere mechanism, the boring fireside chats of *The Green Hills of Africa*, the pointless violence of *To Have and To Have Not*, the self-dramatization slipping into self-parody of *Across The River and Into The Trees*, and on top of this the public folly of his cultivation of a public presence, which becomes an epitaph in the posthumous embarrassment of *Islands in the Stream*. *The Old Man and the Sea*, however, marks one last real high-point. In creating Santiago, Hemingway also created an environment and established its universality, allowing it to stand as an image of the environment of man, rendered in all its richness and complexity. The result is one of the significant milestones in the literature of environmental realism, one of the achievements of which has been the triumphant "placing" of man in a total setting in which his humanity can be reaffirmed, with a deeper humility, in terms of all the forms of life of the biosphere.

PART THREE

Environment and Consciousness in Hardy, Wells, and D.H. Lawrence

CHAPTER ONE

Thomas Hardy's Image of Nature: The Honest Countryman and the Incomplete Universe

And yet the village-churl feels the truth more than you,

> Who's loath to leave this life
> Which to him little yields —
> His hard-taks'd sunburnt wife,
> His often-laboured fields,

The boors with whom he talked, the country-spot he knew.

> But thou, because thou hear'st
> Men scoff at Heaven and Fate,
> Because the Gods thou fear'st
> Fail to make blest thy state,

Tremblest, and wilt not dare to trust the joys there are!

> I say: Fear not! Life still
> Leaves human effort scope.
> But since life teems with ill,
> Nurse no extravagant hope;

Because thou must not dream, thou need'st not then despair!

— Arnold, *Empedocles on Etna*

1. Wessex, *Under the Greenwood Tree* and *Far From the Madding Crowd*

Tracing out the action of Hardy's Wessex novels on a map of the West Country, one sees how the locale covered slowly expands. Beginning at Mellstock we are carried into the wider sphere of a coherent region, but no sooner is this regional note sounded, in *Far From the Madding Crowd* (1874), than a discordant clash of elements is heard. Between 1874 and 1878, Hardy's perspective has changed: the integral community gives way to the disrupted community, and the image of the field is over-shadowed by the sense of the sublime nature of Darwinism. In this context, all sorts of transformations, many of them previously noted by the critics, mark the passage from early to late Hardy: "pristine" imagery

105

yields to imagery reflecting a sense of ageing; the irreconcilability of ideals and environment becomes more acute; the very speed and manner of human movement from place to place is radically altered. With all this, we have the operation of different "natures" that has often confounded the critics.[1] A writer of "idyllic" country tales seems to have been transformed by modern thought into an intellectual pessimist; an upholder of the virtues of the integral community life is apparently compelled by a sense of truthfulness to admit the tragic decay of that life. Hardy, it seems, had a sense of "beneficent nature" in his countryman's blood, and got a mote of the nature of struggle in his speculative eye, until the whole universe blurred and darkened.

This underestimates, however, the toughness of the early books and misreads throughout Hardy's plain view of "the way it was". In *Under the Greenwood Tree*, Hardy portrays Wessex as a structured, self-sufficient community in which there is an intimate sense of the land, one in which the value of harmony is suggested in the vision of a life integrated in terms of work and festival. Hardy's "image of the field" brings out precisely the strength of a community rooted in the natural processes without which civilization cannot grow. Yet, from the beginning, Wessex is also seen as a rather vulnerable social unit, all too subject to disturbing influences from without, and not really intellectually or spiritually vital enough to evolve appropriate responses to meet the challenge of the new thought.

Under the Greenwood Tree (1872) successfully renders the enclosed agricultural community with its roots in the past of Christian Europe, limited in space and perceived as relatively unchanging. Most of the action takes place in "Mellstock" and environs, and the furthest journey in the book takes us only to the market town of Budmouth, ten miles away. The action is circumscribed by nearly a year: the book opens at Christmas and carries through to the following autumn. At the beginning Dick Dewy stands in the dark wood waiting to meet the choir, and at the end, under a spreading tree, his wedding dance goes on. The characters are all village dwellers, with very little social distance separating them, and the disruptions which create the comic flavour by no means threaten the general pattern of village life, though they point at significant and perhaps disturbing currents in that life.[2]

The narrator distances himself from the basic material in several ways. First, we are given the characteristic Hardy retrospect, the action being set in about the 1840's. Second, there is the general comic tone.[3] Third, and following from the comic positioning, there is the lack of any serious identification with the "inner" life of the community. This last fact is extremely significant, for, as we have seen, one of the typical strengths of the novel of the enclosed community is a direct narrative reflecting the dark side of peasant life, an evocation of the timeless world of suffering and redeeming ritual. Hardy's approach is different. He passes over the possibility of identification with the community at such a serious level and renders its everyday life with complete knowledge, but from the point of view of a more sophisticated observer. The general tone is balanced with extreme skill between an appreciation of the virtues of the way of life depicted and a sense of the quaintness of it all. The villagers are seen as practical, shrewd, and quite un-mysterious, clinging to tradition because it is comfortable and familiar.

What kind of village life, then, is Hardy describing in this novel? It would be a gross distortion to suggest that we are being shown some kind of idyllic or ideal life. What we see in fact is a community of considerable coherence and vigor, one with relative economic security and the promise of stability ahead, but one that is also something of a backwater. This estimate seems confirmed by the effect of Fancy and Parson Maybold on the community. Fancy, though a local product, has been educated else-where, while Parson Maybold, relatively sophisticated and idealistic, comes from outside to attempt in a mild way a few reforms in the village. The plot brings together these two disturbing influences. Maybold will replace the traditional choir, and Fancy will play the new organ; at the end they nearly unite as lovers. Hardy writes comedy without producing a novel of character. The little difficulties are solved, and the normal life of the community is restored; the comic license is revoked without any character being inwardly transformed.

Yet is it true to say, as some critics have done, that the community has assimilated the disturbing elements?[4] Even at this level can Hardy be asserting some elemental power of traditional life to stabilize deviants? It seems clear that D.H. Lawrence is right when he suggests that Fancy is far from being reconciled to submission.[5] Everything in the last chapter makes clear that she will continue to lead Dick a merry chase. The split between the serious, businesslike, unfrivolous man, and the spirited, socially ambitious woman that plays itself out in the later novels is more than hinted at here, though it is far from breaking out of the formal boundaries Hardy set for himself.

It would be too much to suggest that *Under the Greenwood Tree* itself dramatizes the disruption of the traditional community, but it clearly reflects a situation in which all is not well. What real power the community has is not any longer in creating an inner life, a *morale*, but in providing models of relationship with the environment.[6] Here, we feel, is a micro-society, a sub-culture with real roots in the locale. True, the basic rituals are extremely secularized and conventional, and the whole village life is limited and circumscribed by formalities which offer the individual very little scope for real integration, but nonetheless, the working daily routine is healthy and apparently secure. Suppose, however, that that working life were to be in any way disrupted from the outside: how well could this community resist collapse? The villagers are fairly prosperous, fond of festival and drink, and proud of their work, but they have little power of resisting change. The new church organ may be harmless enough as an innovation, but the villagers give up virtually without a struggle, summoning all their courage to secure even a postponement. Clearly, they could do nothing against greater and more sweeping changes. The community represented by Mellstock, with its resistance to change and inner coherence, is clearly seen as in need of transformation, a transformation that Hardy will later suggest is not within the power of Victorian liberal idealism to effect. Success can only come if the matrix world is restored from within, through the power of the enlightened individual. This, at least, is what Hardy seems to suggest in his next novel of the agricultural life, *Far From the Madding Crowd*.

Far From the Madding Crowd does more than portray a local agricultural community; it creates a region. We range, with characters who are fairly mobile, from Norcombe to Weatherbury to Casterbridge, sensing as we go the many links that hold this world together — the connections between man and nature, the exchanges between farm and town, the traditional rituals that bind the present to the past. *Far From the Madding Crowd* covers twice as much geographical space as *Under the Greenwood Tree* and there is a corresponding increase in complexity. The characters reveal themselves more fully and freely, and the landscape is seen to exhibit more variety, while the total achievement stands against the reader's possibly complacent sense of what the art of "the good little Thomas Hardy" can accomplish.[7]

Despite its richness of effect, *Far From the Madding Crowd* was seen by Hardy in his preface of 1895-1902 as a picture of regional life, as the story of a community nurtured by a particular relation to nature. With his usual lack of nostalgia, Hardy refers there to the novel's vanished world, arguing that the preservation of "legend, folk-lore, close inter-social relations, and eccentric individualities" has as an "indispensable condition of existence" the "attachment to the soil of one particular spot by generation after generation". Although the general lines of Hardy's success in this novel have been understood from the first, its specific excellences, the depth and unity of its vision, have been blurred by critical views that take too little account of the context of the performance. Hardy's challenge here was to render the human possibilities of the rooted community. *Far From the Madding Crowd* is a thesis novel, one in a great tradition. For in Gabriel Oak Hardy creates a convincing focus for the wisdom of long-established ways which are born anew in this kind of exceptional man. The ironic distance between the writer and his material shrinks and Hardy joins the select circle of Wordsworth, Tolstoy, and the few others who have shaped our vision of the "organic" man.[8]

While the dominant natural scene in the novel is present in what we have called "the image of the field", this is enriched by contrasting angles of vision, which take us back to the central setting with renewed

108

understanding. The grand vista of nature which Hardy was to invoke in *Two on a Tower* and *The Return of the Native* is here no threat. On Norcombe Hill Gabriel does not feel overwhelmed by the stars; standing as he does, with his feet on the ground and his mind steadied by traditional knowledge of the environment, he is both craftsman and contemplative spectator. Troy, by contrast, struggles with the sea, performs his typical "conjuring act" and disappears. Nature, in other cases, can be linked to human emotion in the manner almost of conventional pathetic fallacy — Poorgrass, driving Fanny's body home, feels the woods as threat; Bathsheba, desolate after her split with Troy, stares down at a seething and turgid swamp.[9] These moments, while not merely incidental, do not distract us from Hardy's central image; they reinforce our awareness of it. Hardy's art demonstrates, however, that a healthy psychic state does not involve a disproportionate separation between feeling and context. Suffering is man's lot, but in the texture of real things it may carry its own dignity. Fanny's death is not absurd, despite the dog, for her steadiness of principle, and her courage, are present even in her agony; "Troy's romanticism", on the other hand, is eccentric, personal, and divorced from the community context. The book's narrative interest depends upon Bathsheba's combination of rootedness and flightiness; her problems become more serious as we go on. At the end, when she is no longer a "match" for Gabriel, she marries him, joining the reality she baulked at before, tamed at last.

Far From the Madding Crowd is a novel about the power of a culture which has not yet divorced itself from the natural environment. Through coherent imagery Hardy renders the "feel" of his world. Many of his figures of speech (which are often similes) take us back to the Old Testament Hebrews or the Homeric Greeks. We are at an early stage in the history of the region; we have still a long way to go to the *fin de siècle* weariness of *The Return of the Native* and *Jude*. Spatially, the sense of an integral world prevails. Though expanded from *Under the Greenwood Tree*, the area described has little sense of "outside". No industrial city fumes on the horizon. When Gabriel and Bathsheba move to Weatherbury, they are "intruders" in only a very narrow sense. Hardy makes little of their move in such terms; he sees the whole area described by the novel as a community, with multiple cross-references of all kinds. He presents the working life of the farm, which involves co-operation with nature, and the shaping of its forces toward human fulfillment. The destructive elements are never played down, but we are shown that over the centuries men have devised ways to control most of these. When the "chance" that is deified in one of the novel's rare obtrusive moralizings breaks in, men and women acting from ready wit and trained perception may blunt its cutting indifference. This argues not an overriding sense of Darwinian struggle (it is absurd to try to turn this into a Naturalistic novel), but an underlying realism about environment that sees nature at

109

various times and from varying perspectives as both hostile and beneficent.

Hardy's famous descriptive contrast of church, castle, and barn, often
rightly pinpointed as a significant center of the novel, reveals the basic
discriminations that mark the depth of his vision of community life.[10]

> One could say about this barn, what could hardly be said of either the
> church or the castle, akin to it in age and style, that the purpose which had
> dictated its original erection was the same with that to which it was still
> applied. Unlike and superior to either of those two typical remnants of
> medievalism, the old barn embodied practices which had suffered no mutila-
> tion at the hands of time. Here at least the spirit of the ancient builders was
> one with the spirit of the modern beholder . . . The lanceolate windows, the
> time-eaten archstones and chamfers, the orientation of the axis, the misty
> chestnut work of the rafters, referred to no exploded fortifying art of
> worn-out religious creed. The defence and salvation of the body by daily
> bread is still a study, a religion, and a desire.

(Chapter Twenty-Two)

Man transforms nature into culture through the field; agriculture is the
primary "root" of the community's higher values. Civilized man, more
and more insulated from the sources of his achievements, must call to
mind the primary reality of the food cycle. Prior to discriminations of
value is the living world itself; man's transformation of nature begins
there, and though evaluations of the systems of politics and religion may
change from age to age, man's ultimate dependency on his food-
producing skills does not. It is fitting, therefore, that this connection be
described in terms drawn from religion, that we understand the hope of
"daily bread" as something that is eternally sacred. Hardy goes on to
describe the actual activities of the sheep-shearing, the relative lack of
change in the country, and the naturalness of the harmony between
workers here and their building. There is no sweeping glorification of
rural life as opposed to the urban; Hardy merely reminds us of the
particular strength of such a community, of the strength of rural life. The
barn is an essential object and also a beautiful one, and our feelings about
its beauty derive from its power of suggesting our origins and depend-
encies in nature. It has a living reality because it remains at the root of our
higher aspirations, which, flowering in a given religious or political
system, eventually wither. The insight is precise and it controls the
unfolding of the book.

Hardy, however, does not cherish the Wessex of this novel as an ideal
culture, but constantly depicts its weaknesses — the incomplete mesh of
spiritual ideal and daily working reality, the relative stagnation of energy.
But to dramatize the positive values prior to the rather sapped energies of
religion and politics, Hardy created a figure who moves directly from the
roots into a wider sphere of social and moral achievement. Through
Gabriel Oak we become acquainted with the link between nature and
culture that gives a community as such Wessex its primal significance.

Oak is slightly larger than life because he is the region's exemplary man; we are carried with him from mere "attachment to the soil" to a viable moral sphere.[11]

How is this done? Almost in the first paragraph Hardy makes clear Gabriel's lack of affiliation with the traditional religion. He is seen choosing a sensible man's moderate position in regard to habits which are often a waste of time, though not altogether pointless. But if Gabriel has only a nodding acquaintance with traditional Christian fervour, he is himself quite a religious man, or rather, Hardy exhibits him in a strongly religious context, though one divorced from conventional piety. Gabriel is shown as the careful tender of his flock, as the Good Shepherd. On Norcombe Hill he stands on a portion of the eternal earth, unawed by night, space, or "the keenest blasts" of the busy wind. Though he wears a watch, Gabriel tells time by the stars. (Gabriel's watch has a defective hour hand; he thus lives more in the minute; yet he keeps his watch with him because it is a hand-me-down from his grandfather. The watch might remind us indirectly of the city worker's transformation from a man into a man-hour; it belongs, of course, to the time of craft and particularly cherished heirlooms.) The ability of Gabriel to have the best of both worlds, to mingle the "natural" and the civilized virtues is his most striking characteristic. Hardy illustrates it in his very walk:

Oak's motions, though they had a quiet energy, were slow, and their deliberateness accorded well with his occupation. Fitness being the basis of beauty, nobody could have denied that his steady swings and turns in and about the flock had elements of grace. Yet, although if occasion demanded he could do or think a thing with as mercurial a dash as can the men of towns who are more to the manner born, his special power, morally, physically, and mentally, was static, owing little or nothing to momentum as a rule.

(Chapter Two)

Gabriel's taciturnity, traditional with the countryman, is accompanied by great sensitivity of perception and an awareness of the difficulty of embodying his perceptions in language, one of the contrasts between him and the quite fluent Bathsheba, whose very glibness makes her a victim of the yet more glib Troy later on. Gabriel "wished she knew his impressions; but he would as soon have thought of carrying an odour in a net as of attempting to convey the intangibilities of his feeling in the coarse meshes of language". If Gabriel walks powerfully and keeps silence golden as only a strong man can, he is richer in appreciation of his special environment than most countrymen, though not given to foolish rhapsodies either. He not only "looks at the sky as a useful instrument" but can regard it "in an appreciative spirit, as a work of art superlatively beautiful". Morally, Gabriel is neither a Darwinian superman nor a Lawrencian instinctualist. He is an "intensely humane man", whose first concern even when he is ruined, is for his suffering sheep. It is a sensitivity bred of his trade, a tenderness that grows directly from his contact with nature that we see operating in his first meeting with Fanny.

111

Touching her hand he knows her to be agitated, for "he had frequently felt the same quick, hard beat in the femoral artery of his lambs when overdriven". Fanny, the victim and fugitive, is safe with Gabriel, but her fear of the conventional aspect of community disapproval prevents her from confiding in him. Nonetheless, their meeting is significant, for Hardy (suggesting a contrast with Troy, whom we are soon to be introduced to) shows Gabriel's knowledge of the animal world leading to knowledge of the human physical signs of distress. The kind of knowledge Gabriel possesses generates charity and compassion, not mindlesss ecstasies. Though it originates in contact with the natural, it is socially and humanly useful.

Gabriel is not simply the man of nature. A true product of the field, he combines the virtues of nature and civilisation.[12] If he has access to an almost instinctive awareness, he also owns a fine compact library, and is described as making use of it. We have the picture of a man of the mean, neither too handsome nor too ugly, neither too hurried nor too slow, a man far from a savage, who has a fresh breath of wildness about him, a man not too civilized or over-refined. Though this portrait may suggest a quite programmatic presentation, the reader of the novel will know how flexible and "free" a character Hardy makes Gabriel seem. He can be noble, but he can also get chagrined; if he is very wise in country ways, he can be foolish too, and Bathsheba has to save him from suffocating in his hut. Though his patience with Bathsheba may seem too good to be true, she is a beautiful woman, and he twice threatens seriously to leave her forever. Though he cannot be said to develop remarkably in any psychological dimension, Gabriel grows as the novel unfolds. Suffering deepens him. After the catastrophe with the sheep, he is seen to be a better man, a man "with a dignified calm" and with that "indifference to fate which, though it often makes a villain of a man, is the basis of his sublimity when it does not".

The scenes that precede the great storm illustrate Gabriel's role. He is alerted to the change of weather by his perceptiveness, which takes in shifts of behaviour in the total pattern of nature, even when these occur among the smaller visible creatures. Because he can read the signs, the "Great Mother" speaks to him directly. Of course it is only because he is the man he is, because he is willing to listen to nature, that he can read the signs correctly. Hardy shows that these various manifestations in nature group themselves in distinctive patterns that can only be put together by human intelligence. This is done in "experimental" fashion, evidence being weighed, and a regular check carried out. Also, a natural threat is best understood by the natural man. Gabriel has not lost touch with the environment: his experience over the years has created an almost instinctive awareness, and his habitual rationality enables him to check out its specific phenomena in a systematic way. His conclusions are the product of both sensitivity on the feeling-level of perception and of logical deduction. (The contrast with Troy, whose addiction to reckless pleasure incapacitates him, and whose self-complacent attitude to the storm is based on bravado and not knowledge — and with Boldwood, who is demoralized with grief — is notable.)

Just because his individualism is a fresh version of the agricultural community's age-old responsiveness to environment, Gabriel earns the respect of Weatherbury. Untinged by any radical self-assertion, his powers suggest the renewal of basic energies by a return to individual perceptions dulled by generations of complacent addiction to customs grown rigid. Wessex is not so far gone as not to recognize a good man when it sees him, however. At Casterbridge, the employers seem at first to reject Gabriel as a kind of wolf in sheep's clothing, but his humility and inventiveness (he plays the flute for pennies) lead him on to the next opportunity. When he succeeds in putting out the hayrick fire, it is precisely because of the community approval of his initiative that Bathsheba is given the necessary self-confidence to hire him. Later, when he appears in the inn at Weatherbury, Gabriel is immediately "placed" because his family is remembered as having lived at Norcombe. This clinches the impression of regional unity, and points up the measure of difference between Gabriel's role and that of the culture-reforming hero, the man who inspires change through rebellion. Gabriel wins the confidence of his peers because he expresses the values they believe in but have grown too complacent to practice.

Gabriel and Bathsheba and even Troy are all part of the same community, but Troy has become psychically disconnected from it. Although he has grown up in Weatherbury, he is clearly in many ways an outsider, and definitely uprooted.[13] The bastard son of Lord Severn and a French governess, he is a soldier of fortune, the roving sergeant, and finally the outlaw Turpin, one who arouses energies that will destroy him. Troy's disembodied Romantic sentiment, continuously defined by Hardy in ways that show its separation from real work and real leisure, lands him ultimately in the wasteland of his own corrupt whims. Gabriel's fidelity triumphs when Troy's magical qualities upset Boldwood's tenuous equilibrium. Deception and repression explode in violence, leaving the field clear for wise passivity and measured energy.

It is Troy's cruelty to Fanny, however, (mixed with concern though it is) that separates him from the householding tendencies of the Weatherbury community. When Gabriel arrives in the town, the community concern is to restore Fanny to the flock. Once again, we have an anticipation of Hardy's later concern, for though Fanny and Gabriel understand and trust each other, Fanny cannot confide in him because of her awareness of having violated a community social taboo. This theme is not played up; what we see rather is Troy's shallowness of feeling expressed in his attempts to buy Fanny off. Suggesting that Fanny deserved her fate, however, because of her failure to appear at the right church, is to take a very hard Darwinian attitude to a book which is stating quite another order of values.[14] Hardy, at this point, is emphasizing neither the social rigidity of the community, nor Fanny's position as victim, but rather Troy's violation of the implicit coherence of local life. Later, when he seems to adopt the role of farmer, he is really perverting the old customs, not adopting them. At the harvest supper he causes the farmhands to drink too much of the wrong stuff, and incapacitates them for the emergency. Troy's swordplay (allowing, too, for its strong phallic implications, often noted) may be ssen as illusory "work", as skill applied without a coherent moral and social framework.[15] Troy has to lie to Bathsheba to get her to stand still while he "enchants" her. His "miracles", magician's tricks, contrast with the real work of Gabriel in his various farming enterprises. While Troy uses his rather deadly and artificial "tool", Gabriel works in contact with the real flesh, touching the sheep, Fanny and Bathsheba with the same tender concern. (In the great storm scene Gabriel and Bathsheba survive the destructive atmosphere, save the harvest, and make tender physical contact, while Troy sleeps.) Ostensibly devoted to farming, Troy continues to look for magical increments through his betting on racehorses. Though it is not specifically mentioned, the image the reader may have in mind here is the ironical failure of the Biblical "swords into plowshares". Troy, putting all his faith in self, and finally losing that faith through the "uncanny" accident of the waterspout, is left as a man of disguises, as a pseudo-person, the image of an image in his role as Turpin, the traditional hero. Troy literally fades away into legend, but even there he is not himself. He indulges in his unstable Romanticism of self-inflation at the cost of real self-development. Here again, the contrast between eccentric isolation and the power of participation is made clear.

Far From the Madding Crowd, rendering the image of the field in a subtle total pattern, suggests the old linking of man and nature summed up in the integral agricultural community. Conflict with the city is still non-existent, though the region is fractured by vagrant opportunisms and held down by inflexible subservience to tradition. If the tone of this novel is very removed from *Under the Greenwood Tree*, this is because of Gabriel Oak. In Oak Hardy depicts the inner life of the integral community as he understands it in its strengths. By removing Oak from the lowest common denominator and yet displaying his contact with the earth and with the community, Hardy presents in a realistic and credible framework a kind of ideal version of the creative traditional man. He shows us the man whose spiritual roots go beyond formalities and whose moral and physical being is bound up with his region. In this favourable presentation of Oak, Hardy turns slightly away from the rather comic and removed tone of *Under the Greenwood Tree* to implicate us in an evaluation with considerable moral dimension.

At the end, however, we are not altogether reassured. Gabriel's and

Bathsheba's wedding is given the approval of the community, though the main interest of the visiting musicians (who drag out the old instruments of the village band) is to have a drop of drink sent to them from the inn. The wedding is celebrated as a renewal and the married pair serenaded in the old-fashioned way, while at the same time we feel the familiar gesture to embody a certain futility. Though Gabriel has found his roots and triumphed in his role of wise steward, his redemptive powers may not be adequate to stay the drift toward decadence. One man's talents, perhaps, never are. Nonetheless, Hardy has made the powerful and enduring point that it is such men as Gabriel, with such values, who make a living community possible.

2. The Return of the Native

There is an immense shift of emphasis between *Far From the Madding Crowd*, and *The Return of the Native*, published only four years later, in 1878. This later novel, as the study of John Paterson demonstrates, represents Hardy's conscious expansion of the integral community into a polarized world of geographical and cultural opposites.[16] While working on the book Hardy gradually built up the significance of the social world outside of the heath. This was at first to be represented by Budmouth, but later Hardy invoked the image of Paris to summarize what Clym has rejected and Eustacia seeks. In one sense, of course, the setting is more restricted than in the earlier novels, since the heath is all we have; but in another, it is far wider, for the modern world of commerce and "fashion" is constantly invoked, and the Old Testament and Homeric imagery of *Far From the Madding Crowd* is here replaced by an "imperial" imagery, making reference to such figures as Napoleon, Frederick the Great, and Cleopatra — to saints, sinners, and politicos of varying stripe.

The Return of the Native is dominated by the abiding presence of the heath, which Hardy treats so as to make us feel that we are definitely on the modern side of the watershed of Darwinism.[17] The heath, despite lingering associations with "the field" is really wild nature, the sublime; whatever links it has to man's industry are overshadowed by its primeval singularity and isolation. In such a natural space, the inhabitants are reduced to the state of man at a fairly elementary level of evolution; at the same time, there is a strong sense of ageing in the novel. The two come together in our awareness of the heath as fossilized survival. We see it as a kind of "sport", which retains the most ancient features and in which only the mere scaffolding of civilization may exist, while at the same time it stands for the world at the end of civilization, for the devolving nature also bequeathed by Darwinism to the literary imagination.

Hardy's monolithic descriptive apparatus yields several strata of meanings. The first group clusters around the image of "night", for the heath itself is an "instalment of night"; the opening sequences of the novel are night-pieces; and only slowly do we become aware of the heath

115

as a place of daylight habitation as well. The first meaning of night in Hardy's emotional geography is dark passion, the night which is summed up in the personified "love" of Egdon and the storm. "Then it became the home of strange phantoms" Hardy writes, "and it was found to be the hitherto unrecognized original of those wild regions of obscurity which are vaguely felt to be compassing us about in midnight dreams of flight and disaster". This "flight and disaster" we shall see later triggered by the phantom passions of Eustacia and Wildeve. Night on Egdon also stands for the "night" of moral darkness. References to "hell" carry us into an underworld of Dantean or Greek dimensions. Fires leap up in the darkness, "the whole black phenomenon beneath" might be Limbo "viewed from the brink by the sublime Florentine", while the peasant dance is "demonic", and various characters, haunted by "Tartarean" glooms, must pick their ways through this landscape without landmarks. Even more pervasive, as already suggested, is the sense of primitive night, of the primeval darkness before (or after) civilization. A series of personifying images picture the heath as it "appeared slowly to awake and listen. Every night its Titanic form seemed to await something; but it had waited thus, unmoved, during so many centuries, through the crisis of so many things, that it could only be imagined to await one last crisis — the final overthrow". This "great inviolate place" is the natural sphere beyond all civilizations. "Civilization was its enemy", Hardy writes, summing up the tension between culture and the resistant matrix of natural energies unharnessed by human effort. By means of a series of "paleontological" images, Hardy succeeds in creating an environment in which man's tenuous encroachments are seen from the vast perspective of prehistory. The reddleman is "a curious, interesting, and nearly perished link between obsolete forms of life and those which generally prevail", the mumming is a "fossilized survival", Clym waits for Eustacia in a landscape that resembles that of the "carboniferous" period.[18]

Part of the complexity of the heath may be attributed to the way in which Hardy controls our apprehension of it. His massive opening description emphasizes the darkly inhuman, whether supernatural or natural. We know from Paterson's study that the *ur*-novel placed a greater weight upon the diabolical and witchlike than the final version allows, nonetheless, the opening still reminds the reader of the *Macbeth* world, with all the eerie tones of its night-music.[19] What is really happening is that two distinct systems of images are being superimposed, one upon the other. When we are first introduced to the heath we see it as both "unnatural" and a supremely "natural" place, a duality strongly present in the image of fire in darkness that pervades this part. Whether "wounds in a black hide", or "scalding cauldrons", the fires are a link between contemporary and primitive. The "superstition" evoked is here encompassed within the terms of the folklore aspect of man's beginnings, which Darwinism would inspire anthropology to explore.[20] Hardy's largely spontaneous use of traditional Christian images is the process of becoming a more self-conscious structuring in which the Christian element is part of the relativistically understood total pattern. Significantly, another passage emphasizes the perennial ''place'' upon which the various rituals are played out:

It was as if these men and boys had suddenly dived into past ages, and fetched therefrom an hour and deed which had been familiar with this spot. The ashes of the original British pyre which blazed from that summit lay fresh and undisturbed in the barrow beneath their tread. The flames from funeral piles long ago kindled there had shone down upon the lowlands as these were shining now. Festival fires to Thor and Woden had followed on the same ground and duly had their day. Indeed, it is pretty well known that such blazes as this the heathmen were now enjoying are rather the lineal descendants from jumbled Druidical rites and Saxon ceremonies than the invention of popular feeling about the Gunpowder Plot.

(Chapter Three)

Hardy's dramatic presentation of the heath allows for a gradual fading away of the sense of horror and witchery and takes us toward an acceptance of it as a natural place, one where each age may practice its peculiar life. This shift may be partially unconscious, but its effect is to give the reader the satisfaction of experiencing for himself the pleasures of ''severity'' and ''chastened soberness'' mentioned in the opening description. As the book unfolds, the mirage of hell fades away, and the heath becomes a certain kind of real landscape. Freed from the view of the frustrated ''prisoners'', Eustacia and Wildeve, the reader learns to live with the heath in its daylight aspects. With Clym, Thomasin and Venn, he begins to see this landscape not as a supernatural threat, but as a challenge to his adaptability. A cleansing of vision has taken place.

The novel charts the triumph of the heath itself, of the enduring environment, but this should not be misread as Hardy's advocacy for some mysterious essence of natural life to which human beings must attach themselves or perish. What Hardy suggests about the heath is quite removed from this. In this connection we might recall the familiar passage about the effect of the storm on two adjacent areas of Egdon: a grove of beeches is being lashed by the wind, which ''merely waved the furze and heather in a light caress.'' Here adaptation is the key to survival; a principle extended to the characters, whose attitude to their world determines their success in it.[21] Clym, we learn, knows the heath very well. While he is ''permeated with its scenes, with its substance, and with its odours'', we find Eustacia a fervent hater of nature, at the pitch of her romantic ardour, ''stumbling over twisted furze-roots, tufts of rushes, or oozing lumps of fleshy fungi''. Wildeve cannot understand Thomasin's affection for the environment which seems to him a trap, but the point is that she can see it as ''impersonal open ground'', and her fears of the place are rational, ''her dislikes of its worst modes reasonable''.

117

Hardy insists that the heath is no place for illusions, that one must come to terms with this environment in a very direct and clear-sighted way, or else court trouble. He suggests that Egdon is a purely natural place of a particular kind, one in which certain efflorescenses of "civilized" life, such as ecstatic idealisms and romantic longings, are useless or even dangerous. Here the possibilities of living are pleasantly static and physically real and invigorating; one has the compensations of disciplin-ed severity and an enduring atmosphere of fine shadings. In order to make real contact with the heath, Clym must give up his reform plans and become a furze-cutter; at another place Hardy suggests that an artist or philosopher might value it. One must either learn to see it clearly, or else sink into its rhythms, grasping it inwardly through the power of art; what one cannot do is to challenge it with idealisms, or attempt to project upon it one's longings and frustrations. Once the heath is accepted as a severe and enduring environment, it loses its fears and romantic trappings, and becomes a place of natural challenge, but also one of peace and simpli-city, lacking, however, any quality of yielding "dark" knowledge.

If Hardy's intimate familiarity with his own locale went into his creation of the heath, he was moved, too, by his desire to fashion an image of nature that would resonate with sublime grandeur in the Burkean sense.[22] In the "Mont Blanc" of his favorite Shelley, nature had been invested with the indifferent power of the inhuman other — and this Shelleyan direction we have seen as one example of many Romantic foreshadowings of the typical landscape of Darwinism. It is of course precisely this sober nature of Darwinism that Hardy represents here. The heath is primarily an image of nature itself as revealed by Victorian science. Hardy characterises it as a bleak round of processes which those who love severity and order may find rewarding, but upon which it would be foolish to project one's longings. No vision of this "world" of the heath should be inflated, no "communion" attempted. The Words-worthian intuition, explicitly satirized in *Tess*, is here implicitly denied. Idealism in the presence of the heath guarantees loss of contact with reality.

Of course the heath is not only nature *per se*, but also the countryside as opposed to the city, though a kind of fossilized prefiguring or skeletal after-image of the field, rather than the working field itself. Clym, the man who has had every opportunity to wallow in the romantic, distant Paris, is determined to see the heath as a potentially viable entity. His flight homeward is at once a return to the simple and an idealistic gesture embodying his hopes of shaping the social evolution of the countryside. The novel of double consciousness is clearly in evidence here. City and country are polarized; nature is opposed to fashion and luxury. The returning sophisticated hero wants to identify with the simple, and by so doing to give new meaning to his matrix world and to his own life. The narrative exploits the ironies of the situation. Clym's idealism is noble, and not sensual or foolish, but it is also dangerous because it is divorced from the facts of the heath environment. From one point of view Egdon is just as bad as Eustacia and Wildeve think, and it is far from being as redeemable as Clym imagines, yet, Hardy seems to insist, it has its points. Liberal-minded reformers with intellectually determined programs miss the significance of real life, not because they fail to grasp some mysterious dark essence of that life, but because they ignore the facts.[23] Clym's blindness in leaping too far ahead of the possibilities of the actual situation must be overcome through his plunge into the tactile world of the heath. With symbolic appropriateness, it is Clym's intellectual devotion, his course of self-teaching that "blinds" him, forcing him to turn to a working life on the heath in which the senses and not the intellect become the focus of knowledge.[24] This accelerates Eustacia's estrangement from him, "the convergence of the twain", so to speak, being revealed for the accidental folly that it is. The powers of sexual selection must be regulated by awareness and not succumbed to with naive fervour. Along most of these lines, a comparison with *Far From the Madding Crowd* is helpful. In the earlier novel, Hardy suggests the possible renewal of the community through the efforts of the man of balance, who works from within the tradition, awakening new energies in the old patterns. *The Return of the Native*, by contrast, invokes irreconcilable disparates: on the one hand, we have a progressivism divorced from environmental reality, on the other, a rootedness that has become fossilized, or which can only express itself as romantic longing. The apparently closed quality of the heath world must not lead us to overlook the psychical fracturing which makes it more of a chaos than a cosmos. A brief examination of the social context should clarify these points.

Clym returns in a futile effort to transform heath society; we have already seen how Hardy places that society at the "primitive" stage, while also suggesting the exhaustion of a declining world. Clym's failure is attributed to his attempt to carry Egdon to enlightenment without any intervening transformation of the skeletal beginnings (or survivals) which are its only social forms. What is lacking, Hardy explicitly reveals, is economic development. The heath is a marginal area, cut off from the surrounding farming districts. The pursuits of the inhabitants may loosely depend upon agriculture, but there is in no sense a coherent order of working life. In so far as Hardy is showing us the rural world in Egdon, he is depicting it as a backwater, as a region with no viable exchange of goods and services. The inhabitants are remarkably isolated from each other, and their meetings occur on specifically social or ritual occasions, but not as part of their working lives. Hardy makes a distinction between two kinds of community participation or ritual. The more tested and enduring customs have some relation to basic emotions that must be fulfilled. These may occur (as in the case of the bonfires) out of an ancient and meaningful connection between man and nature. To light such fires,

119

Hardy tells us, "indicates a spontaneous Promethean rebelliousness against the fiat that this recurrent season [or winter] shall bring foul times, cold darkness, misery and death". Such a custom retains its power because it continues to fulfill an emotional need in relation to the environment. Hardy seems to have some respect for what Pareto (the great Italian sociologist, who was an almost exact contemporary of his) called the residues, the lingering human need for self-expression in certain situations; out of these grow time-tested ritual forms, and while the explanation of the forms may change (as the fires of the Britons are later dedicated to Woden and finally associated with Guy Fawkes) the residual need for lighting them persists.[25] Similarly, the superstitious fear and hatred that Susan Nunsuch feels for Eustacia, is channeled into a ritual burning of her effigy. This act may be evil, but it is a living one, full of emotional energy, and therefore exempt from the irony which Hardy bestows on the mere social survivals, such as the mummers' play, about which he can write: "A traditional pastime is to be distinguished from a mere revival in no more striking feature than this, that while in the revival all is excitement and fervour, the survival is carried on with a stolidity and absence of stir which sets one wondering why a thing that is done so perfunctorily should be kept up at all".

The heath society, then, lacking any working routine, is marked by both primitive rituals embodying perennial aspects of the relationship between man and environment, and by such events as the mummers' play, which Hardy describes as a "fossilized survival". Not only the heath itself but its social life carries the double image of primeval beginnings and remote conclusions. Clym's efforts to transform the heath engage neither the surviving energies of the ritual, nor the stagnant customs. His liberal educational passion is almost comically inappropriate. Hardy *might* have written about a community in process of transformation with the resulting loss of traditional values and customs but with the gain of a modernity and efficiency, however dubious. Such a novel is quite typical of his kind of writer attempting to mirror this stage of nineteenth-century life (see, for example, Johan Bojer, *The Last of the Vikings* or Willa Cather, *O Pioneers!* and *A Lost Lady*). Hardy's skepticism may be measured by the degree to which *The Return of the Native* pictures a world of hopeless disparates, one in which passions and ideals are inevitably misdirected in relation to the realities of social and natural life. In Egdon, progress is not ironically treated, because there is no progress at all.

The main Clym story, then, is a tragedy based on his failure to recognize the indifference of the yokels, the stubbornness of his mother, or the ideals of Eustacia, all working against his drive for reform. The fatal relationship between Clym and his mother reinforces the larger sense we have of the impossibility of his return to the matrix. In his blindness Clym wreaks havoc with the very home he wishes to secure and bring light to. Yet he is one of the survivors, because he, like Diggory, can adapt to the heath.

This man from Paris was now so disguised by his leather accoutrements, and by the goggles he was obliged to wear over his eyes, that his closest friend might have passed by without recognizing him. He was a brown spot in the midst of an expanse of olive-green gorse, and nothing more . . .

His daily life was of a curious microscopic sort, his whole world being limited to a circuit of a few feet from his person. His familiars were creeping and winged things, and they seemed to enroll him in their band. Bees hummed around his ears with an intimate air, and tugged at the heath and furze-flowers at his side in such numbers as to weigh them down to the sod. The strange amber-coloured butterflies which Egdon produced, and which were never seen elsewhere, quivered in the breath of lips, alighted upon his bowed back, and sported with the glittering point of his hook as he flourished it up and down . . .

(Book IV, Chapter One)

Clym's success here tells us much about Hardy's scheme of values, but it has been sadly misunderstood. In no sense are we shown him in contact with "dark" knowledge, or in tune with some mysterious essence of heath life. The first thing we notice is that he is actually working; this is virtually the only description of real work in the book, and we may notice that "the full swing of labour" makes him "cheerfully disposed and calm". Hardy shuts out the immense sublimity of the heath, and creates a human space that is carefully delimited by the sweep of a man's arm. This is not an Edenic enclosure but a re-creation of the working sphere of the traditional countryman. The integration of living forms occurs not merely in consciousness but in devotion to specific tasks; Clym is ecologically but not spiritually related to the insects, snakes and rabbits. His own aching modern soul is calmed by a concrete physical operation in a real environment. What Hardy shows us is that though ideals may fail, it is still possible to find value in perception of minute particulars. This may seem an excessively modest achievement for a man who wants to transform a society, but Hardy's description convinces us that it must be the beginning of wisdom. Clym's destructive energies cannot operate while he is in touch with specific realities; they are a product of his will and his ideal vision. It is necessary and valuable to return to the matrix, if this means returning to an awareness of the specific conditions of human existence in a world which is beautiful, even in its indifference to human aspirations. Everything significant must start from a concrete perception, from an assumption of basic rhythms; this is the wisdom of the poet, and it is Hardy's meaning here.

To D.H. Lawrence the tragedy in *The Return of the Native* lies in the futile purpose of man, pitted as he is against the "fecund body of the heath" carried by his ideals away from the "passionate purpose that issued him out of the earth into being."[26] Hardy, however, does not seem to extol the forces beneath the threshold that Lawrence himself calls attention to. Hardy is aware of the passionate drives, but he does not accept the vision of certain of the Naturalists, and show these forces leading man to the apex of experience. On the contrary, these forces, summed up often for Hardy in what we might call "sexual selection", are preferably to be channeled and controlled by human intelligence lest the inevitable disaster follow. Hardy is no primordialist. Everything in his depiction of Clym's drive toward Eustacia and Eustacia's drive toward Clym, is tinged with irony; surely, if ever there was a mismating, this is one. This does not mean, of course, that Hardy's characters are divorced from nature; they are not, they cannot be. But their relationship to nature, as Hardy sees it, should be concrete and physical, and should not involve a Romantic "leap" of consciousness. Lawrence is of course quite correct in his assumption of Hardy's suspicion of the ideal life-ambitions of Clym; but he is surely wrong in assuming that Hardy's novel shows Clym's failure as one involving a lack of contact with the depths of "terrific unfathomed nature".

The tragedy in *The Return of the Native* compasses a vision of neutral nature, together with a sense of the failure of social forms and the inadequacy of thought alone to transform these. Hardy assumes that man is mortal and that life is full of suffering; yet happiness is possible too, given an existence focused on creative interaction with men and environment, a life in which reason constantly modifies social relations without destroying traditional forms that retain their psychological or moral validity. Egdon Heath is a backwater, a socially static community, badly in need of transformation. Yet through certain rituals it manages to allow men to express innate feelings which help to ease their sense of frustration before the cosmos. The fire-lighting is mysterious and beautiful, and even Susan Nunsuch's sorcery is at least for her a release of feeling; it does not really harm Eustacia. What the community needs, however, is a renewal of life, a social transformation that would lead all men to some of the joys of real contact with nature, work, and each other. What is tragic in Hardy is that no such renewal seems possible. For the men of reason like Clym cannot integrate mind and body but move from splendid aspiration to humble ineffectiveness. At the stage of history perceived by Hardy in this novel, the social coinage of intellectual enlightenment can only be Victorian liberalism, a force that has lost its contact with the community it seeks to reform. Desperately, that community needs saving. The old integral base of the pyramid of civilization must somehow survive to transmit the wisdom of its particular strengths. The alternative is the rootless life in which each individual feels the dull "ache of modernism" and not the throb of life. Yet Hardy sees no immediate hope of a solution. The present suffering must be endured, and changes wrought slowly in society, but with no exaggerated hope of success. Everything else is the stuff of presumption and invites the tragedy of unfulfillment.

The depths of "terrific unfathomed nature" offer man no easy resource, and the higher he pitches his aspirations the more likely it is that he will come to grief, simply as a matter of statistical probability. What the novelist can do is to dispel illusions by rendering nature objectively, and by showing how the limitations of social life must inevitably add to human unhappiness. This is the sober wisdom of *The Return of the Native* and in his novels of the eighties Hardy would not essentially alter his vision. Only two novels from this next decade require brief mention in connection with our theme.

3. The Mayor of Casterbridge and The Woodlanders

The Mayor of Casterbridge (1886), lacking any sustained detail of natural description, nonetheless exhibits an environment of town integrated with land and suggests in the mayor, Henchard, a representative figure of the old order, though Hardy is far from indulging in any simplified allegorical identification.[27] Henchard's character grows with an unparalleled density of effect, despite all the clumsiness of the narrative, until we become aware of its symbolic overtones.[28] In Henchard, Hardy embodies the peasant world and dramatizes the peasant consciousness, and his passionate, but extremely limited character sums up the virtues and the defects of the traditional modes of feeling and knowing, seen in the book to be inadequate in the modern, practical world, though splendid in their hints of richness. Henchard is a figure of ruined magnificence. Coiled round in a maze of his own contriving, the mayor becomes a victim of the excesses of his way of being, in which feeling sinks to sentimentality, and physical knowing degenerates into destructive self-indulgence. His limitations are precisely those which Hardy pictures everywhere as part of the narrowness of the old order. Above all, Henchard is confident of his in-touch-ness with the spontaneous nature in which he moves, though too inarticulate expressly to frame such a confidence. At the beginning Hardy reminds us that aspects are deceiving; the relationship between man and nature is not to be judged on a moment's glance. Henchard lacks the power of rational discernment, is incapable of adaptive behaviour. His trust in the weather-prophet is appropriately a key part of his final downward turn. At every point he is counter-pointed and checkmated by the emotionally underdeveloped but much more flexible Farfrae. The conclusion must be that *The Mayor of Casterbridge*, far from being merely a lament over a vanishing world, is a detailed and concrete exposure of the inadequacy of that world to survive without spiritual renovation.

In *The Woodlanders* (1887), Hardy falls back on his power of description to create a region isolated from the wider world but shot through with the same tangle of unpredictable motive and event. Hardy builds up Little Hintock from several real settings, dropping his usual rough topographical realism to construct a kind of hothouse or laboratory Wessex, in which he can demonstrate the workings of the Unfulfilled Intention.[29]

> It was one of those sequestered spots outside the gates of the world where may usually be found more meditation than action, and more listlessness than meditation; where reasoning proceeds on narrow premises, and results in inferences wildly imaginative; yet where, from time to time, dramas of a grandeur and unity truly Sophoclean are enacted in the real, by virtue of the concentrated passion and closely knit interdependence of the lives therein.
>
> (Chapter One)

Here we see implied exactly the contrast I have been trying to emphasize between a cultural integer with certain patterns of adaptation, and the outside world where rationality and a certain looseness of relation dominate. The true inhabitants of Little Hintock, the natives Giles and Marty, are just as subject to a world of chance and struggle as anyone else, yet they are constantly described as embedded in a matrix of custom and labour which guarantees them an "intelligent intercourse with nature". The novel describes the hopeless split between the scientific and rationally trained Dr. Fitzpiers, who fails completely in reason and self-knowledge, and the true Woodlanders, related to local reality but doomed because the very narrowness of their integration. In this situation Grace Melbury becomes the returning native who fails to establish herself fully in either world; she carries the note of "double consciousness" that Hardy also makes clear in the narrative voice:

> They went noiselessly over mats of starry moss, rustled through interspersed tracts of leaves, skirted trunks with spreading roots whose mossed rinds made them like hands wearing green gloves; elbowed old elms and ashes with great forks, in which stood pools of water that overflowed on rainy days and ran down their stems in green cascades. On older trees still than these huge lobes of fungi grew like lungs. Here, as everywhere, the Unfulfilled Intention, which makes life what it is, was as obvious as it could be among the depraved crowds of a city slum. The leaf was deformed, the curve was crippled, the taper was interrupted; the lichen ate the vigour of the stalk, and the ivy slowly strangled to death the promising sapling.
>
> (Chapter Seven)

Here, the metaphor of space close-enwrapped by protective trees that on the one hand builds up our sense of seclusion and sheltering is turned, on the other, into an image of relentless natural process. It is not enough to be, as Giles is, the good woodman, physically immersed in the environmental reality, part of the traditional cultural relationship that shapes attitudes and action to nature in a certain way:

> He looked and smelt like Autumn's very brother, his face being sunburnt to wheat-colour, his eyes blue as corn-flowers, his sleeves and leggings dyed with fruit stains, his hands clammy with the sweet juice of apples, his hat sprinkled with pips, and everywhere about him that attitude of cider which at its first return each season has such an indescribable fascination for those who have been born and bred among the orchards.
>
> (Chapter Five)

Giles and Marty fail because their self-sacrifice and fidelity are no longer effective in a social setting in transition from the old ethic of Christian charity and pagan fullness to the present life of economic struggle and legalistic niceties. Yet they are seen as perhaps more worthy of the reader's sympathy than Grace with her "modern nerves and primitive emotions", or than Fitzpiers, with his operative self-interest. Once again, however, there is no idealization and no lament. Giles and Marty should have adapted to the situation, and could have done so with no sacrifice of moral energy. It is their fate to become noble victims, caught under the weight of their own passivity. In the world of Little Hintock, the sexual impulse is rampant — at points conveyed by Hardy's oblique reference to the phallic trees — but true fulfillment escapes everyone. Natural impulse is seen to be badly in need of intelligent and considerate modification; the power of sexual selection is just as poorly exercised here as in *The Return of the Native*. While Marty represses and hides her feelings, Giles is prevented by his unbending chivalry from making the requisite gesture to Grace, and Fitzpiers indulges himself in his every whim. Everyone is frustrated, because neither the old morality nor the new freedom encourages just the precise flexibility that might steer a course toward some limited happiness.

The Woodlanders is a novel of circumscribed space in which the characters play out a drama often crudely manipulated in the name of a "truth" for which Hardy might have found more coherent expression. In his first novel of the nineties, *Tess of the D'Urbervilles*, there is at first sight a similarly puzzling narrative contortion, though the spatial dimensions are larger and more varied. The whole of Wessex, in fact, seems to be involved (yet not involved) in Tess's fate. The integral community has been transformed, not indeed into an urban wasteland, but into a kind of no-man's-land of the spirit: the burning plain of modern life.

4. Tess of the D'Urbervilles

The narrator of *Tess of the D'Urbervilles* (1891) who is in some ways the fourth main character of Hardy's greatest novel, comments again and again on the actions of the central trio. This obtrusive "voice" serves the overall coherence of Hardy's novel by establishing for the reader the sense of life as it really is. Only the narrator sees the state of things as they are; he watches the dooming events from above, measuring his insights by a knowledge initially lacking in the struggling persons of the drama. In spite of some potentially ambiguous phrasing, the narrative voice of the novel is consistent. It reveals a world without metaphysical consolation, a world in which Christianity is dead, and chance rules. It mocks the very idea that there should be a sympathetic First Cause, and embodies the forces opposing Tess in a self-consciously artificial trope ("President of the Immortals"), putting us in the frame of mind of a secularized society in which a religious designation is linked almost casually to modern

125

political terminology and consequently undermined. In this narrative, the relationship between nature and society as assumed by the characters and the average Victorian reader, is one of the central tissues of error, and as such always is subject to correction, by overt commentary if necessary.[30] All attempts to find objective beneficence in nature are seen as foolish. Nature itself, the grand continuum of growth processes of which man is a part, makes no moral or social distinctions, yet precisely because man can resist the thrust of this "world" energy his life is truly human, and potentially tragic. For his resistance takes the form not only of wise intellectual channellings of the *Grundstoff* of impulse and desire, but also expresses itself as strange perversions of a force which will be denied only at the price of human narrowness. The key, the narrative implies, is neither a compulsive affiliation with the essentially unknown and extra-human forces of nature, nor the cultivated blindness of those who pretend that man has no animal side. It is rather a resilient shaping of matrix energies toward human fulfillment, an achievement, the narrator assumes, that under "present conditions" can only be fraught with tragedy.

Spatially, the novel coils outward, exhibiting contrasting landscapes of the field, and culminating in a vision of the sublime nature that challenges man's assertion of values. Combining psychic evolution and reversion, the novel expresses a maximum tension of "double consciousness" as the "returning sophisticated hero" tries to affiliate with the country life, whose simple embodiment is at the same time struggling to cast away the heavy endowment of her origins. Flung together for a moment by the endless whirlpool of events, their meeting takes place at last as an achievement of love that has hardly any social (or even "natural") sanction in the pitiless daylight of modern life.

Here, the Wessex of *Far From the Madding Crowd* is both expanded in space and, at the same time, shattered in substance. A slow sinking of *morale* accompanying social and economic disruption reveals the promised land as a potential waste land, and while the note of metaphysical distress is sounded clearly, movement in both directions leads to a dead end: for the gifted native escaping there is no escape; for the gifted native returning there is no return.

The Vale of Blackmoor of Hardy's opening pages seems at first a pleasant rural backwater, still untouched by modern life, one that the visiting Clare brothers can see only as a typical country environment. yet the colourful "club walking" dance, Hardy lets us know, is itself a focus of ideal and real, and we are soon led beyond appearances. It is the comic-pathetic "Sir" John who represents the real state of things, for after the dance Tess must return to a Marlott household mired in poverty. The sense of decline is created both by references to the older and more psychologically vital social customs and to the former greatness of the d'Urbervilles. At this point the narrator makes one of his first thrusts of exposure, commenting on Tess's failure to get a dancing partner with the

126

sweeping assertion that "pedigree, ancestral skeletons, monumental record, the d'Urberville lineaments, did not help Tess in her life's battle as yet, even to the extent of attracting to her a dancing-partner over the heads of the commonest peasantry. So much for Norman blood unaided by Victorian lucre." The conception of a "life's battle" prepares us for the thorough-going Naturalism of the descriptions that follow, the bitter reference to money is the beginning of a continuous underlining of the social helplessness of the Durbeyfields, while the "blood" image Hardy quickly expands to express one of the central ironies of the novel.[31]

From exterior prettiness, to interior dreariness — the initial shock over, we are prepared to accept the Vale of Blackmoor as a world of dubious coherence. Lack of employment, large family, physical weakness and drink, handicap the Durbeyfields in the struggle for existence. Hardy is not far from Zola in his emphasis on the "curse" of inheritance and on the defeating environment; his Naturalism encompasses the usual aspects of dreary "low life", including blatant sexual exploitation and violence. The Darwinian nature understood as grand process in *The Return of the Native* is here rendered in terms of the Social Darwinism of struggle and exploitation. In his "Prolegemena to *Evolution and Ethics*", published in 1894, T.H. Huxley would insist that natural selection could be imagined to operate most forcefully on the lowest levels of society, despite the hoped-for growth of "ethical man" at other levels.[32] Anticipating this vein, Hardy develops an ironic parable that almost gives credence to Huxley's sweeping assumption.

Describing "The Slopes", "a country-house built for enjoyment pure and simple" Hardy exposes the failure of money to provide social integration. The redbrick intrusion, later to haunt E.M. Forster and Lawrence, is contrasted by Hardy with the old landscape in which human effort modified the land-base without blatantly imposing itself upon it. The yew-trees "not planted by the hand of man" convey a contrast between what can be "made" (like money) and what must come about through natural processes of growth. The passing reference to the bows hints at the yeoman archer, image of English greatness, and prepares us for the later explicit description of the destruction of the yeoman class in Wessex, whose representative, Tess, is about to be seduced by Alec d'Urberville.[33]

Behind the flashiness and decadence of "The Slopes" lies a newly barren working life. Hardy suggests the monotony of machine labour, in which the field workers lose their natural rhythm in the environment to the demands of a production-style operation. Fixing on the brutal social reality exposed in our time by Steven Marcus and others — the new and unregulated dominance of the Victorian land-owner over the very person of his employees — Hardy creates a subtle parallel between the raped land and the "possession" established by its exploiters over the women who work it for them.[34] Tess's personal "harvest" at this point is

"Sorrow the Undesired", whom the narrator's epitaph baptizes in pity. But lest we take the d'Urberville presumption as singular, Hardy repeats the situation later with Farmer Groby of Flintcomb-Ash, who persecutes Tess because she resists him when his indications are that she should be "fair game" for more than his economic drives.

At Flintcomb-Ash, too, the working life is no longer a human occupation; its drudgery soon reduces the field-women to the level of martyrs without a saviour. The dehumanization is made clear by the rendering of the landscape of earth and sky as blank faces; the work which should confirm the links between energy systems is a matter of meaningless drudgery engaged in for the sake of inadequate yet badly needed wages. Later, we see the machine, once again in the character of a "red tyrant". Watched over by a tranced and dar-grimed guardian, it binds human rhythms to its own imperious and inflexible demands. This "infernal machine" bears no relation to the countryside it serves; it is part of a system of economic control exercised on a hire-basis.

Nothing in Hardy's published observations on the agricultural situation would invite a Luddite interpretation here, however. His satire is directed at a situation in which the introduction of the machinery proceeds in the name of the profits of the farmers and industrialists, while only adding to the misery of the farm-workers on the job. At the same time, the new methods exert a final disastrous pressure upon an already shattered social world, where quality is by no means served. The local beer has declined, the farm milk is watered for city consumption, and the threshing machine itself achieves poorer results than the old hand-methods. Tess eventually returns to Marlott, and Hardy becomes explicit in his description of the process of de-population; economic stringency, forcing migration to the towns, destroys any real possibility of vital life, while those who remain are transformed from permanent inhabitants of a given locale into migrant labourers.

Tess's passage from Blackmoor to Flintcomb-Ash is ironically "upward" in space, though it is clearly "downward" from the apex of her Froom experience. Froom is warm and fruitful; Flintcomb-Ash is high and bleak, and above all, cold — the Naturalistic image of Arctic severity Hardy makes his own with descriptions such as that of the "doom birds", cared for by no one, decimated by winter, flying south to stop at this "starve-acre" place:

> After this season of congealed dampness came a spell of dry frost, when strange birds from behind the North Pole began to arrive silently on the upland of Flintcomb-Ash; gaunt spectral creatures with tragical eyes — eyes which had witnessed scenes of cataclysmal horror in inaccessible polar regions of a magnitude such as no human being had ever conceived, in curdling temperatures that no man could endure: which had beheld the crash of icebergs and the slide of snowhills by the shooting light of the Aurora; been half-blinded by the whirl of colossal storms and terraqueous distortions; and retained the expression of feature that such scenes had engendered. (Chapter XLIII)

128

The "dumb impassivity" of the birds, their driven hunger, mirrors the predicament of Tess herself, trapped as she is on this barren ground; and while Marian can "shriek with laughter" at the flinty, phallic-shaped stones, Tess suffers in silence. Hardy here gives us a fore-glimpse of the final landscape of Tess's "fulfillment"; in this vision of Arctic wastes the dominant sublime nature of vast, inhuman spaces is evoked amid ironical "asides" aimed at man's stark sexual assertion.

In between the two dreary "field" landscapes is the long evocation of the Vale of Froom, or Var, where a quite different set of conditions reigns. Unlike Blackmoor which is best viewed from a distance, Tess must *descend* into Froom to understand it. Her own arrival there does nothing but startle a heron, yet the swarms of cows ripe with milk conjure up a richly intimate and productive life of relationship to the earth, one relatively free of mechanical restraint, and marked by the supple yielding quality of feminine responsiveness. The "plowing and reaping", for the moment are over; the note is one of cooperation, placidity, and leisure.

In Froom, Hardy pictures a pristine world, not nostalgically, but in terms of a recognition of basic linkings. We are at the point where natural and social meet with least abrasion, close to the ecological base of things. The imagery reminds us of the Biblical world of *Far From the Madding Crowd*, and the mention of Dick Dewy, a character cross-reference rare in Hardy, reminds us of his earlier rural world of Mellstock. Significantly, it is the recital of the story of Dick Dewy taming the bull with his fiddle which elicits the first extensive words we hear from Angel Clare in this section: "It's a curious story; it carries us back to mediaeval times, when faith was a living thing". The contrast between the life of reflection and the life of mythopoeic participation is expressed in these very words of Clare. Froom is not really a world in which one can lose reflection, but it is a world where the "power of viewing life . . . from its inner side" can be activated. How far this power, linked to "the great passionate pulse of existence", can carry the individual is at this stage a moot point. What Hardy wants us to grasp is the functioning of a healthy community, defined not as a social state of suspension of nature's laws, but as a human-centered entity, which allows for a psychological responsiveness to moods, atmospheres, and intangible influences that may take the form of a pagan or animistic mythology. In such a community the typing of individuals under such descriptive generalities as "Hodge" becomes impossible. Economic health is based on real people working together with the land, the land animals, and with each other. A median point is established, "the happiest of all positions in the social scale being above the line at which neediness ends, and below the line at which the *convenances* begin to cramp natural feeling . . ." Nor is there in Froom any domination of the "male" aggressiveness Hardy discerns in the other, machine-dominated regions. Love and work can go together, for Clare woos Tess "in undertones like that of the purling milk — at the cow's side, at skimmings, at butter-makings, at cheese makings, among broody poultry, and among farrowing pigs —..." Their relationship develops on multiple levels of reality, and it would be a gross over-simplification to interpret it, on the basis of the self-deception involved, as illusory.[35] Whereas in Blackmoor we are confronted with an "either-or" situation in which degradation lies behind conventional images of rural contentment, here Hardy allows for the luxury of a complex shifting of perspectives: the ideal becomes a living embodiment; the ordinary takes on the excitement of perfect clarity:

> Or perhaps the summer fog was more general, and the meadows lay like a white sea, out of which the scattered trees rose like dangerous rocks. Birds would soar through it into the upper radiance, and hang on the wing sunning themselves, or alight on the wet rails subdividing the mead, which now shone like glass rods. Minute diamonds of moisture from the mist hung, too, upon Tess's eyelashes, and drops upon her hair, like seed pearls. When the day grew quite strong and commonplace these dried off her; moreover, Tess then lost her strange and ethereal beauty; her teeth, lips and eyes scintillated in the sunbeams, and she was again the dazzling fair dairymaid only, who had to hold her own against the other women of the world.

(Chapter XX)

The beauty is there, at many levels, but so is the possibility for dreaming self-deception. Though we cannot overlook the specific reality of the protecting atmosphere, Hardy seems to remind us that actions should be based on other knowledge too, that Tess *is* a relatively helpless dairy-maid, that the diamonds of moisture, transformed into the false gifts of a twisted soul, may "give a sinister wink, like a toad".

The Talbothays Dairy interlude in Tess's life cannot be summed up as either a purely contrasting episode (that is, as a "paradisal" experience opposed to the "Darwinian" reality of the rest) nor can it be treated as an ironic excursion, intensifying the tragedy of the final destruction of the end.[36] What Hardy demonstrates in this section is no suspension of his overall view of nature's indifference, but a *scale* on which human exchange can function with the least harmful distortion of the basic natural forces. Tess and Clare enter Froom with already wounded souls, and in the end they are not able to establish their destined love-relation without tragedy, but while they remain in Froom, they are clear of the worst kind of social disasters. Hardy is not being ironical when he credits Angel Clare with gaining a precious knowledge in Froom, the knowledge of "the seasons in their moods, morning and evening, night and noon, winds in their different tempers, trees, waters and mists, shades and silence, and the voices of inanimate things". He is not suggesting a downward transformation when he records that "amid the oozing fatness and warm ferments of the Var Vale, at a season when the rush of juices could almost be heard below the hiss of fertilization, it was impossible that the most fanciful love should not grow passionate". The passionate impulse, felt as part of a rich unfolding of natural things, is not in itself evil; nor is the knowledge of physical processes that may be quickly transformed into the myth which is the stuff of poetry, a handicap in anyone's "life's battle". But when clarification on other levels fails, no magic essence in these achievements will prevent disaster, though a society which has fostered them may be the best place to endure what must be. The ecologically-rooted, communally responsible Froom is seen by Hardy as a vastly better place in which to face nature's worst than the mechanically-dominated and fractured worlds of either Blackmoor or Flintcomb-Ash. Froom has its possibilities of ecstasy, though they are indeed hedged in by the limitations of man's fate.

In the famous garden scene, for example, we are made aware of the tension between the real ecstasy of Tess, the unitary sense suddenly bestowed upon her as a free gift, and the unmitigatedly "rank" surroundings of the garden itself.[37] Without undermining the value of Tess's feelings, Hardy shows us an environment which itself is far from being gathered up in the sweep of the human joy, though elements in its profusion of life seem to echo or underline that joy. One feels in Hardy's curious alternation of commitment to and removal from Tess's experience, his awareness of both the value of human ecstatic communion, and his sense of its limitation in a time-bound, Darwinian world. Thus the environment in which Tess assimilates the message of Angel's song, though it lends itself to her mood, has its own disparate reality, with which she is necessarily "stained", and to which at some point she must pay attention. The spiritual communion between Tess and Clare that is confirmed a moment later itself emphasizes the "ache of modernism", the "numbers of tomorrows just all in a line" that threaten to erode any presumption of bliss. The bliss is not invalidated, but we are reminded of the isolation and vulnerability of the human pair wrapt in a love which challenges the pitiless decrees of time. A loss of contact with reality, a failure of the sense of the very real natural matrix, is precisely what sends Tess and Clare spinning away from each other, and their reunion comes only in the sweep of a very different music, as a desperate togetherness under the shadow of an eternity without consolation.

Tess demonstrates clearly that Hardy is by no means as convinced as his Romantic predecessors about the beneficent potentialities of nature. Yet his is not a wavering among points-of-view, but rather an assertion of the necessity of human self-determination against a background of natural energies that demand intellectual and moral shaping. In *Tess*, Hardy moves toward an existential position in regard to human responsibility, and throws his weight behind the necessity for social reform. At the same time, he emphasizes the biological context of man, suggesting in the image of Talbothays the basis of the good community in the actual processes of man's cooperation with nature. Nature is not intrinsically "good", but man is imbedded in it, and if he remains close to the sources of his energy, perhaps the chances of human distortion based on ideal falsification will be fewer.

131

We are now in a better position to understand the character of Tess herself, and to relate it to Hardy's encompassing meanings. Tess cannot be understood merely as the veritable embodiment of the traditional countrywoman, or of the rural and simple life. Notable in Hardy's presentation is the sense of upward striving; Tess's richness of nature includes the power of self-transformation.[38] No more than Gabriel Oak is she the static image of the old rural order. What is important is that while she emerges from that order, and expresses some of its strengths, she also has the power of adaptation. Comparing her with Joan Durbeyfield Hardy makes this point almost at once. "Between the mother, with her fast-perishing lumber of superstitions, folk-lore, dialect, and orally trans-mitted ballads, and the daughter, with her trained National teachings and Standard knowledge under an infinitely Revised Code, there was a gap of two hundred years as ordinarily understood". In Tess, we see the innate intelligence responding to bitter experience of life, with a resulting power of discrimination far beyond the average. Although Tess is connected with the land, and possesses a sensitive tenderness for life, and the skills of her trade, she is also a spiritually aware and evolving consciousness. Rising out of suffering and a false sense of self-degradation to the point at which she can assert herself as a loving partner and spiritual equal to Angel Clare, she demonstrates her greatness of soul. Since the pressure of social disapproval is all against Tess, we can rightly see her as Hardy's representative modern soul, as the individual who takes on moral re-sponsibility against the distortions of ideal consciousness, who follows her nature's cravings not with a blind primordial thirst, but in the name of moderation and self-effacement. In the end Hardy makes us see that Tess is the foiled saint of his new existential order in which balance and intelligent perception combine with a capacity for the true idealism of self-sacrifice to produce an individual far superior to the codes which drag her down.

As we begin to construe something of Hardy's culminating effect, we can better understand the deeply ironical tone which so shocked his contemporaries. Not only is Hardy daring to present the evolution of innate quality in a manner to confound the superficial determinant of class, but he is suggesting the complete inadequacy of his own contem-porary world to receive such an heroic bequest. All along, the narrator reminds us of the image of the bird in the trap, of the enclosing social penalties of such a human transformation, all along, he reminds us of the pressures operating against Tess, forcing her into the role which her struggling consciousness refuses to accept.[39] At first it seems that Tess has in fact failed to escape the nets that surround her, for she sinks backward into the arms of Alec, and then murders him. Is Hardy suggest-ing that her evolution has taken a downward turn to the primitive which he links so artfully with Alec, using the trope of a "blood relationship" and creating a series of colour links in red? The final "sacrifice" at

Stonehenge might lead us to think so, yet that sacrifice seems also to be something positive, a reconciliation with Clare that is almost beyond tragedy, and certainly beyond the narrow confines of a Naturalistic primal ritual.

Angel Clare is projected backward toward the country, even as Tess moves outward in the other direction. Angel is another version of the sophisticated consciousness grown away from its roots and seeking to find them again. Angel's failure is first of all a failure of perception. He sees Tess as the pure milkmaid because he is motivated by the wrong kind of intellectual fervor. His first impulse is to love an ideal, not a woman. In Froom we see a gradual awakening of what Lawrence would call "other centres" of knowledge in Angel. Eventually, he is passionately drawn to Tess, but his integral nature is still not completely involved. "Within the remote depths of his constitution, so gentle and affectionate as he was in general, there lay hidden a hard logical deposit, like a vein of metal in a soft loam, which turned the edge of everything that attempted to traverse it". As Tess insists, in the most penetrating psychological observation in the book: "It is in your own mind what you are angry at, Angel; it is not in me". Angel, the apparently emancipated bearer of "an ethical system without any dogma" is himself bound up with social distortions, and turns against Tess with the epithet "peasant" when she tries to reason with him. At this point Angel seems to have plunged into the Valley of Froom with little result, for he sacrifices experience to conventional mental forms; lacking self-knowledge, he is victimized by the impulses in himself which he has not come to terms with. He betrays Tess's love in many ways, even at one point inviting Izz Huet to take her place with him on the trip to Brazil. Yet Tess and he have been drawn together, both physically and spiritually, and his attraction finally overcomes his scruples. Tess waits faithfully for "her husband", enduring the resumed pursuit of Alec, ironically reactivated partially because her honest transmission to him of Angel's views on morality has been perverted to justify Alec's own pleasure. This doctrinal link between Angel, the false prophet and Alec, the failed evangelist, is a significant example of Hardy's view of the destructive role of religious positions in particular, and of formally assumed systems in general. Between the over-scrupulous Angel and the unscrupulous Alec, Tess's humanity wastes away until she is propelled into a kind of will-less motion, "like a corpse upon the current".

Yet Tess's moral power is triumphant in the end. Though she sees Angel as godlike, she is not wantonly unfaithful to her god, to the human relationship which is all that can still give meaning to existence in Hardy's twilight world. Angel slowly recovers from his malaise of principled narrowness. This occurs only when he returns from Brazil as a kind of physical shadow of his previous self. Hardy suggests the power of suffering to create a resurrection of moral energy in sensitive souls. In

133

Froom, Angel really had been touched physically by Tess, and their spiritual kinship had been established. In the end, these factors, reflected on from the point of view of a suffering consciousness, draw him back to her. Now Hardy unfolds his deepest irony. Angel's return awakens Tess from the dreamlike state of her relationship with Alec. Once again, the possibilities of action confront her. Yet now she finds herself trapped, forced into acquiescence to Alec by his persistent sophistry. Alec has convinced her that he is her "true husband" and exercised his superior social power to conquer her again. Tess seems at last the hopeless victim of the evil system of distorted impulse that we have described earlier. Yet Alec is destroyed in a sudden act of violence which has been anticipated from the first moment of their relationship. His taunting words drive Tess to strike out at the restrictions that have now become unbearable. She had done this not as part of a Naturalistic primordialism, but out of the desperation of love, in defence of Clare, whom Alec had just insulted by calling him "by a foul name". The murder of Alec suggests that Hardy saw not only the true psychological threat here, but also the inevitable end of hopeless social repression in violence. This murder is the measure of Hardy's despair about the possibility of the evolving, self-determining spirit finding a place in the contemporary world of restricting social and mental forms, and corrupt economic power. [40] Tess can only break free by an act which confirms her death at the hands of the system.

The natural setting created by Hardy in the final Stonehenge episode is that of plain, and sky stretching to infinity. Darkness shrouding the lovers disperses to reveal the monolithic stones rigid against the sky. Man's imposed order is unyielding and ancient. He builds his social structures in a necessary effort to relate to the cosmic energies, but too inhumanly. The ancient order embodies the dark labyrinth of human narrowness. In terms of Hardy's Victorian world the male double-standard, a phallic assertiveness, dominates the real possibilities of love. The stones of this hideous order do nothing to shield man from the emptiness of infinity; rather they emphasize the nakedness of his self-assertion. [41] In a better society, human communion would be nourished and not defeated by social enactments. Angel's harp could sound over the disordered garden in Froom, creating for a moment the sense of connection with Tess that redeems them both; but here the massive pillars of law sing out the tragic music of the spheres. The glimpse of the caretaker who earlier spied out Angel and Tess in loving sleep together, however, assures us that something has been won. Passionate love realized seals the pact of souls against the threatening social and cosmic domination, yet the trap is closed. The anonymous encroachers, not too far from Kafka's various interlopers, re-assert the Law in all its naked injustice.

From the beginning, the narrator has acted to bring us into a perspective from which we could see beyond the limited views of the characters. In this world of shattered omniscience from on high, he has assumed the god-role. Protecting Tess wherever he can, mediating between the sophisticated and the simple, interpreting so as to lead the reader into a transformed view of the reality he has probably misread, the narrator has carried on a running rhetorical battle with the "unsympathetic First Cause" hatched by the grotesque metaphysics of the "forces opposed to Tess". Now, at the end, he offers us a tenuous hope for the future in the acceptance of the "pact" of personal love by Clare and Liza-lu, though this must remain a symbolic gesture, an act of piety, until, if ever, it is transformed into real love. With the death of Tess, the narrator's case against the "god of this world" is complete. In the very phrase "justice is done", the old system condemns itself. The narrator has exposed the sterility of the traditional metaphors of relationship between man and nature, between character and fate. These metaphors describe a way of being, a view of life that should be entombed, even as the d'Urbervilles lie entombed in the past. Great novels can be very disturbing in their challenges to our conventional social and moral assumptions. Tess's sacrifice calls out to the reader, against all risks, to create his own being, to speak a new language if he can, in the name of passion and truth.

5. Hardy's Nature: The Within and the Without

Some of the good criticism of Hardy's writing centers on his role as creator and interpreter of the "Wessex" world, while certain other perceptive analyses explore the question of Hardy and "modernism", seeing the fiction as prophetic of an existential situation common to his successors. At the heart of both these approaches, whether explicitly dealt with or not, is the ambiguous term "nature".[42] In Hardy "nature" is clearly present in the visible processes among which the characters move, and with which they are subtly intertwined — we need only think of Knight clinging to the cliff, of Dick Dewy's wedding under the "spreading tree", of Gabriel and Bathsheba in the storm, of "haggard Egdon", of Tess in the field, or Arabella and the pig's bladder — to name a diversity of instances from a variety of works. At the same time, "nature" in Hardy often refers to a larger abstraction, either the Darwinian universe of struggle and mechanism, or that "terrific un-fathomed nature" which some critics have credited Hardy with seeing as "beneficent". Unfortunately, the very *width* of Hardy's view of nature has seemed to add to the critical confusion, rather than offering a maximum opportunity for understanding.

Any attempt to define the image of nature in Hardy's fiction might well echo John Wain's observation that Hardy, practically speaking, had the vision of the peasant.[43] This can be modified to read that Hardy was in fact a regionalist by birth, whose artistic perceptions reach one of their strengths in depicting the peasant consciousness. One must not, of course, overemphasize the naive element in Hardy's rural vision, but

135

keep in mind, too, his demonstrated awareness of the Arnoldian world of culture and poetry and of the Darwinian world of mechanism and natural law.

Looking over his subject from the point of view of "The Dorsetshire Labourer" and the prefaces of the nineties, Hardy could rightly see his achievement as first of all that of one who had "inside" knowledge about a way of life that was vanishing. To say this is quite a different thing from deciding that Hardy's works represent in any real sense of lament for this vanishing way of life. In neither the Wessex novels themselves, nor in the prefaces, does Hardy offer much more than a wry smile by way of regret over what is being lost. And in "The Dorsetshire Labourer" (1883), after discussing the whole question of the losses and gains of the agricultural workers under the changing conditions, Hardy sums up, as follows: " . . . new varieties of happiness evolve themselves like new varieties of plants, and new charms may have arisen among the classes who have been driven to adopt the remedy of locomotion for the evils of oppression and poverty — charms which compensate in some measure for the lost sense of home".[44] This kind of sentence, representative as it is of Hardy's overall view, must be kept in mind when we evaluate his image of country life.

To understand Hardy's novels one must grasp the exact relationship of Hardy's community to the nature that sustains it. Hardy is in no sense "Wordsworthian", if this means (as it only loosely does) that he sees nature as an objective repository of some kind of beneficent "spiritual" principle. There is almost nothing in Hardy to suggest such a state of affairs and literally hundreds of passages to deny it. Hardy accepts the view that nature is a proces "indifferent" to man, within which man can exist only by "adaptation". Webster, and others, have made clear Hardy's close attention to the Darwinian controversy and the furore surrounding the publication of *Essays and Reviews* in 1860.[45] Hardy, arriving in London in the very year of the publication of Spencer's *First Principles*, and remaining in contact with "liberal thought" as he did through his unfortunate friend Horace Mosley Moule, was so forceful in his expression of "brute" nature that he was sometimes taken to have gone beyond the sense of merely "neutral" nature to a concept of a malicious creator. Toward the end of his life, he had to insist to Alfred Noyes that his summing up of the forces opposed to Tess was meant as an allegory of personality, not as a literal reading of the metaphysical horizon; and earlier, to invoke the Hardy-ism most beloved by Professor Morrell, he had bluntly called nature "an arch-dissembler".[46] There is no doubt in my mind about the necessity and force of Professor Morrell's attack on those who would turn Hardy's nature into a specifically "beneficent" environment. Yet I think it is a great mistake to move from this very justified sense of Hardy's "neutral" nature to the conclusion that his characters are therefore necessarily "divorced" from nature, and quite wrong to turn Hardy, without further qualification, into a kind of

136

modern existentialist for whom all values have shifted to man the rebel.

Some critics have been deceived by Hardy's location of characters in the nature-relation sustained by the traditional community into reading a sense of beneficence into Hardy's view; others have ignored or distorted the real sense of tradition in Hardy in order to accommodate the strong emphasis on Darwinian nature. But Hardy's view is both "Darwinian" and one that emphasizes the power of the traditional community; nor is there any conflict between these views whatever. Hardy's characters are not divorced from nature; they are in it, and it is in them. If they are country people they experience nature through traditional forms, in terms of field work, festival, or ceremony; if they are more sophisticated, they still have the power, like Clym as furze-cutter, to adapt to the necessities of the situation, and so survive. Nature is indifferent to man, but man can achieve a certain stability if he knows how to adapt. The traditional community is above all an instance of such adaptation; Hardy's "image of the field" reveals a socio-natural entity summing up patterns of adaptation. The traditional community is not to be sneered at, precisely *because* it embodies viable forms of relationship between man and the environment. To Hardy Wessex is not an ideal, but an example.

Hardy knows very well, from the beginning, that the community expressed in his Wessex novels is debased and static, but that even so it sums up certain instinctive forms of relationship between man and nature, without which the individual is cast adrift. Nature is *within* Hardy's characters, but this does not make him a primordialist. The will, the impulses summed up in such matters as "sexual selection" are not automatically destructive, or creative.[47] Hardy's novels suggest that mind and impulse must be balanced. Once again, the traditional forms are useful precisely because it is in them that the "irrational" needs are expressed and brought into focus, so that they may be dealt with by the community. Hardy understands that there are forces or impulses in the individual which defy the control of ordinary reason, but he does not exalt these forces or seek meaningfulness through them alone. On the contrary, he sees them as potentially destructive, unless they are regulated by rational choice which takes account of things as they are, including nature as it is: impersonal, stimulative, but no standard for human action. The "irrational" can be creative in Hardy when it is embedded in traditional forms which are still viable. But the overall picture is tragic, for Hardy sees no human community truly relevant to contemporary life.

Here is where we become aware of Hardy's unique position as sophisticated observer of the peasant consciousness, as a writer who has an objective perspective on the traditional community and its relation to nature. For Hardy understands the implications of the new thought, the effect of the higher criticism upon faith, and of the new science upon the old image of man. What the new thought does is to lead the individual to dissent and to frame ideals; what it fails to do is to recreate the community

137

that will embody the new adaptations. For to Hardy faith in mind is always reckless unless it is accompanied by a clarity of actual vision. The desire to stand outside the community may be a tragic necessity for his ·lonely heroes, but it will also be the means of their destruction. Hardy is very much aware that he is writing in a time of transition when the old thought has played itself out and the new thought must speak to all reasonable men. There is no easy alternative, however, to the rooted patterns of centuries, though these badly need to be transformed. (Their harshness comes through in some of the images of terror incidental to the novels, in the man-trap in *The Woodlanders* that nearly wounds Grace, for example.) What must be done is to stay alert for possibilities; to face the truth of the situation, and work toward a new and better relation of man to man in nature. If the community is reformed in time, the human tragedy will not be so harsh — this is above all the message of the later novels. In so far as the new thought reforms the community it is useful, but the difficulty is that it has eroded belief without reforming or clarifying moral vision, as we see above all in Angel Clare. While the heroes of the new thought, like Clym, are right not to stand still within the traditional community, they cannot by themselves offer a full alternative, precisely because the "unconscious" assumptions of any community flourish beyond thought. Hardy's major novels suggest the limitations of intelligence when it is divorced from the practical realities of adaptation. The later novels attack existing social forms, not out of some kind of "Wordsworthian" faith in the "natural man", but in the name of a new and saner relation between society and nature. They suggest the necessity of an adjustment of social reality to the facts of life in an indifferent universe; society should not condemn the individual for failing to conform to its outmoded conventions; it should be reformed so that it achieves contours acceptable to the rational man, who knows, at least, what nature *isn't*. Hardy's central faith despite his sense of its limitations is in human reason.

Meaningfulness in Hardy, therefore, may be said to be of two kinds. First, there is the meaningfulness of the rational sense of fact — the limited but real power of the human mind to work out patterns of survival in a given environment, taking into account the indifferent universe. Secondly, there is the meaningfulness of that kind of creativity which expresses itself in rituals of order that allow for communion of man with man, and the expression of feeling in relation to nature. Hardy does not envisage a strictly intellectual adjustment to life: thus his constant and loving attention to certain forms of traditional life, his *example* of the Wessex society with its manifold social "adaptations", which offer a possibility for a limited human happiness.

If we go to one of the most striking passages of natural description in Hardy, the scene of Knight and Elfride on the cliff in *A Pair of Blue Eyes* (1873), we can see, even at such an early stage, an illustration of Hardy's complex awareness of both the value of original intelligence and of traditional forms of response to nature. Knight is one of Hardy's rationalist heroes, an idealist, a former Oxford student, who knows the dangers of clambering carelessly about Beeny Cliff, but who nonetheless is caught by the effects of a shower, and nearly falls to his death. Clinging to the cliff, Knight feels time close up "like a fan" before him, and is brought face to face with the "terrible muse" of geology, as he stares at a fossil embedded in the rock before him:

He saw himself at one extremity of the years, face to face with the beginning and all the intermediate centuries simultaneously. Fierce men, clothed in the hides of beasts, and carrying for defence and attack, huge clubs and pointed spears, rose from the rock, like the phantoms before the doomed Macbeth. They lived in hollows, woods, and mud huts — perhaps in caves of the neighboring rocks. Behind them stood an earlier band. No man was there. Huge elephantine forms, the mastodon, the hippopotamus, the tapir, antelopes of monstrous size, the megatherium, and the myledon — all, for the moment, in juxtaposition. Further back, and overlapped by these, were perched huge-billed birds and swinish creatures as large as horses. Still more shadowy were the sinister crocodilian outlines — alligators and other uncouth shapes, culminating in the colossal lizard, the iguanodon. Folded behind were dragon forms and clouds of flying reptiles; still underneath were fishy beings of lower developments; and so on, till the lifetime scenes of the fossil confronting him were a present and modern condition of things. These images passed before Knight's inner eye in less than half a minute, and he was again considering the actual present. Was he to die?

(Chapter Twenty-two)

The straightforward effectiveness of Hardy's description is remarkable. Knight, the thinking modern man, experiences his own insignificance in the form of a panorama of devolution, which exposes the primitive origins of his state of "enlightenment", and which shakes him out of the self-centered complacency of the bright young man to whom death is merely a distant possibility. Knight, caught up in the "space-terror" of the cliff on which he may be dashed to pieces, undergoes the "time terror" of an evolution in reverse, which reminds him how tenuous is his own spark of life, and how all human culture still stands on a "present and modern condition" of innate helplessness before relentless nature. Survival is and has always been a matter of adaptation, and Knight in fact answers the question of his fate by action; his quick intelligence does come to his rescue, and he and Elfride escape the danger. Hardy affirms the practical need of specific, contextual response, the "cunning" of Darwinian lore; yet at the same time, a moment later, he reminds us of the possibility of collective and communal reaction to this kin of danger, when he describes the peasant attitudes to the natural environment:

To those musing weather-beaten West-country folk who pass the greater part of their days and nights out of doors, Nature seems to have moods in other than a poetical sense; predilections for certain deeds at certain times, without any apparent law to govern or season to account for them. She is read as a person with a curious temper; as one who does not scatter kindnesses and cruelties alternately, impartially, and in order, but heartless severities or overwhelming generosities in lawless caprice . . .

Such a way of thinking had been absurd to Knight, but he began to adopt it now.

(Chapter Twenty-two)

The ''primitiveness'' of the peasant attitude, the dark side of which is represented by stagnation, superstition, and ignorance, has also the virtue of fostering a collective awareness of nature's capacity for seeming personal maliciousness. The peasant is intimately aware of what seems to be ''her pleasure in swallowing the victim''. The ''locals'' are protected from the dangers of the cliff by their traditional respect for nature's caprice. Knight must be brought face to face with the primitiveness of his state of being and must respond personally and effectively to the seriousness of the situation; the peasants are usually saved from such accidents by their actual collective awareness of the danger. Living in ''a present and modern condition'' of primitive awareness, they are perhaps incapable of the kind of action habitual to Knight in an emergency, but for them the emergency may never come, simply because of the pre-existing shield of their integral culture.

6. The Last Novels: Hardy and Naturalism

Thomas Hardy's last books take up the question of escape from a social and moral impasse through the projected psychic evolution of the representative figure of the traditional world. Hardy had to examine the complexities of social and natural interaction in the late-Victorian context in terms of a wider panorama of possibility. What kind of human development was possible, and to what extent could it accommodate the strengths of the concrete perceptions of the rooted community? In *Jude the Obscure* (1895) we see the complete disruption of the traditional order resulting in a world which leaves the individual isolated from social forms. The characters move against a background which they are really not part of, constantly in motion, and victimized because they cannot integrate their ideals and their lower drives. Society is understood negatively as a kind of conspiracy against originality and freedom, and the class system is attacked, yet there is left a faint hope of possible evolution, Jude and Sue being (unfortunately for them) ''fifty years'' ahead of their time. Behind society is the relentless mechanical order, which is indifferent at best and at moments of tragedy seems almost hostile. Jude himself is lured by the ideals of self-education and humane learning of Victorian liberalism, but at the same time he is emotionally vulnerable. He represents incompatible elements, and, lacking cunning and adaptive powers, suggests Hardy's final judgment on the noble foolishness which is the last gesture of the dying sub-culture. The hoydenish Arabella, vastly over-rated on the positive side in Lawrence's criticism, is a

140

coinage of opportunist "low-life"; her triumph and Sue's decline at the end offer little consolation. Jude and Sue express for the last time the old Hardy antithesis of the slow, earthy man, and the quick, elusive woman, but here the contrast extends into many levels of meaning: it becomes a commentary on disrupted social-sexual roles in an inflexible society, and an expression of unintegrated modes of being that must be conjoined if modern life is to be worth living. *Jude the Obscure* continues to suggest the necessity for intelligent adaptation as the key to human happiness, and offers the hope of an eventual "evolutionary meliorism", but it is conclusive on the failure of synthesis between the old and the new in terms of the then present England. The field landscape, shrunken in scope, is dominated by Naturalistic emblems of decline, Arabella and her pigs being central. Jude is thrust "unborn" to any new being into an urban world whose social rigidity is reiterated in the repeated imagery of lonely human figures dominated by some overarching domestic structure, whether house, church or college. In Hardy's last major novel, natural space nearly disappears and nature itself becomes the punitive lever of events exerting its force upon individuals locked up in the hopeless social entrapment.

At this point it is possible to explore the relationship of Hardy to Naturalism, which seems to call attention to itself in the last two great novels in particular, though Hardy in his private statements played it down. Morton Dauwen Zabel attempts to distinguish Hardy's art from that of the Naturalists by insisting on his diversion from the naive goal of simply reproducing reality.[48] This, however, is taking the Naturalist claims at face value, something that can hardly be done, because the actual effect of the Naturalist novel often lies outside its theoretical aims. Hardy realized this, as "The Science of Fiction" demonstrates. In this essay of 1891, he emphasizes the differences between story-writing and the scientific processes: for one thing, the writer simply doesn't know all the facts. Hardy seems to doubt the claims of the Naturalist critics, that fiction might be truly scientific, and develops his own criteria. The novel must *seem* to be true, "and when the old illusions begin to be penetrated, a more natural magic has to be supplied".[49] The aesthetic and moral factors come together when we think of the folkways of Wessex as an essential reservoir, not only of modes of adaptation to environment, but of patterns of "natural magic", which take on a concrete form and allow the novelist to enrich his vision of reality with elements that suggest a dimension beyond the narrowly rational. Writing specifically of *The Mayor of Casterbridge*, Robert B. Heilman suggests how "by a whole range of devices . . . [Hardy] . . . expresses his sense of the extraordinary, the unpredictable, the contradictory; of non-rational, non-naturalistic phenomena that challenge patterns and defeat expectations; of the wonderful that undercuts the familiar laws and probabilities of everyday life."[50] This is one of the strongest arguments for Hardy's acceptance of the importance of the intuitive side of life, which we have tried to suggest he values (and finds in Wessex) though he is aware as well of the need for rational adaptation to the Darwinian world. Hardy was not convinced by Bergson's early work, yet an example from the French philosopher's last book enables us to pinpoint an important element in Hardy's fiction. Bergson observes that when a mere accident involves the human presence, our evaluation of it changes. A boulder falls from a cliff upon an empty path and we call it chance; but if it falls upon a man walking along that path, we are inclined to suspect intention, to call the event not a chance event, but one involving Luck.[51] Hardy the thinker knows the universe of chance but Hardy the artist evokes the universe of luck, underlining the strange intersection of human hopes and natural patterns that science largely ignores. Hardy once put this another way when he wrote: "My opinion is that a poet should express the emotion of all the ages and the thought of his own."[52] The mental enlargement we look for from fiction depends upon "intuitive conviction and not upon logical reasoning". In "The Science of Fiction" he asserts further against "mechanical" realism that "a sight for the finer qualities of existence, an ear for the 'still, sad music of humanity', are not to be acquired by the outer senses alone, close as their powers in photography may be". Reminding us of his connection with the great humanistic English tradition, in particular with Wordsworth as aesthetician, Hardy invokes the principle of the "pleasure of telling a tale". "The determination to enjoy" was in all nature as at least a hidden tendency and should be in art. Hardy once wrote:

> We tale-tellers are all Ancient Mariners, and none of us is warranted in stopping Wedding Guests (in other words, the hurrying public) unless he has something more unusual to relate than the ordinary experience of every average man and woman. The whole secret of fiction and drama — in the constructional part — lies in the adjustment of things unusual to things external and universal. The writer who knows how exceptional, and how non-exceptional his events should be made, possesses the key to art.[53]

The many "Naturalistic" features of *Tess* and *Jude* in particular, should not force us to attempt an easy categorizing. Discussing Naturalism itself, I emphasized earlier that the whole movement has the aspect of a struggle to bring meaning out of the mechanistic nature that science seemed to insist on as the true order of things. Hardy is one of those who retained in his work the force of contact between the personal and the universal, the latter often embodied in a vision of natural space, whether of the nature of the field, or of sublime distance. Yet Hardy's art never loses the specific human focus. As he himself made clear, man was his principal concern. "An object or mark raised or made by man on a scene is worth ten times any such formed by unconscious Nature. Hence clouds, mists and mountains are unimportant beside the wear on a threshhold, or the print of a hand". "The beauty of association", in short, "is entirely superior to the beauty of aspect". "Nature", he

142

asserted, "was played out as a Beauty, but not as a Mystery", its "deeper reality" was related to the "tragical mysteries of life".[54]

It would be foolish to take these remarks as an excuse for denigrating the part played by natural scenery in Hardy's fiction, for it goes without saying that the artist's primary concern is man; Hardy was clearly responding here with the usual end-of-century revulsion against exaggerated Wordsworthianism. Hardy understands man in terms of a larger environment. His novels at first manifest a concern for the environment of the traditional agricultural community and finally describe its break-up under the thrust of the mechanized urban world of the new science. Hardy accepts this change, but demands the re-creation of the specifics of human values conceived of originally in terms of a particular community's concrete relation to nature. This "nature", however, must now be understood in new terms, and the values must accordingly be transformed though still rooted in concrete experience. The "field" in Hardy's novels is precisely that area where man has learned to cooperate with indifferent nature, where he has shaped usages that enable him to live in that indifferent nature and find a way to human richness and fulfillment. The new fulfillment, however, must come in new terms and in a new environment. If *Jude* is devoted to exposing the impasse in late-Victorian society, and offers merely a few general statements of hope about the possible meliorism of the future, *Tess* grapples specifically with the redemption of the space that science has turned into a threatening vastness. The conclusion of the novel, we argued, dramatizes a real meeting of souls in the flesh. Love persists, suffering brings a measure of insight, delusions vanish under the weight of experience. Tess and Clare shelter one another on the darkling plain. Like Conrad, Hardy refuses to search for the balancing "within" in nature herself; unlike Lawrence, he does not pinpoint the "unconscious" in terms of the body, though the body is released and sanctioned. Hardy lets us entertain a vision of possibility in the two lovers, who now know the artificiality of a particular social restraint, as they "know" one another in the concrete embodiment of the moment. Hardy's final vision is not one of pure reason, but of the power of the love that knows, that has been freed from a specifically binding order of values. Hardy's redemption of space is tentative, but it is strongly based on the power of suffering to clarify the vision and purify the affections. Going far beyond the programme of Naturalism, Hardy shows us the realization of a truly human space, which, however, is still outlawed by society and threatened by vast nature. The individual, under the monstrous indifference of sublime nature, must create his own community of values, trusting in balanced mind and instinct to cure "the ache of modernism".

As *Jude* shows, however, the passage to real freedom lies through a wasteland of contemporary life, and Hardy's present world remains dark with the shadows of the past. Although Hardy would later affirm that, in

143

the words of Zabel, "the role of man in the universe is a role of emergent exoneration and supremacy", in the novels that emergence and supremacy is only barely foreshadowed. [55] The overriding moral climate is rather one of struggle, ironical misapprehension, and shattered illusions, held short of despair only by Hardy's great capacity for a negative capability in the face of those "uncertainties, mysteries and doubts" belonging to the modern era almost as a birthright.

CHAPTER TWO

H.G. Wells: The Claustrophobia and
Vertigo of Scientific Space

"Wells's achievement was that he installed the paraphernalia of our new environment in our imagination; and life does not become visible or tolerable to us until artists have assimilated it".

V.S. Pritchett

1. The Time Machine: Entropy and One Faint Hope

H.G. Wells's Time Traveller makes what is indeed "the longest journey". Leaving the year 807,701 he ranges forward through time until he finds himself a witness to the natural rites that mark the end of our solar system. In a remarkable passage Wells suggests the bleakness of a dying world.

> The darkness grew apace; a cold wind began to blow in freshening gusts from the east, and the showering white flakes in the air increased in number. From the edge of the sea came a ripple and a whisper. Beyond these lifeless sounds the world was silent. Silent? It would be hard to convey the stillness of it. All the sounds of men, the bleating of sheep, the cries of birds, the hum of insects, the stir that makes the background of our lives — all that was over. As the darkness thickened, the eddying flakes grew more abundant, dancing before my eyes; and the cold of the air more intense. At last, one by one, swiftly, one after the other, the white peaks of the distant hills vanished into the blackness. The breeze rose to a moaning wind. I saw the black central shadow of the eclipse sweeping towards me. In another moment the pole stars alone were visible. All else was rayless obscurity. The sky was absolutely black.

(Section Eleven)

This is a great distance to have come from the polite drawing room scenes of the opening of the story, yet the trajectory of the narrative is inevitable. Wells keeps his story under control at every point, producing a masterpiece which is a landmark in the history of science fiction, and in the rendering of natural space.[1]

The Time Machine (1894) was Wells's first book, and its initial drafts

145

date from as early as 1887, while he was still an enthusiastic science student. While Bernard Bergonzi, the excellent critic of the early Wells, suggests that science is relatively unimportant in this story, one might regard it, on the contrary, as central. Not only is the story "lauched" by the imagined new technology of the time-machine itself, but, more importantly, the myth of the story is based directly upon scientific concepts, and the bite of the story on the social level takes us straight from the present to a future which illuminates the present.[2] Bergonzi, rightly aware of the multiple symbolisms in this remarkably open-structured work, points out its affiliations with fantasy and traditional myth, and analyzes the quality of its ironic commentary of the then present world; yet this hardly obliterates the scientific center which distinguishes such a fiction from works which may be "ironic myths" of quite another character.[3]

In *The Time Machine* man's destiny is understood in Darwinian terms. Not only does T.H. Huxley's individual interpretation of certain Darwinian concepts inspire Wells's partial counter-vision of the society of the Eloi and the Morlocks, but it controls the whole trajectory of the narrative. We are led inevitably through the unfolding of what Huxley calls "the great year", as the universe "runs down" in the manner prescribed by the scientific vision of the century.[4] Bergonzi is mistaken when he describes Wells's Darwinism as being secondary to his Marxism. On the contrary, his Marxism functions within a Darwinian context which evades the orthodox Marxist premises. This is made clear by the evocation of the Eloi and the Morlocks, totally fragmented in what first appears to be a manner predicted by Marxian theory. The Time Traveller sees the Eloi and the Morlocks as descendents of capital and labour respectively. During the course of time capital has become so cushioned from social hardships that its representatives have lost all drives but those concerned with pleasure-seeking, while labour, immured in its subterranean misery, became adapted to the bestiality of struggle. In effect, two species of man evolve from the social division, with one species, the rulers, paradoxically being the physical food of the ruled species. Dominated by the Eloi for thousands of years, the Morlocks were transformed by their physical environment into a specialized hunting species, while the Eloi, softened by their conquest, were exposed to the danger of a growing effeteness, and eventually succumbed. Huxley's famous lectures of the eighties and nineties directed against the Social Darwinists emphasize the necessary and critical distinction between society and nature, but Huxley does hint that the lower classes in society are most subject to the laws of natural selection and mentions that this group seems to be rapidly growing.[5] Because he posits an evolution by the "ethical man" in society, and admits that, despite social achievements, the cosmic process must eventually resume its sway, Huxley falls short of making a clear case for his distinction. The ambiguities allow Wells to suppose a natural selection which operates differently upon the two polarized elements within society. These reached at one state, we are told, a relative state of equilibrium, but when this began to fail, it was the Morlocks who were able to respond to the challenge, precisely because their environment demanded that they keep themselves more mentally and physically vigorous. Wells thus goes beyond Huxley's attempted fine intellectual distinction between nature and society and dramatizes a kind of Social Darwinism in action, though he shows this to be ironically destructive of the original "top dogs", whereas the Social Darwinists of the time were using their theory most often to justify the laissez-faire economics of rampant capitalism.

The world of the Eloi and the Morlocks (we learn from the sustained interpretative commentary of the Time Traveller) is a world which has come about as a result of too much successful adaptation.[6] Man limits positive evolutionary development by attempting to arrest the struggle for existence. Getting rid of pain and suffering, eliminating cunning, destructiveness, energy, violence — man decreases his possibilities of survival. Our noble striving toward the ideal, in so far as it succeeds, ensures our doom. Since this is the Time Traveller's judgment, to which the narrative allows no riposte, we must take it as normative for Wells. Our conclusion must be that his Marxist vision of class struggle is framed by a rather typical Naturalist assumption of "purification by struggle". At one point, for example, the Time Traveller explicitly comments: "What, unless biological science is a mass of errors, is the cause of human intelligence and vigour? Hardship and freedom: conditions under which the active, strong and subtle survive and the weaker go to the wall . . ." This occurs before he meets the Morlocks, and prepares us for their terrible dominance, which he explains on the basis of this Darwinian principle:

> It is a law of nature we overlook, that intellectual versatility is the compensation for change, danger and trouble. An animal perfectly in harmony with its environment is a perfect mechanism. Nature never appeals to intelligence until habit and instinct are useless. There is no intelligence where there is no change and no need of change. Only those animals partake of intelligence that have to meet a huge variety of needs and dangers.
>
> (Section Ten)

Now clearly, Wells had no conscious intention of demolishing the Marxist position of the necessity of social engineering, any more than he was explicitly exposing the limitations of Huxley's distinction between the social ethic and the natural struggle. *The Time Machine* reveals, however, that his commitment as novelist was to the dramatization of the pervasive Darwinian struggle, even though his views as a social thinker might be bringing him slowly toward a Fabian position.[7]

This commitment to Darwinism, and to related scientific theory, underlies the powerful structuring Wells is able to give his story. The vast reaches of space and time are suggested, and human history is placed in a

147

truly cosmic perspective. We sense a rigorous honesty about man's fate, and though faced with doom the human race (emblemized in the Time Traveller) commands our respect. Though Wells's vision seems inextricably bound up with the science of his day, like all imaginative projections it carries its own mystery and meaning. The more closely we look at the scientific context, the clearer this becomes.

T.H. Huxley's Darwinism, for example, foretold the eventual degeneration of all life on the planet.

> The theory of evolution encourages no millenial anticipations. If, for millions of years, our globe has taken the upward road, yet, some time the summit will be reached and the downward route will be commenced. Long since, I ventured to point out that if our hemisphere were to cool again, the survival of the fittest might bring about, in the vegetable kingdom, a population of more and more stunted and humbler and humbler organisms until the "fittest" that survived might be nothing but lichens, diatoms . . .[8]

The Time Machine creates an imaginative picture of the devolution of all life seen as possible by Huxley; Wells leads us from the human to the "post-human" society of Eloi and Morlocks downward to the butterflies and crabs, and to the lichen, humblest of plants. In the final scene in the future, "the red beach, save for its livid green liverworts and lichens, seemed lifeless". The round tentacled thing "hopping fitfully about" in the shallows at the water's edge is a deliberate reminder of the animal which first crawled from the ocean to begin evolution upon dry earth, and by evoking this parallel of the process at its terminal point, Wells emphasizes the circular negativity of evolution. The dying sea, formerly the green fertile source of life, is now "blood-red", and death-still. The ominous eclipse which casts a dark shadow over the sun is a powerful image of finality. Here we seem to see fulfilled the negative possibilities in Darwin's vision of transmuted life-forms.

Certainly, *The Time Machine* dramatizes the finite future of man, though the predictable death of the solar system alone does not warrant this. We know that long before the zenith of human civilization travel to other planets will very likely have made the death of the earth an occurrence which would by no means threaten the extinction of all human life. Wells's *The First Men in the Moon* demonstrates his recognition of the possibility of human life successfully existing on other worlds. This possibility is not explored in *The Time Machine*. At the end of the book, all hope of human life is lost, and the sense of devolution implies an approaching extinction of all things. The Time Traveller goes no further than thirty million A.D., and the implication is that he is approaching the final stop. As Anthony West writes, "a cosmic catastrophe is impending which will finally obliterate the material context in which such concepts as mind, consciousness, and value can possess any meaning".[9] Wells, describing the end of the solar system, suggests the demise of the whole intelligent universe.

This demise, imagined as it is in terms of the apparently failing energy of the sun, suggests an acceptance of projections made from another major stream of nineteenth century science, one that has been consistently interpreted so as to emphasize the ultimate hopelessness of human pretensions.

There is no clear evidence that Wells made a close study of thermodynamics. He wrote about his student days that "at that time (1887) the science of physics was in a state of confusion and reconstruction, and lucid expositions of the new ideas for the student and general reader did not exist".[10] But these "new ideas" to which he refers must have included thermodynamics, since the definition of its laws formed some of the most controversial and well-publicized physical ideas of the nineteenth century; and, — lucid explanation or not — it is quite probable that Wells knew something about the work of Carnot, Mayer, Clausius, and Boltzmann.[11] The discovery of the law of the conservation of energy and the heat-transfer law that could be expressed in terms of entropy, the first and second laws of thermodynamics, makes an involved and highly technical chapter in the history of nineteenth century science, but the implications drawn from entropy and extrapolated into cosmology were of a kind that no enthusiastic science student with a literary flair could miss. Even assuming Wells was not directly familiar with the more technical aspects of thermodynamic theory, he would have been aware of Lord Kelvin's published speculations of 1852 on the dissipation of energy in the universe and his conclusions about the necessary end of the solar system.[12] In fact, Kelvin's time-estimate for the end of the solar system is used in *The Time Machine*, and his influence (as well as the Time Traveller's "earthbound" state) accounts for Wells's limiting of his *Götterdämmerung* to our specific region of cosmic space.

Now current theorizing about the eventual "heat death" of the universe still centers precisely on the second law of thermodynamics, which states that the entropy of a closed system increases with time.[13] This law seems to be absolutely fundamental since everything in the radiative processes of physical nature implies irreversibility, and points in fact to unidirectional time. On the assumption that the universe itself is a closed system, science has envisaged an overall levelling-out, a disorder that would mark the end of the cosmic heat-process that has made all human achievement possible in the first place. From such a perspective, it is conceivable that all life, including man's, involves a quest for order that is ultimately self-defeating. By the end of the century, such negative conclusions seemed to have the full authority of a science that was sure of its perfect reflection of the physical world, as against the "sentimental" assertions of more human-centered viewpoints, and such reflections no doubt contributed to the *fin de siècle* pessimism that Bergonzi notes as relevant to the early fiction of Wells.[14]

Certainly, Wells's description of the end of the world, allowing for its reference to the still-burning stars in the background, seems not inconceivably an artistic visualization of the entropic nightmare as hatched by nineteenth century science. The atmosphere of sad quiet which pervades Wells's concluding description, suggests inevitability. *The Time Machine* images the spectre of life falling back into the black silence of ultimate disorganization. Disregarding the counterentropy of the evolutionary complexification of living forms, Wells seizes upon Huxley's Darwinian idea of the obliteration of higher life by a shift of environmental conditions. He creates his vision of the end of the world by wedding Kelvin's doomsday predictions about energy to Huxley's doomsday predictions about devolution. Wells makes a choice among theoretical possibilities to create a particular effect, and here, as in *The Island of Doctor Moreau*, he hits upon the most pessimistic options. (And just as evolutionary science today would see the element of struggle in *The Island of Doctor Moreau* as exaggerated, so today there is not general agreement among physical theorists about the inevitability of a heat-death which must end all life in the universe.)[15]

If at first the ability to travel in time seems to offer man a remarkable freedom, yet the overwhelming sense that grips the reader of the novel is not finally one of freedom. The "underground" future of the Morlocks, for example, is the nightmare space of the helplessly trapped victim, and Wells touches some raw nerve ends when he gets down to describing it:

> . . . while I stood in the dark, a hand touched mine, lank fingers came feeling over my face, and I was sensible of a peculiar unpleasant odour. I fancied I heard the breathing of a crowd of those dreadful little beings about me. I felt the box of matches in my hand being gently disengaged, and other hands behind me plucking at my clothing. The sense of these unseen creatures examining me was indescribably unpleasant.

> (Section Six)

Undergoing such experiences, the Time Traveller first feels as a "man might feel who had fallen into a pit", and then, more precisely, "like a beast in a trap, whose enemy would come on him soon".

Now the Morlocks in the context of their world are clearly an ironic projection of the "demonic workers" and, as such, their mythical affiliations are rich and significant.[16] Yet this is not all, for both the Time Traveller and the reader feel overwhelmingly the horror of the Morlocks and their dark world, just because Wells renders them as a race given to "primordial" bestiality. In terms of their extremely "close" physical presence, and their hideous environment of darkness, the Morlocks are images of the half-human side of humanity itself — they represent the "buried" side of human nature, one that suggests the nightmare of instinct.[17] This is the cannibal shadow haunting man's upward progress, and significantly, it is linked to the machine. In typical Naturalist fashion, Wells associates work and the lower drives of the struggle for existence, denying them, however, the slightest redeeming quality of "energy" and reducing them to quotients of some desperate equation of horror.

150

Just as he is physically drawn into the shafts, those transit tunnels to the primordial — drawn, that is, by the "higher" faculty of curiosity, and guided by the rationality which is strained but not broken by his experiences, so too the Time Traveller is metaphorically pulled down into the struggle for existence; he combats the Morlocks on their own terms, savouring for a moment the joy of the struggle that is implied in Wells's equation of "effort" with high civilization. "The strange exultation that so often seems to accompany hard fighting came upon me. I knew that both I and Weena were lost, but I determined to make the Morlocks pay for their meat. I stood with my back to a tree, swinging the iron bar before me". This iron bar he has recovered from a machine in the museum, realizing that he "longed very much to kill a Morlock".

The Morlocks are clearly, and in many senses, a dead end, yet their presence compels attention. They are the shadows which wait to devour the rational man, who can only combat them in the depth of their own darkness. Wells is suggesting the ironical split between aspiration and instinct in each individual, and the necessary disharmony of the struggle for survival. For if man rests too easily he begins to resemble the effete Eloi, who are the fatted calves of their enemies, while any acceptance of violence in the name of self-preservation kills the distinction between what he imagines himself to be and what he may fear to become. The claustrophobia evoked by the Morlocks is the threat of negative instinct, the threat of some legitimate challenge that may lead man into a veritable death-trap in which he is victimized by his own darkest impulses.[18]

Against this challenge the Time Traveller asserts the Promethean response, carrying fire into the darkness.[19] The precious matches play a critical role in the combat between the Time Traveller and the Morlocks, for they transform the environment from primitive horror to one in which the Time Traveller can preserve his sanity, and his actual effectiveness. There is here another irony, however, for the Time Traveller's only "human" contact, his relationship with Weena, is broken by his own reckless turning to the fire as weapon. As he watches its effects on the wood, and the fleeing Morlocks, Weena is snatched away. He retains just a few matches, and when these fail to strike, his last crisis comes, but he is able nonetheless to slip away into time and freedom, though alone.

Earlier, on the night before coming upon the "later day South Kensington" museum, the Time Traveller had taken consolation from a direct vision of the reaches of sublime nature, the sky transformed but recognizable, offering him the "friendly comfort" of a contrast with the claustrophobia of the underground wood.

Looking at these stars suddenly dwarfed my own troubles and all the gravities of terrestial life. I thought of their unfathomable distance, and the slow inevitable drifts of their movements out of the unknown past into the unknown future. I thought of the great precessional cycle that the pole of the earth describes. Only forty times had that silent revolution occurred during all the years that I had traversed.   (Section Seven)

Their points of light set against the darkness, these stars mark the distance traveled by Promethean man, who has "borrowed" their kind of energy to carry on his adventure. But the Time Traveller's reflections are tinged with nostalgia and then with horror. He realizes that man as he himself represents him is finished; and with a shudder comes to the first full realization of the cannibalism of the Morlocks. In one short passage we are first set free and then brought back inexorably to the "claustrophobia" of primordialism.

With such preparation, the great ending takes its full dimension as a commentary on the aspirations of the human species. Here, at the end of time, the sun itself sinks into darkness. The source of all light and life fades, and the cold night advances. The Time Traveller, representing the whole human species, suffers a kind of ultimate claustrophobia. Wells's "time machine", which (as Philmus rightly suggests) is the imagination itself, has led us from the comfortable hearthfire of the opening sentence to this sinking fire of the cosmic drama.[20]

As the epilogue asserts: "one cannot choose but wonder". The final images suggest both a forward and backward motion — the primordial world of the "grotesque saurians" and the nearer ages "in which men are still men" — but, perhaps — "with the riddles of our own time answered and all its wearisome problems solved". The narrator sets his more optimistic view against that of the Time Traveller, whose pessimism was literally confirmed "in time". We must "live as though it were not so" suggests the narrator, confronting the negative possibilities, and he calls to mind the flowers as a testimony to the "gratitude and mutual tenderness" that "still lived on in the heart of man".

How are we to read the meaning of the ending? The final image of the flowers reminds us of the great strengths and weaknesses of Wells's story. For the flowers suggest the relationship with Weena, which seems ludicrously inadequate to encompass human fidelity through the ages, a self-indulgence on the part of Wells, or the revelation of some psychical oddity.[21] Yet, though this touch fails, and with it a certain consolation, we can hardly say that the story is ultimately nihilistic. For one thing, most readers find themselves thrilled and not depressed by the final vision. Partially no doubt, this is a question of the old effect of purgation, which may operate at the high level of tragedy or at the more popular level of the horror story. At the root of our "delightful terror" as we read the latter may be an all-too-human masochism, a mild self-torture that we find, on the whole, quite pleasant. From this point of view what could be more delightful than the destruction of the whole world? Then too, it is possible that we simply cannot feel depressed by a vision of the end of the world which is projected so far into the future, and, of course, some of us may be aware that such a projection is rather dubiously premised on many scientific factors, the modification of which may negate it in the end. Perhaps the truest estimate is that we are in the presence of several elements that create a particular effect on us, so that we feel at last both exhilaration and a kind of despair. For Wells's sense of claustrophobia depends ultimately upon his measure of man, and the success of the Wellsian nightmare is partially a testimony to the failure of Wells to create a truly meaningful human space, one that would forcefully counteract the "malady of space-time". A literary work in which the "person" is not understood in full richness and subtlety, or in which the real complexity of human experience is not otherwise suggested, cannot shed nightmares brought on by an over-abstract view of man. Just by being most richly and most characteristically itself literature can dispel the suggestion that man can be summed up by slogans or statistics. Wells's future is more depressing than Joyce's Dublin because it is not inhabited by any fully human consciousness. Yet though he is ultimately a type of Man, and not a fully human presence, the Time Traveller is a worthy representative of human energy face to face with the ultimate reaches of the sublime space that is engendered in our necessary experience of space-time. *The Time Machine*, though inspired by and controlled by the scientific theories we have described, is a search for the meaning of man. The dying of the sun is only significant, in literature, when a witness is provided. Literature, as part of human culture, may serve as an evaluation of the attempts of other aspects of that culture to chart man's place. Wells confronts the future as charted by science and almost redeems it with the presence of a man whose violence and near despair are balanced by his courage, ingenuity, and human fidelity. Even in the face of the Time Traveller's vision, the narrator suggests, the human adventure is worth pursuing.

2. Wells and Evolution: **The Island of Doctor Moreau**

The vividly rendered local space, that landscape of the Home Counties that is so prominent a feature in Wells's early work, should not deceive us: Wells is the first great novelist to carry us into cosmic space. His early work is notable because it leads us away from the social world of the typical nineteenth-century novel to that space that was being created by nineteenth-century science. Wells is one of the great poets of "Darwinian sublime", the creator of a literature of high visionary power, one that reflects the shape of our new environment, and attempts to give it human dimension. Other writers, at least as far back as Milton, had been affected by the magnified vistas of the astronomical revolution, but Wells was one of the first to see the new distances in Darwinian terms, to make the competition of life-forms in space central to his work.[22]

Evolution is the key to the early work of Wells, but it must be understood in two aspects, biological and cosmological. One side of evolution involves the equation of man with the other animals, the sense of man as a biological phenomenon to be understood in relation to a particular place, with certain powers and limitations derived from the interaction of *bios* and environment. This aspect of Wells's work is related to the Naturalistic Novel, but there are at least two key differences between Wells and the mainstream Naturalists. First, unlike the Naturalists, Wells did not usually limit himself to metaphors of struggle in largely urban settings; rather, using the cosmic vision of science, he set about creating *new* environments either by launching his various ''travellers'' into quite new settings, in which the dominant descriptive vision is that of science; or else by bringing something hatched by science from outside the normal round of nineteenth century social life, into conflict with that life. Secondly, Wells almost never took the common Naturalist line of ecstatic celebration of ''life itself''. Quite the contrary — one of the chief aspects of ''nightmare'' in his work is precisely this efflorescence of life-forms. To Wells, the biological emphasis usually suggests a closing of space, a psychic narrowness and the depiction of fierce intensities, in short, the Naturalistic ''beast man'', but without any Naturalistic reveling in that grotesque creation.

The second aspect of Wells's Darwinism serves to counterbalance his tendency to see biology as nightmare. This is his depiction of the changing forms in space-time. The main *motif* here is one of flight. The imagination is given rein, and seeks to realize man at great distances of space and time. Initially, this open space may suggest freedom, ecstasy, or escape. Eventually, however, a limit is reached and we are brought back to the enclosing dimensions of man's failed transcendence. In this aspect of Darwinism, we meet another key idea of nineteenth century science: entropy. For whatever evolution may lead to, it must eventually sink back upon a tide of receding energy; it must freeze to an equilibrium, or perhaps run down. The *devolution* of forms in the future is nearly as certain as their *evolution* from the past.

To understand Wells's work we must picture a time-stream running from distant past to distant future. As you move back through visions of shifting forms you approach the primordial state of struggle and anarchy, the pre-human past that man carries in his biological nature. When man himself appears, the picture shifts slightly, for his social forms remove him from the primary area of struggle in nature, and give permanence to his self-expression, but even here the gain is more apparent than real. For man is powerless against the second law of thermodynamics, and his societies tend in any case toward stagnation attendent upon over-specialization and collectivity. So to go ''forward'' is ultimately the same as going ''backward''; we run up against the same ''primordial'' element, the same anarchy, or else lapse into an all-too perfect order, which is death. Thus, though Wells invokes astronomical and chronological distance to rescue man from the claustrophobia of the Darwinian nightmare, the issue is not in doubt. The conclusion is tragic, but since the number of given ''presents'' seems practically unlimited, the issue is not critical for any single moment. This is so because for almost any given

154

moment, flight is possible, and refuge may be sought "in the stars".

In the early Wells novels and stories struggle dominates everything, and the paradisal space is treated ironically.[23] The biological claustrophobia we have mentioned is often literally rendered in terms of enclosed space. Collectivism and specialization appear with the machine-functioning which is related to the primordial, for Darwin's sense of the rule of chance taken in conjunction with a view of the universe as something to be analyzed reduces animal forms to the status of machines. In the openness of space-time, literally rendered as the sublime distances of planetary and cosmic space, man the adventurer may find a certain freedom; his consciousness may expand in a kind of ecstasy which suggests that mind is after all the primary reality. Thus Wells, like many of the Naturalists proper, is tempted by a dualism which Darwinism (taken literally) would banish. (One thinks of Zola, or Hardy's later work, and of Jack London's *The Star Rover*, that strange blend of Darwinism and metempsychosis. My point is that such recalcitrant or covert "dualisms" only illustrate the constant tendency of writers to seek values in a scientific "myth" which sought to exclude them. This struggle for values, however, might be seen as more successfully related to Darwinism in the "process" vision of a writer like D.H. Lawrence.) Final resolution of the tensions implicit here, however, does not occur, for Wells fails to achieve trust in either body and mind —: body is a down-dragging link with the primordial; while mind, though it sometimes raises man to the skies, robs him of his earthly humanity.

A brief examination of a number of early works of various kinds will confirm the patterns described above. In the short story "The Star", for example, we see the whole earth threatened by an "invasion" from outer space. Vast distances are evoked, creating an ironical perspective between the daily trivia of human life and the mysteries of the cosmos. In this case the intruder is an alien body, a star or comet, but Wells sometimes makes use of the other kind of invaders and suggests — most frighteningly of all — how tenuous is the "dominance" that Darwinism ascribes to human life. *The War of the Worlds*, "The Sea Raiders", and a number of other stories, achieve their most disturbing effects by showing this dominance contested. What is most significant is the bringing together of the threatening primordial (usually expressed as reptile, insect or bird) that haunts such stories as "Aepyornis Island", "The Empire of the Ants", and "The Crystal Egg", with the threatening machine of such pieces as "The Land Ironclads", and "The Cone". As we shall see, when these function together — as, for example, in *The Time Machine*, *The War of the Worlds*, and *The First Men in the Moon*, Wells mirrors a particular nightmare bequest of nineteenth century science. And when his characters react to such nightmares, they demonstrate the oppressive sense of entrapment or the exhilaration (or terror) of flight that are so clearly the essence of the "lay-out" of a good Wells story in the science fiction genre. Flight followed by entrapment occurs in *The Time Machine*, "Pollock and the Porrah Man", "In the Abyss", and "The Country of the Blind", among others, and sheer entrapment in "The Story of the Late Mr. Elvesham", *The Invisible Man*, and "The Plattner Story". Later, when Wells de-emphasizes the scientific or mythical context, he is moved to retain this sense of claustrophobia and release in his most convincing social novels, *The History of Mr. Polly*, and *Tono Bungay*.

If we stop for a closer look at several of these earlier productions, we can see just how Wells's art organizes itself in the ways I have described. "Under the Knife", a story first published in 1896, begins with the earth-bound conventionality of an impending surgical operation. The coming operation causes the narrator to think about the relationship between the physical side of man and the "higher emotions, the moral feelings". He wonders how the spectre of death's destruction of the body affects the spiritual side. A series of fantasies interrupted by the tug of the real world precede his operation. During the time he is "under the knife" he experiences a vivid "out of the body" sensation. He can float away from the scene of the operation, read thoughts, experience emotion. What is striking in the descriptions that occur at this point in the story is the way Wells uses astronomical space, created in detail, to "stage" the man's experiences. Seeing one of the doctors make a wrong cut, the narrator thinks he will die, but instead he sails up into a grand spatial vista. He feels "such release, such serenity as I can compare to no mortal delight I have ever known". The description that follows is remarkable; I quote only part of it:

The sun was incredibly strange and wonderful. The body of it was a disc of blinding white light: not yellowish as it seems to those who live upon earth, but livid white, all streaked with scarlet streaks and rimmed about with a fringe of writhing tongues of red fire. And, shooting half-way across the heavens from either side of it, and brighter than the Milky Way, were two pinions of silver-white, making it look more like those winged globes I have seen in Egyptian sculpture, than anything else I can remember on earth. These I knew for the solar corona, though I had never seen anything of it but a picture during the days of my earthly life.

When my attention came back to earth again, I saw that it had fallen very far away from me. Field and town were long since indistinguishable and all the varied hues of the country were merging into a uniform bright grey, broken only by the brilliant white of the clouds that lay scattered in flocculent masses over Ireland and the west of England. For now I could see the outlines of the north of France and Ireland, and all this island of Britain save where Scotland passed over the horizon to the north, or where the coast was blurred or obliterated by cloud. The sea was a dull grey, and darker than the land; and the whole panorama was rotating slowly toward the east.

The description continues, a tour de force of strange power, as the sick man is carried to such macrocosmic distances that "the little universe of matter, the cage of points in which I had begun to be, was dwindling, now to a whirling disc of luminous glittering, and now to one minute disc of hazy light''. He knows that ''in a little while it would shrink to a point, and at last would vanish altogether''. This strikes him with a sense of ''overwhelming terror''; he is horrified just because ''the covering of the body, the covering of matter'', has been torn from him: what he feels now is a sense of nothingness and despair. His delight in grand vistas has been transformed into a desperate anxiety. However, as Wells concludes the story, we see that the man is saved; what he takes to be the ''hand of God'' turns out to be the hand of the physician: from the macrocosm he slips back into human scale, and returns to a happy existence.

This story not only demonstrates Wells's habit of dramatizing his meanings in spatial terms, but shows his typical shift from local to cosmic, and above all, suggests his uneasiness with disembodied ecstasies and his resolution of the temptation of the visionary in favour of a decision for the earthbound. ''Under the Knife'' illustrates the power of science on Wells's imagination (not of course in the operation, but in the descriptive passages inspired by astronomy) but it also shows the characteristically ambivalent relation of the Wells hero to scientific revelation. What is preferred is not after all the new vision, but the ordinary life of the median between extremes, what is rejected is the perspective of science as a generator of ''spiritual'' energies: the surgeon's hand must not be seen as the hand of God.

Not that anyone would be quick to give either science or the surgeon an exalted role after reading Wells's grim novel of this period, *The Island of Doctor Moreau* (1896). Here we have a nightmare of the claustrophobia of instinct, an anatomy of the ''Morlock'' level of human nature. The book's central power is in the masterful rendering of the transformation of the hero Edward Prendick, who is ''changed'' from average man to the deeply marked protagonist of the human predicament itself, the *homo normalus*, who is also *homo homini lupus*, as he comes to realize. The figure of Moreau, lying in wait for the innocent Prendick, is the new magus of science, and his horror-show is more than simply the drama of struggle envisaged by Darwinism.[24] In this white-haired scientist Wells has captured (long before he became the dominant figure in western society) the technician, the manipulator to whom conscience is a secondary consideration. ''Our little establishment here contains a secret or so, is a kind of Bluebeard's chamber, in fact,'' Moreau graciously explains to Prendick, and adds: ''Nothing very dreadful, really, to a sane man''. The novel will go on to define ''sanity'' in finer terms than Moreau is capable of. Yet it is a great mistake to call him ''a mad scientist'', for Wells's point is not that Moreau's research is totally destructive of other aspects of his personality, but that it is carried on without reference to any wider scale of human values. Moreau is concerned and very patient with the near-hysterical Prendick, but has learned to shut out from his mind the howls of pain of his unfortunate ''objects''. These he refers to at one

157

point as "inimical phenomena", distancing them to abstractions, with the "intellectual passion" of the investigator. "The thing before you is no longer an animal, a fellow creature," he confides, "but a problem". "The study of nature makes a man at last as remorseless as nature".

Prendick is transformed from a rather passive observer, one who hardly realizes the "nature of things", to the point where he shoots the Leopard Man and finds himself drawn directly into the struggle for existence.[25] In this situation, though he attempts to exercise a moral choice in the name of sanity, he commits an act of violence that reinforces his complicity in the whole "painful disorder" of the island. His development seems to mimic the stages of transformation of the consciousness of many educated late Victorians who were forced to come to terms with the new image of man suggested by Darwinism, and who, far from wishing to take the plunge into "primordialism", saw the whole direction as terrifyingly destructive of all moral possibilities. Probably because it was not far from his own generally concealed fears of the worst, Wells is able to chart this course of initiation into the new "dark knowledge" with unfailing skill. Prendick is carried through several further stages, escaping from the claustrophobic island only to find its disorder repeated in the world as a whole.

Moreau himself turns out to be a false god in two ways. First, he demonstrates in the ends he achieves the limitations of man's power to modify nature through exercise of technical ingenuity alone. His death expresses the terrible fact of what we might metaphorically denote as "nature's revenge", and seems to be a sardonic comment on T.H. Huxley's hope for social progress. Secondly, if we take the figure of Moreau to represent some kind of "godstuff" shaping evolution, we can only conclude that Wells is debunking the notion of this god.[26] For Moreau's powers of modification fail; he is thwarted from both directions. "The beast creeps back", and "there is an upward striving in his creations" that mocks him. Prendick's half-hearted effort to maintain a sense of the "spiritualized" Moreau is soon given up. Here, Huxley's attack on those who would deify nature is vindicated. *The Island of Doctor Moreau* in total, supports Huxley's arguments about the folly of assuming that natural evolution is operative in society in terms of moral direction, because it supports Huxley's premise that nature is basically amoral. It does not, however, lend much credence to Huxley's suggestion that the "ethical man" will be a bulwark of social stability, holding back the "state of nature". For the "law" seems a thin veneer over the savagery of the human beast. And Huxley, as scientist and "modifier", could take little comfort in the fate of Moreau, the wielder of the scalpel. (There are many incidental similarities between *Moreau* and *The Tempest*. Prospero's ethical philosophy, moral discipline and white magic, however, contrast with Moreau's "objectivity", his amorality, and his dark skills. The effort to raise humans to higher nature by alchemy and example has become the effort to raise beasts by a scalpel to the shadowy level of the semi-human. The world has become an island peopled with Calibans.)

Prendick's final retreat from biology is one the reader quite sympathizes with, after the horrors of Moreau's island. Phrased as it is — as a search for "whatever is more than animal within us" — it seems to be an understandable "spiritualizing" of experiences following on the shock of a direct encounter with all that is bestial in humanity. Yet Prendick's turn is not, as we might expect, either to the inner life, or to the spirit as something rising through or above matter, but rather to matter itself, to its "vast and eternal laws", embodied in the starry night. This is the same gesture away from the primordial that the Time Traveller makes, a looking up and out of the human predicament, in the direction of great space and steady motion. It is as if, despairing of the realization of Kant's treasure of "the moral law within", the Wellsian heroes have leapt to the farthest distance possible, in fact, to Kant's "starry skies without". Their great necessity is to escape the psycho-physical microcosm, and they do so by invoking the most inhuman vastnesses they know. In this they are not untypical of many post-Darwinian heroes who are placed in a context from which the struggle for existence is "redeemed", either because "life itself" is sacred or because the very mechanism which seems to condemn them, is suddenly, from another angle, seen to be open to "spiritual" possibilities.

Looked at more closely, Prendick's retreat seems to make sense psychologically, and even philosophically, though it is extremely vaguely played out on the page. Psychologically, the necessity is to take some of the pressure off the animal self-consciousness created by the tale just told, to preserve sanity and perspective. Philosophically, though we know all human values must be humanly relevant and cannot reside in a desperate invocation of mere matter, we see that the universe may be capable of creating energies outside of the human environment and biological heritage that may help save humanity from itself, that is, from the evolutionary down-drag so terrifyingly presented in the earlier parts of this very novel. Prendick's final gasp is more than a pious wish, though it may strike the reader as a great deal less forcefully rendered than what has gone before. Are we to agree with V.S. Pritchett, who suggests (in *The Living Novel*, p. 129) that Wells underestimated "the habits, the moral resources, of civilized man"? Does Gulliver's humanity, for example, really stand out above Prendick's final misanthropy? We know that if Moreau and practically the whole cultured world of the late nineteenth century, chose at certain moments to see themselves as Yahoos, they could find in Darwin a ready witness. But is Prendick at the end really pinned helplessly to such an angle of vision? No; he is still searching, exercising his chastened reason toward the goal of balance. And if he finds in the stars the same entropic doom as the Time Traveller, he has at least shifted his perspective away from the claustrophobic sense of man as beast. The real balance would not come in the end from the heavens, but from a more sane view of man, from a more distanced view of "struggle" and "instinct". Wells himself much later could write: "Nature is a great friend of cooperation; it is a gross libel upon her to say she is always 'red in tooth and claw'." *The Island of Doctor Moreau* plumbs one extreme of Darwinian metaphor but leaves us with a man seeking balance, the balance that comes of knowing extremes.

A more overt translation of Darwinian evolution into fiction by the "early" Wells occurs in those two interconnected tales, "A Story of the Stone Age", and "A Story of the Days to Come" (1897). As in the case of *The Time Machine*, the Thames Valley is seen in widely separated epochs; though here there are only two, and they are not explicitly linked by a single traveller. "A Story of the Stone Age" is precisely that, and a generally excellent piece, though one in which a self-conscious humour keeps things rather low-keyed. The tale dramatizes the life of a tribe of primitives in a typical Naturalistic vein. Struggle is the essence of life; the successful individual, Ugh-Lomi, invents the axe, learns to kill the hitherto invincible bear and is the first man to ride a horse. Man the toolmaker is emphasized — what Wells is showing is an evolutionary leap, a new mastery of environment. This is accompanied by violence, a product of man's animal past which is ritualized rather than eradicated by his skeletal religious conceptions. Only with a reading of "A Story of Days to Come", however, can one grasp the ironies implicit in the total conception. The second tale sets us down in the society of the twenty-second century, in a world in some ways startlingly familiar, thanks to anti-Utopias such as George Orwell's *1984* and to the march of events. Wells's vision is predictably fixed on the way in which the transformed environment is dominated by the machine, and the pressures felt by the young couple who are the main characters are economic rather than political. Though the story has some affiliations to *When the Sleeper Wakes* (1899), it is much more successfully realized. We are carried dramatically from the natural "jungle" of the first tale to a mechanized urban "jungle" which now occupies the same space.[27] Evolution, long ago shifting from the physical to the cultural focus, has seen the primitive hand axe of Ugh-Lomi transformed into a vast urban complex which houses about thirty-three million people (cf. *When the Sleeper Wakes*). This literally enclosed space is gradually revealed as a stratified brutally competitive social unit, as "the city that had swallowed up mankind". From this the young couple (who mirror the primitive couple in the first story) must flee, also as a result of a love rivalry. They escape the city via the super-speed "Eadhamite" roads, past the neat sterilized patches of the Food Company, seeing sheep for the first time and settling in a "deserted village" which turns out to be a new sphere of the primitive. With the sword their romantic notions have led them to carry along, they

160

must fight off the wild dogs that contest the ruins of the village with them, but unlike the couple in the first story, their adventure shows them to be fugitives rather than culture-makers, and they must go back. Slowly they sink into the poverty of the lowest classes (who are virtual wage-slaves of the system) and are only saved when their persecutor, a jilted millionaire, relents and leaves them his fortune.

Wells sees struggle as a permanent feature of man's state, and, as the young hero's many "scraps" reveal, the struggle remains at a brutal physical level. The "bestial" is a permanent human affliction. "To think of all who have gone through with it", as Denton, the hero, exclaims about life — "all the generations — endless — endless. Little beasts that snapped and snarled, snapping and snarling, generation after generation". Snarling, however, can be almost a relief, as Denton learns after a successful "scrap". "His blood seemed changed to some sort of fluid fire, his limbs felt light and supernaturally strong". He goes on to suggest a kind of mystical belief in struggle, one rejected immediately by his wife, Elizabeth. Wells condemns the whole trend of social "progress" as "the monstrous fraud of civilization . . . a vast lunatic growth, producing a deepening torrent of savagery below and above ever more flimsy gentility and silly wastefulness". The world of the future combines mechanism and primordial bestiality; implicitly dominating everything is Wells's version of "the god of the machine". "In the darkest corner stood the press whose servant Denton had now become; it was a huge, dim, glittering thing with a projecting hood that had a remote resemblance to a bowed head, and, squatting like some metal Buddha in this weird light that ministered to its needs, it seemed to Denton in certain moods almost as if this must needs be the obscure idol to which humanity in some strange aberration had offered up his life".[28] The fabled world of the first story, the world of speaking animals and of men taming horses and feasting after the hunt has become a "retribalized" world where phonographs have replaced books, a world where men travel on moving sidewalks, and communally eat pleasantly coloured pastes instead of lions, a world where the "free range" is obstructed and sewage systems are more important than rivers. Sinking downward into the underworld of the proles, the young couple suffers greatly, their baby dies in a communal creche, and such release as they get comes in returning to the airship landing platform where they met and from where the open space of sublime nature is still visible. Under the stars, they are able to escape for a moment the brutalization of material life. As Denton says: "down there [that is, in the city] it would seem impossible to go on living if one were horribly disfigured, horribly crippled, disgraced. Up here — under these stars — none of these things would matter. They don't matter . . . They are a part of something. One seems just to touch that something — under the stars . . ." And he continues: "After all we are just poor animals rising out of the brute, each with a mind, the poor beginning of a

161

mind. We are so stupid. So much hurts. And yet . . .'' This hopeful note is
struck again at the end, as after the rescue the couple sits on a balcony
with a view of the whole Thames Valley, translated by Denton into a vista
of man's development:

> "After all — there is a long time yet. There have scarcely been men for
> twenty thousand years — and there has been life for twenty millions. And
> what are generations? What are generations? It is enormous, and we are so
> little, yet we know — we feel. We are not dumb atoms, we are part of it —
> part of it — to the limits of our strength and will. Even to die is part of it.
> Whether we live or die, we are in the making . . ."[29]

In these two stories Wells has created sharp contrasts by means of a
shifting space-time perspective. The wild nature of the first story is used
to link man to his origins; what claustrophobia is present exists in the
sense that the primordial is seen to be so deeply ingrained even as man is
about to make the leap to higher culture. In the sequel, a nightmare world
incorporates machine-life and beast-life, with only faint attempts at
affirmation, in the shape of, first, a momentary sense of ecstasy in the
physical energy of violence, and, more pervasively, as an escape from
claustrophobia into the changing forms in space-time. The lingering
irony here is the suggestion that we have seen it all before. If man has
"progressed" so dubiously between the "Stone Age" and the world of
the twenty-second century, can we really take the concluding pious hope
very seriously?

3. Mechanism and Life: **The First Men in the Moon**

It is not only in the creation of new environments that Wells excels, but
in the juxtaposition of extremely local and familiar ones with those quite
alien and unknown. This point is well-made by Norman Nicholson, who
observes that Wells's imagination "always made its strongest flight
when it had a small patch of solid earth from which to take off".[30] What I
am referring to here, however, involves not so much a "takeoff" as an
invasion. Part of Wells's great originality is that he does not simply
translate the scientific perspectives of Naturalism directly into contemporary social settings, as do most of the Naturalists. Just as en-
amoured of the myths of science as they, Wells uses them to lead us away
from the ordinary social space of the fiction of his contemporaries, or
embodies them in factors which disrupt that social space, and throw it
into a broadened, sometimes cosmic, perspective.

This latter procedure is best observed in those two masterpieces, *The
Invisible Man* (1897), and *The War of the Worlds* (1898). *The Invisible
Man* has as one of its strengths the concreteness of the local setting.
Nicholson observes that though you may not be able to see Griffin, "at
least you know what you will see when you look through him".[31] What
one notices is the ordinary man-in-the-street being terrorized by the
hidden but immensely real power of science. The life described is tinged

with an almost ludicrous sense of attachment to the familiar. Even Kemp, who is also a scientist, imagines himself in a known world of familiar views and friendly neighbours only to wake up one morning as virtually an animal of prey in a landscape of struggle. It is Griffin, indeed a "fabulous beast", who triggers the change, because Griffin is no man at all but a fixed egotistic will wedded to a voice which can haunt the unbeliever and finally explode at him in a sudden orgy of violence. Although physical contact is pervasive in Wells, in *The Invisible Man* one might say that he outdoes himself, depicting the encounter of an unstoppable *idée fixe* with an immovable conventional public, and all in terms of the absurd comedy (or farce) of slaps, pinches, kicks, punches and bites. The key here is the claustrophobia of Griffin who is trapped in a limiting social situation but who sees the possibility of an escape into "the mystery, the power, the freedom". This "shabby, poverty-struck, hemmed-in, demonstrator" seeks to escape his trap by becoming invisible, but this turns out to be the worst trap of all. The mind and fixed will seeking isolation achieve only bestiality. Griffin is hunted like an animal, and he hunts in turn. The conventional English countryside is transformed into a sphere of Darwinian nature and what appears to be the most liberating act, the escape from the body, turns out to be the most restricting, because assumed in the name of a perverse ideal.

The War of the Worlds, bringing the Martian invaders down upon the unsuspecting countryside around greater London, achieves its effects by the contrast of the alien and the familiar, and shows the philosopher-narrator at the mercy of the mechanized primordial — catapulted from his leisured middle-class existence into the panic of flight and the concealment of the trapped animal. The blood-drinking Martians, a central image in Wells's series of variations on the motif of cannibalism, are notably "primeval":

> The peculiar V-shaped mouth with its pointed upper lip, the absence of brow ridges, the absence of a chin beneath the wedge-like lower lip, the incessant quivering of this mouth, the Gorgon groups of tentacles, the tumultuous breathing of the lungs in a strange atmosphere, the evident heaviness and painfulness of movement, due to the greater gravitational energy of the earth — above all, the extraordinary intensity of the immense eyes — culminated in an effect akin to nausea. There was something fungoid in the oily brown skin, something in the clumsy deliberation of their tedious movements, unspeakably terrible . . .

> (Book One, Chapter Four)

At the same time, the sophisticated technology of the invaders is described in such a way as to blur the reader's sense of its difference from its organic wielders:

> At first, as I say, the Handling Machine did not impress me as a machine, but as a crab-like creature with a glittering integument, the controlling Martian, whose delicate tentacles actuated its movements, seeming to be simply the equivalent of the crab's cerebral portion . . .

The contrast between the swift and complex movements of these contrivances and the inert, panting clumsiness of their masters was acute, and for days I had to tell myself repeatedly that these latter were indeed the living of the two things.

(Book Two, Chapter Two)

As the critics have often noted, Wells skillfully refers these strangest of beings back to the distortions of human development itself.[32] What we see is described as a brain absurdly overgrown, in conjunction with the most primitive of appetites, and in possession of the most "advanced" technology (which is also the most absurdly "primal"). A kind of inspired linking of elements produces the spectre of human science turned against civilization itself:

To me it is quite credible that the Martians may be descended from beings not unlike ourselves, by a gradual development of brain and hands (the latter giving rise to the two bunches of delicate tentacles at last) at the expense of the rest of the body. Without the body the brain would of course become a more selfish intelligence, without any of the emotional substratum of the human being.

(Book Two, Chapter Two)

A large part of the novel's irony derives from the helplessness of the ordinary human types (the philosopher-narrator, the soldier, the clergyman) before the onslaught. The very success of our civilization's adaptation has weakened it immeasurably and some new challenge may test it beyond endurance. The ordinary gifts of the ordinary man, while comforting in their very mediocrity, are absurdly inadequate in the face of a crisis of this magnitude. The everyday life of the masses becomes the mob hysteria of those who can only "carry on" during the near devastation of civilization. Wells reminds us that an exceptional situation requires exceptional solutions, which must come from exceptional men, men who are capable of an imaginative response to a new challenge.[33] If the Martians are evil "supermen", embodying all the horrors of a scientifically-based reign of terror, then the other characters are "submen", just because they cannot break their addiction to the ordinary round of pleasure and pain. This is the meaning of the futile card games played by the narrator and the artilleryman shortly after they have "solved" the problem of confronting the Martians. Their solution, of course, to be put into effect, would have required an immense act of discipline and courage, one that Wells suggests is far from forthcoming on the beleagured earth. The threat to mankind of specialized knowledge and dehumanizing technology (though countered by the utopianism of other of Wells's works) is in these early science fiction stories unanswerable. In these stories we may be comforted by Wells's various images of ordinary men reasserting their belief in the everyday reality of flesh-and-blood humanity, but we can hardly be altogether reassured when we know that this very humanity is threatened by the cannibalizing tendencies in itself.

In *The War of the Worlds* the spatial structure is critical. Macro- and microcosmic perspectives, shifted ominously, underline a lack of human control. The earth's people are to the Martians merely as "infusoria" under a microscope; yet they are saved by "the humblest things that God, in his wisdom, had put upon earth". The telescopically-distanced opening gives way to a close human-scaled vision of a specific regional life, a comfortable everyday life, which is disrupted beyond recognition by action from the larger perspective. The disruption is conveyed in terms of a breakdown of social cohesiveness and a rebirth of the war of species against species. Men are driven underground, and a large central portion of the book exploits the claustrophobia of entrapment. At the end, the perspective is opened again, though the mood has changed. Without that hubris of the mediocre and the self-satisfied, which to Wells is one of great human temptations, man can still aspire to the vision of "life spreading slowly from this little seed-bed of the solar system throughout the inanimate vastness of sidereal space". Such a view is seen to be hedged round with dangers, and mocked by the ironic after-image of the terrible threat just overcome. In the light of the whole vision of man that Wells demonstrates in these early works, it would be foolish to over-emphasize the optimism of such a potential release in the future. Even the most visionary future must be built on an actual present, and in the present man lives in almost perpetual bondage to his own nature and instincts.

All the themes of the early Wells novels are summed up in what turned out to be Wells's last unqualified success in this fictional genre. *The First Men in the Moon* (1901) stands out among the early novels for its richness, its poetic power, and the structural ingenuity with which it holds quite diverse elements together. It is, of course, another journey book, and generates immense interest from the fact that its predicted journey has now been made. Far from nullifying the spell of the book over the reader, the onrushing history of man's technological achievements allows us to feel its specific power more strongly than ever. Wells put more of his manifold "selves" into this novel than into any of his other books; if it falls short of being his most artistically perfect work, it is without doubt his most representative, the most perfectly "Wellsian" of his novels.

Yet again, some critics have denied that Wells's understanding of science affected *The First Men in the Moon*. Jules Verne, for example, dismissed the book by sneering: "I make use of physics. He invents."[34] Admittedly, "cavorite" is a patently gimcrack invention; it carries very little "ontological" weight in the novel. We must ask, however, whether the question of how much science controls Wells's vision is to be decided only on the basis of the plausibility of the trigger mechanism of his plot. Science fiction demands that technology or science "trigger" and then control an explicit situation. Bedford and Cavor reach the moon within the terms of an extremely sketchy technology, but it is still technology, and not magic. If the borderline here is thinner than usual, it should be noted that the ambience of the novel is strongly rational and "realistic"; cavorite may be a rather fantastic invention, but we are a long way from pure fantasy. Even if we assume that, in terms of technological plausibility, Verne's cannon shot is more "scientific" than Wells's cavorite (and the margin is probably slight), Wells's "realism", his concern with biological and psychological reality, his power of projecting a recognizable social milieu, places him far beyond the self-congratulating "physics" of Verne. Wells is not "unscientific" because he does what a good novelist should do, that is, turn our attention to the human questions as quickly as possible. When technology serves as a "trigger" as it does in *The First Men in the Moon* we may ask that it be as well imagined as possible. Both cavorite and the shield of Achilles are imaginative projections from the technology of their day, yet the Homeric shield is a far profounder conception, because it incorporates more of the reality of its culture than Wells's cavorite does of ours. The "real" existence of either the shield or the cavorite, however, is not the question. Furthermore, cavorite seems particularly irrelevant in the 1980s, because we are so saturated with the specific apparatus of the real moon trips. Cavorite may seem less implausible when the detailed modes of the first moon trips are known only to specialists. In short, cavorite is not at all as unscientific, as, for example, a magic carpet would be.

Verne's "science" serves to launch his journey without tearing us away from the world we know, but Wells's art keeps us in the world we know in more ways than Verne's art or science ever dreamt of. The critics who are anxious to show that science plays little part in Wells's vision seem sometimes to be almost tacitly assuming that for science to play a key role in a novel, the novelist must have the scientific grasp of a competent worker in that field. They seem to demand in science fiction a "realism" that never was. Wells must not only write convincingly of a trip to the moon; he must *really* tell us how to get there, and not just plausibly imagine us there. If we insist on the obvious and suggest that a novel is always "a fiction", if we remember that Ishmael never went to sea, that Henry Fleming did not go to war, or Strether to Paris, it is clear that we are belaboring the obvious. Of course Wells "invents", as Verne insisted. And Wells is a far greater writer than Verne because of his far richer and more profound invention. But the richness and profundity of this invention should not blind us to the fact that Wells is consistently imagining along the lines of the form he virtually created, that he is writing a novel in which his own kind of "realism" is maintained throughout, though one which can draw to itself also the perspective of fantasy that the mainstream novel does without, or achieves by other means.

The First Men in the Moon, like so much of Wells, leads us from the parochial to the cosmic. This is a novel dominated by environments, both familiar and strange, and its theme is how organisms adapt to a given space and what happens when they encounter the alien thing. Though he launches us easily into such general terms, Wells registers everything according to its human relevance. One of the miracles of his achievement here is that it did not leave us waiting until the real moon landing to raise certain questions that only an "unearthly" perspective could raise.

It all begins in a very localized earthly Kentish countryside, in the "clay part of Kent", where "outside the doors of the few cottages and houses that make up the present village, big birch besoms are stuck to wipe off the worst of the clay". From this world of inns, and credulous landladies, of "brick-making and motor cars and the cricket of last year", we are carried swiftly into perspectives of the earth and moon, both suddenly visible as spheres in the dark and inhospitable vastness of space. Yet the tiny sphere that ferries Bedford and Cavor wraps them round in a humanly bearable area, crazy in its weightlessness, but delimiting and protective, and enclosing both *Lloyd's News* and the *Complete Works of William Shakespeare*.

Coming in for a landing, they get their first close view of the moon, and Wells turns his genius to the creation of the concrete substance of an alien environment, one that was already in his day "known" (from a distance, of course, and through the measurements of science).[35] Yet after Wells, man could claim to know something more about that grand abstraction, "alien environment". For in this great description (and those that follow) Wells renders the experience of an alien environment as no astronaut has yet succeeded in rendering it. He creates even while invoking them what photographs of scientific significance notably lack — the sense of the human presence, the penumbra of emotion by which our own earth came most fully alive, even in its shadows. One of the devices of Wells's descriptive magic is to invite the reader to help him imagine the scene which he wishes to evoke. Here, to give us the poetry of a new landscape, he leans on the reader's assumed knowledge of the moon's general appearance. From this, he sweeps us easily into a sharpened sense of the glittering contrasts of a landscape, in which, whatever it may conceal, we can apprehend stark beauty.

When the sphere bumps down (and the contrast between Wells's primitive technology and his remarkably sophisticated grasp of the environment is most evident here), the travellers emerge to experience their new world. Fixed on the idea that Wells is not really influenced by science, one could easily draw the wrong conclusion. Instead of calling attention to the obvious lack of seriousness in his technological scaffolding, one should be noticing how he is transforming the information of a few hundred years of scientific investigation into the coherent image of a place which is not made up of the whole cloth of fantasy, but rendered in a coherent relation to the presumed earthly visitors, one whose mystery emerges from rock-forms, the patterns of sunlight and darkness, and culminates in a particular "chain of life" consistently imagined in terms of a particular environment.

Wells's moon-world, like all his imaginative landscapes, is dominated by Darwin's sense of the competition of forms in space. Seen from a distance, the rocky ramparts appear to overwhelm everything, but Wells shows us that the key is energy, the life-creating power of the sun. Through this we move to the living forms, beginning with the seeds of humblest plants — which feed the mooncalfs — which feed the Selenites. The excited descriptions of the sunrise and of the finding of the tiny seeds of life remind us that to Wells the miraculous is a flowering of the ordinary, that consistency is part of the magnificence of the real vision of a science that is in no sense earthbound, but rather capable of carrying us from our own backyard to the wide reach of the cosmos.

The book discloses a total environment of three habitable spheres. The earth is the first of these, the familiar daylight world, summed up in one specific locale to which men have bound themselves by centuries of associations (Wells mentions something of the history of his Kentish countryside, the Roman settlements, and so on). Leaving the surface of this sphere, the travellers enter the narrow space of the cavorite "viewing platform". This carries them to the third sphere, which is also one to be entered, but which offers no possibility of the re-creation of a familiar environment. By stages they approach the alien; by stages Bedford is released from it, for it is through Bedford that these significant contrasts chiefly emerge. On the way back to earth he looks out from the delimited artificial environment of the cavorite sphere, and senses the vastnesses of the cosmic surround, testing certain new evaluations of his conventional image of mind and body. He imagines himself to be part of a larger "mind" ("like some god upon a lotus leaf") that simply tenants the rather trivially limited body of Bedford. (This exploration of dualism was suggested earlier by the conversation between Bedford and Cavor after their first view of the Selenities. Bedford had argued that communication with the moon-creatures was impossible because they, the Selenites, were of "another clay", a vivid image capturing his own "earthly" predelictions. Cavor, on the other hand, pointed out that mind-stuff is a common primal factor which makes intelligent exchange among different planetary beings possible.)

In the chapter "Mr. Bedford in Infinite Space", however, we are shown the possibility of a "spiritualization" of experience, in which the all-too-human energies of this doughty imperialist are transformed for a moment into a kind of meditation. The visionary power is here reasserted within a Darwinian context, the inner life suddenly blossoming in an act of relation to the farthest vistas. Like the Naturalists, Wells could recover the heritage of Romantic affiliation between inner and outer — in certain limited moments at least, harking back to the primal power of mind to transcend the level of environment as threat.[36] Yet he is well aware, too, of the negative side, of the dwarfing of human consciousness by the pressure of an immense and pitiless natural scene. Bedford, fighting his way back to the sphere after losing Cavor, had felt just such a pressure:

> Over me, about me, closing in on me, embracing me ever nearer, was the Eternal, that which was before the beginning and that which triumphs over the end; that enormous void in which all light and life and being is but the thin and vanishing splendour of a falling star, the cold, the stillness, the silence — the infinite and final Night of space.

(Chapter Eighteen)

This is the familiar claustrophobia, from which Bedford soon escapes, though not by opting for mysticism. His direction is toward physical safety, translated finally into the terms of the most conventional creature comforts. Drawn into this adventure half against his will and thanks to an especially strong acquisitive sense, he desires neither self-transcendence nor a plunge into the primordial, though he endures both. What he finally longs for is the average life of the rather well-off bourgeois citizen of earth, specifically of the British Empire. Clichés of the ''white man's burden'', and his murmurings about the ''imperial'' prospects of the trip, do not at all sum up Mr. Bedford, but they underlie the kind of life he chooses, they caricature but do not belie his goals.

As for Wells's third sphere, the inner moon, this is a gigantic trap, and its horror is expressed in terms of claustrophobia, yet so large are some of its inner spaces that the travellers can suffer from ''giddiness'' as well, and it is in fact their inability to walk across a plank bridge covering an ''utterly void and black'' gulf that incites them to escape. The vastness and complexity of the inner moon world, however, does not blunt our sense of it as a terribly restrictive enclosure. Cavor's later descriptions of the ''Central Sea'' only add to our horror of the labyrinthian depths of this world, which even the Selenites have not fully reclaimed for their own species:

> The caverns and passages are naturally very tortuous. A large proportion of these ways are known only to expert pilots among the fishermen, and not infrequently Selenites are lost forever in their labyrinths. In their remoter recesses, I am told, strange creatures lurk, some of them so terrible and dangerous that all the science of the moon has been unable to exterminate them.

(Chapter Twenty-two)

Coming out of the dark spaces after their first entrapment, the explorers feel that the moon surface by comparison has become a friendly place, one that they can greet ''with the emotion a home-coming exile might feel at sight of his native land''. ''The air was intensely hot, and we were in grat physical discomfort, but for all that we were no longer in a nightmare. We seemed to have come to our own province again, beneath the stars''.

The underworld of the Selenites, like the underground of the

169

Morlocks, is an expression of the primordial in terms of darkness and restrictive space. Yet here the complexity is greater, and the effect more devastating. The punning humanity of the Beast Folk is repeated in the Selenites, but in terms of a concrete symbolism of space, and with a much greater social complexity. Here the programmed society is seen arising from a specific and graphically drawn environment: the necessity of escaping from the sun leads the Selenites to adapt to the interior vastness; their society is a projection from the microcosm of the anthill or beehive, but with the relationship between instincts and intelligence subtly shifted, so as to create a sense of freedom yielding itself up to specialized horror. The encounter between the earthmen and the Selenites is played out in terms of the struggle for existence. Bedford and Cavor recognize that their captors know the basic elements of life: "food, compulsion, and pain". Plunged into this experience, Bedford in particular is quick to resort to the primitive authority of the club, but both travellers feel the pressure of their own needs, the ravenous hunger, the misery of the trapped animal, and it is Cavor who announces that later the "struggle for mastery" between the earth and the moon societies is inevitable.

The finest stroke in the narrative is the shift of emphasis from the quick emotional responses of Bedford to the rational assimilation of data described in Cavor's messages. This is crucial because by allowing us to feel Bedford's horror of the claustrophobic world, Wells has implicated us in Bedford's convictions about the alien nature of the moon society: we think we see two chains of life rising to radically diverging apexes. But the underlying Darwinism is consistent; both societies are subject to natural laws; they must organize in terms of the environment, feed themselves, perpetuate themselves. Cavor's sympathy for the moon society allows us to feel an increasing connection between it and our own human one. Wells's procedure is to suggest apparently outrageous modes of Selenite behaviour and then to create an immediate link with the earth-world. For example, the controlled growth of the young Selenites in jars is described, and Cavor comments: "That wretched-looking hand sticking out of its jar seemed to appeal for lost possibilities; it haunts me still, although of course, it is really in the end a far more humane proceeding than our earthly method of leaving children to grow into human beings, and then making machines of them". Speaking of the worker-drones Cavor observes: "To drug the worker one does not want and toss him aside is surely far better than to expel him from his factory to wander starving in the streets". The reader, at first seeing the Selenite world from a protected distance, is slowly drawn in; learning the ways of these intelligent "insects", he is forced to an awareness of his own inadequate humanity.

There is an even greater subtlety in Wells's procedure, however. It is Cavor's rationality, which we have seen as a radical contrast to Bedford's impulsive energy, that draws him into communication with the Selenites.

170

The rather dry Cavor, whom Wells describes as something of an insect and something of a machine, seems the ideal interpreter of the Selenite world, which is both a world of primordial horror, and a world of the machine. While Bedford recovers from the first jolting experience of the "Selenite's Face", it is Cavor who is hankering after "strange knowledge" and crediting the Selenites with a "high degree of intelligence". Through Cavor, our glimpse (via Bedford) of the "infernal machine" becomes an awareness of a whole society in which "each is a perfect unit in the world machine". Comparing Wells's description of the explorers' first sight of the machine, with Cavor's later description of the Selenites, we see a connection between forms that is shocking.

A nightmare of nineteenth century science is evoked. The world could increasingly be seen as comprehensible in terms of mechanistic materialism; the universe was a structure of parts operating together: a machine. Darwin's discovery of the chance shuttle of natural selection had annexed the human to this order. This might be concealed at the level of man in society, but a look at the primordial soon made it clear. Man too, anchored as he was to the mechanism of the body, could be understood as the end-point of the "forces" which controlled all matter alike. The logical step from here would be to make sure that the function for which he had evolved would be fulfilled finally by translating this material knowledge into social terms. Against such a line of thought T.H. Huxley's fine distinctions would seem pedantic quibbling. Once again, Wells touches disturbingly upon science's unique power of dehumanization. But Wells's insight cuts deeper still.

For Cavor's view of the Selenite society is far from static. He begins in curiosity and eager sympathy, continues in patience and intelligent comprehension — but, slowly, his grip begins to fail. As he enters the great cavern to converse with the Grand Lunar, he confesses, "just for a space I had something like the 'horrors'". His recounting of the ways of Selenite society to earth, is now balanced by a recounting of the ways of earth society for the benefit of the Grand Lunar. Again borrowing a page from Swift, Wells builds up the tension of contrast to its maximum point. The reader, increasingly revolted by the Selenite world, yet increasingly drawn into it by implication, is now confronted by a direct analogy to his own earthly society. At the same time, he is probably relieved that he is not part of the "rational" society of the Selenites. His earthly "chaos" seems suddenly preferable to the perfection for which he pays such a price. We are aware, too, that only a man of Cavor's single-minded, narrow devotion to intellectual classification could be so naive as to unfold the story quite like this. He has let himself in for what follows, and the reaction of the Selenites is a perfectly comprehensible outburst against things put quite this way. At the point at which Cavor describes the human addiction to warfare the tension breaks. The outrage has gone far enough. Now the whole tone of Cavor's narrative shifts; his sympathies seem to dissolve. He bitterly regrets the scientific objectivity which led him to tell the Grand Lunar the truth about human society. The interruptions in Cavor's messages take on a sinister tone: the "truth" has led too far, ultimately to silence. We must not miss the tremendous point that Wells makes here. For Cavor represents science and the scientific view of things; and he uses scientific discourse. What he has told us about the lunar society, what he tells the Grand Lunar about the earth, is the descriptive truth of generalization, the classifying truth of categories and abstractions. There is nothing human in Cavor's narration, no impulse of individual concern that is sufficient to break the spell of the objective comparison of function and structure. And in terms of Cavor's discourse the two societies come together: they come together as comparative structures, as social organisms, as participants in and mechanisms of the universal struggle for existence. Cavor's terms indeed have their usefulness, but he has relied on them too far, and he finds to his misery that they lead not to the "communication" he had hoped for, but to something else, to a kind of entropy, a breakdown in communication.[37] As Bedford vividly puts it, they lead Cavor ultimately only backward, into the pit of his own logic, "into the dark, into that silence that has no end".

So it is to Bedford's vision that we return after all. And Bedford, with his eminently human and average predilections, is an immensely agreeable character, one with whom we can all-too-easily sympathize. For if Bedford has turned away from the ecstatic vision of mind expanding across the cosmic spaces, he has also turned away from the hostile threat of those spaces, and has manifested a complete revulsion at the claustrophobia of the primeval which Cavor's reason paradoxically led him into. Bedford, indeed, offers us something of the human, but, as Wells makes clear, it is a very limited kind of humanity after all. For Bedford's values, though they include the specific and the impulsive, lack a moral dimension, and any deeper kind of self-knowledge. We can feel at home with Bedford because he *feels*, because he has the quick of sympathy that we instinctively take as essential to any definition of the human. Bedford, in short, is a fleshly man, not in any sense an insect, or a theorizing monstrosity. Nonetheless, he is finally inadequate to quiet the reader's doubts about humanity set in motion by the grand journey. For the reader knows, as Wells would have him know, that Cavor's hint about Bedford being after all something of "a bounder", is on the mark. Bedford's instability, his self-satisfaction, his ultimate narrowness and social opportunism do very little to reassure the reader who is sunk in nightmare by the vision of human lunacy and mechanical futility the whole book encompasses. If Wells hints at an escape into dualism through Bedford, he also hammers home that such a route is impossible for such a man. If he glories in Bedford's fleshly self, he is also too honest to present it as an adequate answer to the dehumanization of the flesh which is one of his overriding themes. For this problem, Wells has in fact no solution.

Despite the humour, the satire, and the inimitable Wellsian "bounce", we are left with very few consolations. Wells, trying both heaven and earth, fails to locate the environment of man.

4. Wells and the New Mythology of Science

What did science really mean to Wells? It meant an escape from a potential dependency upon "trade", it meant ideas, a framework for a life's vision, and, perhaps, at the same time, a certain kind of nightmare. There is nothing really surprising in Wells's engagement with science. Caught up in the new magic of its promise, at the end of a century that had come to believe in progress through technological change, he steered himself away from a limiting childhood and youth toward the open prospects of London. When he began to turn to literary expression, it was natural that his work should reflect the impact of the ideas which had graced his liberation. Yet, as he began truly to assimilate these ideas, he would find them far from consoling, and the tensions that may have led him to write in the first place, the fear of social entrapment and failure, would find an echo in the pessimistic vision of the limitations of man that lay beneath the superficial allure of nineteenth century science. [38] It may not be fanciful to suggest that the real emotional power of many of Wells's early writings originates in a personal sense of claustrophobia seeking appropriate expression in the ambiguously-toned presentation of a science which was in fact both thrilling and also rather frightening in its prospects. Like that mythical animal "Western Man", Wells had moved almost miraculously "upward"; his works catch a gleam of the glory of ascent but also hint at possible catastrophes. This kind of tension, embodying a precarious balance between exhilaration and despair, would be especially tempting at first, before the routines of success became habitual. It would encompass a vision of possible traps, a sense of the limitations of inherited gifts, and perhaps, a fear that these seemingly miraculous gifts might become mechanical. After a frantic ten years or so of impressive creative activity, Wells had just about exhausted the inspiration of such youthful tensions. From then on, still devoted to science, he could set himself to use it (and his other sources) more ratiocinatively in the prescriptive and expository vein; his novels would be loosely strung together fictions about his reading and his interests of the moment. But the passion would be gone, because the passion in this case stemmed from a peculiar angle of vision, from a pressing awareness of personal gifts and a sense of the possible frustration of these — a theme, which, cast in the imagery of the science whose language he had assimilated, allowed Wells to speak for his time as well as for himself.

Such a view seems to me necessary to supplement the kind of "history of ideas" tratment given to Wells's connection with science by even so good a study as that of W. Warren Wagar. Wagar concisely summarizes Wells's relation with T.H. Huxley, and goes on to outline Wells's views on man's place in the nature hatched by the new scientific world view.[39] Implicitly understanding literature in such cases as a simple rendering of scientific ideas, Wagar suggests that Wells, along with most of the other post-Darwinian writers of significance, simply "took over" the bleak nature of Darwinism. This seems to distort the complex exchange that actually occurred, the exchange that defies easy categorization in the multi-levelled works in question. While it is an absolutely correct generalization to place Wells's writings within a Darwinian context, criticism only begins there. To argue that Wells launched "a case against nature", for example, is acceptable, provided one is simply coining a catch-phrase to sum up his anti-Romanticism; but it is misleading if it is taken to mean that Wells depicted nature as completely negative in relation to the human search for values. In fact, as we have shown, although Wells rejects the traditional ordered nature of Western metaphysics, he *does*, in certain limited ways, seek values in nature. And while it is true to say that Wells sought larger vistas than the personal, it is surely, in the light of the typical affirmation of the ordinary in most of his important fiction, quite an over-statement to affirm (as Wagar does) that Wells was "intellectually indifferent to life at the level of the individual".

Wells, the man of his time, found his mind enriched by the exciting ideas of science, and took it upon himself to express his vision of the world by making use of these ideas. But as a writer of fiction, dependent upon the ambiguous and emotionally rich language of words, Wells went about transforming science into myth, creating modern science fiction, which, as Frye notes, is supremely fitted to express a vision of those "high powers" beyond human control, which humanity must nonetheless reckon with.[40] The tradition of "romance" literature (from which science fiction partially derives, and to which it is closely allied) suggests the dominance of structure over character development and individual psychology. *Frankenstein*, the archetypal modern science fiction novel, illustrates this tendency perfectly. And Wells's stories too, are brilliant fables that seldom encompass a full range of character development and psychological insight. The transformation of science into such mythological structures was an extremely valuable enterprise, leading to the development of modern science fiction, clearly one of the freshest paths of twentieth century literature.[41] But there is also a one-sidedness in Wells's reliance on myth and in his failure to probe very deeply into the complex life of the individual. For the science which forced Wells to his confrontation with the implicit present and the probable future seemed to offer him no values which its own radical delimitations did not immediately revoke. That despite this, he fulfilled the writer's most demanding recent task — to render the human dimension of each new step that carries the species further into the unknown — is the true measure of his greatness. Lifted from the conventional social space of the

174

nineteenth century novel, we are transported by Wells to a number of remarkably realized places. We enter, not the landscape of fantasy, but the landscape of the total biosphere as theorized by science. This is not a turn away from "realism" but rather a turn to the realism vindicated by science — the miraculous twists of the literary mind saturated with science suggesting not fanciful escapades, but possible adaptations of men to environments. If we examine the spatial dimensions of the new universe depicted by Wells we find both a positive and a negative direction. Torn from the conventional human scale, we may experience exhilaration and the bliss of freedom in flight through space and time. But carried beyond a certain point, we become dizzy with vertigo, or oppressed by the claustrophobia of the primordial, or of the running-down universe. Wells, having brought us so far, can only hurry us back to the conventional human-scaled world, where, sadder and wiser, we may bury ourselves in a round of pleasure and money making, or search the stars for a deeper clue. In making the imaginative leap from the theory of pure science to the myth of science fiction, Wells was testing science for its human relevance. Ultimately (in the early fiction), he finds it wanting, for he can imagine no human inner life sufficient to meet the challenge of its vast constructions in space and time and if, in translating the new science to the level of myth, he sometimes evokes the older myths, the pathos and irony are great, because, where these contained always a kernel of consolation and pointed to a link between the human and the godlike, the new myths, as Wells presented them, left man struggling to redefine his essential nature. Science, directed by the pressures of his personal predicament, fed Wells's imagination and struck a central chord for his age and ours. If it required writers with a wider vision than Wells to move through both the rapture and terror inspired by that science to a steady perspective on man, his best art captures the excitement of a new experience and fixes a vision that, for all its limitations, will endure.

175

CHAPTER THREE
D.H. Lawrence and The Struggle for a Human Space

Never, if you want to live and grow, never will you be able to say to matter,
"I have seen enough of you; I have surveyed your mysteries and have taken
from them enough food for my thought to last me for ever". I tell you: even
though, like the Sage of sages, you carried in your memory the image of all
the beings that people the earth or swim in the seas, still all that knowledge
would be as nothing for your soul, for all abstract knowledge is only a faded
reality: this is because to understand the world knowledge is not enough, you
must see it, touch it, live in its presence and drink the vital heat of existence
in the very heart of reality.

Teilhard de Chardin, "The
Spiritual Power of Matter"

1. The Early Novels: A Tentative Realism

The oft-noted lucky accident of D.H. Lawrence's birth in a mining
community not yet radically separated from the old England of field and
hedgerow made it possible for him to develop a literary realism that
would exclude neither the natural world nor the modern urban world of
industry and commerce.[1] In Lawrence's realism "nature" and natural
space, however, take on special significance; they are understood as
dynamic elements, capable of inducing necessary social transformations
when the human spirit becomes attuned to them through connections
made at the deepest, most primary level of physical existence. For
Lawrence nature is not so much a *scene* as a field of energy, and the
sexual imperatives of his novels argue as much as anything the inescapable character of Darwinian struggle and flux, which certain moments of
redeeming value may transform and even sanctify.

Lawrence's realism — his love of the social detail, his concern for the
truth of history, even his focus on the consciousness-in-process in the
natural setting — these qualities — partially traceable to the influence of
Naturalism — are often at war with an aestheticism that was the common
bequest of his era. It is the aestheticism — the self-conscious renderings
of atmosphere, the poetic indulgences, the unconvincing "spiritual"

aura — that ruins that promising early novel, *The White Peacock* (1911), which takes most of what strength it has from Hardy.[2]

In *The White Peacock* we do certainly encounter the old agricultural England, quite forcibly presented in the rabbit-hunting and potato-planting scenes and in the image of the barn as sheltering refuge. George Saxton, in fact, may be seen as a kind of pale Henchard dragged down by his own weakness, or as a fainter Jude, unable to be born to the higher life, but though his decline is potentially the central dramatic stuff of *The White Peacock*, it is rendered without the full marshalling of the psychological and social evidence that might have made it truly moving. The young Lawrence's self-indulgent presentation of the swooning sensibility of Cyril Beardsall further blurs the relationship among the curiously diverse elements that never quite mesh in this novel; yet summed up rather baldly some of the themes are worthy of the mature Lawrence (or Hardy).[3] One way to describe the limitations of *The White Peacock* would be to say that it is an attempt at what I have called the novel of double-consciousness ruined by the mishandling of the Beardsall figure, and on a deeper level, by Lawrence's too tentative rendering of the integral agricultural community, a failure that would be set right in *The Rainbow* some years later. And though the reader will identify, and dismiss, the compulsory post-nineties descriptive passages that mar the narrative in many places, there are also brief attempts (unsuccessful but interesting) to use the natural setting to dramatize a tension between the ''earthly'' quest for value and the emptiness of ''vast'' space:

> The sky was glittering with sharp lights — they are too far off to take trouble for us, so little almost to nothingness. All the great hollow vastness roars overhead, and the stars are only sparks that whirl and spin in the restless space. The earth must listen to us; she covers her face with a thin veil of mist, and is sad; she soaks up our blood tenderly, in the darkness, grieving, and in the light she soothes and reassures us. Here on earth is our sympathy and hope, the heavens have nothing but distances.

> (Part II, Chapter Five)

Sons and Lovers (1913), although it is hard to see it at this distance, was first of all a triumph of courage — Lawrence the young working-class writer sloughing off the false persona of the aesthete and seizing material directly at hand in the life of his family and community. It involves precisely the same kind of literary self-knowledge as Hardy's *Far From the Madding Crowd* and roughly parallels that work in terms of Lawrence's own career. Reading backwards from the perspective of his mature fiction, the novel seems curious in its ordering of the elements of nature and mechanism, male and female, city and country, but understood in terms of Lawrence's oedipal obsessions and in relation to the various literary problems afflicting *The White Peacock*, the elements fall into place.

In *Sons and Lovers* the Naturalistic themes and images are in process of being transformed. The frank sexual approach clearly suggests a concern for self-realization, for existential rooting, rather than being presented as illustrations of the power of raw instinct. The fight with Baxter Dawes is not simply a battle of rival male "animals", but a complex rite of passage confirming that life is struggle and physicality and at the same time accelerating the "drift toward death" that is Paul's spiritual condition because of his excessive attachment to his mother. Early in *Sons and Lovers* (Chapter VI) as Paul sketches the mines, we are presented with a transformation of the Naturalistic "beast" image — the mines are like "a big creature you don't know", but "wonderful" because of such aliveness. This reverses Zola's kind of emphasis (see *Germinal*) on the coalmine as a devouring evil monster.

Sons and Lovers is both vital and "vitalistic". Vital in its evidence of Lawrence's suddenly acute grasp of the visual world, demonstrated not only in the natural descriptions but throughout, his achievement here contrasting sharply with the shopworn literary attempts that mar most of *The White Peacock*.[4] Vitalistic in its delineation of an energy system that includes Walter Morel's violent drives, Paul's finally unleashed sexual potency, the internal conflicts and celebrations of the Moral family, the life of the mine itself, and nature in various forms and moods.[5] Much of the complexity, and some of the confusion of the novel, however, lies in the way Paul himself is placed in relation to these vitalistic elements. In social terms, it is quite understandable that he will be drawn to the "genteel" world of his mother, and later, of Miriam. In both cases, however, the sexual element, though present, is perverse and ultimately dooming of Paul's further development. His mother's is not the matrix world, but, ironically, a mirage obscuring the real freedom that lies in Paul's commitment (made in desperation and very tentatively only in the final passages of the novel) to "life". By making aestheticism and "sensibility" elements in the dramatic clash of values, and by revealing the ambiguous nature of "beauty" (which is sometimes stultifying, sometimes life-enchancing), Lawrence gives explicit and implicit testimony to the values of "realism" and Naturalism. But, to reiterate, it is a Naturalism transformed that is in question. One has only to look at the relationship between Paul and Clara to measure the special intensity of Lawrence's treatment. Clara and Baxter Dawes may be seen as a married couple mirroring the Morels; Paul's passion for Clara is a legitimized (though extra-marital) flow of those very energies blocked and dammed up by social prohibitions — he cannot sleep with his mother and Miriam's character causes her to take on the pseudo-mother role of genteel, naive temptress. Yet even with Clara there are many complexities — just because of its quality of substitution Paul's relationship with her soon plays itself out; Baxter is the father-rival who drives away the faltering son-lover. And Clara is only part, "a speck" of that nature that draws Paul away from the matrix and toward "life", as the scenes on the Lincolnshire coast show. The "horizontals" mentioned to Miriam in one of their "aesthetic" discussions (Chapter VII) are experienced with Clara (their relationship is relatively free and "open") but the imagery suggests a journey theme that is to be taken up more fully only in the evolutionary context of *The Rainbow*.

Paul Morel, a "modern" person, emerges from the vital subculture of Bestwood because he must pursue the development of higher consciousness instilled in him by nature and education. Bestwood's vitality has to do with its earthiness, its contact with real work, with nature, and with the quality of life of the miners, who are not unrelated to the old England of the agricultural order, despite their often depressing working environment. Because Paul is a "conscious" person, he cannot simply rest in the subculture, but the vitality that draws him, often against his will, is ironically linked to that subculture, thus ensuring that his escape to freedom will be marked by a peculiarly modern kind of "angst". In terms of our delineation of traditional patterns, the "paradisal" in this case is the false paradise of the dominating mother (a true place of beauty but one that must be left behind). In the walk to the Leivers' farm in Chapter VI we see how Gertrude and Paul share the intensity of the natural setting, while their outright flirting and implicit sexual attraction (they are more like lovers than mother and son) give warning of danger. Immediately, the fourteen-year-old Miriam appears, in the rural setting that could itself be liberating were it not for her developing aesthetic pretentions and her repressed sexual nature. When the relationships with both Miriam and Clara fail, and his mother dies, Paul is left alone in the "vastness and terror of the immense night", i.e., face to face with all the pressures of existential anxiety attendant upon one who has found no permanent source of vitality in nature. Only his own anchoring sense of a valid physicality and "being" holds against that wave of existential terror visible in the image of sublime nature Lawrence makes us see in the final pages of this novel. The city, not yet taken as the "enemy" of Paul's own self-intuited, fleetingly grasped, sense of vital life, can be accepted both as a challenge and as a future test.

In *Sons and Lovers*, Lawrence makes a great advance toward that "process" sense of reality that will emerge fully in *The Rainbow*. Nature is not a great sea that swallows the characters, as in extreme Naturalism, nor is it fully subject to manipulation by the civilized "aesthetic" sense bent on dominating it. When, early in the novel, Mrs. Morel stands in the moonlight, she experiences herself as one at the centre of a complex inner-outer continuum. Her feelings, inchoate and overt, her physical body, the child in her womb, the flowers, the landscape and the moonlight fuse to a moment of unique consciousness which becomes an ecology of intense human experience. (We are made to see and feel how all the separate elements are interacting, how they are interdependent, and to what extent the climax and peak experience remains a "whole" not reducible to a set of various stimuli and responses).

She hurried out of the side garden to the front, where she could stand as if in an immense gulf of white light, the moon streaming high in face of her, the moonlight standing up from the hills in front, and filling the valley where the Bottoms crouched, almost blindingly. There, panting and half weeping in reaction from the stress, she murmured to herself over and over again: "The nuisance! the nuisance!"

She became aware of something about her. With an effort she roused herself to see what it was that penetrated her consciousness. The tall white lilies were reeling in the moolight, and the air was charged with their perfume, as with a presence. Mrs. Morel gasped slightly in fear. She touched the big pallid flowers on their petals, then shivered. They seemed to be stretching in the moonlight. She put her hand into one white bin: the gold scarcely showed on her fingers by moonlight. She bent down to look at the binful of yellow pollen; but it only appeared dusky. Then she drank a deep draught of the scent. It almost made her dizzy.

Mrs. Morel leaned on the garden gate, looking out, and she lost herself awhile. She did not know what she thought. Except for a slight feeling of sickness, and her consciousness in the child, herself melted out like scent into the shiny, pale air. After a time the child, too, melted with her into the mixing pot of moonlight, and she rested with the hills and lilies and houses, all swum together in a kind of swoon.

(Chapter One)

Now the reader who looks carefully at this whole passage (of which I have quoted only the central part, including the sentence at which Lawrence seems to come very close to the "melting" and blurring graces of high-toned aestheticism) will, I think, understand its novelty of approach, its closeness to the "quick" of experience, and will also connect it with that later passage which occurs just before Paul announces his break with Miriam. Both passages reveal how Lawrence reactivates the Romantic sense of intense communion with nature, without failing to convey the terror and "otherness" of nature made clear by Darwinism and occasionally by Naturalism.

A corncrake in the hay-close called insistently. The moon slid quite quickly downwards, growing more flushed. Behind him the great flowers leaned as if they were calling. And then, like a shock, he caught another perfume, something raw and coarse. Hunting round, he found the purple iris, touched their fleshy throats and their dark grasping hands. At any rate, he had found something. They stood stiff in the darkness. Their scent was brutal. The moon was melting down upon the crest of the hill. It was gone; all was dark. The corncrake called still.

(Chapter Eleven)

Sons and Lovers, though it looks back to Hardy and even to Dickens for aspects of its social realism, and borrows from Naturalism some measure of its fascination with both physical energy and sexuality, begins to reveal Lawrence's conviction that nature, perceived dynamically, might point the way to an authentic modern life of the spirit. The pleasure of reading and re-reading this novel lies partially in the excitement of its sharply rendered physical detail, partially in its (related) power to dramatize experience as process, and in its vision of a potent nature, not yet perceived as part of a Utopian quest for social transformation and amelioration. At the end, Paul stands in a large and threatening spatial universe, subject indeed to what Teilhard called "the malady of space-time", yet nourished by the knowledge that he, a "speck of flesh" is not entirely "nothing". It is only in his next novel, *The Rainbow*, however, that Lawrence depicts the actual complex struggle for selfhood in this wider, more frightening universe beyond the sheltering subculture.

2. The Rainbow: Evolution of Consciousness

The Rainbow (1915) begins at Marsh Farm, firmly rooted in the old agricultural order, but the movement of the action quickly grows complex. Lawrence takes up Hardy's main trajectories in his own way: the "field" is to be both a refuge and a starting point. The main structure of *The Rainbow* involves first of all an arch figure centered usually "forward" in time, an arch through which the present leads to the uncreated future.[6] At the same time, there is the image of the human pair or group in the foreground, these being in a state of relatively "free" relation in space to the arch, so that at times it may recede from them, while at other times, it actually touches them. The rainbow is the arch seen in terms of value. It is the unity between the flesh and the ideal, an image of selfhood in that it dramatizes the beauty of the moment which promises to blossom with a sense of value beyond mere struggle. In the rainbow itself Lawrence finds an image which refers to a natural phenomenon while having strong Biblical connotations.[7] This kind of blend is typical. The quest pattern of the novel carries us away from a world which is conceived in terms of a Gothic absoluteness, into the modern world. Evolutionary social development is thus connected with the Biblical "Journey" motif. The two "arks" referred to in *The Rainbow*, though strictly Biblical in derivation, are significantly related to the evolutionary unfolding.[8]

Lawrence uses the image of the Ark of the Covenant to suggest the new formulation of the sacred in the modern world.[9] In his work, sacred space is no longer clearly defined within rigidly enclosed limits: the hierarchic gives way to the inner; the person becomes the temple of Lawrence's Holy Ghost, whose presence is as fleeting as that of Yahweh's. Modern man, cast out from the shelter of the traditional order, becomes a traveller seeking God's presence in the wilderness of the space-time universe.

Noah's Ark, on the other hand, is an image used by Lawrence in connection with the positive-negative security of the human group, especially the family. The human pair, if they turn the Ark into a mere refuge, lose touch with the possibilities of the rainbow. In Darwinian terms, life is a relentless process in which adaptation on all levels is a basic necessity:

This is sin, this tying the knot in Time, this anchoring of the Ark of eternal

182

truth upon the waters. There is no ark, there is no eternal system, there is no rock of eternal truth. In Time and in Eternity, all is flux. Only in the other dimension, which is not the time-space dimension, is there Heaven. We can no more *stay* in this heaven than the flower can stay on its stem. We come and go.[10]

In Lawrence's terms, the cathedral is a temple from which God is absent. It is brought into play in contrast to the two arks, and represents not simply the outmoded past, but, specifically, the reign of Love. This modern world of the historically exhausted "Love" is, in *The Rainbow*, only gradually revealed in all of its ramifications. When we finally know it in its full nothingness and sterility, at the end of the novel, we realize the necessity for the turning of the cycle which the self-creation of the characters has been working toward all along. (Yet nothing in Lawrence's personal writings seems to justify any supposition of a millennium realized in history, or of a Teilhardian transformation of matter into spirit. On the contrary, Lawrence is constantly emphasizing the persistence, indeed, the eternality, of time. Lawrence's conception of historical "epochs" implies a psychic dynamism and relativism, that different qualities will be called for in different eras.)[11]

The opening paragraphs of the novel establish the Brangwen relationship to the land in terms of the peasant consciousness: a cyclical seasonal round has dominated their lives for generations. The horizontal perspective of the field, however, is interrupted by the verticle axis of the church-tower, which stands for the fixed aspiration of the epoch of Love. From time immemorial, the Brangwens have flourished in a coherent world of ecological fullness and inter-dependency. The men especially, married to the earth, have existed in a rich "blood-consciousness", in the tactile sensually knowing world of physical immediacy. This world, however, cannot really be conceived of as permanent, or as the final state of truly human awareness. In the women is another king of knowing, one quite different from the peasant way. This is "the power of thought and of comprehension".

Yet Tom Brangwen, who becomes at once the focus of the narrative, is a *locus classicus* of the inarticulate peasant who " . . . knew that his brain was a slow hopeless good-for-nothing", but who, at the same time, is " . . . more sensuously developed, more refined in instinct" than his clever classmates.[12] Tom Brangwen, pushed on by his mother's desire that he "know", is hopeless with the "linear" world of the printed page. Seeking to fulfill himself sensually, he comes again to a dead end, but meeting the foreign man and girl at the hotel, he senses the world beyond. Through Lydia Lensky these two possibilities are brought together.

Lydia, in contrast to Tom, moves "inward" from the life of the city toward the sheltering agricultural world.[13] Here, she and her husband live out a life of real but limited validity: real, because each achieves self-awareness in the relationship, and both are thrust into that sense of the "third thing", which is the objective and authentic world they create between them; limited, because they are rescuing themselves from meaningless rather than creating a new meaning, and because they are living in the security of a fossilized order rather than meeting the challenge of a new adaptation.

In the relationship of Tom and Lydia, Lawrence describes at one point a release in the flesh, the experience of a totality beyond the mind's abstractions.

> Their coming together now, after two years of married life, was much more wonderful to them than it had been before. It was the entry into another circle of existence, it was the baptism to another life, it was the complete confirmation. Their feet trod strange ground of knowledge, their footsteps were lit up with discovery. Wherever they walked, it was well, the world re-echoed round them in discovery. They went gladly and forgetful. Everything was lost and everything was found. The new world was discovered, it remained only to be explored.
>
> (Chapter Three)

Exploring the flesh, releasing the body's unconscious energies, the individual counteracts the modern "malady of space-time". In passages too numerous to quote here, Lawrence sets Tom Brangwen against the great spaces on the burning plain of modern life. In relation to the actual modern existential life, he remains a fugitive, despite his validation of the blood-consciousness, and the flood of that life destroys him. But the rainbow signifies that the flesh will no more be destroyed by the flood.

The vastness of the "infinite world" is no longer the predominant factor, yet the journey imagery suggests a passage through the wilderness to a goal not yet reached. The emphasis is partially on the child Anna, because the parents will not themselves arrive at the terminal point enclosed by the novel's vision. Though they are raised out of the time-dimension altogether by their new knowledge in the flesh, they continue to exist at a certain phase of development in relation to the modern world, being merely the transmitters of the "blood" knowledge buried in the rural past.

In Lawrence's study of Anna and Will's marriage, which is the most detailed, the most fiercely knowledgeable rendering of a relationship in the novel, we are carried to the next phase of the quest for meaning. In their first significant meeting as lovers, in the "moon-harvest" scene, Anna and Will engage in a ritual conflict which initiates them into a lifetime of marital struggle. The preliminary courting between Anna and Will makes passing use of an animal imagery that Lawrence will develop further; however, the most significant point is that for Will, unlike Tom, the expedition into the body darkness *itself* seems fearsome and is mixed up with the threat of that vast space which is being negated. The situation between the lovers is adventitious; their work is not really part of the traditional rural pattern. Yet the farm is there, around them, and they take possession of the field without the necessity of seeking it out. Attached to the field in the only way they can be, neither as true inheritors nor as outsiders, their experience is a considerably less self-conscious version of Levin's encounter with the matrix world. Nonetheless, despite Lawrence's use of the term "work" to describe the activity of Anna and Will in stacking the sheaves, their situation differs greatly from Levin's, or, for that matter, from the experience of Clym Yeobright on the heath. For it is not the peasant consciousness as such that is activated here — Tom Brangwen's world is unavailable to them — but the blood-consciousness separated from the context of working life that enclosed its previous manifestations. Lawrence is suggesting a transitional phase in which the knowledge of the old order, narrowed to a more specifically sexual content, is available to counteract the one-sidedness of the epoch of Love. The human meaningfulness buried in acts of relation to this environment, the physical knowledge characteristic of the traditional agricultural order, is summoned up in this moment of the two lovers, who are no longer part of that world. That is how compelling environment can be, Lawrence seems to tell us: old connections can be rediscovered in the name of a new orientation. This love-ritual in the field gathers old knowledge to a new purpose.

The summons, however, is ignored. The rhythm of physical intimacy in the stacking is increasingly interrupted by Will's tense compulsion. As the work goes on we learn that "His will drummed persistently, darkly, it drowned everything else. Into the rhythms of his work there came a pulse and a steadied purpose". As they draw together, Will becomes paralyzed so that the moment of true contact is broken; when the conflict passes we are told that "something fixed in him forever".

After the marriage, when the couple settle into their village house, occurs their only true realization of the experience of "timelessness". Though they too are raised by the power of the flesh into what Lawrence would later describe as an experience of the "fourth dimension", Anna and Will remain unable to translate their discovery into terms that would hold good for everyday life; their marriage fails to elicit a higher consciousness, a deepened selfhood that would carry them beyond the limitations of their given environment. [14]

The final metaphorical summary of this part of the modern quest is stated in that unique style, both Biblical and evolutionary, which singles this novel out among Lawrence's works. We see Anna standing on Pisgah mountain, overlooking the promised land seeing "a faint gleaming horizon, a long way off, and a rainbow like an archway, a shadow-door with faintly coloured coping above it". The perspective suggests a future in which the limitations of the present will be resolved in a release of the flesh that will span the horizon with its value. The tensions between near and far, flesh and mind, action and passivity, doing and serving, will be resolved in the near future, as part of the generative power of Anna herself. She will hold up the child, Ursula, who will walk through the fiery furnace, asserting that faith in the spirit which could not be fully stated in the present. The natural cycle goes on, leaving Anna part of the past, but through the power of birth she retains a connection with the future in which she herself can take no direct part.

Yet the Ursula-Skrebensky relationship, with which Lawrence carries us into the modern urban world, is a vexing one for the characters concerned, and has been so as well for Lawrence's critics. [15] Because Lawrence never fully articulates the distinction between "creative" and "destructive" energies in the relationship between Ursula and Skrebensky, there is a formal blurring, and a discrepancy within the overall pattern, which the reader realizes by the end, when the "rainbow" vision appears again. (This is true even though the actual depiction of the relationship is extremely vivid and powerful). We are not really given clear reasons why Skrebensky is an inadequate self, and have to assume these from Lawrence's moral trajectory, which I think we can fairly do, but ought not to be left to do. Even so, one can argue that Lawrence's failure with Skrebensky is one of tone and form and not one of intrinsic vision, and we need not take this failure as a key to some flaw in his sense of the organic world of growth and corruption.

In the second moon-harvest scene we are once again made aware of Lawrence's vision of evolutionary transformation. The modern world encroaches and the gap between the individual consciousness and the processes of traditional human life-in-nature is seen to be great. The farm is the setting for a social event, not a point of contact with rhythms integrating man and the environment. Here, the dynamics of psyche and nature are rendered so as to emphasize the uncontrollable, the ecstatic, and the destructive in human consciousness: the psycho-physical order shaped by traditional patterns of work in nature does not apply. Instead, Lawrence dramatizes Ursula's acceleration toward the future: "She must leap from the known into the unknown". This is as it should be, for the enclosing limitations of the modern world have made the old rural rhythms inaccessible, and to realize herself in knowledge through the flesh, Ursula must reach beyond the social world of polite evening chatter. "The darkness seemed to breathe like the sides of some great beast, the haystacks loomed half-revealed, a crowd of them, a dark, fecund lair just behind". This reference reminds us of the "primordial" level to be struck by the key image of the "Darwinian" beasts later. Here, Ursula senses at once the possibilities of psycho-physical release into the widest possible future. "It was as if a hound were straining on the leash, ready to hurl itself after a nameless quarry in the dark. And she was the quarry, and she was also the hound. The darkness was passionate and breathing with immense, unperceived heaving". Dancing with Skrebensky, she is caught up in this flux of movement that should thrust them into the darkness of a new sense of knowledge. With the rising of the moon, her arousal reaches a peak of intensity, but here there is a shift from positive to negative feeling, for Skrebensky is unable to face up to this demand for release. As the dance ends, he sees her among the corn-stacks in a magic conflagration of light amid darkness. She is sealed with the deeper unconscious knowledge, and he is annihilated by this vision, all the more aware of his nothingness. The images of fire and water, darkness and light that predominate suggest the atmosphere of potential for newly fused selfhood, but, as the conflict between the lovers develops, these images seem more and more to evoke a world of inorganic hardness.[16] The description thus contrasts sharply with the ''organic'' tone of Ursula's girlhood awakening, and even with the tone used earlier to characterize the struggle between Anna and Will. Such ''chemical'' impersonality points ahead to the final sterility of exchange in the last moon scene, after which the relationship of Ursula and Skrebensky collapses. While this earlier scene suggests the magic potential in the meeting of the lovers, it betrays the lack of warmth in Skrebensky, his failure to kindle Ursula and himself to a new knowledge, and Ursula's ''demonic'' reaction to this.

Lawrence's next three chapters, ''Shame'', ''The Man's World'' and ''The Widening Circle'' depict the inadequate alternatives in action for the still unrealized self. What is emphasized throughout is the power of dehumanization in capitalistic mass society. Lawrence's vision is not directed simplistically against the machine as such, but against the failure of man to create himself in machine society.[17] While the agricultural world of the past provided a measure of opportunity for the development of consciousness-transforming work, the modern capitalistic machine-world is paralyzed by greed. (''The most moral duke in England makes two hundred thousand a year out of those pits.'') As Lawrence wrote in the Hardy Study: ''There is half an eternity of pure leisure for mankind to take, if he would, if he did not think, at the back of his mind, that riches are the means to freedom.''[18]

At this point, Lawrence develops two kinds of natural image that serve to dramatize the strengths and weaknesses of Ursula's position. First, there is a series of fleeting visions of the horizon, usually at dawn or sunset; these sum up Ursula's knowledge of a beauty and reality outside of the brutally materialistic world into which she has plunged. At the same time we can read them as pathetically disembodied versions of the crowning unity of heaven and earth that cannot be attained except through the flesh. There is an ironical dimension here, as with Blake's ''Sunflower''; a sense of futile longing, though also a vision of promise. The second image is the false Eden offered by the faun-like Anthony Schofield. Seeing herself as a ''traveller'' Ursula escapes the latter; but how is she to embody her ''rainbow'' longings?

In fact, her entry into the university, which occurs at this time, is central to her further discovery of what her future must be. The university is affiliated with bygone religious fervour: ''Her soul flew back to medieval times, when the monks of God held the learning of men and imparted it within the shadow of religion". It is revealed also as in complicity with the materialistic present: "It pretended to exist by the religious virtue of knowledge. But the religious virtue of knowledge was become a flunkey to the god of material success". Now Lawrence allows us a glimpse of Ursula's state of being at this critical moment, summing it up in a passage full of portentous and striking imagery:

> That which she was, positively, was dark and unrevealed, it could not come forth. It was like a seed buried in dry ash. This world in which she lived was like a circle lighted by a lamp. This lighted area, lit up by man's completest consciousness, she thought was all the world: that here all was disclosed for ever. yet all the time, within the darkness she had been aware of points of light, like the eyes of wild beasts, gleaming, penetrating, vanishing. And her soul had acknowledged in a great heave of terror only the outer darkness. This inner circle of light in which she lived and moved, wherein the trains rushed and the factories ground out their machine-produce and the plants and the animals worked by the light of science and knowledge, suddenly seemed like the area under an arc-lamp, wherein the moths and children played in the security of blinding light, not even knowing there was any darkness, because they stayed in the light . . .

(Chapter Fifteen)

Despite the preponderance of the dark-light contrasts which create the ambience of a traditional dualism, we should proceed with caution in locating radical divisions in the reality depicted here. What is suggested, perhaps, is two kinds of knowing, with Ursula struggling to extend her range beyond the common and conventional knowledge of "the world in which she lived". Ursula's struggle is depicted in natural images. She is like a seed which is not yet caught up in the "new germination" which is mentioned later, at the very end of the novel. She is like a person living in the circle of an arc-light, who sees around her a luminous darkness. The arc-light represents mental consciousness, everyday life, the modern urban world, and even the mechanical or automatic side of nature. The darkness represents the unconscious, a living world which is rich in mystery, power and danger. Lawrence's reference to the campfire evokes a world of Darwinian primitivism. Ancient man is surrounded by wild beasts, but is himself already conventionalized, since no one dares to throw a fire-brand into the darkness. (Anyone doing so would become an outcast, like Johannes Jensen's Darwinian culture-heroes.) The wild beasts we may take at this point as the physical primordial side of humanity itself, as the apparently "lower" instincts which, however, shine forth with positive values of a religious kind. The "gleam in the eyes of the wolf and hyena" is also "the flash of the sword of angels, flashing at the door to come in." The angels themselves are "not to be denied, like the flash of fangs."

Lawrence is here directly engaging the tradition of Darwinian primordialism, but he is not simply exalting an ordinary and callow primitivism in the manner of many of the literary Naturalists. This passage shows of course that he shares certain assumptions with them: the sense of a tension between civilized and primordial worlds, an imagery of carnivorous violence, an emphasis on physical energy, and an overriding sense of man as a species. He goes beyond his inheritance of Naturalism, however, in several respects. For one thing, the passage shows us Lawrence's heavily Biblical tone creating a more complex frame of reference, leading beyond the purely biological level to a new expression of the "numinous". Something must renew civilized man; he must be reborn in the vitality of "life itself", yet his transformation must not be merely an evasion of the modern world. The brave man would cast a firebrand into the darkness in order to illuminate the darkness; he does not want to obliterate the arc-light world, but to extend it. The passage suggests not a simple-minded escapism, but the difficulties implicit in a genuine search for selfhood in the modern world.

In order to understand what Lawrence means by selfhood, we must examine another passage reflecting Ursula's experience, one that occurs just a few pages after the "Darwinian" one. Here Ursula discusses "life" with one of her teachers, Dr. Frankstone:

No, really," Dr. Frankstone had said, "I don't see why we should attribute some special mystery to life — do you? We don't understand it as we understand electricity, even, but that doesn't warrant our saying it is something special, something different in kind and distinct from everything else in the universe — do you think it does? May it not be that life consists in a complexity of physical and chemical activities, of the same order as the activities we already know in science? I don't see, really, why we should imagine there is a special order of life, and life alone —"

The conversation had ended on a note of uncertainty, indefinite, wistful. But the purpose, what was the purpose?

. . .For what purpose were the incalculable physical and chemical activities nodalised in this shadowy, moving speck under her microscope? What was the will which nodalised them and created the one thing she saw? What was its intention? To be itself? Was its purpose just mechanical and limited to itself?

It intended to be itself. but what self? Suddenly in her mind the world gleamed strangely, with an intense light, like the nucleus of the creature under the microscope. Suddenly she had passed away into an intensely-gleaming light of knowledge. She could not understand what it all was. She only knew that it was not limited mechanical energy, nor mere purpose of self-preservation and self-assertion. It was a consummation, a being infinite. Self was a oneness with the infinite. To be oneself was a supreme, gleaming triumph of infinity.

(Chapter Fifteen)

In this encounter, two kinds of language are set side by side. Dr. Frankstone's description of life is an outside description, having nothing to do with the sense of life proper. She uses the language of abstraction and non-involvement, which automatically excludes us from the mystery

189

and the sense of awe that are part of a fully human perspective.[19] Lawrence is not unfair to the fleetingly evoked Dr. Frankstone, but he immediately renders the domain of that mystery which her language passes over. We experience with Ursula the leap which takes her beyond a partial or analytic view to a grasp of the totality.[20] Life cannot be understood merely in terms of descriptive reduction; there must be as well the testimony of consciousness tuned to the "quick" of complex structures. The "unicellular shadow" visible to Ursula is directed from its own center, or at least describable as if it were so directed. Ursula is more concerned with herself as a vehicle of unity, capable of sensing higher unities, than she is with herself as an assembly reducible to part-functioning.

If we return to the Darwinian passage for a moment, then, we can understand the angels and beasts of darkness more fully. They are not so much Jungian archetypes as representations of the biological "soul": for D.H. Lawrence, the self is not so much a psychic principle to be apprehended through the articulation of essentially mental images, as for Jung; rather it is a biologically-derived principle of spiritual direction, a nodalisation of quintessential body-impulse which must be called into play if the individual is to escape mechanism.[21] Calling this soul fully into play means, most often, sexuality free from the trammels of mental consciousness. ("Sex is pure blood consciousness.") The dark shadow-shapes are indicators of the body-factor to be encountered inevitably in successful sexual exchange, an exchange which is for Lawrence the key medium through which violence can be exorcised and sterility and stagnation of spirit brought to an end.

Ursula's vision of the depths of life-as-experience caught in the episode of the Darwinian beasts and the sense of a possible "consummation" of self and the infinite inspired by the microscope slide, turn her toward "the new world", that post-modern world in which "Skrebensky was waiting for her".

Their reunion occurs under the promise of a passionate "darkness" which is described in a flurry of positives that seal its significance; yet at the same time there are qualifications: "the pleasure, the spontaneous joy was not there any longer" for Ursula.

Their first complete sexual encounter is the third described by Lawrence in terms that evoke the timeless world. In the "roaring circle" of the tree, Ursula passes into "the pristine darkness of paradise". Through the flesh she has been carried "to the eternal, changeless place" in which it seems as if she has received "another nature". Yet it is clear that this paradisal moment in nature is enjoyed by the lovers on the edge of the modern world, and that the "roaring circle" of the tree is an enclosure pressed upon by "the lights and the machine glimmer" of the working world that has assaulted Ursula and captured Skrebensky. This moment of leisure in nature carries the lovers upward to other dimensions of knowledge; but their attempt to move creatively through the arc-light world fails. The paradisal moment flowers in the Darwinian struggle for existence, but the mechanism and rigidity of the "lower" order eventually routinizes the motions of the flesh. Ursula's desire "to be gone" has been fulfilled, but during the next weeks she finds the sense of "death" and the horror of "not-being" in her lover, and falls herself into a negative pattern which cannot help him. Skrebensky grows as "tense" and "fixed" as the social order by which they are surrounded, even in their attempt to restore the paradisal moment on the downs. Ursula's longing for freedom reawakens; there is somewhere "beyond", "where the old restraints had dissolved and vanished, where one moved freely, not afraid of one's fellow man". Lawrence's counterpoint of spatial elements grows complex: on the one hand we have the modern arc-light world and its natural equivalent, the burning plain of modern life; on the other, the enclosure of the flesh-in-nature, which re-creates the moment of value in the flux against the intrusion of the chaos of sublime space and beyond the mechanism of the epoch of Love. Yet this enclosure can give way, perhaps must give way, to a more destructive experience, and the lovers must survive such destruction in order to prove themselves for the future.

The book's third moon-scene, one of the great, stark passages in modern literature, marks the final failure of their struggle toward a positive resolution. Lawrence introduces this scene with a summary of the impasse to follow. Ursula's yearning arises again at evening; she is caught up in the rhythm of moon and tide, but bitterly, because the "vast suggestions of fulfillment" that touch her deepest centers amid this "field" of physical-psychic energy, cannot be realized in the "personi-fication" of Skrebensky. Together, that evening, they go among the dunes, out onto the bare beach, to re-enact, but with what a difference, the Arnoldian vision of lovers clinging together on the burning plain of modern life. A few powerful paragraphs establish the failure of the "struggle for consummation". Images of fierce animal combat are combined with stark contrasts of light and dark, and with metaphors of fusing and melting. The "high blast of moonlight", the "glare of white light" dominates everything, and drives Ursula to a frenzy of restlessness. In the moonlight is virtually fulfilled the prophecy made about Anna's offspring, that "the child might walk there, amid the burning coals and incandescent roar of heat". Ursula is in fact "a witness" to the need of the flesh, but when the flesh of Skrebensky fails to answer hers, the struggle that ensues becomes purely destructive. The moonlight welds Ursula to a beyond *apart from* Anton; she wants "to go", and the tension builds up because she cannot do so either with him or without him. She cannot reach the fullness of her being apart from the creative contact he should offer her; he can only crouch in the darkness which is the flesh with all possibilities of the "beyond" removed from it. Their physical contact leads not to freedom and a further meaning, but to a corpse-like state of rigidity in which consciousness sinks to a blankness for Skrebensky and the moon and sea do not exist for Ursula. The sublime space that should be humanized by love which touches the heights of timeless being and sends a new vision flashing forward in time, is alive only with the "glare of white light" that signifies nothingness and non-being. Consciousness must lapse out for a moment's release from the strain of such experience. Just as the splitting apart of the light and dark signifies here the irreconcilable difference of two modes of flesh-relation, the one abundant with spiritual direction and ready for selfhood, the other defensive, limited and static, so the actual physical struggle of the lovers, depicted in terms of the Darwinian furies, leaves us with a hopelessly one-sided and brutal version of "adaptation". Here, there is no combat reconciled on a higher plane, but merely a foray of one against the other, mutual aggression that goes beyond what is humanly invigorating, and which results in the symbolic death of both the partners. The images of fusing and melting furthermore introduce a sense of inorganic, "chemical" transformation, mostly of a negative kind, toward nothingness rather than being, while Ursula's "metal" face and her salty tears are the reverse of what is human and "quick". She wants to travel toward the "eternal", but it is those tears that gather and travel at last on her "motionless, eternal face". The total effect is of an open space saturated with overpowering forces which, without the establishment of any intimacy and union, the lovers cannot even consciously face. In addition, there is a crushing sense of sterility and mechanism; the spectacle of a dehumanized inner and outer environment. Where there should be self-development toward knowledge of life as a total experience, there is a failure of animal vitality and a complete sense of alienation. The barren landscape of this third "moon scene" is in sharp contrast to the rural enclosure discovered in the stacking scene between Anna and Will, and further removed into anonymity from the previous moon-dance scene of this pair. We witness from scene to scene a gradual accretion of mechanism and a de-specifying of the environment. In terms of the Biblical metaphor, we find ourselves truly in the "wilderness", in the desert with God absent from the ark of the person, and the promised land not in sight. The world of Love, the abstract, infinite world of struggle and non-flesh threatens at this point to engulf Ursula, whose destiny should be to find a new way to the future. Her vision collapses and she is tempted to follow her mother's way, to give up the quest. The encounter with the horses, however, changes all this. It is a powerful scene in every way, one of Lawrence's famous passages, and has been subjected to various readings. [22]

In my view it stands first of all as a striking example of Lawrence's unique ability to render the total world of inner and outer so that we understand human life and consciousness as overflowing conventionally determined boundaries: nowhere in this novel is there a clearer example of Lawrence's grasp of the individual body as sensitized within a web of relationships on many levels of knowledge. The real environment of the woods above Willey Water is not either Ursula's mental state, nor is it a pre-determined set of abstractions, forces, objects, or energies: it is a process in which what we call "mind" or "psyche" and what we call "body" or "matter" are inextricably bound together. Lawrence neither evades the brutal physical reality of nature, nor does he simplify Ursula's interaction with her environment to the point of turning her into an object. This image of natural space is not reducible to the landscape of dream. The horses, in their movement and vitality, are rendered as a kind of fiery presence, shimmering and flashing in the dreary rain. This is simultaneously a stalking, a wooing, and a nightmare pursuit. Ursula is forced out of her acquiescence and complacency, into a direct physical response. "In a sort of lightning of knowledge their movement travelled through her, the quiver and strain and thrust of their powerful flanks, as they burst before her and drew her on, beyond." The fiery horses may be associated with the body-energy of male sensual power — this we would know even without Lawrence's gloss and the Yoga theorizing, merely from the descriptive emphasis on the power of their flanks and haunches, and through the suggestive imagery of tumescence that permeates the passage. We can also take for granted Ford's point that this is for Ursula an experience of "panic", an encounter with those natural energies which Lawrence would later see as a "glimpse of the living untamed chaos". The precise relevance of these fiery horses to the whole line of the story, however, lies not quite in either of these identifications, but in the way they revivify our sense (and Ursula's sense) of what kind of selfhood she should be seeking. For the horses, from one point of view energetic, potent and alive, are yet dangerous and unruly, captured without being really tamed. They recall the Darwinian "beasts", and stand for the primal physical and organic kind of knowing that must underlie all "higher" knowing. Yet, at the same time, these horses are prisoners of their own level of existence; they are "only" instinctual, and they flash forth from the dark past of the blood, vital, yet not in themselves a proper model for this Brangwen girl, who is also in love with the higher world, and in search of unity. To realize herself, Ursula must not marry Skrebensky, for that would be to deny the primal element that the horses embody, but neither can Ursula merely sink to the level at which the horses plunge and rear, the dark blood level of the Brangwen past, which is pre-moral and pre-civilized. Somehow, Ursula must carry what the horses awaken in her through the arc-light world, without letting it be tainted by mechanism; she must establish a new organic connection with a new lover in a relationship that will lead to a creative higher consciousness denied by the pressures of the epoch of Love. Unlike the horses, she need not go on "running against the walls of time, and never bursting free''; in her, the impulse in the flesh translates into a new knowledge.

> She was the naked, clear kernel thrusting forth the clear, powerful shoot, and
> the world was a bygone winter, discarded, her mother and father and Anton,
> and college and all her friends, all cast off like a year that has gone by, whilst
> the kernel was free and naked and striving to take new root, to create a new
> knowledge of Eternity in the flux of Time.

(Chapter Sixteen)

Lawrence's imagery illustrates his grasp of the old rhythms and rootedness, and the relation of these to the discovery of wholeness in the Darwinian world of struggle and change. The epoch of Love does not offer the final summary of man's position in the wider universe: its husk of limitations, its mechanisms and ugly compulsions must be dissolved. Ursula understands for the first time the true promise of the rainbow, that "the flesh will not be destroyed" by the flood of modern life, for the rainbow is arched in the blood "and would quiver to life in the spirit". Man can redeem the empty space of the heavens with a new vision, fitting to it "a living fabric of Truth" which, though it begins in the personal relationship, can be extended to all of society so that a new epoch will come about. If the reader must, to a certain extent, take this wisdom on faith, if Lawrence, in *The Rainbow* itself and in terms of this final relationship especially, raises as many questions as he answers, yet the poetic thrust, the overarching form of the book, is consistent.[23] Lawrence depicts the removal of modern man from rural life to the city, and shows the cyclical round of the field giving way to the open space and time of sublime nature. Vastness rendered in terms of the modern scientific universe must be met with the assertion of the value of the flesh which the old, closed order affirmed, and which can be reaffirmed in the paradisal moment which is not merely an escape from time, but a gathering of meaning out of struggle that makes the next stage of the human endeavour possible.

Lawrence's study of the three generations of the Brangwen family emphasizes struggle, adaptation, inheritance and environment, though these are taken beyond the usual narrow limits of classic Naturalism. It is because Lawrence could go beyond the concept of a life-mechanism to the sense of a life-process that he could escape the metaphorical "bind" of such a writer as Wells, for whom the animal and the machine blend together in the shape of a post-Darwinian nightmare. Lawrence's characters inhabit a "multi-dimensional environment" in which things are not static entities but rather "events". In Lawrence, as in other moderns, the social world of the traditional novel is dissolved into "centres of experience", but *The Rainbow* is most original in its comprehensive rendering of man's place in a universe in which the dynamic relation of the "within" and the "without" is sustained. Lawrence's characters are not psyches consuming all reality in the name of consciousness, but individual bodies sensitized to a web of relationships on many levels of cognisance. Lawrence's sense of man's place in nature is comprehensive, but perhaps its greatest profundity lies in his rendering of value as an essentially "ecological" experience, with the human person at the peak of awareness discovering himself or herself to be an intuitive, intelligent body at the center of a living world.

3. Women in Love: A Desperate Balance

On the 24th of May, 1916, Lawrence wrote to Lady Ottoline Morrell about the novel that was to be a sequel to *The Rainbow:* "It comes rapidly," he confided, "and is very good". He went on: "When one is shaken to the very depths, one finds reality in the unreal world. At present my real world is the world of my inner soul, which reflects on to the novel I write. The outer world is there to be endured, it is not real — neither the outer life."[24] The spectre that haunts the final stage of the relationship of Ursula and Skrebensky in *The Rainbow*, the possible loss of the "quick" of selfhood and the accession of an empty, mechanical mutual destructiveness is a pervasive threat in *Women in Love* (1921). As soon as we examine the use of natural setting in the latter novel, the pattern becomes clear.

There are four central clusters of natural imagery in *Women in Love*, though these are not all similar in kind. As the negative poles we have the Alpine overworld of inhuman frigidity and the swamp underworld of the muddy depths of instinct. On the positive side, there is the human-spaced enclosure of the middle distance of wood, field or water, one in which the lovers begin to re-create a paradisal space in the midst of the Darwinian flux of struggle. Finally , there is, beyond everything, what Lawrence perceives as the ultimately inhuman world of the "incomprehensible", which is Janus-faced: it is a creative mystery that can be positively apprehended, though to those simply disgusted with human corruption it stands out as an apocalyptic threat. The Alpine overworld and the swamp underworld suggest two aspects of the divided self of the modern man whom Lawrence sees as typical. Such a man, given over to merely analytical and abstract knowledge, will be at the mercy of the most destructive unconscious impulses. The overworld and the underworld are in subtle alliance: frigidity and removal breed corruption. In terms of Lawrence's pinpointing of the malaise in social terms, exploitative, divisive knowledge is linked to the destructiveness of orgiastic primitivism; the most coldly mechanistic consciousness will also be the most savage.

On the other side, the attempt to re-crate the humanly viable and spiritually resonant space in which "freedom together" is a real possibility, demands not only a disengagement from the evil social world, but a positive contact with the creative mystery which has to be found anew in the extra-human. The paradox or contradiction is only apparent: *Women in Love* strains for a humanistic vision through strategies of circumvention of the existing evil. This means getting in touch with centers of meaning presently repressed, overlooked, or simply undiscovered. The battle for selfhood grows more complicated as the milieu grows more subtly evil. Birkin and Ursula must seek to re-establish the organic connection in a society in which the very springs of action seem to be poisoned. Action *within* the society causes the person acting to be caught up in the very destructiveness he seeks to avoid. Birkin's answer is to preserve himself and those he cares about by a kind of passive resistance to the dominant death-mode. His mediation between extremes is expressed in his cultivation of that kind of passivity which is called "star-polarity", a relationship between man and woman in which exploitative reduction of the other person is abandoned in favour of "free, proud singleness". However, since star-polarity involves only the monad of the couple, a wider social base must be envisaged and Lawrence tries to suggest this in his concept of *Blutbrüderschaft*, which is a convenient term for the emotion-charged relationship of Birkin and Gerald. *Blutbrüderschaft*, absurdly inadequate though it may be in effect, has the value of disturbing the monad of the couple in favour of the re-establishment of the human relationship between man and man, in which a whole new social structure might begin to emerge.[25] Both of these relational styles, however, imply an escape from destructive orgy and the mechanical reduction of experience. The proper assimilation of the dark knowledge of the non-human world will lead to that human rebirth in the quick of the creative mystery, without which the evolutionary process will dispense with the human experience altogether. Put another way, it may be said that the novel demonstrates how man's failure to continue to make himself in terms of his total natural environment, how his failure to extend and deepen his awareness of his place in the life-process, must inevitably extinguish his claim to pre-eminence within it. Lawrence's "unreal world" is therefore only unreal in terms of a ubiquitous and brutal mechanism, while the world of his "inner soul" includes the sense of interiority, or the value of the "within" in a vision which is far from excluding the total biosphere.

The subject of *Women in Love* is therefore first of all the process of disengagement, the movement toward "freedom together" that is Birkin's goal.[26] Extricating oneself from the destructive cycle of the modern world is a very difficult feat, however, for it involves leaving behind the disease which one is manifestly afflicted by; but the second stage of the new self-realization is perhaps even more difficult. For when one has escaped into "our own nowhere", one has tempted the demons of solipsistic self-indulgence beyond measure and landed oneself in an unreal world indeed. Birkin's opinion that a "perfected relationship" could do duty for a locality seems to the casual reader perhaps a profundity of common sense, yet Lawrence's total vision declares it to be somewhat naive. Human beings cannot cut themselves off from that web of relationships in which they exist as "ultimate physical facts".

* * *

196

Birkin cannot be described merely as the good man in the bad society — his problem is slightly different, for he is the would-be organic man in the determinedly mechanistic society. His powers are strained because he is up against a whole social order which conceives of itself, more and more, in terms of the machine. And this is not merely an external fact but a temptation of his own conscious and unconscious being. Birkin is a prophet enmeshed in the evil he decries; like Hamlet, he dallies amid corruption, and, like Lear, he lends vehemence to chaos.

Nonetheless, the industrial phenomenon in *Women in Love* is more than Birkin's nightmare: it is presented as an objective evil. Its characteristic environment is created first in the walk the sisters take in the opening chapter. Theirs is a funereal landscape: with its geometrically imposed squalor, and its aboriginal tenants, it is a powerful version of the "underworld" that Wells rendered in his own way. We are shown at the same time Gudrun's attempt to repress her knowledge of it, and then led immediately to contemplate the "arctic" being of Gerald, seemingly far removed from the darkness that surrounds the wedding. Yet the association of Gerald with the "wolf totem" reminds us of his primitive, carnivorous nature; he too, has an "aboriginal" side which will be further revealed. The book will lead us through the underworld to the frozen mountains of death. The ice-destructive knowledge in the head yields inevitably the dark knowledge of the underworld, the two are linked. Western civilization may be doomed by its position athwart unintegrated sensual and abstract knowledge. As we learn much later in the "Moony" chapter, "the destructive frost mystery" is the particular fate of "the white races"; but the novel's profundity is to probe the depths of the psychical and social dynamic where extremes sometimes meet. The actual symbolic patterns are reinforced by outright discussion and argument, so that eventually we see how closely linked are the "ideal" and the real brutality of everyday life — in this respect, we might think of *Heart of Darkness*. Gerald's complicity in the underworld, his personal darkness and chaos are the inevitable concomitants of his arctic "wolf nature". Yet the "social being" and the "private self" can be split, Gerald argues. It doesn't matter what your social commitment is, your private being can remain untouched. Lawrence shows that this is self-deception. Having uncovered the hypocrisy, he carries out the famous and devastating exposure that makes up most of the chapter "The Industrial Magnate".

Gerald's father Thomas Crich is seen trying to put the idea of separateness into effect. He is destroyed by it. Gerald himself takes another line: one of cynical bravado. He gives up any pretence to Christianity and substitutes the ideology of pure mechanism for the old religion. God is dead, and the machine will become god with Gerald as its embodiment. "He found his eternal and his infinite in the pure machine-principle of perfect coordination into one pure, complex infinitely repeated motion,

197

like the spinning of a wheel; but a productive spinning, a productive repetition through eternity to infinity''.[27]

When the symmetry of the book brings in Loerke to replace Gerald, Loerke's own affiliation with the unyielding work-principle is seen as even more single-mindedly corrupt. Loerke explains at one point: "No, it is nothing but this, serving a machine, or enjoying the motion of a machine-motion, that is all. You have never worked for hunger, or you would know what god governs us". Loerke's granite frieze for the factory is described as a kind of parody *kermess*, a debased fiesta, a caricature of leisure and letting go. While Gerald *lives* in a world which tears him apart, Loerke *expresses* that world, its nothingness and innate schizophrenia. Significantly, it is he and Gudrun who hatch the vision of the evil apocalypse: the only future they can imagine is the crowning horror of a world which is a projection of their divided selves:

> As for the future, that they never mentioned except one laughed out some mocking dream of the destruction of the world by a ridiculous catastrophe of man's invention: a man invented such a perfect explosive that it blew the earth in two, and the two halves set off in different directions through space, to the dismay of the inhabitants: or else the people of the world divided into two halves, and each half decided *it* was perfect and right, the other half was wrong and must be destroyed; so another end of the world. Or else, Loerke's dream of fear, the world went cold, and snow fell everywhere, and only white creatures, Polar bears, white foxes, and men like awful white snow-birds, persisted in ice-cruelty.

(Chapter Thirty)

In a society that is based on a monumental repression, and in which the very roots of human tenderness are allowed to wither, extreme social violence is inevitable. The sense of violence in *Women in Love* is disquieting. Gerald has killed his brother and tries to kill Gudrun; Hermione "smashes" Birkin; Minette slashes the young man in the café; Diana strangles her young man fighting for life in Willey Water. These are only a few of the hostile outbreaks in a novel in which all the relationships are tinged with violence. The work-society at its most elemental is a version of the Darwinian world of brute struggle. Not that Lawrence sees all struggle as evil; like Wells, he has a sense of the creative side of physical contact — which is evident in the wrestling scene between Birkin and Gerald. Unlike Wells, however, Lawrence has also a vision of primal struggle being transformed into spiritual energy in an order radically different from the plane of Darwinian survival. While Wells exposes the thin veneer between civilization and savagery, and shows the beast lurking in the ordinary social man, Lawrence distinguishes between the healthy confrontations of human beings within a physical energy-system, and the sick aggressions of those who are driven to extremes by the failure to admit a basic physical reality. In Lawrence's view, idealism and not bestiality is at the root of destructive violence.

This is why some of the most powerful scenes in the book reveal specific aggressions against the natural in a context of mental rigidity. Gerald forces his mare to stand by the train as it roars past: such a heartless imposition of mechanism and a straining inhuman will marks the relationship of the "industrial magnate" to living things and, like Vronsky's breaking of the mare's back, Gerald's cruelty to his "mount" shows an underlying sexual tension.[28] Gudrun's dance before the cattle manifests the same rigidity and fixity of pattern, and she and Gerald are inevitably drawn together, in a pact of violence. Gudrun leads the way into the dance of death, in which sexual wooing takes on the form of a contest. Both partners are strung up to a remarkable tension. Gudrun will not be intimidated by the "domineering smile" on Gerald's face; she "strikes the first blow" and promises to strike the last, feeling "in her soul an unconquerable desire for deep violence against him". The flux of Gerald's consciousness from rigidity to chaotic release is vividly described: "It was as if some reservoir of black emotion had burst within him, and swamped him".

A satanic bargain is struck in the blood-initiation of the well-known "Rabbit" chapter.[29] The question immediately arises as to why Lawrence should combine a sense of the "daimonic" with pervasive images of aggression, as he does there and elsewhere in describing the relationship of Gerald and Gudrun and of Hermione and Birkin. Certainly, in his presentation of the "lovers" at this point as gloating spectators over the caged and frightened rabbit he transforms the naturalistically-derived image of animal energy into something far more sinister.

> The rabbit made itself into a ball in the air and lashed out, flinging itself into a bow. It really seemed demoniacal. Gudrun saw Gerald's body tighten, saw a sharp blindness come into his eyes.
> "I know these beggars of old", he said.
> The long, demon-like beast lashed out again, spread on the air as if it were flying, looking something like a dragon, then closing up again, inconceivably powerful and explosive. The man's body, strung to its efforts, vibrated strongly. Then a sudden, sharp, white-edged wrath came up in him. Swift as lightning he drew back and brought his free hand down like a hawk on the neck of the rabbit . . .

> (Chapter Eighteen)

A moment later, we find that the scream of the rabbit in the struggle "seemed to have torn the veil" of Gudrun's consciousness. She and Gerald look at each other in "mutual hellish recognition". Lawrence presents them as "implicated with each other in abhorrent mysteries". "What the devil!" Gerald exclaims, referring to the rabbit, as Gudrun shows him the "long, shallow red rip" which "seemed torn across his own brain, tearing the surface of his ultimate consciousness, letting through the for ever unconscious, unthinkable red ether of the beyond, the obscene beyond".

There is more than a touch of primitivist violence here; it is a scene dependent upon the trope of the "red rage", or the seizure of upper

consciousness by the "bestial" impulses, that we know from Naturalism. Lawrence's transformation of the image is, however, dramatic and
striking. As we know, the "quick of self" in his vision depends upon the
release of the body-consciousness; this is precisely what is impossible
however, in the constricted, rigid machine-world of the epoch of Love, in
the world of what Erich Neumann calls the "sclerotic consciousness".
Writing of the difficulties of self-transformation, Neumann makes a few
observations that are extremely relevant to Lawrence's text. He tells us
first, that "Repression by the sclerotic consciousness creates an underworld with a dangerous emotional charge, which tends to erupt, to
overpower and destroy the world of the victors; this underworld is
inhabited by the vanquished and suppressed gods, the demons and
Titans, the dragons, which form the perilous substructure of the dominant
world of the victors". Neumann goes on to explain how rigidity and
chaos form a kind of polar negative factor in relation to possibilities of
self-transformation.

> For Satan as antithesis to the primordial living world of transformation is
> rigidity — the rigidity which our conscious culture, for example, ordains so
> sternly in its hostility to transformation but at the same time he appears as its
> opposite, as chaos . . .
>   The rigid, unequivocal self-certainty — in this connection one should say
> "ego-certainty" — which eludes transformation and all creativity, includ-
> ing revelation, is a thing of the Devil . . .
>   But the other side of the Devil, the exact reverse of his rigidity, is chaos.
> We know only too well by our own example, as individuals and as a whole,
> how this "other side" of rigid consciousness looks. We engender within
> ourselves this structureless, blurred, impure amorphousness, this mass
> formlessness and aversion to form, wherever the Devil's rigidity dominates
> our consciousness and our life. The smooth, undifferentiated fixity of the
> one is inseparable from the molluscous, undifferentiated chaos of the
> other.[30]

In the "Rabbit" chapter, Lawrence's depiction of the bestiality of primitivism is comprehensive.[31] Tension resolving itself in pure struggle
catapults us from a level of stringent repression into a chaos of instinct, to
the lowest and most inhuman level of the Darwinian order. In terms of
Lawrence's value of wholeness and self-realization, the body must be
released cleanly for the spirit to emerge and point the way forward in the
human adventure. The ritual described here, however, is rather comparable to Conrad's "unspeakable rites", in that it is really part of a
distortion of the ideal motive: the activation of repressed elements that
have a purely destruction function in relation to civilization. Since
Lawrence, however, unlike Conrad, has an actual process of biological-
ly-related transformation in view, and is not making merely an ironical
commentary on the limitations of ordinary awareness, he can show the
perversions of instinct as peculiarly blasphemous. Gudrun and Gerald
allow themselves to be "possessed" by an evil caricature of Lawrence's

200

cherished life-instinct. In going from extreme to extreme they are sinners against "the Holy Ghost", and are unforgiven.

At this point it is possible to deal with Lawrence's dramatization of the "death instinct", which is so central to the novel, and which exists as the other side of the emphasis on "life" that we have noted throughout. Like Freud, and like the "aggression" ethologists, Lawrence's orientation is biological, and of course, Darwinian, but as a novelist he uses language to carry us to perspectives from which we can begin to understand struggle and aggression and even death in quite another sense than theirs.

Women in Love explores the various possibilities of death with great intensity, if not precision. It makes use of the traditional religious concept of transformation, the "dying" to the old life that marks the beginning of the new. In addition, there is the satirical reversal of our usual expectations: death can be beautiful, we learn, above all in comparison with life which has become mechanical. This is evident in the passage relating to Ursula, and elsewhere:

> But better die than live mechanically a life that is a repetition of repetitions. To die is to move on with the invisible. To die is also a joy, a joy of submitting to that which is greater than the known; namely, the pure unknown. that is a joy. But to live mechanized and cut off within the motion of the will, to live as an entity absolved from the unknown, that is shameful and ignominious.

(Chapter Fifteen)

Here the evil will is associated with a certain kind of knowing. To be a prisoner in the epoch of Love is to have lost touch with the creative motions of the "nuclear unconscious" of the body. "Life" in the epoch of Love is a living death; death, however, may be the way of re-entry to the unknown; it is something that analytical knowledge does not encompass, and so, paradoxically, may be more "alive" than the living death of mechanism. This leads us to a second consideration. "Death" is a term used to describe the impasse of mechanized being in the epoch of Love; but it is also a biological fact, and a fact of experience. The impasse of mechanized being offers only the experience of nothingness, while the experience of biological death has a *content*, which is "corruption", or "dissolution".[32] Biologically, death is "devolution", as Lawrence calls it, and, (here is the difficult part!) it leads "onward", out of the impasse of mechanized consciousness. If we choose to discount the "spiritualist" tinge of some of the passages in question, we can see the compatibility of this emphasis with the evolutionary perspective in general. Life, Lawrence insists, is not limited to human life as we know it; man may be surpassed, or improved upon. Individual biological death is the dying of one member of the human species; the death of all the members of that species as it now exists might *not* be simply the end of life's adventure in consciousness. Death is part of the process of evolution, which may cleanse itself of human imperfections and produce something quite new and striking.

201

On this point, the narrative must be read from a double perspective, precisely because Lawrence's apocalyptic vision is marked by an ironic bite, which destroys the even tenor, though not the coherence of the total poetic statement. If man forfeits the creative lead and plunges into the mechanical death-process, he will be caught up in the whole aggression-masochism pattern predicted by Freud, and will succeed in destroying the species. This will reintroduce the flux of organic life and death, but not for humanity. Birkin's satiric rage against inadequate consciousness drives him to the point of accepting the destruction of the only vehicle of higher consciousness that we know. If this is misanthropy, it is served by a grand and scientifically acceptable vision. Questions of entropy apart, eternity offers time enough for the universe to evolve novelties of conscious life. Such a perspective may be far too inhuman and invite the application of a futurism in which all moral questions dissolve. Yet nowhere does the novel acquiesce in the passing of human responsibility; rather it puts forth a savage warning about the possible issues of man's narrowness. That Romantic perversity, man's near pride in his wanton destructiveness, his conceit that his end will mean the end of the universe, is discounted. But this is not because the positive apocalyptic transformation has been lost; it is because the state of mechanical death is so vividly rendered that a monumental disgust hovers over the narrative. The possibility of further human creation is weighed in the balance against the destructive element; there is no real resolution. Either man will find a new way, or he will destroy himself, but his destruction will not be the end of life.[33] Darwinism enables Lawrence to satirize the human pretension of bringing the whole universe to a fall. Once man becomes aware of his place in the whole energy system, once he recognizes the beauty in "pure creation", he may break the impasse of sclerotic consciousness, and rejoin the flux of life and death.

In the "historical" or mythical context this means regaining the equilibrium between the two extremes represented by "snow annihilation" and the "African process". Another meaning of death is evident here, when in connection with the latter, Lawrence refers to a kind of "mystical death", in which "the relation between the senses and the outspoken mind had broken". In Lawrence's holistic grasp of being, full life means mind-body together; breaking the unity of perception is a kind of "death", in which an extreme is followed until there is an inevitable reaction against it. The African process has led to a long primitivistic sleep, in which knowledge is of one kind only, knowledge of the senses, which can only grasp disintegration and dissolution. Now, as we have just described it, such a knowledge is not an utter dead-end; it is simply one-sided, closed and repetitive, and here Lawrence comes close to the Wellsian linking of instinct and mechanism, save that his positive evaluation of the biological side causes him to stop short of characterizing the African process as simply evil. The African process is not evil, but one-sided, and backward. In so far as it is a *sensual* process, however, it is not altogether negative. The "white races", however, by which Lawrence means the industrial west, will go through a different process, though it will also be a process of "dissolution".

Lawrence's vision of the African process and of the process of "snow abstract" annihilation may be related to his myth of the two successive phases of human experience, which must be affirmed in a newly creative relation to the third epoch, that of the Holy Ghost. The primitive is repetitive and mechanical, and the abstractions of the epoch of Love lead to chaotic sterility. If, in Lawrence's terms, the African process is more positive, it is because it is closer to the organic, yet this point is never made directly. *Women in Love* is unique in its exploration of the characteristic Lawrencian phases of human possibility, because it emphasizes that side of modern life in which extremes of "intelligence" and "instinct" meet in uncreative death. The African process is not available to those caught up in the snow abstract world, and it is brought into the novel as a kind of footnote, suggesting, perhaps, the matrix of the more complex (and destructive) primitivism of the snow abstract annihilation phase of western society.

We are now in a position to understand the phenomenon of "aggression" in *Women in Love* in relation to the Freudian formulations and in terms of ethological theory, represented by Lorenz. All three perspectives are based on a biological orientation. Freud's instinctual theory of aggression demands a differentiation between the libido drive and what he ultimately termed the "death instinct".[34] The latter is the expression of the tendency of organic life to return to the inorganic. Since the self-destructive drive is directed at the tension perceived in life itself, the pleasure principle is maintained as the Freudian ideal, and the movement away from consciousness itself leads toward the ultimate peace of death. Aggression and eroticism function as part of the essentially self-destructive drive: there is a tendency to attack others who get in the way of pleasure; and, more fundamentally, a masochism in which the pleasure of self-destruction is enjoyed in non-lethal form. In *Women in Love*, as we have seen, aggression is first of all the result of a fettered life-instinct. Escape from tension is not generally a Lawrencian ideal; quite the contrary, for self-realization in the flux involves precisely awareness and tension. However, in *Women in Love*, the existence of a society which has repressed the bodily side so as to deny itself the possibility of creative tension in the flux, leads to a strategy of escape, which might be affiliated to the Freudian sense of passivity in death. Furthermore, the vision of apocalyptic destruction in the achievement of "ice destructive" knowledge amounts to a death-drive, and is definitely an attempt to move away from human consciousness, though not to the inorganic. The pattern of masochism and aggression against others visible in Birkin could be interpreted in Freudian terms as the will-to-death expressed in a form less

203

final than suicide. That this would be a distortion only becomes clear when we take into account the goal of "star-equilibrium" and recall, amid the tensions and excesses, the underlying struggle of the novel toward a viable life-center for the fulfilled human being.

The distance Lawrence has travelled from the naive formulations of classic Naturalism becomes evident when we pursue this question of instinct and aggression along the lines developed by Lorenz and other contemporary ethologists.[35] The literary tradition emphasizing Darwinian struggle in its creative aspect has now to contend with the nightmare of a society haunted by war and torn apart by aggressions springing from biological energies seemingly irrelevant in the modern context. *Women in Love* finds mere reason inadequate in the solution of the problem of destructive instinct; as we have pointed out again and again, it condemns narrow rationality as itself the perpetrator of bestial excesses. Lawrence would agree with Lorenz that "Man as a purely rational being, divested of his animal heritage of instincts, would certainly not be an angel — quite the opposite".[36] Yet the problem, as Birkin says at one point, is not "too much mind", but rather "not enough mind". Birkin's struggle is to activate an awareness that feeds upon the deepest human emotional sources, without invoking the destructive energies with which they are bound up. To do this, he must go beyond the traditional social rituals and work out the tensions of human relationships in a newly ritualized context. He must combat the narrow rationality (and bestiality) of the dominant society through a re-establishment of the physicality which has been left out of the given formulations. His is not a blind groping toward salvation in the irrational, however, but an attempt to broaden human knowledge so that the new human phenomenon of the next stage of evolution will be realized, as *The Rainbow* foretold. *Women in Love* meets the complexity of the modern situation by going beyond the presumption that a mere return to the flesh will necessarily solve anything. The epoch of Love is to be surpassed through the creation of a new equilibrium in which flesh and ideals will no longer be destructively linked. In the modern industrial world, Darwinian struggle can no longer be looked upon as a casual necessity: the work-society must break out of its tensions and seek new formulations of emotional exchange, based on a deeper grasp of human nature. Tension will be retained, but the worst forms of aggression, in the name of sanity, must be eliminated. A more complex sense of the bindings of consciousness and environment must be created, or else western society will fulfill itself in a purely destructive sense, and a post-human landscape, in which man is not even a memory, will become the next setting for life's advance.

* * *

It is now possible to go further into the connections between the inner life of the characters in this novel, especially their experience of sexuality, and the landscapes in which their lives unfold. Gerald and

Gudrun above all are affiliated with both the swamp underworld and the Alpine overworld, those sinister extremes that betoken the failure of creative balance. The establishment of the bond between them by the edge of Willey Water is marked by their mutual adherence to the muddy depths of the chaotic unconscious:

> Gudrun has waded out to a gravelly shore, and was seated like a Buddhist, staring fixedly at the water-plants that rose succulent from the mud of the low shores. What she could see was mud, soft, oozy, watery mud, and from its festering chill, water plants rose up, thick and cool and fleshy, very straight and turgid, thrusting out their leaves at right angles, and having dark lurid colours, dark green and blotches of black-purple and bronze. But she could feel their turgid fleshy structure as in a sensuous vision, she *knew* how they rose out of the mud, she *knew* how they thrust out from themselves, how they stood still and succulent against the air.

(Chapter Ten)

When Gerald appears a moment late, he seems to be Gudrun's "escape from the heavy slough of the pale, underworld, automatic colliers". His whiteness, however, is an ambiguous quality, for Gudrun is also "aware of his body, stretching and surging like a stem". In this encounter, the mental-physical rigidity of the lovers is manifest: Gudrun's perception of the plants on the intellectual plane is quite different from that expressed in the Chinese drawing, where the artist has reached a spontaneous and full knowledge of the natural being of the goose; and quite different, too, from Ursula's "unconscious" identification with the "jewel life" of the butterflies. Birkin on the island says he will mow down the "jungle of rank plants" that confronts them. He launches into a long discourse about humanity as the "Dead Sea Fruit", something which creation can do without. The swamp-fascination of Gerald and Gudrun, their participation in the rottenness of the rigid and abstract epoch of Love, is countered by Birkin's appeal to the creativity of life itself, an appeal both satirical and optimistic. It should be noted that Birkin's chief fury is directed not at the individual, who "may sometimes be capable of truth", but against the abstraction of "humanity", those who function in comfortable hypocrisy in our epoch of Love. His emphasis, one notes, is on creativity and life-direction. Man has taken a false turn, "like the ichthyosauri":

> "Do you think that creation depends upon *man*! It merely doesn't. There are the trees and the grass and the birds. I much prefer to think of the lark rising up in the morning upon a humanless world. Man is a mistake, he must go. There is the grass, and hares, and adders, and the unseen hosts, actual angels that go about freely when a dirty humanity doesn't interrupt them — and good pure-tissued demons: very nice".

(Chapter Eleven)

According to Birkin, man is "not proud enough". What is clear in his partially occult and partially Darwinian jeremiad is the disgust directed at the crawling and floundering being of those who accept the compromise of divided selfhood.

Later, at the water party, when Gerald dives to attempt to rescue his sister, he feels the cold horror of the underworld he will soon morally drown in: "But it's curious how much room there seems, a whole universe under there; and as cold as hell, you're helpless as if your head was cut off". Gerald has decapitated himself by too much of the wrong kind of mind; he becomes the victim of the most sinister kind of "no mind". As for Gudrun, "she was suspended upon the surface of the insidious reality until such time as she also should disappear beneath it". The lovers descend into an orgy of pure sensationalism. They combine mental coldness with a deep self-indulgence in chaotic sexuality, a sexuality which is purely exploitative, and which represents aggression on a personal level deriving from frustration. This sexuality is inextricably bound to that mechanical death they have everywhere embraced. We have already observed how their aggression against the natural order demonstrates the unfixed relation between spontaneous feeling and imposed will that is their characteristic failing. Unable to function naturally in a context of physical relatedness, they must whip themselves up mentally to feel anything at all. In their case the Freudian relation between masochism and aggression applies: they struggle to escape the life-tensions that have become unbearable, thus hastening the negative apocalypse that will mark the end of man before it marks the beginning of anything else. Their relationship becomes the text of Birkin's sermon of despair, from which he draws what to some may be the scant consolations of biological fecundity.

After the evil pact of the "Rabbit" chapter, we see Gerald and Gudrun driven relentlessly toward the release which is merely the final explosion of all their tensions. If their ultimate death-struggle takes place in the white Tyrolean fastness, the point of entry is through yet another version of the underworld. Lawrence describes Ursula's arrival on the continent at Ostend: "Strange and desolate above all things, like disembarking from the Styx into the desolated underworld, was this landing at night... It was all so strange, so extremely desolate, like the underworld, grey, grey, dirt grey, desolate, forlorn, nowhere — grey, dreary nowhere". It is Gerald and Gudrun, however, who are propelled in spirit from the underworld to the snowy height, passing from one ecstasy to the other in a process of negative fulfillment which Lawrence enables us fully to grasp.

The snow that Ursula sees as unnatural fascinates Gudrun. She stares at it in a kind of pained rapture, while Gerald, "icy vapour round his heart", sees "the blind valley, the great cul-de-sac of snow and mountain peaks under the heavens". He realizes that there is "no way out. The terrible silence and cold and glamourous whiteness of the dusk wrapped him round, and she remained crouching before the window, as at a shrine, a shadow". The whole final struggle is to be played out in the blank space of the mountains, which with singular appropriateness, represents no free space in which the spirit can soar, but rather a claustrophobic mirror-version of the enclosing underworld: "In front was a valley shut in under the sky", Lawrence writes, "the last huge slopes of snow and black rock, and at the end, like the navel of the earth, a white-folded wall, and two peaks glimmering in the late night . . . This was the centre, the knot, the navel of the world, where the earth belonged to the skies, pure, unapproachable, impassable".

The late stages of the relationship of Gerald and Gudrun are marked by unbridled aggression and their final encounter is marked by sexual conflict and by a rhythm of violence building to a climax authentic but failing in satisfaction: "The struggling was her reciprocal lustful passion in the embrace, the more violent it became, the greater the frenzy of delight, till the zenith was reached, the struggle was overborne, her movements became softer, appeased". Gerald wanders away, realizing that he does not "care enough" about Gudrun "to kill her". In a final nausea, seeking the peace of non-existence, he is obsessed by a fantasy that he is about to be "murdered". The "half-buried" crucifix reminds us of the hidden roots of the epoch of Love, of the heritage of the elder Crich and his failure, and of the descending line of Gerald's desperation after the old man's death. The crucifixion of the body by the mechanical will is complete; the masochistic-aggressive pattern is fulfilled under the "unremitting" moon that is not locked in to the sensual earth-power, but rather serves as a kind of lamp of final consciousness on the ultimately "barren" tragedy, played out in the blank whiteness of the snow. At the end, is complete dehumanization, the "frozen carcass of a dead male" beneath the still unclimbed peaks of the mountain.

* * *

Birkin's relationship with Hermione leads him close to the "ice-destructive" knowledge of modern life, which he combats by a devotion to self-transformation that circumvents abstraction and chaotic sensuality. In the classroom, Hermione's gloating wilfulness is exposed, and Birkin announces the necessity of "lapsing out", of activating the "dark involuntary being", which is "death to one's self" but "the coming into being of another". Hermione's charge of "satanism" Birkin meets with a retort that is worth remembering in connection with the "daimonic" play of Gerald and Gudrun that we have already examined: "You are the real devil who won't let life exist". It is the "knowledge of things concluded" that Birkin sees as limited, and which he overrides in favour of the fuller knowledge of the Chinese drawing of the geese: "I know what centers they live from — what they perceive and feel — the hot stinging centrality of a goose in flux of cold water and mud — the curious bitter stinging heat of a goose's blood, entering their own blood like an inoculation of corruptive fire — the fire of cold-burning mud — the lotus mystery". This is not exactly mysticism, but a testimony to the organic knowledge of the whole texture of an experience that comes about through the awakening of the body; it is in specific contrast to the divisive knowledge of the epoch of Love, and derives from the yoga-istic side of eastern wisdom, which Lawrence took for granted, despite his dislike of the eastern "systems".

Hermione's explosion of violence against Birkin, described in the witty terms of a parody of sexual encounter, shows her to be part of the negative process of tension-aggresion we have seen in Gerald, and reveals the actual evil that between this couple is mostly subdued into verbal exchange. Birkin's effort is to avoid the final battle to the death with Hermione, to disengage himself from her with a minimum of damage to his own impulses. We learn at one point that "he would never, never dare to break her will, and let loose the maelstrom of her sub-consciousness, and see her in her ultimate madness". After being "smashed" by Hermione at Breadalby, then, Birkin retreats into the vegetation, there to play out the masochistic sequence in a relatively controlled way. Birkin's ritualized immersion in the vegetation suggests a number of meanings that spring from its ambiguous display of subtly mixed elements of both pleasure and pain. His flight is first of all a way of escaping his fatal embroilment with Hermione; instead of being driven to a retaliation against her, which would further enmesh him in the destructive pattern, he allows his tensions to be "conducted" away into an immediate physical experience that is impersonal. The vegetation is in definite contrast to "the old ethic", to the mentally rigid world of abstract fulfillment. If Birkin's enjoyment of its punishing qualities is in one sense due to the frustration of the libido drive in the relationship with Hermione, however, such "masochism" is not simply an expression of the Freudian will-to-death, or the pleasure of self-destruction expressed in a non-lethal form. The masochism here is in fact part of a creative disengagement from the unfeeling human distortions of the epoch of Love: it is associated with the awakening of the physical energies of the body in nature, which such people as Hermione cannot sanction. What Birkin enjoys is not really self-injury linked to a drive toward extinction, but a sharpening of physical awareness through moderate aggression against the body, and the ritual release of social guilt in a natural setting. Birkin punishes himself not by perpetuating the death cycle with Hermione, but so as to stimulate a new sense of life that can later emerge in a more human context. His agony, however, is to begin to feel the authenticity of his physical being from the center of an extreme state of isolation and pain, so that he half doubts the validity of his own perceptions, and accuses himself of being "mad". The scene may be said to function as an anticipation of the later "paradisal excurse" with Ursula, in that it presents an alternative to "orgiastic" and destructive sensuality, and thus to mechanism, through the awakening of the body in a natural environment, the reality of which has been violated in the existing social order.

In Birkin's complex relationship with Gerald, it is worth noting to what extent a similar pattern prevails: how the tension of conflict which threatens to draw Birkin into a destructive reciprocity with his doomed friend is eased. Once again, the exchanges are mostly verbal, until the actual physical encounter of the "gladiatorial" scene brings the situation into fresh perspective. The wrestling actualizes the contact that is otherwise taboo, and serves to break the bind of mental consciousness; it projects the men onto a new plane of communication, and functions as a ritual release of their pent-up aggressions. Critical studies making interpretations of the novel with homosexual behavioural models in view can only distort Lawrence's cultural focus.[37] The corruptive grip of mechanism on heterosexual marriage (visible in both central relationships in *Women in Love*) can be cured only by a relaxation of the whole person in all his relationships. Lawrence concentrates on the male predicament, not only for personal reasons, but because of his concern with the healthiness of work, which must be carried beyond the Darwinian or Social Darwinian level of struggle, toward a level of creative self-development. In his eyes men, (and not women) are still the central working members of society. Gerald, as is clear from the "Man to Man" chapter and elsewhere, is unable to break out of his social role and to relate to Birkin directly on the human and physical level. In the wrestling episode they strip in order to "fight" and get a "mutual physical understanding". Gerald, no longer like a "machine that is without any power", comes alive in a struggle which makes both him and Birkin more "whole".

Biological reality is recognized in this ritual combat which is similar to the fights of animals, ethologically perceived, precedence being established without the ultimate death-struggle. Birkin senses a physical rhythm in which his body and spirit are separated, and then reunited so that an instant of intimacy and recognition between him and Gerald grows out of an inadvertent touch. The frustration of impulse in a false social order is mitigated by the release of energy in a non-destructive form; the "love" that Birkin feels for Gerald, the concrete and specific act of emotional commitment that he consistently makes, and which lifts their relationship out of the sphere of material necessity, is finally expressible beyond the boundaries of narrow convention. Lawrence's descriptions of parody orgasms exposing the failure of real satisfaction in the epoch of Love are parallelled here by a description of symbolic sexual fulfillment: Birkin wrestles for Gerald's soul, that it should be released in the body to make that whole man which the industrial magnate can never be. The taint of *outré* futility which in general mars Lawrence's concept of *Blutbrüderschaft* is overborne in the poetic truth of this transformed image of Darwinian struggle, in which the innate quality of "mastery" is revealed in Birkin as inextriably bound up with his power to free Gerald from the cycle of death. The social distance that reappears with the resumption of conventional roles in the conversation immediately fol-

lowing the combat is not unbridgeable; there is a warmer understanding
between the two men, though this is not strong enough to carry Gerald
through the trauma of his father's death. Birkin's central commitment to
Ursula, his struggle for his own survival as an integral being, leaves him
unable to woo his friend's potential beyond this point. yet despite its
ambiguities and hedged-in quality, this encounter between the two men
functions as an alternative ritual in the flesh to the sterile routines of the
industrial world, and, unlike the "daimonic" pact of Gerald and Gudrun,
it does not answer rigidity with the chaos of primordial instinct.

It is above all the actual physical brightness and spiritual potential of
Ursula herself, however, that enables Birkin to carry out his campaign of
disengagement from the "ice destructive" world of Love. Ursula's
spontaneity is emphasized throughout: in the first description of her look
of "sensitive expectancy"; in the vision of her life as a "shoot that is
growing steadily, but which has not yet come out of the ground"; in the
unconscious identification, already mentioned, with the "jewel life" of
the butterflies beside the pond; and in the final remarkable contrast with
Gudrun's fixed destructiveness in the Alpine scenes. Of all the characters
Ursula has the easiest and most intimate connection with living things. It
is she who protests most directly against Gerald's treatment of the horse,
arguing with him that the mare "has as much right to her own being, as
you have to yours". Birkin asserts the principle of resignation of the will
to the "higher" life, and mocks what he sees as her sentimentality and
rebelliousness, until she defiantly asserts that she is "a bolter" among
"mares". The misunderstanding is partially resolved in the "Mino"
chapter that follows, when Birkin explains that the "will" he has in view
is not the *Wille zur Macht* but the tension of equilibrium between two
beings that can fuse each into creative rapport with the other. Later,
Birkin's fixation on the "dark river of dissolution", which we have seen
as part of his rather ambiguous organic argument against the mechanical
death-stream, is met by Ursula's anxious life-assertion; refusing to be a
"flower of corruption", she insists that she is "a rose of happiness".

At last, in the "Moony" chapter, a ritual encounter takes them both
utterly beyond "the dumb show" of words to where the "gesture in the
blood" can be felt directly.[38] Ursula, her spontaneity dampened, is
described as cut off from any human relation. Bound more deeply than
ever by the coils of "nothingness" that surround her, she is still alive to
the "magical" world of the animals, but clings with grim purpose to the
example of their "singleness of being" and unsociability, and not to the
magic of their physical life. In a mood of destruction, she sets off to
Willey Water, disturbed by the "white and deathly smile" of the risen
moon. There, Birkin engages in a furiously intent "game" of stone-
throwing at the image of the moon in the pond, until Ursula feels
"dazed" and "spilled out", like "water on the earth". The moon in the
water is of course only a semblance, an image of the cold heights

suspended over the murky depths, and described in terms that evoke a hard brilliance that is completely inhuman. Birkin's assault on this semblance is a ritual destruction of the evil conjunction of the polarities of the cold, abstract head-knowledge and the murky sensual knowledge of the epoch of Love. His action breaks up the imposed pattern and re-establishes for a moment the creative flux, transforming the rigid lines of the reflected moon into images of fire and rose petals. The moon that Birkin seeks to smash represents the feminine demand for a kind of ghastly "love", inevitable in the context of that "ice-destructive" knowledge created by modern man. Birkin's gesture of stone-throwing is in one sense futile, for he cannot by himself prevent the image of the moon from reassembling itself; he cannot by himself destroy the evil conjunction of elements that characterizes the modern world. yet his action may be taken as another form of ritualized aggression, by which violent energy is released in a form that can bring the individual to a new and fruitful inner realization. The transformation here is wordless, but of great significance, for at the conclusion Ursula feels herself no longer bound up with the deathly moon, but flowing creatively like the water which spills onto the earth and starts the shoots of life in motion.

Thus, the dead flower-husks Birkin throws upon the pond at the beginning may signify a rejection of Ursula's old self, and of the terms of their previous relationship, with its incompatible commitments to "life" and "charity". The issue is not settled at Willey Water, because the positive power of transformation has not yet come into view, and the lovers remain unconnected, suspicious, and in a phase of confused exhaustion, while the modern world stands complacently in its power of mechanical momentum. Birkin, however, now proposes more concretely than ever, "another way", the "paradisal way" that involves spontaneity, objectivity, and "free proud singleness". This is an alternative that demands a "spiritual" purpose that will not evoke the "ice-destructive" knowledge of the northern cycle, and which calls for a physical relationship, but not the "Dionysic ecstatic" one that is "like going round in a squirrel cage". While Birkin here at last takes concrete action ("They must marry at once, and so make a definite pledge, enter into a definite communion"), Ursula is resistant. Following upon a comic interlude describing Birkin's "proposal", Lawrence shows her turning away to her own singleness, and welcoming Gudruns's highly critical analysis of Birkin's domineering manner. Two experiences, however, cause a softening of this attitude. First, Ursula has a vision of some yellow-hammers ("so uncanny and inhuman, like flaring yellow barbs shooting through the air on some weird, living errand") that enables her to throw off the influence of Gudrun's "anthropomorphic" caricature of a robin as "a little Lloyd George of the air". Ursula concludes that: "Rupert is quite right, human beings are boring, painting the universe with their own image. The universe is non-human, thank God". Thus, although she still

211

insists that love is "everything", Ursula has taken a large step toward accepting Birkin's view of the priority of the "life-quick". She has "seen around" the abstract conventional patterning of reality, and has suddenly grasped a wider dimension: the physical energy-system which must serve as a reference point for human values, if cultural schizophrenia is to be avoided. Ursula, without being fully aware of it, has been prepared for the experience of a love that returns to the source, for the awakening of the "dark body" which feels itself part of the "living quick" of the whole natural world.

The chapter "Excurse", which is in many ways the thematic center of *Women in Love*, is written in a disappointingly laboured fashion, which does little to clarify Lawrence's vision of positive self-transformation.[39] Because the intensity of the novel is in general so sustained, this failure leaves us perilously close to bathos. yet there is, even here, success enough to enable the reader to appreciate the implications of Birkin's paradisal strategy, provided he has understood the symbolic contrasts between "nature" and "mechanism" that appear throughout.

Another scene of combat precedes the reconciliation in the star-polarity that Birkin has been advocating verbally almost from the first. What seems mere jealousy of Hermione turns out to be Ursula's perception of and protest against the strangeness of Birkin's demands. She throws away the rings in a fury of reaction against his spiritual "depravity" and mocks his "pleasure in self-destruction", yet later returns bringing a flower, her aggressions spent in physical motion. She has expressed her naturalness, after all, and found beyond words another token "of the reality of beauty, the reality of happiness in warm creation". They drive to tea, and a contrast is built up between their state of being, with its new physical awareness, and the world of Love, represented by Southwell Cathedral, "like dim bygone centuries sounding". Ursula finds that "the world had become unreal. She herself was a strange, transcendent reality". A series of passages follows in which the imagery shifts radically, and in too random a fashion, evoking Biblical, natural and scientific comparisons to describe the transformed awareness of the lovers. The emphasis is on Ursula's exploration of what in yogaistic terms would be Birkin's "lumbar ganglion" and "sacral ganglion" regions of "primal consciousness"; in previous encounters it was Ursula and not Birkin who shied away from such love, and here we witness her reciprocity of commitment. Lawrence strains to render the exact tone of a single experience. comprising religious awe, organic wholeness, plenitude of being, accession to the more-than-human, activation of a new physical knowledge and energy, and intouchness with the ultimate life-source.[40] All of this, "before the taking of a toast and tea", may be summed up as a "spiritual" euphoria accompanying a break with the tension and combatativeness characteristic of modern life; such euphoria is possible because the tightly circumscribed limits of mental consciousness have been obliterated through a gentle communion of touch. Both lovers participate in a widening of consciousness, which Lawrence attempts to convey through various metaphors of transformation-toward-increase: awakening, being born, being overwhelmed, opening, flowing, releasing, flooding, and so on. These mark the realization of the "lotus-mystery" of the Chinese drawing, and of the "Egyptian" knowledge of the epoch of the Flesh; the "deepest physical mind" is brought into play against the knotted consciousness of modern life, and the way is prepared for the final exchange of "star-equilibrium" in the forest.

This "ultimate marriage", described at the beginning as "some one *really* pure single activity", is defined further throughout the novel, and finally by Ursula in the Tyrol when she says that she believes in "something inhuman, of which love is only a part". Unlike certain other passionate exchanges between Birkin and Ursula described by Lawrence, the one in Sherwood Forest finds the lovers fulfilled in "this star-equilibrium which alone is freedom". The awakening of the "dark body" occurs in an enclosed natural setting, in the paradisal space of the woods, where the theme of non-exploitative, balanced sexuality adumbrated in the afternoon wooing scene is continued. What occurs is best understood in terms of the well-known exposition of "passive" sexuality given by Alan Watts in his book *Nature, Man and Woman*.[41] Sexuality may be thought of as the most intimate trans-personal act of the human being, to whom the other, the lover, is nature, that is, part of the living world. This view in its ramifications is rather alien to traditional Christianity, with its radical division between nature and spirit, and difficult to credit in a mechanistic age, in which exploitative appropriation colours the human attitude to sexuality, the other person being a vehicle of release of tension rather than a revelation of the power of relaxation-in-a-totality. The problem comes back to the adherence to abstract consciousness, to the repression of feeling, and its subsequent release in aggressiveness and forced pleasure. In "star-equilibrium", however, Lawrence creates a symbolic non-exploitative sexuality, one dominated by a "singleness" which becomes overwhelmingly a new kind of total union. The bliss of aimlessness succeeds brutal aggression, and the schizophrenic consciousness is grounded again in the primal body of pleasure. Peace and leisure and a contemplative awareness mark an experience in which the contours of the world too sharply defined by the mental consciousness, dissolve. Lawrence's restoration of sacrality to the sexual act makes for a further link with systems such as Tantric yoga, for both the Lawrencian vision and that of this particular eastern system originate from an attention to physicality and a charting of the feelings in relation to specific body-centers. In addition, both make use of the concept of the union of opposites, and suggest the playing-out of ritual sexuality within a circumscribed space. Far from confusing sacred and profane modes, Lawrence is answering the bankruptcy of the dissociated

sensibility of western society with a reformulation of the sacred within
the profane, describing possibilities of restoration of existential wholeness through a renewed sense of being-in-nature lost in the epoch of
Love.[42] Alan Watts, though not referring specifically to Lawrence, sums
up the Lawrencian view when he writes that "sexuality is a special mode
or degree of total intercourse between man and nature. Its delight is an
intimation of the ordinarily repressed delight which inheres in life itself,
in our fundamental but normally unrealized identity with the world".
Watts concludes:

> The height of sexual love, coming upon us of itself, is one of the most total
> experiences of relationship to the other of which we are capable, but
> prejudice and insensitivity have prevented us from seeing that in any other
> circumstances such delight would be called mystical ecstacy. For what
> lovers feel for each other in this moment is no other than adoration in its full
> religious sense, and its climax is almost literally the pouring of their lives
> into each other. Such adoration, which is due only to God, would indeed be
> idolatrous were it not that in that moment love takes away illusion and shows
> the beloved for what he or she in truth is — not the socially pretended person
> but the naturally divine.[43]

Birkin and Ursula, achieving "star-polarity", break the circuit of
aggression and restore the power of the libido to create, not the unconsciousness of escapism, but the texture of a wider knowledge. They pass
out of the Darwinian sphere of struggle into the temporary, but essentially
valuable, paradisal sphere of cooperation and mutual interdependency.
Lawrence's language carries us beyond the "physical" obsessions of
Naturalism, without denying the physical. The body is manifestly present
and active, but no longer perceived as an instrument of willfulness or
divisive consciousness; it is the center of a field of delight in which the
biological energies are released so as to create a world whose significance
is known directly. To Lawrence, the "dark body" is the body aware of
itself as an outflowing of the "protoplasmic" energy of life; it is the body
as realized self, as unified consciousness alert as well to the inflowing
sources of energy: in short, the body as terminus of a set of signals from
the whole biospheric mass, and as "translator" of those signals into a
further life, one that is "directed" and not merely an automatic movement. Birkin and Ursula at last get beyond the viciously narrowed sense
of love present in the predominant society, and recognize that human
connectedness with the environment which must be cherished if man is to
remain "the expression of the incomprehensible". That "something
inhuman" which the perverse vision of a humanity striking at its own
vital sources turns into an image of fear can also be an image of cosmic
magnificence. In the paradisal space in which integration with the other is
part of an integration with nature itself, in the feeling-centered bliss of
passivity and acceptance, lies the answer to the threat of the ice-
destructive world hatched by perverse consciousness. Through the positive visionary transformation that originates in the body, Birkin and

Ursula set up a counter-world to the predominant, mechanized society. In doing so they re-introduce the potential of space as plenitude and make a start toward banishing the spectre of the negative apocalypse, in which man would disappear after forfeiting the creative lead to other forms. Lawrence's paradisal enclosure involves no evasion of the Darwinian world of struggle or pain; it suggests, however, the one-sidedness of pure materialism, and dramatizes the significance of leisure, passivity, and of the biological pause in which vision can begin to function. Birkin and Ursula have recovered a human scale and a human sense of values in a world dominated by vastnesses of negation. They have not "retreated" into a never-never land of private sensibility, but have found the way back to the abiding reality of the life-quick which is more than human, but can only be realized *by man* when he is being honest to his own physical nature. The paradisal enclosure in *Women in Love* restores the "ultimate physical facts" and through these man's connection with the "creative mystery". Ursula's feeling that "the universe is non-human, thank God", may be taken therefore as a rejection of the mechanized society, as a tribute to the majesty of the total system in which man must adapt or die, and as an anticipation of the objective quality of the experience that Birkin claims must be a "third thing" between two subjectivities. Yet life unfolds; there can be no standing still: the evolutionary point-of-view of *The Rainbow* is by no means abandoned. Birkin and Ursula do not "lapse out" of responsibility and knowledge, they reach an achieved equilibrium; this is the peace of balance, not of obliteration. Their paradisal experience reminds them of the splendour of life forgotten in the routine of everyday existence. Without escaping the flux of change, they can see beyond it, toward the unfolding of a new "adventure of consciousness" in the human future.

They cannot, however, re-enter the working world of the epoch of Love, for this would be to forfeit once and for all the power of contemplation won by their commitment to the spontaneous flowering of their physical selves. Taking tea at the inn, they agree to seek out a place where they can be "free". But of course such a place does not as yet exist. It must be created in a "perfected relation between you and me, and others"; a mere seeking out of some locality is pointless. The epoch of Love must be transformed by positive apocalypse, by a reconciliation in the flesh, which brings man back into touch with the creative energies of the living world in which he has bodily form and existence. It would be a distortion to over-emphasize either the inner or the outer thrusts of the necessary revolution, for the significance of Lawrence's art is that it forces upon us the sense of man's complexity, and of the inter-relatedness of those aspects of himself that he arbitrarily divides into "physical", "mental", "spiritual", and so on. For Birkin and Ursula to live in true humanity, a new environment must be created, one that allows man to express his visionary ardour without the crushing of his deepest animal nature, and outside of the binds of a falsifying socialization. This means newly ritualized experience in a newly perceived physical nature, and the destruction of both the evil compulsions and the ugly environment of the existing world of Love.

4. Lawrence, Science and "The New Human Phenomenon"

Lawrence's overriding sense of the physical world demands that the human body itself be central to the evocation of "higher" values; in fact, the body is for Lawrence the anchoring point of the "unconscious". Lawrence struggles hard against the dualistic separation of spirit and nature. Nothing in Lawrence's "pollyanalytics" has been so misunderstood as this, however, possibly because of his expression of this aspect of his thought, which falls back on references to yoga and to the "blood consciousness".[44] Yet when one looks with a firm eye at what Lawrence means by the blood consciousness, and when one looks into his use of the yoga-istic chakras, one finds very little that is alarming. To Lawrence, the unconscious "is never an abstraction, *never to be abstracted*. It is never an ideal entity, It is always concrete".[45] The true unconscious Lawrence identifies with the body, and he suggests that *direct* experience is the first form of knowing. " . . . We realize that the unconscious contains nothing ideal, nothing in the least conceptual", he writes in *Psychoanalysis and the Unconscious* (1921) and goes on to affirm that "this is our answer to materialism and idealism alike. The *nuclear unconscious* brought forth organs and consciousness alike. And the great nuclei of the unconscious *still* lie active in the great living nerve centers, which nerve centers, from the original solar plexus to the conclusive brain form one great chain of dual polarity and amplified consciousness".[46]

Lawrence affirms a region of "perfect primary cognition". We know first of all through our whole experience of being what we are: our living, as-yet-unanalyzed first experience as bodies in space. If this Lawrencian concept seems *outré* and difficult, it is perhaps only a measure of how hard it is for us to break out of our conventional preconceptions. If we think for a moment of ourselves not thinking, if we conjure up a moment of real experience and real knowledge, one in which the whole texture of reality surprises us before we begin to capture it in our conceptual and verbal nets, we shall perhaps come close to what Lawrence refers to.[47]

And, as Lawrence made clear in his 1919 "Introduction to These Paintings", such real experience and whole knowledge underlies the creative efforts of both the artist and the scientist:

Any creative act occupies the whole consciousness of man. This is true of the great discoveries of science as well as art. The truly great discoveries of science and real works of art are made by the whole consciousness of man working together in unison and oneness: instinct, intuition, mind, intellect, all fused into complete consciousness, and grasping what we may call a

216

complete truth, or a complete vision, or a complete revelation in sound. A discovery, artistic or otherwise, may be more or less intuitional, more or less mental, but intuition will have entered into it, and mind will have entered too. The whole consciousness is concerned in every case.[48]

In this essay Lawrence was taking for granted the modern definitions of science, and relating them to his own conception of creativity, a procedure which brings him remarkably close to the most advanced theory of scientific imagination of our own time.[49] Lawrence worked out in his own terms a criticism of the post-Renaissance determination to stand at all costs outside of the phenomenon; yet when he came to think more deeply about the question of thinking itself, he could begin to see that science at its elemental and formulative level could incorporate a *physical* grasp of reality that gave it its authenticity and cohesion. When science tells us that water is "H_2O" we rebel, he asserted, because such a formula does not "occupy" the whole consciousness.[50] It is more correct to say that water under certain circumstances produces two volumes of hydrogen and one of oxygen — with this we find ourselves in agreement, because we have not been asked to sacrifice the *experience* of the entity "water" in the name of a mental abstraction. Apprehending the phenomenon water involves more than playing with its qualities carried off to a high degree of abstraction; and Lawrence assumed, with some degree of truth, that even scientific creation could not dispense with the "concreteness" that the artist always took for granted.

Lawrence's supposed hatred of science resolves itself really into a question about the importance of substantiality. Even that technology which arouses Lawrence's most ferocious denunciations is criticized above all because it is so often destructive of the knowledge which is immediate, physical and personal. The scientific image of the universe is too often a projection of only one aspect of human knowledge, a confession of man's limited self-formulation.[51] It is destructive of the human sense of being a part of the whole, terrifying in its invocation of mere abstractions. In "The Crown" Lawrence explains that "these 'laws' which science has invented . . . they are all prison walls, unless we realize that we don't know what they mean".[52] Since we can't *experience* such laws, they fail to convey the mysteries they point to. In "Dragon of the Apocalypse" (1930) Lawrence directly confronts Teilhard's "malady of space-time".

I have read books of astronomy which made me dizzy with the sense of illimitable space. But the heart melts and dies — it is the disembodied mind alone which follows on through this horrible void of space, where lonely stars hang in awful isolation. And this is not a release. It is a strange thing, but when science extends space ad infinitum, and we get the terrible sense of limitlessness, we have at the same time a secret sense of imprisonment. Three dimensional space is homogenous, and no matter how big it is, it is a kind of prison . . .

In astronomical space, one can only *move*, one cannot be.[53]

217

The point is that "when we describe the moon as dead, we are describing the deadness in ourselves. When we find space so hideously void, we are describing our own unbearable emptiness". The "male" principle of the epoch of Love is to blame,

> Which conception reached its fullest in Turner's pictures which were utterly bodiless; and also in the great scientists or thinkers of the last generation, even Darwin, Spencer, and Huxley. For these last conceived of evolution, of one spirit or principle starting at the far end of time, lonelily traversing time. But there is not one principle, there are two, travelling always to meet, each step of each one lessening the distance between the two of them. And Space, which so frightened Herbert Spencer, is as a Bride to us. And the cry of man does not ring out in the Void. It rings out to Woman, whom we know not.[54]

Lawrence wants man to "be alive", "with a goal in the *creative*, not the *spatial* universe". This requires the flesh-knowledge which art cannot dispense with and science disregards at its peril. In the apocalyptic act of the artist, flesh and spirit are one. Lawrence argues that literature has the power to organize outer reality in terms of its own mode of speech. Becoming the word in the process, it disputes the "single principled" view of extreme science, and goes beyond the order of abstraction. Space and time can be filled up with the real being, the substance of art, which depends upon man's power to know in a primal way, through the body. The physical unconscious, in touch with the magnificence of the living world, will create those new symbols which will enable us "intuitively and instinctively" to feel the truth of the laws which science announces from on high.

And perhaps Lawrence bridged the gap implied in such a "separatist" formulation in even more direct terms. I return to the question of the substantiality of art, as taken up in "Introduction to These Paintings". Here, Lawrence credits Cezanne with rediscovering reality in a very specific sense.

> . . . Cezanne's apples are a real attempt to let the apple exist in its own separate entity, without transfusing it with personal emotion. Cezanne's great effort was, as it were, to shove the apple away from him, and to let it live of itself. It seems a small thing to do: yet it is the first real sign that man has made for several thousands of years that he is willing to admit that matter *actually* exists.[55]

The reader who is distracted by Lawrence's apparent reversal of the standard art-history interpretation of Cezanne is missing the more important point — Lawrence's reversal of the post-Romantic primacy of the "abstract self", his opening up of a common world of substantial being which the mythopoesis of art and the abstracting power of science may both take account of. " . . . We realize finally", he writes, "that matter is only a form of energy, whatever that may be, in the same instant matter rises up and hits us over the head and makes us realize that it exists absolutely, since it is compact energy itself".[56] Before one throws down the charge of "scientism" to Lawrence's appropriation of the abstraction

218

"matter", Lawrence himself intervenes to make clear the "contact point" of inner experience with outer nature, and reminds us that artistic knowing is an affirmation that "there is no invisible mind to be related to a visible reality . . . for thought is of the same kind as flesh". Lawrence's terms suggest that every successful act of creation is a testimony to the inextricable unity of body and mind within a process extending beyond the individual. And something of the same affirmation seems to lie at the heart of the "realism" of certain projections of scientific thinking, which is now described as the discernment of "gestalten that are aspects of reality", something that presumably involves a much more physically committed perception than is available to the "mental consciousness" in isolation. And as to "matter" itself — it is precisely the great opportunity of the writer to make such an orphaned word *mean something* in terms of the way in which it "rises up and hits us over the head". It is the plain duty of the writer to break out of the convenient thought-forms and to perceive with the freshness of Cezanne, in his own measure, to break the optical cliché. When the writer learns how to render matter as palpable, sensible, and natural, he will not be giving the lie to science, but only rendering an account of reality in terms that remain closer to the body's primal grasp of the situation than is commonly useful in scientific communication.

In the "Study of Hardy" (written 1914) Lawrence praises Boccioni for "trying to state the timeless abstract being of a bottle", but damns him for attempting to represent simple motion, for trying to give expression to the bottle in terms of the laws of mechanics.[57] Here too, Lawrence's concern seems to be for a kind of objectivity. The "timeless abstract being" of the bottle, in view of the appended qualifications, seems to suggest a concretely realizable bottle, not a Platonic form, but a reality that can be captured in its essence, though only by a total engagement on the part of the artist. Lawrence's bottle, if not Boccioni's, belongs in the "real world" that is eminently *graspable* by both science and art.

This point may be supported by the testimony of the famous letter to Edward Garnett, usually taken as one of the central statements of the Lawrencian aesthetic.

> Somehow that which is physic — non-human in humanity, is more interest-ing to me than the old-fashioned human element, which causes one to conceive a character in a certain moral scheme and make him consistent. The certain moral scheme is what I object to . . . When Marinetti writes "It is the solidity of a blade of steel that is interesting by itself, that is, the incomprehending and inhuman alliance of its molecules in resistance to let us say a bullet. The heat of a piece of wood or iron is in fact more passionate for us than the laughter or tears of a woman —" then I know what he means.
>
> He is stupid as an artist, for contrasting the heat of the iron and the laugh of the woman. *Because what is interesting in the laugh of the woman is the same as the binding of the molecules of steel or their action in heat*: it is the inhuman will, call it physiology, or like Marinetti, physiology of matter, that fascinates me.[58]

Just as there are allotropic states in elements, that is, different physical properties of the same element in various compounds (two kinds of sulphur in different compounds, still sulphur); or using Lawrence's example, just as the element carbon underlies the very different surface fact of diamond or coal, so in human beings there is "another ego" (the unconscious or the more primal self), which is *consciousness expressing itself through matter in the shape of the body*. Lawrence's aesthetic metaphor compels this reading. "Ego" implies a conscious center — "another ego", a conscious center related "allotropically" to the consciousness of this or that individual person. In terms of the "physiology of matter" this could only be the knowing body, or consciousness in matter, delimited as the person. Lawrence has found the perfect metaphor to express what seems to be a "process" conception of the knowing body-mind. The "inhuman will" sounds frightening, but Lawrence is probably thinking of some cohesive force at the root of solid matter as underlying also the woman's laugh — in distinction to some relatively superficial social cause. To describe the "carbon level" is to describe the individual mind-body at the point where it is most free of its social colouring. In the same letter to Garnett he speaks of looking for the "new human phenomenon" — this means charting the deepest interiority of the individual human self where it is closest to natural energies. Lawrence, like his own later hero, Cezanne, realizes that "matter exists" and goes about rendering it at the point at which it can be seen "infolding upon itself", to borrow a Teilhardian phrase. Lawrence is determined to escape from the disabilities of Romantic dualism, with its "spiritualized" unconscious. The Darwinian universe offers him the great challenge and opportunity of describing man in terms of a coherent environment which is not merely a projection of the mind. He ends up by finding terms to describe a configuration of psychic energy at bottom related to physical energy, but of more importance to him as an artist, because it cuts more deeply into reality as perceived by the whole man. Thus it can quite justifiably be said to be "the new human phenomenon" that Lawrence describes. In other terms, we can credit Lawrence, in his most original moments, with uniting the dynamic unconscious as discovered by the Romantics and by psychoanalysis, with the very real world that science forces upon our attention, the world we grasp as a direct experience or "bump into" rather than the mentally atomized world of the imaginative physicist. Without depriving us of meaningfully directed characters capable of the free play of consciousness in a complex world, Lawrence holds to a basically naturalistic context; he captures above all the subtle margin on which thinking beings are most enmeshed in a more than personal flux, in that fiery crucible of sheer physical energy where "we and the cosmos are one".

5. D.H. Lawrence: The Struggle for a Human Space

Dramatizing the passage of western man from the rural matrix to the urban world, D.H. Lawrence contradicts the assumptions implicit in the actual transformations of modern society, and reveals himself as a revolutionary struggling to sustain both a literary realism and an Archimedean point from which to criticize the society he wishes to change. "Nature" as we have already defined it, serves him as such a point, but, apart from failures of realization in the novels, there are problems in this perspective. Let us characterize Lawrence's "nature" as an inheritance of antinomian Romanticism, to which is added a strong sense of the actual struggle for life that is owed to Darwin. Lawrence, unlike some of the Naturalists, is fully aware of the necessity of attempting to transform the scientific world-view and unlike other late Romantics, he largely evades the perils of extreme dualism in his secure placing of the consciousness factor in the body. His Darwinian perspective therefore constantly tempers the antinomian and Romantic side of his vision. Even so, his position carries its own strengths and weaknesses, and these must now be considered. Lawrence's morality, based as it is on man's connection with the circumambient universe, is a life-morality of impressive dimensions. No one can be free unless he activates his real, spontaneous self. When one acts with energy and ardour, cutting through doubts and unconscious pressures, when the whole self is mobilized in an action, that action is virtuous. The false categories, the mental binds, are obliterated in a direct commitment to a concrete moment. Let us try to set this morality in relation to two possible antitheses, the Enlightenment morality of the Socratic man, on the one hand; and the Christian morality of the fallen man on the other.[59] When the Enlightenment began to undermine the Christian order, it attacked the "false" categories of religion, but proceeded to substitute its own parameters, insisting that only within these could rational discourse take place. "Reason" often meant a retention of the assumptions of Christianity without its spiritual dynamics, and the uncritical acceptance of certain kinds of meaningfulness deriving from a fairly narrow conception of man. The Lawrencian morality is based on that Romantic position which is critical of both "Reason" and Christianity. In such a position, values are no longer from on high but man is exalted, so that the superman is not far away. The poet is elevated to the role of priest. Blake's Christ, for example, ceases to be a traditional figure, and becomes a symbol of the human imagination. The *nomos* of custom is overruled by the *physis* of the personal impulse, and the test of morality lies in the freedom of the individual to live abundantly in the released senses. In this situation, harmony must come out of the clash of opposites to which one submits oneself unprotected by prior moral categories. Energy and joy become the characteristic emotional tones of the truly liberated self.

What is immediately significant for our purposes here is that a strong criticism of this position emerges in Romantic literature itself. Man so exalted as to dare all without the guidance of formal categories lives in a moral realm in which it is sometimes difficult to distinguish creativity from crime. Lurking beneath the Romantic sense of liberation is the uncertainty inseparable from a "cosmic" morality which leaves out distinctions that become significant once the moral lines are drawn in a tighter mesh. Blake's maxim "Sooner murder an infant in its cradle than nurse unacted desires", even when we allow for overstatement and recognize the metaphorical sense of this (that one is bound by the springs of action, willy-nilly), nonetheless makes us uneasy to the extent that it links a certain kind of liberation to a specific evil. If the dimension of "my neighbor" and the social order do not somehow appear, such a morality is in danger of becoming no morality at all. With the Romantic sense of personal release in the ecstasy of instinct we are one step from Raskolnikov and his imagined superiority, which results not in self-liberation, but simply in the murder of two old ladies. I would argue that as early as "The Ancient Mariner" we have a study of the complex predicament of the man who plunges into the world of experience in the sense defined above. It may be true, as the Romantics assert, that "only the ideas you live have any value", but Coleridge's great poem, among many other things, makes us aware of the difficulty of morally productive action in the soul divorced from society and committed to a lonely plunge into uncharted experience.

No wonder, then, that nineteenth century intellectual history offers us the spectacle of ideologists clashing over this sensitive and difficult question of natural morality. We know of Christianity's continuous resistance to it; and we can see the force of such milestones as Mill's essay "Nature", and the later writings of T.H. Huxley. Huxley conjured up his "ethical man" to counteract the post-Darwinian spectre of the natural man with his all-too-unreliable "instincts". For of course pure Darwinism, which in its scientific aspect is a product of the Enlightenment tradition, seemed to undercut the antinomian option from one side, just as Christianity, seemed to undercut it from another, while the Freudian model of the unconscious threw the whole question into a new perspective. Traditional antinomian naturalism, of course, involves the assumption that evil is an illusion of matter which the mind can rid itself of; from a certain point of view the cosmos will take shape and everything come right. The natural morality emerging from Darwinism inspired, by contrast, dark ruminations inseparable from a view of the world which emphasized struggle and dispensed with any spiritual dimension. Yet, as we have seen, this dimension could be reaffirmed in a naturalistic context, the struggle for value being carried on at the level of "nature" rather than at the level of "super-nature". Thus, we have the curious split in Darwinian-tinged value-systems — "whatever is, is right" — but does this mean a morality of the stronger; or a conviction that nature must be "right", and that, in the end, good will somehow evolve from ill? Lawrence's post-Darwinian dilemma in going to the "standard of nature" is clear: at his best, he turns the values of "the quick" of consciousness against social forms that pervert the best powers of the natural man; at his worst, he indulges in a perverse violence supposedly sanctioned by nature's immoral energies.[60] If the "within" is the product either of a nature red in tooth and claw, or of a species mired in original sin, or is afflicted by tensions deriving from the family matrix itself, then the natural man is in a precariously defended position indeed.

Nonetheless, the actual state of freedom depicted in naturalistic ethics, its insistence on spontaneity and its cultivation of a sense of oneness with the universe, remains appealing. After all, "the ethical man", the Christian in a state of grace, and the patient emerging from a successful psychoanalytic process may all be indistinguishable from this kind of "natural man", in so far as the immediate emotional tone is concerned. The problem, of course, lies in the roots of one's perception of the human animal. Lawrence's goal of spontaneity and freedom seems a particularly useful one in view of his struggle against the unthinkingly mechanizing and analytic phase of western society.[61] It is also a desirable root morality, a useful first principle. (No one should be out of touch with the universe.) Appearing as it does in the context of the "second wave" of European Romanticism, we can see its connection with the naturalistic morality of such eastern systems as Zen, espoused by writers like the late Alan Watts. C.H. Waddington, in *The Ethical Animal*, quotes with approval certain remarks of Alan Watts on the necessity of an encircling "natural" morality, but qualifies his approval in the following significant statement:

> Nearly all such forms of thought pay insufficient attention to the fact that a fully-developed human being is inconceivable in isolation from society. Human individuality only arises within a social framework, and its maturation depends essentially on the social means of communication, that is to say, conceptual thought and language. An attempt to do without intellectual thought, and to handle the affairs of life "naturally" and "spontaneously" as we move our bodies in walking, must if pushed too far, lead to the abolition of one of the most important elements in human nature. The use of reason is as natural to us as our heartbeat. A satisfactory way of life has to comprise them both.[62]

Waddington's point is sharply evocative of Lawrence's ethical tightrope walk. For it seems to me undeniable that Lawrence in fact understood the necessity of retaining reason and the social dimension as a narrower mesh inside which moral decisions must ultimately be made. But from his point of view the most important thing to be said to the epoch of Love was that its abstractionism and "statistical morality", lacking a prior awareness of the very roots of man's being in nature, and failing to provide a sufficient ground of value, must be insufficient, and ultimately destructive. A concrete morality, he thought, would always be able to distinguish the false note in the rigidity of social or rational categories set up on too narrow a conception of human possibility. Lawrence wanted the mind to be part of a wholeness with the body, he wanted "knowledge" to include the art-speech that reflected the body-consciousness and its immediate perceptions. And he attempted to create a social matrix for the individual by moving from the "one" directly to the "two", to the monad of the couple, which could retain the flesh-knowledge that is a guarantee of a certain reliability. Yet it was not his commitment to "nature" that got Lawrence in difficulty, but his inability to bring the necessary ethical discrimination out of the context of sexuality, which became, probably for personal reasons, more and more poisoned for him during the "leadership" period. The existence of the Lawrencian superman indicates a disruption of that tenuous male-female balance created in the great early novels. Such a superman falls into the ultimate trap of the naturalist ethic because he can develop no real relation to that "other" in whom society begins. Left at the mercy of his "instincts", he fails to make that passage suggested in the earlier novels; the movement from struggle to a point of self-realization through concrete knowledge never occurs. In *The Plumed Serpent* (1926) Kate says of Cipriano: "What do I care if he kills people? His flame is young and clean". But Cipriano does not exist either as a character or as a moral entity; Lawrence is unable to create here that density of physical, mental, and social relationship that distinguishes his earlier novels. Cipriano's morality would be unthinkable if "real" people, either literary or actual, were involved. In a limited context, the definite sense of the other would forbid such callow extremism, and the religious peace deriving from the achieved and concretely realized paradisal relationship would not leave room for such an unqualified glorification of irrational violence. For even if the superman can do without Eliot's humility that is "endless", he cannot, in Lawrence's own terms, do without the discriminating sense of every *actual* situation in which he is enmeshed, nor avoid relating his own physical perceptions to a wider dimension of intellectual and social life. Lacking the true spontaneity of free-flowing energy and a language to render it, Lawrence's implicit Darwinism emerges in the middle novels as a strained and destructive force; it becomes simply a self-justifying version of the incomplete ethics of Naturalism in which the "stronger" survive and the "weaker" go to the wall. Such Darwinism seeks to uphold the "natural" life against the pressure of conventional society by an unconvincing formula, as if destruction accompanied by a naturalistic ideology must somehow really be creativity in disguise. But the false logic of Lawrence's perverse and ungrounded mental consciousness is unequal to the true logic of Lawrence's sense of the creative "quick", and an instinctive revulsion at what is being created appears alongside the mechanical literary impulse that moves *The Plumed Serpent* forward. Happily, Lawrence's final works breathe a spirit directly opposite to extremities of "struggle" and "domination"; the key perspective becomes one of "tenderness", and this term largely excludes any self-indulgent exploitation of the other.

This does not mean, however, that the late works are fully successful. *Lady Chatterley's Lover* (1928) offers the solution of a "paradise of the common day" to the problem of evil as Lawrence perceived it in the contemporary world. Yet however notable the book as a cultural force, in none of its three incarnations does it seem a really satisfying novel. The opening chapters of the final version are very heavy-handed in their satire; the language is loose and slangy and marked by a kind of twenties smartness that doesn't lend itself to the seriousness of the theme; on the other hand, where there might be real comedy, there is only shrillness. Nor is the Mellors-Connie relationship one that fully breaks free of the ironclad paradigm implicit in Lawrence's metaphysic of love of the senses. Lawrence's presentation of the gamekeeper embodies a comic disparity not resolved by any narrative irony; Mellors is such an inveterate verbalizer that we grow weary of him and skeptical of his paean to a concrete doing and giving. Even the flavour of his earthy dialect does not excuse the constant preaching and teaching, or the coy references to the male and female organs, an approach that from our perspective seems to be almost insufferably self-conscious.

In *Lady Chatterley's Lover* the paradisal and human-scaled enclave of the wood is set in radical opposition to the reality of the modern world, but since the latter is conveyed mainly through a rhetoric of denunciation, the structure of the novel loses tension. The critics who have seen this novel as a kind of fairy tale, a variation on the theme of Sleeping Beauty, are indirectly testifying to the escapist quality of the natural setting depicted here. Although it avoids the excesses of *The Plumed Serpent*, *Lady Chatterley's Lover* does not match the reverberating perceptions of *The Rainbow* and *Women in Love*.

"Man is tormented with words like midges," thinks the protagonist of *The Man Who Died* (1929), "but beyond the tomb they cannot go." Confronted by severe illness and the knowledge of his own approaching death, Lawrence achieved a new dimension in style, and created a short novel whose valedictory pathos is lightened by a punning wit quite unique in his work. To go beyond words, he uses words like some Buck Mulligan improving the tone of an Oscar Wilde parable. It is precisely the underlying humour, the self-probing mockery, the "faint remote smile" in the heart of suffering, that saves this fable from the shallows of pretentiousness. The outrageous use of the "escaped cock" to sum up the missing part of Christianity (the rooster as resurrection symbol, but with a difference) is only one example of the audacity with which the New Testament symbols and phrases we all know by heart are played upon to produce a specifically Lawrencian context. And one must remember that if Lawrence finds puns in the gospels, he is only following in the tradition

225

of the gospel writers themselves: "Peter" as the "rock" upon which the church is built, for example, almost invites a Lawrencian riposte.

The meeting between Lawrence's Christ-figure and the priestess of Isis takes place in the classic Mediterannean setting first discovered by the Romantics, one which Lawrence uses with skill as a timeless image abstracted from a world he knew so well — the real world of the south, which was just then on the verge of being given over to the expansionist plans of the rising fascist states. The "mythical" setting not only removes us at once to the widest dimensions of western history, but also makes possible the specific import of Lawrence's encounter. This is Lawrence's revision of the gospels in terms of his triadically conceived mythology of human spiritual evolution. At the point at which Christianity was destined to introduce the reign of "the spirit", and in lieu of the Christian miracle of the resurrection, Lawrence asserts the reborn flesh, thus "forcing" the third phase (the era of the Holy Ghost) in place of the "abstract" Christian era. Directing this parable at his own time, the waning days of the epoch of Love, Lawrence tries to show, not so much that the beginning of the Christian era might have been different, but that the present can be. There is no need to assume that love involves denial of the body, that thought demands suppression of the concrete experience of the senses. Whereas *St. Mawr* had evoked the Pan experience in connection with aspects of sublime nature, pointing to fundamental energies absent from male-female relationships in the modern context, *The Man Who Died* shows an archetypal Jesus coming to terms with the complexity and richness of the phenomenal world. Lawrence uses that favourite Romantic word "plastic" to suggest the vast, intricate and complex spaces of nature, of which the reborn Jesus feels himself to be a part. The interpenetration of man and nature is dependent upon an acceptance of sexuality and physicality; it cannot be merely an idea or a disembodied emotion. Struggle and even death must be accepted, entered into, and transcended.

Lawrence's "redemption" of Christianity, then, assumes a living through of physical reality necessarily apprehended in a post-Darwinian context. And this is true even in those tales in which elements of fantasy seem to encourage something less than a face to face encounter with contemporary existence. Neither a callow Social Darwinist, nor a failed Utopian, Lawrence attempts, often with sharp success, to elicit the grain of higher consciousness that sets man apart from the raw struggle for existence in nature. Though his grasp of social reality in the novels occasionally fails, or yields to other purposes, and though his impatience with common human failings seems often far too extreme, it is surely a gross error to try to dismiss his total vision as a perverse Naturalism, with little relevance for present or future social development. On the contrary, many of his perspectives are more than ever relevant in our age of manifoldly perceived ecologies.

Lawrence's evolutionary awareness, emphasizing sudden mutations of value systems, never leads him into the trap of "futurism". Part of his sense of the concrete involves an absolute focus on the "now", so that he stands in this respect quite apart from evolutionary ethics of the more conventional kind. Lawrence in fact is much more comparable with a Christian thinker and poet like Teilhard than he is, for example, with Sir Arthur Keith, Olaf Stapledon, or Bernard Shaw. Though he would scorn Teilhard's vision of a teleological evolution toward point Omega, Lawrence writes of a universe that is centered in man, and in which man's growth demands the assimilation of a more and more complex reality. Teilhard, as an emergent evolutionist and Christian, suggests a progressive liberation of the spirit from matter and a socialization of reality involving a climax in which "God is All in everyone", whereas Lawrence retains a naturalistic perspective within his process view, connecting the mind with the body in time, and hailing the spirit as it appears in matter under the terms of that pantheism and pluralism from which Teilhard so assiduously fought to keep himself free.

For Wells, the Darwinian universe of forms competing in space could "allow but a little consciousness", and the primordial option suggested at best a momentary energy propelling the human endeavour "forward". The more pervasive fact of primordial bestiality (which was also "mechanism") made certain the human fate that was in any case determined by the Second Law of Thermodynamics. Hardy sets the concrete world of the traditional peasant consciousness against the vast and humanly meaningless round of modern space-time, sanctioning both reason and certain modes of adaptation in nature, and rejecting the unleashed instincts. Even more significant perhaps than his later leaning toward evolutionary futurism is his affirmation of the power of the suffering consciousness to win through to concrete knowledge, and to a near-tragic acceptance of life's necessary incompleteness.

Lawrence, from his post-Darwinian perspective, is committed from the beginning to taking seriously that actual physical "nature", which is an arena of extra-human energy on which man nonetheless depends. The individual psyche is examined first in the context of the subculture, where Lawrence's inner drama of the transformation of nature (sheer "matter" and "distance") into the human value of wholeness (body and spirit) points toward the revolutionary future beyond the dying capitalistic phase. This takes the form specifically of a paradise of the "common day" set within the flux as a human encounter radiating values and knowledge beyond mere mechanism. *The Rainbow* carries us from "once upon a time" right into the modern world, but beyond only in a paroxysm of vision that is not fully worked out in terms of human relations. In *Women in Love* the spatial world dominates over the temporal, and struggle is pervasive. The psyche, contaminated by "the world of Love" that is now revealed up and down the scale of horrors,

227

becomes self-destructive. Nonetheless, the paradisal is again asserted, under conditions of great tension. Here nature too is often reflected as a destructive force (perceived thus by the wounded psyche), and in the exchange between mind and nature there are elements that remain corrupt, evil and ambiguous. Nonetheless, a ritual of release provides the nucleus of a new world, which remains, however, to be created as an ethical reality, beginning in terms of the male-female relationship of Birkin and Ursula. *Women in Love*, however, like *The Rainbow*, ends without a complete resolution. The separation from the mainstream of western society hinted at here is accomplished, at a great price, in the succeeding novels. While no finality can be demanded of a vision so tinged with the Utopian as is Lawrence's, it is clear that a failure of balance turns the primitive quest into an evasion of the ethical answers set by Lawrence's own thundering questions. The antinomian naturalism that is always subject to further qualification in moral terms, lacking a real drama of relationship, and undermined by the exoticism of the middle period, degenerates into a Darwinism of violence, above all in *The Plumed Serpent*. From here there is a recovery, a working toward an ethic of "tenderness" and a re-creation of the paradisal option which stops short, however, of being part of a real engagement with the complexities of the western society Lawrence had met head on in the earlier and greater novels.

Despite his limitations, however, Lawrence is nonetheless the true inheritor and transformer of the nature of literary Naturalism, to which he added a sense of the within, generated by the unconscious knowledge of the body itself. In his best works he achieves a language of impressive complexity and creates a drama of the self in nature that is highly relevant to every serious attempt to understand the world we live in. With all his contradictions, Lawrence stands as the type of the creator envisaged in the theory that underlies this whole work — for he demonstrates the power of literature to redeem the abstractionism of science, and responds directly to the challenge of his time, seeking an image of man in his wholeness in an age of fractured sensibility. Lawrence may be seen as a phenomenon parallel to the great Romantics, who met the challenge of the mechanistic science that preceded them, and who attempted to create an image of man as an active consciousness in touch with a meaningful world. Our age is still engaged in the huge task prophetically pointed to in Lawrence's best work, a task which centers on the recovery of a human order in the nature bequeathed to us *via* the symbolism of the overridingly potent world-view of science.

SUMMARY AND CONCLUSION

The history of man's relationship with nature from ancient times climaxes in the western world's development of science and technology, a fortunate passage which went too far in assuming that truth could be established only in axiomatic, abstract propositions. Inevitably, literature's mythopoeic way of knowing nature in its immediacy and physical splendour was devalued. As post-Renaissance mathematics and scientific models veer away from the world of experience, literature for a while magnificently and defiantly explores the concrete world of the newly discovered locale and of the vast spaces of the cosmos itself. The Romantic movement in particular achieves a synthesis of "spiritual" and "natural" which breaks apart, however, because of its own misconceived dualism and the renewed pressure of a mechanist philosophy that denied the possibility of human values in nature entirely. In Realism and Naturalism the attempt to mimic the materialism of science is but a theoretical ploy which covers a multitude of strategies, mainly designed to find values in the new sense of struggle brought finally into the heart of the human environment by Darwinism in league with a technological brutality previously unknown in human history. Symbolism, for its part, retreated from the common world to exalt the art-work itself and laid the basis for a new prose literature which emphasized imagination instead of mere reporting. By this time, too, science was just beginning to achieve a greater awareness of its own imaginative commitment, and was casting out the presumptions of naive realism, and literature proceeded to go almost too far in a one-sided reflection of consciousness, just when it might have performed a more useful function in a world in which its "holistic" insights were needed more than ever. Having tried and failed to mimic science's pretended "realism", literature tried and succeeded in mimicking science's real "psychologism". The Joycean and post-Joycean novel accompanied physics into the uncertainties of the subjectively perceived microcosm, not without benefit, but at the price of losing their power to centralize an image of man in a society already fractured by ideological divergencies that seemed unbridgeable.

Those who accept the Wordsworthian idea of literature's cultural centrality, and its character as a necessary reservoir of values cannot be complacent about such "scientistic" fragmentation, subjectivity, and psychologism when these become the main mode of a whole age. They hope for the rediscovery of such alternative traditions as the one I have named "environmental realism", in which there is complexity of relation between inner and outer without a complete dissolving of human experience into the microscopic elements of the subjective consciousness unanchored in everyday society and primal nature. In this respect, they hope that literature will not go too far toward imitating that science whose energies are so often fragmentative, and whose traditional neutrality in relation to values gives it an awesome but quite inhuman grip on its own kind of truth. The truth of literature is less remote and more homely than that of science, and even more marvellous. It is the truth of a virtual experience of human beings whose most important knowledge often occurs as a complex awareness of physical and sensory input, in an emotional and intellectual process that is not simply the sum of these stimuli, but which depends upon them and defines itself through them. Such a process cannot be charted in the ''outside'' rational terminology of science, but this does not make it ''irrational'', or suspect, though it makes it individual, ambiguous, and difficult to relate to formal systems of logic. The power of the literary image of nature is partially the power of the word to render this concrete experience, and to suggest that it too must be taken into account when man decides what his environment fundamentally is. And if science has in recent years seemed willing to enter into discourse about values as never before, literature has never ceased to conduct this most important of dialogues between the self and the world. In short, literature has its own image of nature, its own human language, and must regain confidence in these, even while continuing to pay attention to the striking symbolisms of the other ''languages'' of human culture. With a new dedication to its own best powers, modern fiction at least could turn the skills of those language games which have so fascinated it in the post-Einsteinian, post-Heisenbergian universe of relativity and uncertainty toward a rediscovery of man that would be significant to readers beyond the confines of an academic and cultural elite.

More than ever literature needs to find language for the outer and inner spaces of the perennial and ever-new human landscape, so that the inter-connections of the ''physical'' and the ''spiritual'' will be further explored and intellectual values will not be divorced from the testimony of the tacitly knowing body-consciousness. Even allowing for its limitations and its false tracks, its failures and its narrowness, the tradition of verbal art I have described here, which establishes literature's power to render the experience of man in the living world of nature, represents one of the centers of our human quest for self-knowledge through the word, and stands against the modern sense of alienation and despair with a testimony of vision, concrete imagination, and energies perceived.

NOTES AND REFERENCES

(Where possible, extended, interrupted quotations from a single source have been referenced by a single footnote. In the discussion of primary texts, all passages cited from full-length books are located by chapter. First publication dates for all primary works are listed at the first mention of each work. References to critics have been avoided in the literary analyses in chapters one through four, Part Two, where a close documentation of every point would have expanded the footnotes unmercifully. The specialist reader will recognize at once the debts of this writer in those chapters, and others should have no difficulty in measuring the accuracy and sensitivity of treatment in each case. Only exceptionally has any attempt been made to deal with material published after 1975.)

PART ONE, CHAPTER ONE:
Natural Space in Literature: An Introduction and Overview *and* **the Idea of Nature in Western Civilization**

1. George Santayana, *Three Philosophical Poets* (New York: Anchor Books, 1953), pp. 56-57.
2. Paul Shepard, *Man in the Landscape* (New York: Knopf, 1967), p. 6.
3. R.L. Gregory, *Eye and Brain* (New York: McGraw-Hill, World University Library, 1973), p. 160.
4. Shepard, p. 36.
5. Gregory, pp. 175-6.
6. This is not to denigrate the many interesting studies based on stylistic analogies, of which Wylie Sypher's *Four Stages of Renaissance Style* (New York: Anchor Books, 1955) is a good example.
7. Has not literary criticism concerned itself too incestuously with contextual and archetypal factors, to the neglect of the environmental basis of language? In the civilizations of the ancient world we know that important myths were often specifically related to environmental perceptions. Some of these would be more meaningful to us if we could experience the environment in which they grew. Others express spatial perceptions which it would be hard for us to recapture. The old story that the earth rides on the back of a turtle may have been a sharply evocative verbal mapping for some cultures, but for us it is a dead image. For us it represents neither a relation between bodies, nor a binding of our feelings to the earth. Suppose we read, however, that "the earth is our mother". We do not take this as literal place-relation, yet we respond. We do so because we are still *ecologically* placed in relation to the earth as a child is to its mother. The analogy is still valid. The environmental situation, therefore, does seem to affect the power of language to move us.
8. Northrop Frye, *Anatomy of Criticism* (Princeton: University Press, 1957), p. 136.
9. Ernle Bradford, *Ulysses Found* (London: Sphere Books, 1963), pp. 87-91.
10. There have been few attempts by critics to deal with structures like natural space in literature. General studies in the traditions of Romanticism, Literary Realism, and Naturalism will often touch upon aspects of the representation of nature in literature, but works like Gaston Bachelard's *The Poetics of Space*, in which all kinds of spatial relation are explored, are rare. Bachelard's phenomonological approach, however, despite its brilliance of specific insight, sometimes seems rather arbitrary and is determinedly a-historical. On the other hand, articles like Joseph Frank's "Spatial Form in Modern Literature" usually lack a sufficient theoretical basis to carry us to the level of general considerations. Cf. Gaston Bachelard, *The Poetics of Space* (New York: Orion, 1964), and Joseph Frank, "Spatial Form in Modern Literature esp. the novel"), *Sewanee Review* LIII (1945), pp. 221-240; 433-456.
11. Alfred North Whitehead, *Science and the Modern World* (New York: Mentor Books, 1953), chapter five.
12. My assumption here is one of critical realism. There is a real world which is not merely the creation of human consciousness, and that world may be legitimately interpreted in some ways but not in others. Human forms, whether expressed as art symbols or science symbols, or in some other way,

are intimately linked to the matrix world, but they do not simply create it. Whitehead explains: "The creed is that the actual elements perceived by our senses are *in themselves* the elements of a common world; and that this world is a complex of things including indeed our acts of cognition, but transcending them. According to this point of view the things experienced are to be distinguished from our knowledge of them. So far as there is dependence, the *things* pave the way for the *cognition*, rather than *vice versa*. But the point is that the actual things experienced enter into a common world which transcends knowledge, though it includes knowledge." Cf. *Science and the Modern World*, pp. 89-96. Modern academic literary criticism, where it derives from neo-Kantian assumptions, will not go far toward being reconciled with science, unless science follows the road of Jeans and Schrödinger toward an idealist metaphysics or theory of knowledge.

13. William Chase Greene, *Moira: Fate, Good, and Evil in Greek Thought* (New York: Harper & Row, 1963), p. 225.
14. R.G. Collingwood, *The Idea of Nature* (Oxford: The Clarendon Press, 1949), p. 44.
15. See A.O. Lovejoy and George Boas, *A Documentary History of Primitivism and Related Ideas* (Baltimore: Johns Hopkins Press, 1953), p. 106.
16. Lovejoy and Boas, p. 113; see also Greene, Chapter VIII, for further details.
17. C.S. Lewis, *Studies in Words* (Oxford: University Press, 1960), p. 38 ff. The Platonic forms were outside of physical nature in the grosser earlier sense of *physis*, though not outside of what Plato meant by cosmos. Cf. Aldo D. Scaglione, *Nature and Love in the Late Middle Ages* (Berkeley: University of California Press, 1963), p. 153, note 4.
18. Lewis, p. 40. See also the same writer's *The Discarded Image* (Cambridge: University Press, 1964), pp. 92-121.
19. E.W. Tayler, *Nature and Art in Renaissance Literature* (New York: Columbia University Press, 1964), p. 73. See also Scaglione, pp. 8, 10-11.
20. Lewis, *Studies in Words*, p. 49.
21. E.R. Curtius, *European Literature and the Latin Middle Ages* (New York: Pantheon Books, 1953), chapter six.
22. Alfred North Whitehead, *Science and the Modern World*, p. 13. Also, as Ian Barbour points out, the doctrine of creation implies that the details of nature can only be known by observing them. Cf. Barbour, *Issues in Science and Religion* (New York: Harper Torchboks, 1971), p. 46, ff.
23. *The Idea of Nature*, pp. 94-95.
24. Cf., for the positive side of this transformation of nature, G.A. Jellicoe, *Studies in Landscape Design* (London: Oxford University Press, 1960), for the negative side, *Hard Times*, "Nottingham and the Mining Countryside", or the essay by Raymond Williams, "Ideas of Nature", in *The Times Literary Supplement*, Friday, December 4, 1970, pp. 1419-1421. Williams points to the role of the country estate as a green place where the exploiting classes would not have to witness the scenes of their devastation.
25. This can be plausibly established by a close study of relevant entries in The Oxford English Dictionary.
26. The traditional astronomical systems already assumed man's relative insignificance in relation to the dimensions of the system, but the "plurality of worlds" and Giordano Bruno's "infinite universe", most authorities agree, made for a new sense of disquiet. See, Grant McColley, "Humanism and the

History of Astronomy'' in Robert M. Palter, *Toward Modern Science* (New York: Dutton Paperbacks, 1969); also Collingwood, pp. 96-7, Lovejoy, *The Great Chain of Being*, pp. 99-108, Herbert Dingle, ''Copernicus and the Planets'' in *A Short History of Science* (a symposium) (New York: Anchor Books, 1959), pp. 23-24, especially. On the ''infinite universe'', see Stephen Toulmin and June Goodfield, *The Fabric of the Heavens* (Harmondsworth: Pelican Books, 1963), pp. 209-214. On the new sense of a universe of ''matter in motion'', see E.A. Burtt, *The Metaphysical Foundations of Modern Science* (London: Routledge and Kegan Paul, 1951), p. 239, and Collingwood, p. 102.

27. A.O. Lovejoy, *The Great Chain of Being* (Cambridge: Harvard University Press, 1936), pp. 316-317. J.H. van der Berg suggests that man only began to notice the landscape when he became estranged from it. See ''The Subject and his Landscape'' in Harold Bloom, ed., *Romanticism and Consciousness* (New York, Norton, 1970), pp. 57-65. This is true in the sense that western poets and painters began to discover landscape in a self-conscious fashion when a this-worldly focus, with all its new glories and lost consolations, slowly replaced the Christian sense of a present ''spiritual'' reality underlying the things of the world. Van der Berg's statement is misleading, however, in so far as it might suggest: 1) that there was virtually no awareness of the natural world *per se* before, say, the Renaissance; and 2) that man's modern discovery of the landscape actually *created* it, or in some primal sense gave existence to an experience that would otherwise not have been felt. Against this idea that a sense of oneness with nature is a Romantic fad and not a human essential molded in different ages in different ways, one must set the enduring fact of the body in the environment, and the testimony of literature and art through the ages to the meaningfulness of ''nature'' and even landscape, to the human animal. See Alexander von Humboldt, *Cosmos* (London: Longman, Brown, etc. 1849), Stanley Burnshaw, *The Seamless Web* (London: Allen Lane, 1969), and René Dubos, *A God Within* (New York: Scribner, 1972). The two latter writers combine an awareness of man's shaping power over nature with a sense of the depth of his biological roots, and discuss the arts as one means of connection with the actual concrete world.

PART ONE, CHAPTER TWO:
Romantic Nature and the ''Exact, Concrete Imagination''

1. For example, that most sane and central anthology-textbook, *The Norton Anthology of English Literature*, warns readers not to take the Romantic interest in nature and landscape too literally. This is no doubt a useful *caveat* for students, but does not Professor Abrams miss a good chance to remind everyone of the undoubted ''realistic'' strain in Romantic nature-description? Considering the influence of more recent commentaries like Harold Bloom's *Romanticism and Consciousness* (with its contributions from van der Berg and de Man), and Northrop Frye's ''The Drunken Boat'', such a reminder might have been timely. Surely criticism has swung too far toward the aesthetic, archetypal and structuralist approaches and surely the dissenting critic is on strong ground when he sees the ''image of nature'' in broader and

234

more "realistic" terms than these. Cf. M.H. Abrams, et al., *The Norton Anthology of English Literature* (New York: Norton, 1962) volume 2, pp. 9-10; Bloom, *Romanticism and Consciousness*; Northrop Frye, "The Drunken Boat: The Revolutionary Element in Romanticism" in *Romanticism Reconsidered* (New York: Columbia University Press, 1963).

2. W.K. Wimsatt, *The Verbal Icon* (Lexington: University of Kentucky Press, 1954), p. 110.
3. *Science and the Modern World*, p. 84.
4. *Science and the Modern World*, p. 93.
5. *Science and the Modern World*, p. 95.
6. *Science and the Modern World*, p. 85.
7. "Prospectus" from *The Recluse*, lines 62-71.
8. M.H. Abrams, *The Mirror and the Lamp* (New York: Norton, 1958), p. 66.
9. *The Mirror and the Lamp*, p. 64.
10. Cf. "The American Scholar", 1837.
11. Joseph Warren Beach, *The Concept of Nature in Nineteenth Century English Poetry* (New York: Macmillan, 1936), p. 201.
12. The poem moves through an image of the child-self and the youthful self to the third "now" and what I call the second crescendo. This crescendo expresses a much broader sweep away from the particular than we experienced in the first (which was an expression of the body's self-delighted knowledge-in-relaxation). This second crescendo dissolves any illusions of process as sheer bliss, though it resolves suffering into a pattern, the *symphony* that humanity makes up. Now the poet is in touch not only with nature as an aesthetic order, not only with nature as a therapeutic necessity, but with nature as the reservoir of humanity in travail, with its moral implications of the relation of man to man in terms of the common fate of men.
13. Henri Ellenberger, *The Discovery of the Unconscious* (New York: Basic Books, 1970), pp. 223-228.
14. *In Memoriam*, III.
15. The secondary imagination as "an echo" of the primary imagination, which is a "repetition in the finite mind of the eternal act of creation in the infinite I AM". *Biographia Literaria*, Chapter XIII. Imaginative minds are as Wordsworth portrays them in *The Prelude*, Book XIV, lines 112-116:
    For they are Powers; and hence the highest bliss
    That flesh can know is theirs — the consciousness
    Of Whom they are, habitually infused
    Through every image and through every thought . . ."
    For a modern criticism from this direction, see Charles Williams, *The English Poetic Mind* (Oxford: Clarendon Press, 1932). Williams faults Wordsworth for failing in ultimate trust in his solitary "visitants from another order".
16. See, for example, David Ferry on Wordsworth in *The Limits of Mortality* (Middletown, Connecticut: Wesleyan University Press, 1959); Lionel Trilling on "The Immortality Ode" in *The Liberal Imagination* (New York: Viking, 1950); W.J. Bate, *John Keats* (Cambridge: Harvard University Press, 1963); C.E. Pulos in *The Deep Truth: A Study of Shelley's Skepticism* (Lincoln, Nebraska: University Press, 1954); and in general, Morse Peckham, *Beyond The Tragic Vision* (New York: George Braziller, 1962).

17. "Goethe and the Idea of Scientific Truth", which must be studied with Heller's concluding remarks on "The Hazard of Modern Poetry", both in *The Disinherited Mind* (New York: Meridian Books, 1959). Cf. also *The Artist's Journey to the Interior and Other Essays* (London: Secker and Warburg, 1966), in which Heller delineates the subjectivity of Romanticism as part of the movement of modern culture toward the private symbol, the "pure inwardness" that feeds on its own creativity, and delicately hints that this passage is one that might better be ultimately reversed.
18. Heller, *The Disinherited Mind*, p. 32.
19. *The Disinherited Mind*, p. 30.
20. *The Disinherited Mind*, p. 31.
21. "There will always be skylarks; perhaps even a few nightingales. But poetry is not only the human equivalent of the song of singing birds. It is also Virgil, Dante and Hölderlin. It is also, in its own terms, the definition of the state of man". *The Disinherited Mind*, p. 287.
22. Heller writes: "For both our faith and our physics are fascinated by the vast voids inside and outside everything that exists, by empty fields of tension, and by the indeterminate motion of particles seemingly speeding around one another in order to hide from themselves the nothingness at the core of things". *The Disinherited Mind*, p. 267.
23. This is to disagree with the interesting argument of Owen Barfield in *Saving the Appearances: A Study in Idolatry* (New York: Harcourt, Brace & World, 1965).

PART ONE, CHAPTER THREE:
The Nature of Literary Naturalism

1. To be more precise, one should perhaps elaborate as follows. There is first of all the association of the novel with the post-Renaissance transformation of consciousness and world-view, resulting in the characteristic "formal realism" so well charted by Ian Watt in *The Rise of the Novel*. There is secondly, in the first decades of the nineteenth century, the movement away from the most fanciful side of Romanticism, this movement, as I have assumed, being one aspect of Romanticism itself. As science develops quickly in the first decades of the nineteenth century, however, and as the "everyday" world becomes increasingly the world of bourgeois values, one may note a tendency on the part of the writer (especially in the later stages of this tradition) to draw explicitly upon science for aesthetic support. Thus, Realism shades off into Naturalism, where the "scientism" of novel theory becomes pervasive and overt. See Ian Watt, *The Rise of the Novel* (Harmondsworth: Peregrine Books, 1963), pp. 9-35. Also, George J. Becker, *Documents of Modern Literary Realism* (Princeton: University Press, 1963), and for Realism in the major nineteenth century national literatures, the special issue of *Comparative Literature*, Volume 3, Number 3 (summer, 1951).
2. Though not the question of the superiority of the artist to the bourgeois world he increasingly wrote about. See *Realism, Naturalism and Symbolism*, edited by Roland N. Stromberg (New York: Harper Torchbook, 1968), pp. XII-XIII.

3. *"Le Roman Expérimental"* was published in 1880. The word "Naturalism" had first been used in the preface to the second edition of *Thérèse Raquin* in 1868. See also Edward Stone, *What Was Naturalism?: The Materials for an Answer* (New York: Appleton-Century-Crofts, 1959).
4. If we take the case of Zola, for example, the situation should be clear. A novel like *Germinal* cannot be accounted for in terms of Naturalistic aesthetic doctrines alone. It manifests mythical, epical and symbolic dimensions that are intrinsically incompatible with the strict scientism of Zola's theory. See, among many others, Harry Levin, *The Gates of Horn* (New York: Oxford University Press, 1963).
5. Cf. Enid Starkie, *From Gautier to Eliot* (London: Hutchinson, 1960); C.M. Bowra, *The Heritage of Symbolism* (London: Macmillan, 1943), and Edmund Wilson, *Axel's Castle* (New York: Scribner's, 1931).
6. See *Mr. Bennett and Mrs. Brown* (London: The Hogarth Press, 1924).
7. The critical wedge against the naive assumptions of some of the "modernists" was driven by Wayne Booth, *The Rhetoric of Fiction* (Chicago: University Press, 1961). I am thinking of the rediscovery of picaresque, and of such various manifestations of an older (and more solid?) realism as we find in Richard Hughes, Patrick White, and Alexander Solzhenitsyn.
8. On Darwin's language, see Howard Mumford Jones in Philip Appleman, et al., *1859: Entering an Age of Crisis* Bloomington: Indiana University Press, 1959), and A. Dwight Culler in Appleman's *Darwin* (New York: Norton, 1970). For the reception of Darwinism in England and America, see, among many others, Alvar Ellegard, *Darwin and the General Reader: The Reception of Darwin's Theory of Evolution in the British Periodical Press, 1859-1872* (Goteberg: Almqvist and Wiksell, 1958), and Thomas F. Glick, ed., *The Comparative Reception of Darwinism* (Austin: University of Texas, 1972).
9. Darwin, of course, adopted Herbert Spencer's phrase "the survival of the fittest", which added yet another touchstone for the metaphorical expansion of Darwin's mechanistic core meaning.
10. Charles Darwin, *The Origin of Species* (London: John Murray, 1859), from chapter four on "Natural Selection".
11. This is the famous conclusion to the 1859 edition of *The Origin of Species*.
12. My point is that literature in its intrinsic character must deal with concrete renderings of experience, that this inevitably involves values, and that, far from being seen as a "distortion" of the pure ideas of science or philosophy, such a rendering of values is essential for advancement of human self-awareness. J.W. Burrow concludes his introduction to the Penguin edition of *The Origin of Species* with the tart remark that Darwin's work "brings to an end countless centuries of more or less animistic attitudes to nature, even though they may persist in some of our more private and instinctive reactions". There is a monstrous confusion here. Knowledge is not simply a matter of intellectual abstraction from experience, and it is precisely those "private and instinctive reactions" which we need to affirm against the "objectivist" delusion that the mind can somehow escape its matrix, or that man is "nothing but" a prototype for the ultra-intelligent computer. There is nothing "illegitimate" in experiencing nature as value, though such ex-

periences must be anchored in the concrete and will also be at some level subject to the perspectives of the whole current of psycho-social evolution, which includes science. One can criticize certain attitudes to nature as "naive" or "archaic", but one cannot simply dispense with man's seemingly universal quest for meaning by suggesting that it should be satisfied by systems and symbolisms which are demonstrably incapable of giving satisfaction, precisely because of their narrowness. See Charles Darwin, *The Origin of Species* (Harmondsworth: Penguin Books, 1968), edited by J.W. Burrow, and especially Burrow's "Editor's Introduction", pp. 47-48.

13. This definition is from Charles Child Walcutt, "Naturalism and the Superman in the Novels of Jack London", *Papers of the Michigan Academy of Science, Arts and Letters*, XXIV, Part IV (1938), pp. 89-107. See also Walcutt's *American Literary Naturalism: A Divided Stream* (Minneapolis: University of Minnesota Press, 1956) for a long and useful discussion of Naturalism, which does not, however, take into account either the specific relation of literary to scientific symbolism, or the intrinsic value-conferring character of literature, and which makes the mistake of trying to sort out the Naturalistic tradition by dealing with literature as a repository of "ideas", the same mistake Beach makes in dealing with Romantic nature.

PART TWO, CHAPTER ONE:
Wild Nature or the Natural Sublime

1. Marjorie Hope Nicolson, *Mountain Gloom and Mountain Glory: the Development of the Aesthetics of the Infinite* (New York: Norton, 1959).
2. Willard Trask, *The Unwritten Song: Poetry of the Primitive and Traditional Peoples of the World* (New York: Macmillan, 1966), Volume I, p. 254.
3. Mircea Eliade, *The Sacred and the Profane* (New York: Harper Torchbooks, 1961), pp. 27-65.
4. This is of course very different from the oriental self-abandonment that expresses man's nobility through his power of sinking into nature, of letting himself be swallowed up by things. An interesting general discussion of man's aesthetic relation to nature, and some comments on eastern art, can be found in Jacques Maritain, *Creative Intuition in Art and Poetry* (New York: Meridian Books, 1955), pp. 3-30.
5. Marjorie Hope Nicolson, *Mountain Gloom and Mountain Glory*, pp. 31, 49 and 143.
6. Cf. Edmund Burke, *A Philosophical Enquiry into the Origin of our Ideas of the Sublime and Beatiful*, edited by J.T. Boulton (London: Routledge and Kegan Paul, 1958), Section VII, p. 39.
7. Boulton, introducing Burke, p. xliii. It is sometimes easier to recognize the difference between the Romantics and their predecessors than it is to describe it in tight, logical categories. In Byron's long letter to Murray of March 25, 1821, he attacks the "Lakers" and defends Pope's "Windsor Forest" as a "seeing" of nature. But neither "Windsor Forest", with its humanized landscape and its mythology, nor "The Seasons" with its carefully distanced descriptive detail, invite the *"participation mystique"* which is the essence of Romantic nature poetry.
8. René Poggioli, "The Oaten Flute", *Harvard Library Bulletin* XI (1957), p. 176.

9. See also C.L. Sanford, *The Quest for Paradise: Europe and the American Moral Imagination* (Urbana: University of Illinois Press, 1961), pp. 140-142.
10. William Wordsworth, *The Prelude*, Book VI, lines 624-640. Unlike "Tintern Abbey" this visionary expression was not written virtually "on the spot", but somewhat later, as Wordsworth reflected on the actual experience.
11. As Shelley's early rhapsodic nature poems of this period show the influence of Coleridge, Byron's indicate not only that he was staying near the Shelleys, but also reading Wordsworth.
12. The controlling focus here, however, remains that of "sublime" power and distance and so Byron's apostrophe to ocean is properly dealt with at this point. There is a positive and negative side to the encounter with wild nature, while the paradisal is in itself a beneficent experience. The distinction between positive sublime and paradisal is this: positive sublime involves at its best the body/consciousness expanding outward into a validly established rhapsodic awareness of space (Wordsworth, "Tintern Abbey", Shelley, "Ode to the West Wind"), while in paradisal nature space is drawn in around the body/consciousness, emphasizing the protected enclosure. In certain cases (Byron's Genevan Cantos; Chateaubriand) we have a "sublime" undermined by the absence of an anchoring body/consciousness, one which is verbal, rhetorical, and "swooning". When the emphasis on the bliss of body-consciousness in a single passage is used to offset the threatening distant spaces described in others, we have juxtaposition of paradisal with negative sublime. Clear examples of the latter effect may be found in Arnold's "Empedocles on Etna", and in *Women in Love*.
13. Cf. A.O. Lovejoy, "On the Discrimination of Romanticisms" in *Essays in the History of Ideas* (Baltimore: Johns Hopkins, 1948), pp. 228-253.
14. Quoted in T.C. Walker, *Chateaubriand's Natural Scenery: A Study of his Descriptive Art* (Baltimore: Johns Hopkins, 1946), p. 14.
15. Walker, p. 174.
16. See "On the Discrimination of Romanticisms" in *Essays in the History of Ideas*, p. 251.
17. All quotations from Johannes V. Jensen, *The Long Journey* (New York: Alfred A. Knopf, 1945), translated by A.G. Chater.
18. Not only mainstream literature, but the literature of travel and science fiction exhibit the kind of encounter with natural space I have described here. While modern painting has largely given up spatial perspective and realism, the same is not true of film, which, like the novel, is committed to a certain formal realism. Cf., for example, the use of the desert in T.E. Lawrence's *Seven Pillars of Wisdom*, and in the David Lean film, *Lawrence of Arabia*. The shift from a geocentric to a heliocentric perspective has made possible the sublime vision of "spaceship earth", while relatively untamed earth landscapes are seen from new angles, thanks to advances in technology. Cf. the comments of Antoine de Saint Exupéry in *Terre des Hommes*, chapter five.

PART TWO, CHAPTER TWO:
The Image of the Field

1. This has been well-charted by German scholarship in particular. Among many significant contributions, cf. Peter Zimmermann's *Der Bauernroman*

(Stuttgart: J.B. Metzlersche, 1975). Here we have a complete analysis of the peasant novel, with the historical and social context, statistics on types and authors, mythologies and ideologies, & etc., although the period mainly covered is 1830 to 1970, and the writer's focus sociological rather than ecological. In different perspective, some of my observations are the commonplace of traditional scholarship on the peasant novel. See, for example, E.K. Bennett's thumbnail sketch of the "country novel" in *A History of the German Novelle* (Cambridge: University Press, 1961), p. 118.

2. Cf. F.M. Barnard, *J.G. Herder on Social and Political Culture* (Cambridge: University Press, 1969), pp. 7-10.

3. "The Ecology of Peasant Life in Western Europe" in William L. Thomas Jr., *Man's Role in Changing the Face of the Earth* (Chicago: University Press, 1956) Volume I, p. 220. The question is whether one is "idealizing" or "mythologizing" "real" peasant experience by drawing upon concepts of "wholeness" and "integrity", as fostered by anthropologists like Redfield. I would deny this, since literature tells also of the actual evils of peasant life and in interpreting the quality of what is good in such life, we need to pay attention to social scientists who come to grips with the issue and who speak a language that names the kind of experience that must have existed but is often neglected in the more overtly "scientific" reports. Cf. Robert Redfield, *Peasant Society and Culture* (Chicago: University Press, 1965), and *Peasant Society: A Reader*, edited by Jack M. Potter, May N. Diaz and George M. Foster (Boston: Little, Brown, 1967), especially, pp. 2-34; 378-383; and 419-437.

4. M.H. Abrams, *The Mirror and the Lamp*, p. 113.

5. "The Ruined Cottage", Second Part, lines 513-525, edited Jonathan Wordsworth. *The Music of Humanity* (New York: Harper Row, 1969).

6. Cf. Wordsworth's letter to the Whig statesman Charles James Fox, of 14 January, 1801, in which he speaks of land as a kind of medium of expression for persons who would otherwise be forgotten, and complains about the decay of rural domestic life.

7. Leo Tolstoy, *Anna Karenina* (New York: Bantam Books, 1960), translated by Joel Carmichael.

8. Emile Zola, *Earth* (London: Elek books, 1954), translated by Ann Lindsay, a few modifications here by this writer.

9. Knut Hamsun, *Growth of the Soil* (New York: Alfred A. Knopf, 1921), translated by W.W. Worster.

PART TWO, CHAPTER THREE:
The Natural Paradise in Modern Literature

1. See A.O. Lovejoy and George Boas, *A Documentary History of Primitivism and Related Ideas*, C.L. Sanford, *The Quest for Paradise*.

2. John Armstrong's interesting study, *The Paradise Myth* (London: Oxford University Press, 1969) posits two distinct paradisal images within the western tradition: one is the earthly Arcadian paradise; the other a myth of the divine precinct, a dynamic paradise incorporating a symbolic tension of tree and snake, which stands for a reconciliation between rootedness and change. In Armstrong's version, the imagination reconciles stasis and kinesis in this latter version only; the earthly paradise is a despicable anti-evolutionary variant of the true paradisal.

3. For documentation of such a possibility from the physiological point of view, see Stanley Burnshaw, *The Seamless Web*. What Burnshaw argues for poetry in general, I would argue for certain kinds of literary expression, specifically, the paradisal image.

4. See George Boas, *Essays on Primitivism and Related Ideas in the Middle Ages* (New York: Octagon, 1966), especially pages 3-7; 15; 30-39; 88-95; and also G.H. Williams, *Wilderness and Paradise in Christian Thought* (New York: Harper & Row, 1962), Norman Cohn, *The Pursuit of the Millennium* (London: Mercury Books, 1962), p. 201 & ff.

5. Henri Baudet, *Paradise on Earth: Some Thoughts on European Images of non-European Man* (New Haven: Yale University Press, 1965).

6. Baudet, p. 13.

7. This is Baudet's thesis. See *Paradise on Earth, passim.*

8. Sanford, pp. 15-16. See also Norman Cohn, *The Pursuit of the Millenium*. Lovejoy and Boas were perhaps the first to point out that the paradisal myth, far from being merely escapist, could function as a criticism of society. See *A Documentary History of Primitivism and Related Ideas in Antiquity*, p. 16; also Baudet, p. 56.

9. For these observations by the Grazia, see, *Of Time, Work and Leisure* (New York: Twentieth Century Fund, 1962), pp. 12-25; and 419-421.

10. Lines 47-55.

11. Mircea Eliade, *Cosmos and History: The Myth of the Eternal Return* (New York: Harper Torchbook, 1959), pp. 154-159.

12. Cf. Desmond King-Hele, *Shelley: His Thought and Work* (London: Macmillan, 1972), pp. 282-3.

13. Lines 498-504.

14. Giuseppe Di Lampedusa, "The Professor and the Siren", in *Two Stories and a Memory* (London: Collins and Harvill Press, 1962), translated by Archibald Colquhoun.

15. "*Et in Arcadia ego:* Poussin and the Elegiac Tradition" in *Meaning in the Visual Arts* (Garden City, New York: Doubleday, 1955), pp. 295-320.

PART TWO, CHAPTER FOUR:
Man in the Biosphere

1. *The New American Bible* (New York: Benziger, 1970), p. 901.

2. Henri Bergson, *Les Deux Sources de la Morale et de la Religion* (Paris: Félix Alcan, 1932), pp. 135-136.

3. I am indebted here to Joseph Wood Krutch, *Great American Nature Writing* (New York: William Sloane, 1950), pp. 8-12 & ff.

4. Cf. E.D.H. Johnson, *The Poetry of Earth* (London: Gollancz, 1966), p. IX, and Joseph Wood Krutch, *Great American Nature Writing*, pp. 44-50.

5. A.O. Lovejoy, *The Great Chain of Being*, pp. 236-240.

6. Ralph Waldo Emerson, "The Naturalist" in *The Early Lectures of Ralph Waldo Emerson*, Volume I, 1833-1836, edited by Stephen W. Whicher and Robert E. Spiller (Cambridge, Massachusetts: Harvard University Press, 1959), pp. 69-83.

7. By, I believe, Alan Watts, in a television seminar.

8. Cf. Alister Hardy *The Living Stream* (New York: Harper and Row, 1965),

pp. 266-7; Marston Bates, *The Forest and the Sea* (New York: Random House, 1960), and John Storer, *The Web of Life* (New York: Devin-Adair, 1956).

PART THREE, CHAPTER ONE:
Thomas Hardy's Image of Nature:
The Honest Countryman and the Incomplete Universe

1. On this theme, cf., especially Lionel Johnson, *The Art of Thomas Hardy* (London: The Bodley Head, 1894 & 1923); Herbert B. Grimsditch, *Character and Environment in the Novels of Thomas Hardy* (New York: Russell and Russell, 1925); John Holloway, *The Victorian Sage* (New York: Norton, 1965), pp. 244-289; Roy Morrell, *Thomas Hardy: The Will and the Way* (Kuala Lumpur: University of Malaya Press, 1965); Jean R. Brooks, *Thomas Hardy: The Poetic Structure* (London: Elek, 1971).
2. Michael Millgate in *Thomas Hardy: His Career as a Novelist* (London: Bodley Head, 1971), p. 54, notes that by the end of the book we sense "something lost"; F.R. Southerington, *Hardy's Vision of Man* (London: Chatto and Windus, 1971), pp. 46-47, names "time" and "sexuality" as obtrusive factors upon this picture of a society embedded in a rural environment.
3. Douglas Brown, *Thomas Hardy* (London: Longmans, 1954), p. 45, calls it "facetious"; he and others find a certain aesthetic uncertainty here.
4. H.L. Weatherby, "Old Fashioned Gods: Eliot on Lawrence and Hardy", *Sewanee Review*, Volume 9, 1967, suggests that harmony is restored by the marriage at the end. Here and elsewhere he seems to overlook the sense of disquiet, and the inability of the traditional community to deal with disruption and deviancy.
5. "Study of Hardy" in *Phoenix* (New York: Viking Compass, 1972), p. 412.
6. Jean R. Brooks, p. 156, notes both a loss of communal involvement in religion and "the sustaining power of ritual close to nature".
7. Henry James's well-known condescension from his review of *Far From the Madding Crowd*, which appeared in *The New York Nation*.
8. Not merely the "natural man", but the man whose natural affiliations combine with other factors to make him balanced or "whole".
9. The swamp scene is more complex, however. Cf. Southerington, p. 73, and Brooks, p. 167.
10. Southerington, p. 63, rightly claims that the barn represents "rural continuity at its best", and Merryn Williams, *Thomas Hardy and Rural England* (London: Macmillan, 1972), p. 131, notes the significance of the barn's practical function. She is right to insist that the barn is not "timeless" in any "romantic or mystical" sense — if she means by that that Hardy is not merely expressing conventional sentiments. On the other hand, the passage is not an auction listing — meanings and significances beyond the *merely* practical carry us to an awareness of what endurance and integrity mean in the context of such a community. For some references to the way the architecture in this novel in general evokes "balance", see C.J.P. Beatty, "Far From the Madding Crowd: A Reassessment" in *Thomas Hardy and the Modern World* (Dorchester: The Thomas Hardy Society, 1974), edited by F.B. Pinion, pp. 14-36.

11. Southerington makes this point clearly and comprehensively. He interprets Oak most persuasively as the adaptive man, the man of balance, and the community guide, pp. 60-75. James Wright in his "Afterword" to *Far From the Madding Crowd* (New York: Signet, 1961) makes clear Gabriel's role as the natural man. Brooks, p. 164, argues that he creates order out of chaos, which is, as I see it, precisely the traditional relevance of the agricultural community *vis à vis* "untamed" nature.

12. Howard Babb's interpretation of the book as fundamentally contrasting "nature" and "civilization" seems mistaken to me. Cf. "Setting and Theme in *Far From the Madding Crowd*", *ELH*, Volume XXX, 1963, pp. 147-161.

13. Cf. Holloway, p. 285: "The great disaster for an individual [in Hardy] is to be *déraciné*".

14. As Morrell does, p. 99.

15. On the sexual symbolism, cf. Richard C. Carpenter, "The Mirror and the Sword: Imagery in *Far From the Madding Crowd*", *Nineteenth Century Fiction*, Volume XVIII (1963-64), pp. 342-344.

16. *The Making of THE RETURN OF THE NATIVE* (Berkley: University of California, 1960), p. 40.

17. Cf. F.B. Pinion, *A Hardy Companion* (London: Macmillan, 1968), p. 34, and Goldberg, "Hardy's Double-Visioned Universe," *Essays in Criticism*, Volume VIII (1957), p. 375. Certain critics, Millgate, for one, pp. 132-3, who is too obsessed with Jamesian point-of-view; and George Wing, *Hardy* (Edinburgh and London: Oliver and Boyd 1963), pp. 52-54, because he misunderstands Hardy's peculiar mythopoesis and the unfolding of this image in the book — refuse to be impressed by the functionality of the heath. I agree with Brooks, p. 177, who hails the Wagnerian grandeur of the opening.

18. Cf. M.A. Goldberg, pp. 374-382, which has much to say that is helpful here. I agree with him on the "neutrality" of Hardy's universe, and on the emergence of a true "poetry" out of the Darwinism, but I fail to understand exactly how the world of "culture" and "science" are reconciled or juxtaposed; I see rather a failure of reconciliation; a schizophrenia between "humane ideals" and "scientific reality".

19. Cf. Paterson, pp. 17-22; 132.

20. Cf. Ruth A. Firor, *Folkways in Thomas Hardy* (New York: A.S. Barnes, 1962), pp. 265-268.

21. Cf. Morrell, pp. 94-98.

22. Cf. Harold Orel, *Thomas Hardy's Epic Drama: A Study of the Dynasts* (New York: Greenwood Press, 1969), pp. 50-65. Orel finds sources for Hardy's "sublime" in Burke, and notes in passing that there is no precise term to cover the long and wide spatial vistas Hardy uses in *The Dynasts*. One of the advantages of the construct of "natural sublime" as set forth in this study is that it enables critics to handle such spatial components as part of an understood and common spatial "effect".

23. Merryn Williams, pp. 136-144 makes good points about the significance of Egdon as "living soil", and stresses its character of rural backwater that needs reforming. I believe she goes a bit overboard on this line, however, and distorts the novel. "Reforming" Egdon is a not unambiguous undertaking, and Clym is not simply a foiled hero of reform; he is also quite foolish, priggish and unrealistic. Furthermore, Egdon's "backwardness" should not

be written off with such "enlightened" assurance that all Egdon Heath needs to set it right is to become a garden suburb. Such a prospect, indeed, is both physically grotesque and spiritually appalling — far more so than Susan Nunsuch's voodoo.

24. Brooks, p. 187, makes the sharp point that Clym is placed here "within the limited area where man can still find certainty".

25. Hardy's friend Mr. Clodd told him in 1890 why "the superstitions of a remote Asiatic and a Dorset labourer are the same": "The attitude of man," he says, "at corresponding levels of culture, before like phenomena is pretty much the same, your Dorset peasants representing the persistence of the barbaric idea which confuses persons and things, and founds wide generalizations on the slenderest analogies". See Florence Emily Hardy, *The Life of Thomas Hardy* (London: Macmillan, 1962), p. 230. Hardy immediately saw the connection of this with poetic expression, but did not go on to draw conclusions about a "myth-making" impulse. The explanation in the text of *The Return of the Native* itself about the fires being an "instinctive and resistant act of man" and the reference to the varying "rational" explanations makes my point.

26. *Phoenix*, p. 415.

27. This line of argument derives from Brown, pp. 63-70; and from his *Thomas Hardy: The Mayor of Casterbridge* (London: E. Arnold, 1964); and is reaffirmed in various measure by D.A. Dike, "A Modern Oedipus: *The Mayor of Casterbridge*," *Essays in Criticism*, Volume II (1952), pp. 169-179; Millgate, p. 233; and Brooks, 196-215.

28. Cf. Robert B. Heilman's "Introduction" to *The Mayor of Casterbridge* (Boston: Houghton Mifflin, 1962), pp. v-xxxviii.

29. Cf. Pinion, p. 369.

30. This is to offer a new and hopefully helpful way of regarding the supposed "intrusions" of Hardy's commentary. Cf., e.g. Millgate, p. 271, and Southerington, p. 125, for other ways of handling this problem.

31. Cf. Elliot B. Gose, Jr., "Psychic Evolution: Darwinism and Initiation in *Tess of the d'Urbervilles*", *Nineteenth Century Fiction*, Volume 18 (1963-1964), pp. 261-272, for a connection of this "blood theme" with Darwinian primordialism.

32. T.H. Huxley, *Collected Essays*, Volume 9, *Evolution and Ethics and Other Essays* (New York: Appleton Century Crofts, 1898), pp. 40-41. See also my chapter on Wells.

33. Merryn Williams, cautioning us about the use of the term "peasant", locates Tess in a specific class range between small farmer and rural proletarian, p. 173.

34. Steven Marcus, *Other Victorians; A Study of Sexuality and Pornography in Mid-Nineteenth Century England* (New York: Basic Books, 1974). Cf. also Merryn Williams on "the theme of seduction", p. 79-99, and the interesting comments on Tess as "victim" in Evelyn Hardy, *Thomas Hardy: A Critical Biography* (London: The Hogarth Press, 1954), pp. 231-235.

35. As Allan Brick largely does in "Paradise and Consciousness in Hardy's *Tess*", *Nineteenth Century Fiction*, Volume 17 (1962-1963), pp. 115-134. Cf. also Morrell, pp. 90-93.

36. Cf. Arthur Mizener, "*Jude the Obscure* as a Tragedy", *The Southern Review*, VI (1940), pp. 193-213 for *both* views. Van Ghent, *The English Novel: Form and Function* (New York: Holt, Rinehart and Winston, 1953),

p. 203 refers to "the sensual dream, the lost Paradise". Brooks, p. 244, tries to twist the meaning of "paradise" to accommodate human limitation, but if we are back in 'everyday" life, why use it at all?

37. Cf. Morrell on the "unweeded garden", pp. 91-92.

38. Cf. Gose, pp. 266-267.

39. Cf. Philip Mahone Griffith, "The Image of the Trapped Animal in *Tess of the d'Urbervilles*", *Tulane Studies in English*, Volume 13 (1963), pp. 85-94. Griffith, however, confuses Hardy's sense of natural and social interaction, and misses the Darwinian implications of entrapment. T.E.M. Boll, "Tess as an Animal in Nature", *English Literature in Transition*, Volume 8-9 (1965-1966), pp. 210-211, further confuses the issue by making out Hardy as an advocate for natural law at all costs.

40. Tess's name, according to Millgate, p. 269, means "reaper" or "carrying ears of corn", but she is not merely a reaper in the old sense; she does develop toward a kind of new selfhood. Thus it seems not quite true to say, as Millgate does, that "her pilgrimage has no possible goal", p. 273.

41. Brick, p. 134, ingeniously contrasts the spatial placement of the characters at the end of this novel with some passages from Arnold, and brings out the objectifying power of Hardy's imagination. In my own comments on Hardy's spatial forms, I have not drawn much on Carol Reed Andersen's "Time, Space and Perspective in Thomas Hardy", *Nineteenth Century Fiction*, Volume IX (1954-55), pp. 192-208, finding her idea that Hardy's technique "appears to be the pathetic fallacy driven to such an extreme that it is no longer a fallacy but an artistic integer" rather unhelpful.

42. Lawrence's vision of Egdon Heath as the "strong and fecund" body of earth begins to project this kind of vision on Hardy, though Lawrence has really another axe to grind. John Holloway offers us a fairly simplified "ecological" Hardy, for whom "it is right to live naturally", which means "to live in continuity with one's whole biological and geographical environment" (p. 281), a view which is a rather limited entrée to the novels, as Roy Morrell has demonstrated in adequate detail. David J. de Laura, trying to make sense of *Tess*, concludes that Hardy is a Wordsworthian despite himself. Cf. de Laura, "The Ache of Modernism in Hardy's Later Novels," *ELH*, XXXIV (1967), pp. 380-399.

43. John Wain, "The Poetry of Thomas Hardy," *Critical* Quarterly, Volume 8, Number 2 (Summer, 1966) p. 170. But see R.J. White, *Thomas Hardy and History* (London: Macmillan, 1974) p. 50 for a contrary point of view.

44. "The Dorsetshire Labourer" in *Thomas Hardy's Personal Writings*, edited by Harold Orel (Lawrence, Kansas: Kansas University Press, 1966), p. 182.

45. Harvey Curtis Webster, *On a Darkling Plain* (Chicago: University Press, 1947), pp. 27-44.

46. *The Life of Thomas Hardy*, pp. 243-244; p. 176.

47. Webster, pp. 68-71 emphasizes the "meaninglessness" of human attractions based on Darwinian sexual selection, but he draws mostly from the poems to make his point. The more complete psychology of the novels indicates something a little different: that "impulse" is valuable but often sadly unaccompanied by the insight and wisdom that would make it truly creative, both in relationships and in society. Cf. Troy's, Eustacia's, Henchard's appealing but destructive "irrationality".

245

48. Cf. Morton Dauwen Zabel, "Hardy in Defence of His Art: The Aesthetic of Incongruity" in *Craft and Character in Modern Fiction*, reprinted in Guerard's *Hardy: A Collection of Critical Essays*, pp. 24-45.
49. "The Science of Fiction" in *Thomas Hardy's Personal Writings*, p. 135.
50. Heilman, p. XVIII.
51. *Les Deux Sources de la Morale et de la Religion*, pp. 151-156.
52. *Life of Thomas Hardy*, p. 386. See also Pinion, *A Hardy Companion*, pp. 143-151.
53. *Life of Thomas Hardy*, p. 252.
54. *Life of Thomas Hardy*, pp. 116, 120, 185.
55. Zabel, p. 37.

PART THREE, CHAPTER TWO:
H.G. Wells: The Claustrophobia and Vertigo of Scientific Space

1. Pritchett says of *The Time Machine*, "It will take its place among the great stories of our language". *The Living Novel* (London: Arrow Books, 1960), p. 125. See the summary of the book's reception in Ingvald Raknem, *H.G. Wells and his Critics* (London: Allen and Unwin, 1962), p. 16.
2. Robert M. Philmus, "*The Time Machine;* or, The Fourth Dimension As Prophecy", *PMLA*, LXXXIV (1969), pp. 530-535, and *Into the Unknown: The Evolution of Science Fiction from Francis Godwin to H.G. Wells* (Berkeley: University of California Press, 1970), pp. 69-78.
3. See Bernard Bergonzi, *The Early H.G. Wells* (Toronto: University Press, 1961), pp. 31-34, and 158.
4. T.H. Huxley, *Collected Essays*, Volume 9, p. 85. On Huxley see also William Irvine, *Apes, Angels and Victorians* (London: Weidenfeld and Nicolson, 1955) and on the Wells-Huxley connection, Norman and Jeanne Mackenzie, *The Time Traveller* (London: Weidenfeld and Nicolson, 1973), pp. 53-59; Mark R. Hillegas, *The Future as Nightmare: H.G. Wells and the Anti-Utopians* (New York: Oxford University Press, 1967), pp. 18-21, and W. Warren Wagar, *H.G. Wells and the World State* (New Haven: Yale University Press, 1951), p. 17.
5. T.H. Huxley, *Collected Essays*, Volume 9, pp. 40-41; 214-16.
6. This anticipates Zamyatin's idea of the danger of social entropy.
7. For Wells's "Fabian" adventures, cf. Margaret Cole, *The Story of Fabian Socialism* (London: Mercury Books, 1963), pp. 117-124.
8. Cf. T.H. Huxley, *Collected Essays*, Volume 9, p. 85. "Devolution" in scientific terms, then, implies simply a transformation of the organism to meet new environmental conditions. It need have no sinister implications such as Wells projects here or in his essay "The Man of the Year Million", which Bergonzi discusses in connection with *The Time Machine*. Bergonzi is surely correct, however, in seeing Wells's use of this idea as connected with a general *fin de siècle* fascination with "degeneration". Again, Wells chooses a scientific possibility that is extreme and explores it for its human implications. He ignores the fact that social evolution makes man's dependence on environment less direct, and the fact that biological evolution seems to be a complexifying process. Cf. also Philmus, "*The Time Machine;* or, The Fourth Dimension as Prophecy" for a discussion of Wells's relevant article on "Zoological Retrogression".

9. Anthony West, "H.G. Wells" in *Encounter*, Volume 8, (February, 1957), pp. 53-54.

10. *Experiment in Autobiography* (New York: Macmillan, 1934), pp. 168-172.

11. "Carnot's cycle" is mentioned in the opening paragraph of "The Lord of the Dynamos" (1894). And Camille Flammarion and other popularizers of astronomy were making much of the spectre of a universal "heat-death". See *La Fin du Monde* (Paris, 1894), p. 115 for a striking illustration.

12. Cf. "On a Universal Tendency in Nature to the Dissipation of Mechanical Energy" by Professor W. Thomson (Lord Kelvin) in *The London, Edinburgh and Dublin Philosophical Magazine and Journal of Science*, Volume IV (July-December, 1852), p. 306. "Within a finite period of time past the earth must have been, and within a finite period of time to come the earth must again be, unfit for the habitation of man as at present constituted, unless operations have been, or are to be performed, which are impossible under the laws to which the known operations going on at present in the material world are subject".

13. "Current" meaning during the last fifty years or so. See, for example, the well-known discussion by Sir Arthur Eddington in *New Pathways in Science* (Cambridge, England: University Press, 1935), pp. 50-71. Compare the more recent statements of G.J. Whitrow, "Time and the Universe", and Richard Schlegel, "Time and Thermodynamics", both in J.T. Fraser, *The Voices of Time* (New York: George Braziller, 1966).

14. Bergonzi, pp. 1-22.

15. Compare the article mentioned in my note 12, above, with, for example, Joseph Needham on "Evolution and Thermodynamics" in *Time: The Refreshing River* (London: Allen & Unwin, 1948), and with the statement in *The Encyclopedia of Physics*, edited by Robert M. Besancon, Second Edition (Toronto: van Nostrand Reinhold, 1974), pp. 463-4. "The principle of irreversibility is *not* an absolute law of nature . . . since Newton's second law of motion is unchanged when -t is substituted for t, and there is no direct evidence that interatomic forces are dissipative . . . In this view irreversibility is a statistical property, which appears to be a general law of nature only because the probability of reversal is extremely small". (Eddington, however, took that into account).

16. Cf. Bergonzi, p. 53; Wagner's Nibelungs offer a striking example.

17. Cf. Bergonzi, pp. 48-9. The Eloi, as a race deprived of creative contact with their instinctual depths (the energetic side of the Morlock nature) are of course effete. We see parts of a fractured psychological totality, which would have to be creatively fused again to make up the truly human.

18. One of the significances of the repeated motif of cannibalism in Wells is its reference to "self-devouring"; the race eating its own substance. It is furthermore a "dark sacrament" of fallen man as he appears in Wells's Naturalistic vision of evil. Cf. Conrad's "unspeakable rites" in *Heart of Darkness*, and the "pact" between Gerald and Gudrun in *Women in Love* for analogous versions of a primordial and post-Darwinian corruption of instinct.

19. On the myth of Prometheus, see Robert Graves, *The Greek Myths* (Baltimore: Penguin Books, 1955), Volume I, pp. 143-149. The Promethean spirit manifests itself in a desire to transform nature and to extend human consciousness. The Promethean act depends on the existence of an energy

source on the physical level, and on man's daring and initiative on the psychological and spiritual level. All science involves Promethean transformation, but, as *The Time Machine* (both through its strengths and weaknesses) helps us to understand, such transformation is not the whole story about becoming human. Pritchett, p. 122, refers to the frequency of fires in Wells. Without belabouring his witty point, one can say that these "anarchic" fires can also be seen as one element in the overriding spatial patterns I have suggested here. Fire is energy and though it may be destructive, it leads onward, to new experience, new consciousness.

20. Philmus, "*The Time Machine;* or, The Fourth Dimension as Prophecy", p. 534.

21. Pritchett describes this memorably as "faint squirms of idyllic petting", p. 125. Cf. Lovat Dickson, *H.G. Wells: His Turbulent Life and Times* (London: Macmillan, 1969) for an account of Wells's own love relationships that confirms the tendency to self-indulgence and the pattern of claustrophobia and assertion of freedom.

22. The views I shall be developing here bear some resemblance to those put forth by the Mackenzies in their chapter "Tales of Space and Time" in *The Time Traveller*, where Wells's "cosmology" is analyzed in terms of "pessimism" and "optimism" and related to the scientific (and in particular, the Darwinian) vision; while Wells's "claustrophobia" is analyzed in Robert P. Weeks, "Disentanglement as a Theme in H.G. Wells's Fiction", *Papers of the Michigan Academy of Science, Arts and Letters*, XXXIX (1954), pp. 439-444. Wells criticism, beginning with the assumption that the "Utopian" Wells was the significant one, has turned in recent years toward a detailed consideration of the darker vision of the early work. Cf. Hillegas, pp. 16-18. For the background to Wells's position as novelist of cosmic space, see J.O. Bailey, *Pilgrims through Space and Time* (New York: Argus Books, 1947), and especially Philmus, *Into the Unknown*.

23. Cf. Bernard Bergonzi, *The Early H.G. Wells*, pp. 49-50; also "The Door in the Wall", which I have already referred to in Part Two, chapter three.

24. There is little indication that Prendick is a "humanist intellectual" as Bergonzi points out, p. 109. Contrary to Bergonzi's opinion, neither Frankenstein nor Moreau is an "alchemist", nor does Prendick seem to represent "science" at all. Moreau has cast out the moral frame of reference in his work; in him Wells captures the dilemma of a science which is devoted to "interfering" with natural things, without being able to place them in a context of human significance. Even the most nobly-motivated activities must be judged by their results in terms of the whole human situation. Cf. Philmus *Into the Unknown*, p. 125-6.

25. By shooting the Leopard Man, "on the impulse of a moment", Prendick seizes the initiative for the first time in the novel. He has decided that death is preferable to torture and has taken it upon himself to cancel out his blasphemous "life" and give it peace. But this act of violence draws him into Moreau's world in a direct way.

26. Cf. Bergonzi, pp. 104-108.

27. This kind of trope was used very successfully (in the form of a match cut) in Stanley Kubrick's famous film, *2001: A Space Odyssey*.

28. On symbolic machinery, see Northrop Frye, *Anatomy of Criticism*, p. 150; and Leo Marx, *The Machine in the Garden: Technology and the Pastoral*

Ideal in America (New York: Oxford University Press, 1964), p. 170 ff.

29. Cf. the impressive concluding speech of Raymond Massey in Wells's film of 1936, *Things to Come*.
30. Norman Nicholson, *H.G. Wells* (London: Arthur Barker, 1950), p. 14.
31. Nicholson, p. 14.
32. Cf. Jack Williamson, "H.G. Wells, Critic of Progress: A Study of the Early Fiction", *Riverside Quarterly*, Volume III, Number 2 (March, 1968), p. 108; also Leo J. Henkin, *Darwinism in the English Novel, 1860-1910* (New York: Russell & Russell, 1963), p. 257.
33. It is fascinating that Orson Welles's broadcast of Wells's novel should have triggered a wave of popular madness and confusion analogous to that depicted in *The War of the Worlds*. Cf., among others, Norman and Jeanne Mackenzie, *The Time Traveller*, pp. 410-412.
34. Quoted in Bergonzi, p. 157.
35. Cf. Marjorie Hope Nicolson, *Voyages to the Moon* (New York: Macmillan, 1948), pp. 249-50, Philmus, *Into the Unknown*, pp. 37-55.
36. This kind of expression seems sincere, in contrast to Wells's more self-conscious public pronouncements in *God the Invisible King* and *The Soul of a Bishop*. As is usually the case with English writers, Wells's connection with Naturalism has not been convincingly charted. But see Raknem, pp. 282-304.
37. Entropy may refer to information theory as well as physical nature. See David Hawkins, *The Language of Nature* (San Francisco: W.H. Freeman, 1964).
38. Though this specific interpretation is not quite made, there is certainly a great deal of evidence for it in the Dickson and Mackenzie biographies, and Pritchett's essay on Wells looks in the same direction.
39. W. Warren Wagar, *H.G. Wells and the World State* (New Haven: Yale University Press, 1961), p. 62 & ff. It should be noted that Wagar is not explicitly concerned with the fiction, and that he states, at one point: "Wells was willing at times to admit that there might be a deeper relationship between human life and the cosmos . . ." Wagar, p. 76.
40. Frye, *Anatomy of Criticism*, p. 33. Cf. also pp. 49, 51, 159.
41. In an excellent essay on the subject, Stephen Toulmin seems unnecessarily dubious about the value of transforming "pure" science into myth. In fact, this is surely one of the essential tasks of the modern writer exploring the scientific universe for its human and "metaphysical" relevance. Cf. Toulmin, "Scientific Theories and Scientific Myths" in A. MacIntyre, *Metaphysical Beliefs* (London: SCM Press, 1957), pp. 20-21.

PART THREE, CHAPTER THREE:
D.H. Lawrence and the Struggle for A Human Space

1. Cf., e.g. F.R. Leavis, *D.H. Lawrence: Novelist* (Harmondsworth: Peregrine, 1964), p. 105, and Harry T. Moore, *The Intelligent Heart* (Harmondsworth: Penguin, 1960), pp. 23-27.
2. See the useful discussion in Julian Moynahan, *The Deed of Life* (Oxford: University Press, 1963), pp. 5-12.
3. Raney Stanford, "Thomas Hardy and D.H. Lawrence's *The White Peacock*", *Modern Fiction Studies*, Volume V, Number 1 (Spring, 1959), pp. 19-28, makes Lawrence's nature too "psychological" in comparison

with Hardy's but clearly establishes the influence of Hardy on Lawrence's "sense of place" at this point. Mark Schorer on "Lawrence and the Spirit of Place" in Harry T. Moore, *A D.H. Lawrence Miscellany* (Carbondale: Southern Illinois University Press, 1959) perhaps reads too much into the description of *The White Peacock*, and certainly misinterprets the use of nature in *Sons and Lovers*, in which there is no opposition of "flower and farm and field to mine and machine and factory" along the lines he imagines.

4. The whole question of nature in *Sons and Lovers* is well-handled by Dorothy van Ghent, *The English Novel: Form and Function* (New York: Holt, Rinehart and Winston, 1953), pp. 49-52. She understands Lawrence's "vital matrix" as the evocation of something basically unexplored or neglected in western society.

5. Moynahan, p. 23.

6. Cf., for example, Arnold Kettle, *An Introduction to the English Novel*, Volume II (New York: Harper Torchbook, 1960), pp. 121-123; and Keith Sagar, *The Art of D.H. Lawrence* (Cambridge: University Press, 1966), p. 45.

7. *Phoenix II* (London: Heinemann, 1968), p. 373.

8. For Biblical imagery in *The Rainbow*, see George H. Ford, *Double Measure: A Study of the Novels and Stories of D.H. Lawrence* (New York: Holt, Rinehart and Winston, 1965), Chapter six. Ford's comments are always helpful, but I am making some new points here and in what follows.

9. Louis Bouyer, in *Rite and Man* (Notre Dame: University Press, 1963), p. 159 writes of Yahweh that he "in the desert freely dwelt with his people, but as a traveller, always retaining his freedom to leave, and never belonging to the land through which he was passing". Despite Martin Jarrett-Kerr's *D.H. Lawrence and Human Existence* (London: Rockliff, 1951), and George A. Panichas's *Adventure in Consciousness: The Meaning of D.H. Lawrence's Religious Quest* (The Hague: Mouton, 1964), the subject of Lawrence and the modern religious consciousness, or of his literary apprehension of modes of sacred space and time, has hardly been touched.

10. *Phoenix II*, p. 413.

11. See his comments in "Books", *Phoenix* (New York: Viking Compass, 1972), pp. 731-734, and "On Human Destiny" in *Phoenix II*, pp. 623-629, in particular.

12. Leavis's point, that Tom Brangwen desires to be satisfied in a less crude way than the animal, and his general characterization of Brangwen, are well-taken, but there is no need to be defensive about the kind of peasant-consciousness I am defining here. Daleski's reference to Tom Brangwen as a "creature of the dark" gives the psychological dimension of my judgment. Cf. Leavis, *D.H. Lawrence: Novelist*, pp. 108-112; and H.M. Daleski, *The Forked Flame* (Evanston: Northwestern University Press, 1965), p. 84.

13. My point is that the peasant consciousness is not simply to be superseded by this "outside" world, which itself is too one-sided, but is rather to be the source of a complementary element that will make possible the transformation of the static urban world into the truly human world of post-capitalistic man. The brilliant essay of Raymond Williams, "Tolstoy, Lawrence, and Tragedy", *Kenyon Review*, Volume 25 (Autumn, 1963), pp. 633-650 argues a separation between Tolstoy and the Lawrence of *Women in Love* on the question of "the discovery of the meaning of natural work and its relations

with other men and with the land''. As Williams suggests, Lawrence ultimately fails to move creatively from sexuality to sociality, from the individual to the social dimension, though I believe this is a personal failure and
not necessarily the fate of his kind of ''counter-culture'' vision, or of our age
in general. Cf. also Scott Sanders, *D.H. Lawrence: The World of the Five
Major Novels* (New York: Viking Press, 1973), where these issues are dealt
with.

14. In ''The Crown'' Lawrence specifically relates Anna's ''dancing before the
Ark'' to the interplay between the epochs of Flesh and Love. Cf. *Phoenix II*,
p. 369. In the same essay, Lawrence describes how the battle of opposites
produces ''the third thing''. Lydia had already warned Anna that the marital
struggle must yield up ''what is neither you nor him'', the love which is ''the
third thing you must create''. Anna's dance signifies the reversal of the
one-sided situation in which she is enclosed by the flesh of darkness; in the
womb the light will grow stronger and assert itself. The Biblical parallel with
David points up the reversal of roles between Anna and Will.

15. Cf. Colin Clarke's grasping of the nettle in *River of Dissolution* (London:
Routledge and Kegan Paul, 1969), pp. 58-59. I am, of course, following
Clarke part of the way here, though attempting to avoid his extremely
one-sided version of these matters.

16. Cf. ''The Two Principles'' in *Phoenix II*, p. 231 for Lawrence's
''alchemical'' musings. The fire-water conjunction of opposites is related to
''times of disintegration, the crumbling of an era'', pp. 234-235.

17. *Pace* the C.P. Snow of *The Two Cultures: And a Second Look* (New York:
Mentor, 1964), p. 84.

18. *Phoenix*, p. 428.

19. Surely the resemblance between ''Frankstone'' and ''Frankenstein'' is not
accidental.

20. Lawrence's biological orientation is first of all ''holistic'' in its insistence on
the dynamic integral character of both physical and personal structures. In
Fantasia of the Unconscious, (Harmondsworth: Penguin, 1971), p. 157, he
insists on the whole nature of the lowly fly, which is not ''a sum of various
things. A fly is a fly and the items of the sum are still fly''.

21. For Lawrence the self involves a ''sense of totality''; knowledge depends
upon the action of the body and its complete energies. *Fantasia*, p. 133. He
conceives of a ''nuclear unconscious'' rooted in the nervous system, which
underlies both organs and consciousness. This is a kind of *élan vital*, or
''spontaneous life motive'', every organism's experience of its ''center''. It
is a self-ordering principle, which Lawrence also calls the ''soul'', and it
precedes and directs the more mechanical ''psyche''. When Ursula reflects
upon the ''will'' of the one-celled organism under the microscope, she is
trying to understand the direction of the ''life-drive'' of this tiny creature.
Lawrence's occasionally vivid attacks on the ''bullying will'' should not
cause us to overlook his understanding of the ''will'' in one sense as the
power which rescues us from mechanism. If not perverted by mental consciousness, the will is a focussing of the ''incalculable impulses'' of the soul.
Cf. *Fantasia of the Unconscious*, and *The Symbolic Meaning*, edited by
Armin Arnold (Fontwell, Arundel: Centaur Press, 1962), p. 163. Although
the terminology seems to be part of a discredited ''vitalism'', I do not believe
Lawrence's thinking can be summed up in this way; what he is getting at is

that consciousness-experience demands a *language* of self-creation. He is not so much "importing" an "entelechy" as trying to render *what it feels like to be "inside"* that "matter" that science measures and dissolves into ever vaguer and more abstract imponderables.

22. Clarke, e.g. pp. 45-6, denies that the scene is properly integrated with the Skrebensky affair, whereas most commentators do make such a connection, and in my view, correctly. Ford, for example, points to the "maleness" of the horses, and their significance as a natural force, for they are an embodiment of the "Pan" feeling that Ursula seems to have lost. Cf. *Double Measure*, pp. 158-160. Daleski, working from an idea borrowed from E.L. Nicholes, suggests that the scene involves a reawakening of Ursula's primal passion, beginning to be lost in the affair with Skrebensky. Both Ford and Kenneth Inniss, *D.H. Lawrence's Bestiary: A Study of his Use of Animal Trope and Symbol* (The Hague: Mouton, 1971), p. 136, rightly emphasize the "naturalistic" tone of this scene, though Ford hedges a bit, and Inniss is committed to a *symboliste* view of Lawrence that I feel to be altogether on the wrong track. On the whole question of Lawrence's kind of symbolism there is Eliseo Vivas's idea of the "constitutive symbol", which seems to be merely a device for fitting Lawrence's art to a neo-Kantian or Cassirer-inspired aesthetic in which it manifestly does not belong. For common sense on this matter we have, fortunately, Spilka's assertion that Lawrence's symbols are "not suggestive evocations of timeless spiritual reality, but material and focal expressions of those vague but powerful forces of nature which occur, quite patently, in time". Cf. Eliseo Vivas, *D.H. Lawrence: The Triumph and Failure of Art* (London: Allen and Unwin, 1961), pp. 273-291, and Mark Spilka, *The Love Ethic of D.H. Lawrence* (Bloomington: Indiana University Press 1955), pp. 39-41.

23. The ending, of course, has been almost universally dismissed as inadequate. Cf. Leavis, p. 148; Hough, p. 90; Ford, with some qualification, p. 162; Daleski, p. 125, and Clarke, p. 67. The general view seems to be: 1) that it is unprepared for; and 2) that it is self-contradictory and rhetorically inflated. While it is true that the personal and social momentum of Ursula's vision remains a potential, the metaphorical circle is closed. We have moved from flesh to spirit, from past to present, and now stand on the edge of the realizable future in which the two polarities may be joined in a creative third phase. The trajectory of the book has led us from the old order of rural man to the city which functions too much as a dialectic opposite; in the future that may come about at any moment is the possibility of synthesis in which a marriage in the flesh, free of mechanism, might guarantee a new truth of the concrete, a truth that can be lived, but which is not merely "dark". This truth could begin in the microcosm of the two and ferment through all society. The visionary eye of Ursula can quite properly relocate the quest-goal in an immediate act that will achieve "the Holy Ghost". For the moment, though, the imagery of corruption and hard brittleness is quite appropriately understood as "triumphant"' Ursula is looking at the "present", in which there is no immediate evidence of escape from it, but, of course, in Lawrence's terms of natural evolutionary transformation, from the perspective of cyclical time, there is no reason why corruption and bloom cannot both be "eternal". A comparison with the ending of Zola's *Germinal* (in which there is a similar

252

purgation of darkness by the central character, and a similar combination of dark and light, mechanical and organic, corruption and fruition) might be in order. Both endings seem to me rather grand and ultimately coherent perorations, interesting conjunctions of character and metaphor, and Lawrence's is certainly not unprepared for, and hardly self-contradictory.

24. Aldous Huxley, ed., *The Letters of D.H. Lawrence* (London: Heinemann, 1932), p. 352.

25. This interpretation of *Blutbrüderschaft* is derived from Spilka, chapter seven; see also Daleski, p. 187, who interprets this Lawrencian gambit not socially, but in terms of a demand for both singleness and union.

26. Cf. W.R. Martin, "'Freedom Together' in D.H. Lawrence's *Women in Love*", *English Studies in Africa*, Volume 8, 1965, pp. 111-120. Martin interprets Birkin's and Ursula's "escape" as a partially successful adaptation to the vital part of "tradition", a very useful point, but one that does not get over the obstacle of "our own nowhere" for those to whom it is an obstacle.

27. Cf. Daniel Bell, "Work and its Discontents" in *The End of Ideology* (New York: The Free Press, 1960), pp. 222-262, for some observations on the role of work as a God-substitute in modern society; Alan Watts, *Nature Man and Woman* (London: Thames and Hudson, 1958), pp. 43-45, for the western roots of the "God of the Machine" idea, and my discussion of the idea of nature in western civilization in Chapter one.

28. This point is made by Raymond Williams, "Tolstoy, Lawrence and Tragedy", p. 644, and, perhaps originally, by Ford, pp. 211-12.

29. The significance of this scene as a pact of violence between Gudrun and Gerald has been well-charted by several critics, including Vivas, 246-251, Moynahan, p. 86, and Daleski, pp. 156-7.

30. Erich Neumann, *Art and the Creative Unconscious* (New York: Harper Torchbooks, 1966), pp. 162-3.

31. I don't think this point has quite been made before, but see David J. Gordon, *D.H. Lawrence as a Literary Critic* (New Haven: Yale University Press, 1966), p. 90, who refers to Lawrence's later work (post *Women in Love*) as exhibiting the perverse vital as a nemesis to a corrupt civilization. Kingsley Widmer in "Our Demonic Heritage: D.H. Lawrence" in *A D.H. Lawrence Miscellany*, p. 20, jocularly categorizes Lawrence's "savage nature" as an "exhilarating nothingness". Neither of these critics is aware of the larger pattern in which the alienation of consciousness from environment through mechanism had led (in a post-Darwinian context) to various versions of a "dark" nature turned against human presumption, nor of the connection between mental rigidity and "bestial" chaos.

32. What follows was written before I came to terms with the implications of Clarke's analysis of "dissolution", and I believe that, at the very least, it represents an important aspect left out of his probing. The centrality of Lawrence's commitment to an "organic" and "naturalistic" way of looking at things makes it desirable that the critic work within these terms where possible. Cf. *River of Dissolution* for Clarke's brilliant reduction of reduction.

33. Cf. the section, "Flimsiness of Civilization" in Shaw's "Preface" to *Back to Methuselah* (1921): "Nature holds no brief for the human experiment: it must stand or fall by its results. If Man will not serve, Nature will try another experiment". Raymond Williams claims as a constant theme in the book

"that man is a mistake as he is, and that the world would be better without him". Cf. Williams, "Tolstoy, Lawrence and Tragedy", p. 648. Richard D. Erlich, in "Castrophism and Coition: Universal and Individual Development in *Women in Love*", *Texas Studies in Literature and Language*, Volume 9 (1967), pp. 117-128, tries to connect the physical relationships with the "castastrophism" Lawrence assumed in nature.

34. In *Beyond the Pleasure Principle* (1920). Cf. Sigmund Freud, *Standard Edition*, volume XVIII, (London: Hogarth Press, 1961), pp. 34-64. On Lawrence and Freud, cf. especially, Philip Rieff, *The Triumph of the Therapeutic* (New York: Harper and Row, 1966), pp. 189-231.

35. That these lines are much disputed should perhaps be noted here.

36. Konrad Lorenz, *On Aggression* (New York: Bantam Books, 1971), p,239.

37. Even though the wrestling is portrayed in terms of sexual consummation, critics have almost universally played down the homosexual implications. As Daleski notes, p. 186, this scene is well-realized in comparison with Birkin and Ursula's "excurse" and this may account for the agreement of the commentators on its "extra-sexual" significance; rather than being merely "obscure", Lawrence here achieves an admirable artistic tension, just because he draws us so far away from the "obvious" content he has so daringly invoked. David Cavitch, *D.H. Lawrence and the New World* (New York: Oxford University Press, 1969), pp. 65-66, misses this point, and treats Lawrence as a "failed" or disguised "homoerotic". Despite Lawrence's Puritanism it is hard to believe he would have baulked at this issue, had it meant to him what Cavitch suggests it did.

38. Clarke's reading of this scene is particularly incisive. Cf. pp. 99-110.

39. On this, among many critics, cf. Hough, pp. 101-102.

40. 1) religious awe ("where the Sons of God saw the daughters of men"); 2) organic wholeness ("the silent delight of flowers in each other"); 3) plenitude of being ("the marvellous fullness of immediate gratification"); 4) accession to the more-than-human ("not a man, something other, something more"); 5) activation of a new physical knowledge and energy ("released from the darkest poles of the body"); 6) intouchness with the ultimate life-source ("the darkest, deepest, strangest life-source of the human body").

41. I do not propose to raise the issue of what Frank Kermode (*D.H. Lawrence*, New York: Viking Press, 1973, pp. 59-60; 75-80) quaintly calls "buggery" here, since it has been well-dealt with by Ford, pp. 203-205, and Daleski, pp. 105-106; 178-179; 303-304. The precise weakness of G. Wilson Knight's appraisal in "Lawrence, Joyce and Powys", *Essays in Criticism* Volume 11, (October, 1961), pp. 403-417, is that it fails to take into account the question of artistic realization. If for twenty or thirty years critics were oblivious of what Lawrence was hinting at in fact in the "burning out of shame" passages, then we must assume that these passages are in a different category from the merely difficult ones, such as Ursula with the horses, or Birkin throwing stones at the moon, which critics have always wanted to understand because they felt them to be powerful and significant. Such curious references to "positions" and private parts may be revelatory of Lawrence the man, but they cannot be the substance of significant criticism if they are so vaguely unfolded in the text as to practically escape the reader's notice. In the case of the alternative to "squirrel-cage" passion, the situation

is very different. We must make some judgment about the content of "star-polarity" just because its thematic relevance is unquestionable. What I have done here is to suggest a kind of analogy for "star-polarity", but it is not merely an analogy, and it is not far-fetched. Emile Delavenay, for example, in *D.H. Lawrence: The Man and His Work* (London: Heinemann, 1975), pp. 262-267, connects Lawrence with Oneida and while Kermode insists that Lawrence does not mention *coitus reservatus*, Aldous Huxley thinks that he does. Cf. Huxley's *Collected Essays* (New York: Harper Brothers, 1958), pp. 82-89. Huxley furthermore links the Oneida practices with Tantric yoga and with the Brethren of the Free Spirit, which reinforces my suggestion that Lawrence's "paradisal" gesture is a kind of "counter-culture" challenge to the distortions of the noble western Christian concept of *agape*. Compare Lawrence's erotic contexts with the descriptions of Tantric erotic ceremony in S.B. Dasgupta, *An Introduction to Tantric Buddhism* (Calcutta: University Press, 1958), pp. 145-188, and in Mircea Eliade, *Yoga: Immortality and Freedom* (New York: Bollingen, 1958), pp. 202-271.

42. While Vivas, pp. 138-9, thinks that to make sex sacred is to make it taboo, he misses the force of Lawrence's challenge to the played-out western religious sense, largely because Vivas himself is too complacent about modern society and the claims of conventional rationality.

43. *Nature, Man and Woman*, p. 188.

44. At this stage of western history it is hopefully no longer necessary to point out the validity and effectiveness of the Yoga-istic conception of the body-consciousness. Among many discussions, see Ernest Wood, *Yoga* (Harmondsworth: Pelican, 1964).

45. *Psychoanalysis and the Unconscious* (Harmondsworth; Penguin, 1971), p. 242. The emphasis is Lawrence's own.

46. *Psychoanalysis and the Unconscious*, pp. 229-242.

47. For analogous conceptions cf., for example, Alfred North Whitehead, *Science and the Modern World*, Michael Polanyi, *Personal Knowledge*, and Maurice Merleau-Ponty, *Sens et Non-Sens*, available as *Sense and Nonsense* (Evanston, Illinois: Northwestern University Press, 1964).

48. *Phoenix*, pp. 573-4.

49. I am indebted for some key observations to John Remsbury, "'Real Thinking': Lawrence and Cézanne", *Cambridge Quarterly* II (1966-67), pp. 117-147.

50. Cf. Michael Polanyi, *Science, Faith and Society* (Chicago: University Press Paperback, 1970), p. 10; also the same writer's *Personal Knowledge*. I believe Lawrence was getting at the concrete, immediate, and personal, nature of scientific intuition — this previously had been underemphasized by theorists in favor of the assumption of a rather naive version of generalization proceeding from "objective" investigation of the facts. Cf. Ian G. Barbour, *Issues in Science and Religion*, pp. 138-9 for a discussion of the fortunes of "naive realism".

51. This kind of thinking we can see mirrored in a diversity of moderns, among whom one might mention Teilhard de Chardin, Jung, Whitehead, and such sixties and post-sixties prophets as Alan Watts, Theodore Roszak and René Dubos.

52. *Phoenix II*, p. 397.

53. *Phoenix*, p. 293.

54. "Study of Thomas Hardy", *Phoenix*, p. 485. Cf. also Mircea Eliade, *Cosmos and History: The Myth of the Eternal Return* for the connection between conceptions of space and existential rooting; also, Teilhard de Chardin, *The Phenomenon of Man* (London: Fontana Books, 1972), pp. 249-252, for "the malady of space-time". C.S. Lewis's traveller, Ransom, has some interesting observations on this question in *Out of the Silent Planet*. Cf. also my chapter one, Part Two, and my comments on Wells.

55. "Introduction to These Paintings" in *Phoenix*, pp. 567-568.

56. That "matter" is "energy" is a useful scientific abstraction. Lawrence's point, however, is about the "solidity" of matter. Some criticism of his writing accuses him of "scientism" or else of dissolving the person in an impersonal flux of consciousness. At his best, surely, he is rendering the human person in depth, reaching up from and back down to the physical world as it emerges in the *Gestalt* of artistic perception. Compare, Remsbury, p. 157, with Robert B. Heilman, "Nomads, Monads, and the Mystique of the Soma", *Sewanee Review* LXVIII (1960), pp. 645-659, the latter suggesting that Lawrence was in flight from humanity into "monadic narcissii".

57. *Phoenix*, p. 464.

58. *Collected Letters*, edited by Harry T. Moore (London: Heinemann, 1962), p. 282.

59. What follows has been influenced by Reinhold Niebuhr, "Christ vs. Socrates", *The Saturday Review* (December 18, 1954), pp. 7-8, 37-39.

60. Cf. G.G. Simpson, *The Meaning of Evolution* (New Haven: Yale University, 1967), Chapter XVIII, and Gertrude Himmelfarb, *Victorian Minds* (New York: Crofts, 1968), chapter XII. Graham Hough in *The Dark Sun* (Harmondsworth: Pelican, 1961) places Lawrence clearly and convincingly within the naturalistic tradition and shows how Lawrence accommodates "struggle" (inherited from Darwinism) as "polarity", which is precisely the kind of post-Darwinian leap into the realm of value that I have been documenting throughout this study. Hough criticizes Lawrence's position mainly from the point of view of its failure to give due weight to "tragedy", which is the weakness of his Utopianism, while my emphasis here is with those critics (Vivas, Daleski, Sanders) who are disturbed by the immoral implications of a naturalism that is unchastened by some kind of ethic of brotherhood.

61. Although I have profited a great deal from Eugene Goodheart, *The Utopian Vision of D.H. Lawrence* (Chicago: University Press, 1963), and Baruch Hochman, *Another Ego: The Changing View of Self and Society in the Work of D.H. Lawrence* (Columbia, South Carolina: University of South Carolina Press, 1970), I have many points of disagreement with them, particularly on the question of Lawrence's sense of social reality. I believe that Lawrence's "rejection" of society was not so total as they imply, and that his attack was specifically on modern bourgeois western society which has developed reason and technics at the expense of concrete knowledge. It may be true, as Goodheart and Hochman would insist, that Christianity and Freud are right about the impossibility of any complete harmony between civilization and impulse; but Lawrence was also right to insist on the creative impulse which seeks to create a closer harmony. Furthermore, it is difficult to see "impulse" as the chief danger of our age, despite the ravages of Nazism, and obscurantist popular culture. Surely, the real dangers of our age are first of all, the

undermining of hope and joy in existence by a sterile intellectualism which destroys values only to have them reappear in hideous disguise; and, secondly, the threat of impersonal and "statistical" oppression by heartless bureaucracies. To those not actually starving, and able to concern themselves with higher values, these are indeed threats, and against them Lawrence's insistence on the necessity of concrete perception and "wholeness" will remain telling.

62. C.H. Waddington, *The Ethical Animal* (London: G. Allen & Unwin, 1960), p. 170. See also Arthur Koestler, *The Lotus and the Robot* (London: Hutchinson, 1960) and especially "Between the Lotus and the Robot" in *Drinkers of Infinity* (London: Hutchinson, 1968), pp. 287-291.

SELECTED GENERAL
BIBLIOGRAPHY

PART ONE
History, Philosophy and History of Ideas

Philip Appleman, ed. *Darwin*. New York: Norton, 1970.

Philip Appleman, et. al. *1859: Entering an Age of Crisis*. Bloomington: Indiana University Press, 1959.

Robert Ardrey. *The Territorial Imperative*. New York: Atheneum, 1961.

Ian G. Barbour. *Issues in Science and Religion*. New York: Prentice-Hall, 1966.

Marston Bates. *The Forest and The Sea: a look at the economy of nature and ecology of man*. New York: Random House, 1960.

--------------------. *Man in Nature*. Englewood Cliffs: Prentice-Hall, 1965.

Henri Baudet. *Paradise on Earth*. New Haven: Yale University Press, 1965.

Daniel Bell. *The End of Ideology*. New York: The Free Press, 1960.

Henri Bergson. *Les Deux Sources de la Morale et de la Religion*. Paris: Felix Alcan, 1932.

J.D. Bernal. *Science in History*. London: C.A. Watts, 1965.

Robert M. Besancon, ed. *The Encyclopedia of Physics*. Toronto: van Nostrand Reinhold, 1974.

George Boas. *Essays on Primitivism and Related Ideas in the Middle Ages*. New York: Octagon, 1966.

Alfred M. Bork. *Science and Language*. Boston: D.C. Heath, 1966.

Louis Bouyer. *Rite and Man*. Notre Dame: University Press, 1963.

E. Bovill. *English Country Life: 1780-1830*. London: Oxford University Press, 1963.

Asa Briggs, ed. *How They Lived: 1700-1815*. Oxford: Basil Blackwell, 1969.

British Broadcasting Corporation. *Ideas and Beliefs of the Victorians: An Historical Revolution of the Victorian Age*. London: Sylvan Press, 1944.

Jacob Burckhardt. *The Civilization of the Renaissance in Italy*. London: Phaidon, 1929.

E.A. Burtt. *The Metaphysical Foundations of Modern Science*. London: Routledge and Kegan Paul, 1951.

Joseph Campbell, ed. *Spirit and Nature: Papers from the Eranos Yearbook* V.1. New York: Pantheon, 1954.

J.D. Chambers, & G.E. Mingay. *The Agricultural Revolution 1750-1880*. New York: Schocken Books, 1966.

Chester S. Chard. *Man in Prehistory*. New York: McGraw-Hill, 1969.

S.G. Checkland. *The Rise of Industrial Society in England, 1815-1885*. London: Longmans, Green, 1964.

V. Gordon Childe. *What Happened in History*. Harmondsworth: Penguin, 1942.

Norman Cohn. *The Pursuit of the Millennium*. Rev. Ed. London: Temple Smith, 1970.

Margaret Cole. *The Story of Fabian Socialism*. London: Mercury Books, 1963.

R.G. Collingwood. *The Idea of Nature*. Oxford: The Clarendon Press, 1949.

W.C. Dampier. *A History of Science and Its Relations with Philosophy and Religion*. 4th ed. Cambridge: University Press, 1961.

Charles Darwin. *The Descent of Man*. London: John Murray, 1871.

--------------------. *The Origin of Species*. Harmondsworth: Penguin, 1970.

S.B. Dasgupta. *An Introduction to Tantric Buddhism*. Calcutta: University Press, 1958.

Sir Gavin de Beer. *Charles Darwin: Evolution By Natural Selection*. London: Nelson, 1963.

Sebastian de Grazia. *Of Time, Work and Leisure*. New York: Twentieth Century Fund, 1962.

Herbert Dingle. "Copernicus and the Planets" in *A Short History of Science*. New York: Anchor, 1959.

P.H. Ditchfield. *Old English Customs Extant at the Present Time*. Rpt. London: Methuen, 1968.

Theodosius Dobzhansky. *Mankind Evolving*. New Haven: Yale University Press, 1962.

René Dubos. *A God Within*. New York: Scribners, 1972.

--------------------. *So Human an Animal*. New York: Scribners, 1968.

Sir Arthur Eddington. *New Pathways in Science*. Cambridge: University Press, 1935.

Loren C. Eiseley. *Darwin's Century: Evolution and the Men Who Discovered It*. London: Gollancz, 1959.

Mircea Eliade. *Cosmos and History: the Myth of the Eternal Return*. New York: Harper, 1959.

--------------------. *The Sacred and the Profane*. New York: Harper and Row, 1961.

--------------------. *Yoga: Immortality and Freedom*. New York: Bollingen, 1958.

Alvar Ellegard. *Darwin and the General Reader. The Reception of Darwin's Theory of Evolution in the British Periodical Press, 1859-1872*. Goteberg: Almqvist and Wiksell, 1958.

Henri Ellenberger. *The Discovery of the Unconscious*. New York: Basic Books, 1970.

Ralph Waldo Emerson. "The Naturalist" in *The Early Lectures of Ralph Waldo Emerson*, Volume I, 1833-1836, edited by Stephen E. Whicher and Robert E. Spiller. Cambridge, Massachusetts: Harvard University Press, 1959.

E. Estvyn Evans. "The Ecology of Peasant Life in Western Europe" in W.L. Thomas, *Man's Role in Changing The Face of the Earth*, Volume I.

R.J. Forbes. *Man the Maker: A History of Technology and Engineering*. New York: Abelard-Schumann 1958.

Franklin L. Ford. *Europe 1780-1830*. London: Longmans, 1970.

Henri Frankfort. *Before Philosophy: The Intellectual Adventure of Ancient Man*. 1949; rpt. Baltimore: Penguin, 1964.

--------------------. *Kingship and the Gods: a Study of Ancient Near Eastern Religion as the Interpretation of Society and Nature*. Chicago: University of Chicago Press, 1948.

J.T. Fraser, ed. *The Voices of Time: a cooperative survey of man's views of time as expressed by the sciences and the humanities*. New York: G. Braziller, 1966.

Sigmund Freud. *Beyond the Pleasure Principle*, Standard Edition, Volume XVIII. London: Hogarth Press, 1961.

--------------------. *Civilization and its Discontents*, Standard Edition, Volume XXI. London: Hogarth Press, 1964.

Etienne Gilson. *Reason and Revelation in the Middle Ages*. New York: Scribners, 1938.

Charles C. Gillispie. *Genesis and Geology: the Decades before Darwin*. Cambridge, Massachusetts: Harvard University Press, 1951.

Thomas F. Glick, ed. *The Comparative Reception of Darwinism*. Austin: University of Texas, 1972.

John C. Greene. *Darwin & The Modern World View*. New York: New American Library of World Literature, 1963.

William Chase Greene. *Moira: Fate, Good and Evil in Greek Thought*. New York: Harper Row, 1963.

R.L. Gregory. *Eye and Brain*. New York: McGraw-Hill, 1973.

J.L. and Barbara Hammond. *The Village Laborer, 1760-1832*. London: Longmans Green, 1927.

Sir Alister Hardy. *The Living Stream: Evolution and Man*. New York: Harper and Row, 1965.

J. Hawkes. *History of Mankind, Cultural and Scientific Development, Volume I*, Parts I and II. New York: Harper and Row, 1963.

David Hawkins. *The Language of Nature*. San Francisco: W.H. Freeman, 1964.

H. Hearder. *Europe in the Nineteenth Century, 1830-1880*. London: Longmans, 1966.

Herbert Heaton. *Economic History of Europe*. Rev. ed. New York: Harper, 1948.

Gertrude Himmelfarb. *Darwin and the Darwinian Revolution*. Gloucester Mass.: Peter Smith, 1967.

--------------------. *Victorian Minds*. New York: Crofts, 1968.

Richard Hofstadter. *Social Darwinism in American Thought*. Philadelphia: University of Pennsylvania Press, 1944.

Alexander von Humboldt. *Cosmos: Sketch of a Physical Description of the Universe*. London: Longman, Brown, Green, and Longmans, 1849.

T.H. Huxley. *Collected Essays: Evolution and Ethics and Other Essays*. Vol. 9, New York: Appleton, 1898.

Edward S. Hyams. *Soil and Civilization*. London: Thames and Hudson, 1952.

William Irvine. *Apes, Angels, & Victorians: a joint biography of Darwin and Huxley*. London: Weidenfeld & Nicolson, 1955.

Geoffrey Alan Jellicoe. *Studies in Landscape Design*. London: Oxford University Press, 1960.

Lord Kelvin. "On a Universal Tendency in Nature to the Dissipation of Mechanical Energy", *The London, Edinbugh and Dublin Philosophical Magazine and Journal of Science*, Volume IV (July-December, 1852).

Arthur Koestler. "Between the Lotus and the Robot" in *Drinkers of Infinity*. London: Hutchinson, 1968.

--------------------. *The Lotus and the Robot*. London: Hutchinson, 1960.

Noel Korn and Fred Thompson, eds. *Human Evolution: Readings in Physical Anthropology*, 2nd ed. New York: Holt, Rinehart & Winston, 1967.

263

Yervant H. Krikorian, ed. *Naturalism and the Human Spirit*. New York: Columbia University Press, 1944.

Claude Levi-Strauss. *The Savage Mind*. London: Weidenfeld and Nicolson, 1966.

--------------------. *Tristes Tropiques*. New York: Criterion, 1961.

Bert James Loewenberg. *Darwinism Comes to America, 1859-1900*. Philadelphia: Fortress Press, 1969.

Konrad Lorenz. *King Solomon's Ring: New Light on Animal Ways*. New York: Crowell, 1952.

--------------------. *On Aggression*. London: Methuen, 1970.

Arthur O. Lovejoy and G. Boas, et. al. *A Documentary History of Primitivism and Related Ideas*. Baltimore: Johns Hopkins Press, 1935.

--------------------. *Essays in the History of Ideas*. Baltimore: Johns Hopkins, 1948.

--------------------. *The Great Chain of Being*. Cambridge, Massachusetts: Harvard University Press, 1936.

--------------------. "Optimism and Romanticism" in James L. Clifford, *Eighteenth Century English Literature*. New York: Galaxy, 1959.

Karl Löwith. *Meaning in History*. Chicago: University Press, 1957.

Steven Marcus. *The Other Victorians: A Study of Sexuality and Pornography in Mid-Nineteenth Century England*. New York: Basic Books, 1974.

George P. Marsh. *Man and Nature*, ed. by David Lowenthal. Reprinted Cambridge, Massachusetts: Harvard University Press, 1965.

Floyd W. Matson. *The Broken Image: Man, Science and Society*. New York: Anchor Books, 1966.

Grant McColley. "Humanism and the History of Astronomy" in Robert M. Palter, ed. *Toward Modern Science*.

Marshall McLuhan. *Understanding Media: The Extensions of Man*. New York: Signet, 1964.

William Hardy McNeill. *The Rise of the West: a History of the Human Community*. New York: Mentor, 1963.

Sir P.B. Medawar. "Imagination and Hypothesis", *Times Literary Supplement*, 25 October, 1963, pp. 849-50.

--------------------. "Science and Literature", *Encounter*, Volume 32 (January, 1969), pp. 15-23.

Bernard E. Meland. *The Secularization of Modern Culture*. Oxford: Oxford University Press, 1966.

James Mellaart. "Roots in the Soil", in *Dawn of Civilization*. London: Thames and Hudson, 1961.

Maurice Merleau-Ponty. *Sense and Nonsense*. Evanston, Illinois: Northwestern University Press, 1964.

R.J. Mitchell and M.D.R. Leys. *A History of the English People*. London: Longmans Green, 1950.

Jacques Monod. *Chance and Necessity*. New York: Alfred Knopf, 1971.

Ashley Montagu. *The Concept of the Primitive*. New York: Free Press, 1968.

Henry Morley, "Conrad Gessner" in Robert M. Palter, ed. *Toward Modern Science*.

Lewis Mumford. *The City in History: Its Origins, Its Transformations, and Its Prospects*. Harmondsworth: Pelican Books, 1961.

264

Joseph Needham. *Time, the Refreshing River*. London: Allen Unwin, 1948.

Erich Neumann. *Art and the Creative Unconscious*. New York: Harper Torchbooks, 1966.

Reinhold Niebuhr, "Christ vs. Socrates", *The Satruday Review* (December 18, 1954), pp. 7-8; 37-39.

F.S.C. Northrop, "Man's Relation to the Earth and its Bearing on His Aesthetic, Ethical and Legal Values" in W.L. Thomas. *Man's Role in Changing the Face of the Earth*.

Christabel Orwin and Edith H. Wetham. *History of British Agriculture, 1846-1941*. Hamden: Archon Books, 1964.

Henry Fairfield Osborne. *From the Greeks to Darwin: an outline of the development of the evolution idea*. New York: MacMillan, 1908.

Robert M. Palter, ed. *Toward Modern Science*, Vol. I, New York: Dutton, 1969.

Morse Peckham. *Beyond the Tragic Vision*. New York: George Braziller, 1962.

--------------------. "Darwinism and Darwinisticism", *Victorian Studies* III (Sept. 1959).

P.J. Perry. *British Agriculture: 1875-1914*. London: Methuen, 1973.

Gottfried Pfeifer. "The Quality of Peasant Living in Central Europe" in W.L. Thomas, *Man's Role in Changing the Face of the Earth*.

Michael Polanyi. *Personal Knowledge: Towards a Post-Critical Philosophy*. New York: Harper Torchbook, 1964.

--------------------. *Science, Faith and Society*. Chicago: Phoenix, 1970.

Jack M. Potter, et al. *Peasant Society: A Reader*. Boston: Little Brown, 1967.

Bernard M.G. Reardon. *Religious Thought in the Nineteenth Century*. London: Cambridge University Press, 1966.

Robert Redfield. *Peasant Society and Culture: An Anthropological Approach to Civilization*. Chicago: University of Chicago Press, 1965.

--------------------. *The Primitive World and its Transformations*. Ithaca, N.Y.: Cornell University Press, 1953.

Hans Reichenbach. *From Copernicus to Einstein*. New York: Philosophical Library, 1942.

--------------------. *The Rise of Scientific Philosophy*. Berkeley: University of California Press, 1951.

Philip Rieff. *The Triumph of the Therapeutic: Uses of Faith After Freud*. New York: Harper and Row, 1966.

J.M. Roberts. *Europe, 1880-1945*. New York: Holt, Rinehart and Winston, 1967.

Theodore Roszak. *The Making of A Counter-Culture*. Garden City, New York: Doubleday, 1969.

Max Ferdinand Scheler. *Man's Place in Nature*. Boston: Beacon Press, 1961.

Richard Schlegel. "Time and Thermodynamics" in J.T. Fraser, *The Voices of Time*.

Paul Shepard. *Man in The Landscape*. New York: Ballatine Books, 1967.

George Gaylord Simpson. *The Meaning of Evolution*. New Haven: Yale University Press, 1967.

Bernard W. Smith. *European Vision and the South Pacific*. Oxford: The Clarendon Press, 1960.

C.P. Snow. *The Two Cultures: and a Second Look*. New York: Mentor, 1964.

John H. Storer. *The Web of Life, A First Book of Ecology*. New York: Devin-Adair, 1956.

265

Pierre Teilhard de Chardin. *The Phenomenon of Man*. London: Fontana Books, 1972.

——————————. "The Spiritual Power of Matter" in *Hymn of the Universe*. New York: Harper and Row, Perennial Library, 1972.

W.L. Thomas, ed. *Man's Role in Changing the Face of the Earth*. Chicago: University Press, 1970.

David Thomson. *England in the Nineteenth Century*. Harmondsworth: Penguin, 1951.

——————————. *England in the Twentieth Century*. Harmondsworth: Penguin, 1965.

Time-Life Books. *The Emergence of Man*. New York, 1972-74.

Stephen Toulmin and June Goodfield. *The Fabric of the Heavens*. Harmondsworth: Penguin, 1963.

Stephen Toulmin. "Scientific Theories and Scientific Myths" in A. MacIntyre. *Metaphysical Beliefs*. London: SCM Press, 1957.

G.M. Trevelyan. *Illustrated English Social History*. Harmondsworth: Penguin, 1966.

Andrew van Melsen. *Evolution and Philosophy*. Pittsburgh: Duquesne University Press, 1965.

Charles Vereker. *Eighteenth Century Optimism*. Liverpool: University Press, 1968.

Conrad Hal Waddington. *The Ethical Animal*. London: G. Allen and Unwin, 1960.

W. Warren Wagar, ed. *European Intellectual History Since Darwin and Marx*. New York: Harper, 1967.

Alan W. Watts. *Myth and Ritual in Christianity*. London: Thames and Hudson, 1954.

——————————. *Nature, Man and Woman: A New Approach to Sexual Experience*. New York: Pantheon, 1958.

——————————. *The Way of Zen*. Harmondsworth: Penguin, 1962.

A.N. Whitehead. *Modes of Thought*. New York: Free Press, 1968.

——————————. *Science and the Modern World*. New York: Mentor, 1953.

G.J. Whitrow. *The Natural Philosophy of Time*. London: T. Nelson, 1961.

——————————. "Time and the Universe" in J.T. Fraser. *The Voices of Time*.

W.P.D. Wightman. *The Growth of Scientific Ideas*. New Haven: Yale University Press, 1953.

Raymond Williams. "Ideas of Nature". *Times Literary Supplement*, December, 1970, pp. 1419-1421.

——————————. *The Country and The City*. New York: Oxford University Press, 1973.

PART TWO
The Image of Nature in Literature and Art

M.H. Abrams. *English Romantic Poets: Modern Essays in Criticism*. New York: Oxford University Press, 1960.

--------------------. *The Mirror and the Lamp: Romantic Theory and the Critical Tradition*. New York: Oxford University Press, 1953.

Lars Ahnebrink. *The Beginnings of Naturalism in American Fiction*. New York: Russell and Russell, 1961.

John Armstrong. *The Paradise Myth*. London: Oxford University Press, 1969.

W.H. Auden. *The Enchaféd Flood*, or, *The Romantic Iconography of the Sea*. New York: Vintage Books, 1957.

Erich Auerbach. *Mimesis: The Representation of Reality in Western Literature*. New York: Anchor Books, 1957.

Gaston Bachelard. *The Poetics of Space*. New York: Orion, 1964.

J.O. Bailey. *Pilgrims Through Space and Time*. New York: Argus Books, 1947.

Owen Barfield. *Saving the Appearances: A Study in Idolatry*. New York: Harcourt, Brace and World, 1965.

Jacques Barzun. *Classic, Romantic, and Modern*. Boston: Little Brown, 1961.

Joseph Warren Beach. *The Concept of Nature in Nineteenth Century English Poetry*. London: Macmillan, 1936.

George J. Becker. *Documents of Modern Literary Realism*. Princeton: University Press, 1963.

E.K. Bennett. *A History of the German Novelle*. Rev. and continued by H.M. Waidson. Cambridge: University Press, 1961.

Harold Bloom, ed. *Romanticism and Consciousness*. New York: Norton, 1970.

Reginald Horace Blyth. *Zen in English Literature and Oriental Classics*. New York: E.P. Dutton, 1960.

Maud Bodkin. *Archetypal Patterns in Poetry. Psychological Studies of Imagination*. London: Oxford University Press, 1963.

Wayne Booth. *The Rhetoric of Fiction*. Chicago: University Press, 1961.

Sir Maurice Bowra. *The Heritage of Symbolism*. London: Macmillan, 1943.

--------------------. *Primitive Song*. London: Weidenfeld and Nicolson, 1962.

--------------------. *The Romantic Imagination*. New York: Oxford University Press, 1961.

Ernle Bradford. *Ulysses Found*. London: Sphere Books, 1963.

Edmund Burke. *A Philosophical Enquiry into The Origin of our Ideas of the Sublime and Beautiful*. Ed. J.T. Boulton. London: Routledge and Kegan Paul, 1958.

Stanley Burnshaw. *The Seamless Web*. London: Allen Lane, 1969.

Douglas Bush. *Science and English Poetry*. New York: Oxford University Press, 1950.

Frederick I. Carpenter. "The American Myth: Paradise (To Be) Regained". *PMLA*, LXXIV, 1959, pp. 599-606.

Sir Kenneth Clark. *Landscape into Art*. Harmondsworth: Penguin, 1956.

James L Clifford. *Eighteenth Century English Literature*. New York: Galaxy Books, 1959.

James Edmund Congleton. *Theories of Pastoral Poetry in England, 1684-1798*. Gainsville: University of Florida Press, 1952.

Ernest Robert Curtius. *European Literature and the Latin Middle Ages*. Trans. Willard R. Trask. New York: Pantheon Books, 1953.

John Francis Danby. *Shakespeare's Doctrine of Nature: a Study of King Lear*. London: Faber and Faber, 1949.

Bengt Danielsson. *Gauguin in the South Seas*. Garden City, New York: Doubleday, 1966.

Basil Davenport. *The Science-Fiction Novel: Imagination and Social Criticism*. Chicago: Advent, 1969.

Fred Alair Dudley, ed. *The Relations of Literature & Science: a Selected Bibliography, 1930-1967*. University Microfilms: Ann Arbor Michigan, 1968.

Gilbert T. Dunklin. *Wordsworth: Centenary Studies*. Princeton: University Press, 1951.

P.H. Epps. "The Golden Age", *Classical Journal*, XXIX (1933-34), pp. 292-296.

Benjamin Ifor Evans. *Literature & Science*. London: Allen & Unwin, 1954.

H.N. Fairchild. *The Noble Savage: a Study in Romantic Naturalism*. New York: Columbia University Press, 1928.

David Ferry. *The Limits of Mortality*. Middletown, Connecticut: Wesleyan University Press, 1963.

Joseph Frank. "Spatial Form in Modern Literature (esp. the novel)", *Sewanee Review* LIII (1945), pp. 221-240; 433-456.

Northrop Frye. *Anatomy of Criticism: Four essays*. Princeton: Princeton University Press, 1957.

--------------------. "The Drunken Boat: The Revolutionary Element in Romanticism" in *Romanticism Reconsidered*. New York: Columbia University Press, 1963.

Lilian R. Furst. *Romanticism in Perspective: a Comparative Study of the Romantic Movements in England, France and Germany*. New York: Humanities Press, 1967.

Richard Gerber, *Utopian Fantasy: a Study of English Utopian Fiction Since the End of the Nineteenth Century*. London: Routledge and Paul, 1955.

A. Bartlett Giamatti. *The Earthly Paradise and the Renaissance Epic*. Princeton, N.J.: Princeton University Press, 1966.

W.W. Greg. *Pastoral Poetry and Pastoral Drama: a Literary Inquiry, with Special Reference to the Pre-Restoration Stage in England*. New York: Russell & Russell, 1959.

Claudio Guillen. "On the Concept and Metaphor of Perspective" in *Comparatists at Work*, ed. Stephen G. Nichols Jr., and Richard B. Vowles.

Jean Hagstrum. "The Sister Arts: From Neoclassic to Romantic" in *Comparatists at Work*, ed. Stephen G. Nichols Jr., and Richard B. Vowles.

J.B. Halsted, ed. *Romanticism: Problems of Definition, Explanation and Evaluation.* Boston: Heath, 1965.

George Haines IV. "Art Forms and Science Concepts" *The Journal of Philosophy* XL (1943), pp. 482-491.

Erich Heller. *The Artist's Journey to the Interior and Other Essays.* London: Secker and Warburg, 1966.

--------------------. *The Disinherited Mind.* New York: Meridian Books, 1959.

Leo Justin Henkin. *Darwinism in the English Novel: the Impact of Evolution on Victorian Fiction, 1860-1910.* New York: Russell & Russell, 1963.

Mark Robert Hillegas. *The Future as Nightmare: H.G. Wells and the Anti-Utopians.* New York: Oxford University Press, 1967.

Robert D. Hume. "Gothic Versus Romantic: A Re-evaluation of the Gothic Novel", *PMLA*, Volume LXXXIV (1969), pp. 282-290.

Aldous Huxley. *Collected Essays.* New York: Harper Brothers, 1958.

--------------------. *Literature and Science.* London: Chatto & Windus, 1963.

--------------------. "Wordsworth in the Tropics", in *Do What You Will.* Garden City, New York: Doubleday, Doran & Company, Inc., 1929.

Edward Dudley Hume Johnson, ed. *The Poetry of Earth: a Collection of English Nature Writings.* New York: Atheneum, 1966.

Arthur E. Jones, Jr. "Darwinism and its Relation to Realism and Naturalism in American Fiction, 1860-1900", *Drew University Bulletin*, 38 (Dec. 1950), pp. 3-21.

Desmond King-Hele. *Shelley: His Thought and Work.* London: Macmillan, 1972.

Gyorgy Kepes. *The New Landscape in Art and Science.* Chicago: P. Theobald, 1967.

Arnold Kettle. *An Introduction to the English Novel.* New York: Harper Torchbooks, 1960.

Robert Kiely, ed. *Man and Nature.* Boston: Little Brown, 1966.

John Kieran. *John Kieran's Treasury of Great Nature Writing.* New York: Houghton, Mifflin, 1957.

William J. Keith. *The Poetry of Nature*, Toronto: University of Toronto Press, 1980.

--------------------. *The Rural Tradition*, Toronto: University of Toronto Press, 1974.

Karl Kroeber. *Romantic Landscape Vision: Constable and Wordsworth.* Madison: University of Wisconsin Press, 1975.

Joseph Wood Krutch. *Great American Nature Writing.* New York: Sloane, 1950.

Diana Laurenson and Alan Swingewood. *The Sociology of Literature.* London: Paladin, 1972.

Harry Levin. "What is Realism?" *Comparative Literature*, III (Summer, 1951), pp. 193-199.

--------------------. *The Gates of Horn.* New York: Oxford University Press, 1963.

C.S. Lewis. *An Experiment in Criticism.* Cambridge: University Press, 1961.

--------------------. *The Discarded Image.* Cambridge: University Press, 1967.

--------------------. *Studies in Words.* Cambridge: University Press, 1967.

Judson S. Lyon. "Romantic Psychology and the Inner Senses: Coleridge", *PMLA*, Volume LXXXI (1966), pp. 246-260.

George Lukacs. *The Meaning of Contemporary Realism.* London: Merlin Press, 1963.

269

Robin Magowan. "Fromentin and Jewett: Pastoral Narrative in the Nineteenth Century", *Comparative Literature*, XVI. 1964, pp. 331-337.

Jacques Maritain. *Creative Intuition in Art and Poetry*. New York: Pantheon, 1953.

Leo Marx. *The Machine in the Garden: Technology and the Pastoral Ideal in America*. New York: Oxford University Press, 1964.

Arthur S. McDowell. *Realism: A Study in Art and Thought*. London: Constable, 1918.

James Walter McFarland. *Ibsen and the Temper of Norwegian Literature*. Oxford: University Press, 1960.

Charles W. Morris. "Science, Art and Technology", *Kenyon Review*, 1 (1939), pp. 409-423.

Henry A. Murray, ed. *Myth and Mythmaking*. Boston: Beacon Press, 1968.

Bernard Myers. *The German Expressionists: a generation in revolt*. New York: Praeger, 1957.

Stephen G. Nichols Jr. and Richard B. Vowles, eds. *Comparatists at Work*. Waltham, Massachusetts: Blaisdell, 1968.

Marjorie Hope Nicolson. *Mountain Gloom and Mountain Glory: the Development of the Aesthetics of the Infinite*. Ithaca: Cornell University Press, 1959.

--------------------. *Voyages to the Moon*. New York: Macmillan, 1948.

Erwin Panofsky, "Et in Arcadia ego: Poussin and the Elegiac Tradition" in *Meaning in the Visual Arts*. Garden City, New York: Doubleday, 1955.

Howard Rollin Patch. *The Other World, According to Descriptions in Medieval Literature*. New York: Octagon, 1970.

Robert M. Philmus. *Into the Unknown: the Evolution of Science Fiction from Francis Godwin to H.G. Wells*. Berkley: University of California Press, 1970.

Robert Plank. "The Golem and the Robot", *Literature and Psychology*, XV (1965), pp. 12-28.

René Poggioli. "The Oaten Flute", *Harvard Library Bulletin* XI (1957), pp. 147-184.

--------------------. "The Pastoral of the Self", *Daedalus* LXXXVII (1959), pp. 686-99.

--------------------. "Realism in Russia", *Comparative Literature* III (summer 1951), pp. 253-267.

C.E. Pulos. *The Deep Truth: a Study of Shelley's Skepticism*. Lincoln, Nebraska: University Press, 1954.

Frederick A. Pottle. "The Eye on the Object in the Poetry of Wordsworth" in Gilbert T. Dunklin. *Wordsworth: Centenary Studies*.

V.S. Pritchett. *The Living Novel*. London: Arrow Books, 1960.

H.M. Richmond. "Rural Lyricism. A Renaissance Mutation of the Pastoral", *Comparative Literature*, XVI (1964), pp. 193-210.

Georg Roppen. *Evolution and Poetic Belief: a Study of Some Victorian and Modern Writers*. Oslo: Oslo University Press, 1956.

Charles Sanford. *The Quest For Paradise: Europe and the American Moral Imagination*. Urbana: University of Illinois Press, 1961.

George Santayana. *Three Philosophical Poets: Lucretius, Dante, Goethe*. Cambridge, Mass.: Harvard University Press, 1910.

--------------------. "The Long Way Round to Nirvana" in *Some Turns of Thought in Modern Philosophy*. Cambridge: Harvard University Press, 1933.

Aldo D. Scaglione. *Nature and Love in the Late Middle Ages*. Berkeley: University of California Press, 1963.

Seventeenth Century Science and the Arts. Various Authors. Princeton: 1961.

Henry Nash Smith. *Virgin land: The American West as Symbol and Myth*. Cambridge: Harvard University Press, 1950.

Enid Starkie. *From Gautier to Eliot*. London: Hutchinson, 1960.

George Steiner. *Language and Silence*. London: Faber and Faber, 1967.

Lionel Stevenson. *Darwin Among the Poets*. New York: Russell and Russell, 1963.

Edward Stone, ed. *What Was Naturalism?: Materials for an Answer*. New York: Appleton-Century Crofts, 1959.

Roland N. Stromberg, ed. *Realism, Naturalism and Symbolism: Modes of Thought and Expression in Europe, 1848-1914*. New York: Harper, 1968.

Michael Squires. *The Pastoral Novel*. Charlottesville: Virginia University Press, 1974.

Wylie Sypher. *Four Stages of Renaissance Style*. New York: Anchor Books, 1955.

--------------------. *Literature and Technology: the Alien Vision*. New York: Random House, 1968.

E.W. Tayler. *Nature and Art in Renaissance Literature*. New York: Columbia University Press, 1964.

Edwin Way Teale, ed. *Green Treasury: A Journey through the World's Great Nature Writing*. New York: Dodd Mead, 1952.

Anthony Thorlby. *The Romantic Movement*. London: Longmans, 1966.

Willard Trask, ed. *The Unwritten Song*. New York: Macmillan, 1966.

Lionel Trilling. *The Liberal Imagination*. New York: Viking, 1950.

J.H. van der Berg, "The Subject and his Landscape" in Harold Bloom. *Romanticism and Consciousness*.

Dorothy van Ghent. *The English Novel: Form and Function*. New York: Holt, Rinehart and Winston, 1953.

T.C. Walker. *Chateaubriand's Natural Scenery: A Study of His Descriptive Art*. Baltimore: Johns Hopkins, 1946.

Charles Child Walcutt. *American Literary Naturalism: A Divided Stream*. Minneapolis: University of Minnesota Press, 1956.

--------------------. "Naturalism and the Superman in the Novels of Jack London", *Papers of the Michigan Academy of Science, Arts and Letters*, XXIV, Part IV (1938), pp. 89-107.

Dorothy Walsh. "The Cognitive Content of Art," *The Philosophical Review*, LI (Sept. 1943), pp. 443-451.

Basil Willey. *The Eighteenth Century Background: Studies on the Idea of Nature in the Thought of the Period*. London: Chatto and Windus, 1940.

--------------------. *The Seventeenth Century Background*. New York: Columbia University Press, 1950.

Charles Williams. *The English Poetic Mind*. Oxford: Clarendon Press, 1932.

George Huntson Williams. *Wilderness and Paradise in Christian Thought*. New York: Harper and Row Publishers, 1962.

Raymond Williams. *Culture and Society, 1780-1950*. London: Chatto and Windus, 1959.

Edmund Wilson. *Axel's Castle*. New York: Scribner's, 1931.

William Kurtz Wimsatt. *The Verbal Icon: Studies in the Meaning of Poetry and Two Preliminary Essays Written in Collaboration with Monroe C. Beardsley.* Lexington: University of Kentucky Press, 1954.

Morton and Lucia White. *The Intellectual Versus the City: From Thomas Jefferson to Frank Lloyd Wright.* Cambridge: Harvard University Press, 1962.

Virginia Woolf. *Mr. Bennett and Mrs. Brown.* London: The Hogarth Press, 1924.

Yevgeny Zamyatin. *A Soviet Heretic: Essays by Yevgeny Zamyatin.* Chicago: University Press, 1972.

Peter Zimmermann. *Der Bauernroman.* Stuttgart: J.B. Metzlersche, 1975.

PART THREE
Hardy, Wells and Lawrence

1) Thomas Hardy

Carol Reed Anderson. "Time, Space and Perspective in Thomas Hardy". *Nineteenth Century Fiction* IX (1954-55), 192-208.

Howard Babb. "Setting and Theme in Far From the Madding Crowd" *ELH, Vol. XXX*, (1963), 147-161.

James Osler Bailey. *Thomas Hardy and the Cosmic Mind: A New Reading of The Dynasts*. Chapel Hill: University of North Carolina Press, 1956.

Joseph Warren Beach. *The Technique of Thomas Hardy*. 1949; rpt. New York: Russell & Russell, 1962.

Edmund Charles Blunden. *Thomas Hardy*. London: Macmillan, 1942.

T.E.M. Boll. "Tess as an Animal in Nature", *English Literature in Transition*. pp. 210-211 (1965-6), 8-9.

Allan Brick. "Paradise and Consciousness in Hardy's Tess," *Nineteenth Century Fiction*, 17, (1962-3), 115-34.

Jean R. Brooks. *Thomas Hardy: The Poetic Structure*. London: Elek, 1971.

Douglas Brown. *Thomas Hardy*. London: Longmans, Green, 1954.

R.C. Carpenter. "The Mirror and the Sword: Imagery in *Far from the Madding Crowd*", *Nineteenth Century Fiction*, 18, (1963-4), 331-345.

Lord David Cecil. *Hardy the Novelist: An Essay in Criticism*. London: Constable, 1943.

Louis Crompton. "The Sunburnt God: Ritual and Tragic Myth in *The Return of the Native*," *Boston University Studies in English*, 4, (1960), 229-240.

Donald Davidson. "The Traditional Basis of Thomas Hardy's Fiction", *Southern Review*, VI, (1940).

D.J. de Laura. "The Ache of Modernism in Hardy's Later Novels," *ELH*, XXXIV, (1967), 380-400.

Robert Y. Drake, Jr. "The Woodlanders as Traditional Pastoral", *Modern Fiction Studies*, 6 (1960), 251-257.

T.S. Eliot. *After Strange Gods*. London: Faber, 1934.

Langdon Elsbree. "Tess and the Local Cerealia", *Philological Quarterly*, XL, (October, 1961), 606-613.

Ruth Firor. *Folkways in Thomas Hardy*. Philadelphia: University of Pennsylvania Press, 1931.

M.A. Goldberg. "Hardy's Double-Visioned Universe", *Essays in Criticism*, 7, (1957), 374-382.

Elliot B. Gose "Psychic Evolution: Darwinism and Initiation in *Tess of the D'Urbervilles*", *Nineteenth Century Fiction*, 18, (1963-4), 261-274.

Ian Gregor. "What Kind of Fiction did Hardy Write?" *Essays in Criticism*, XVI (1966), pp. 290-308.

Phillip Mahone Griffith. "The Image of the Trapped Animal in Hardy's *Tess of the D'Urbervilles*". *Tulane Studies in English*, 13 (1963), 85-94.

Herbert B. Grimsditch. *Character and Environment in the Novels of Thomas Hardy*. New York: Russell and Russell, 1925.

A.J. Guerard. *Hardy, A Collection of Critical Essays*. Englewood Cliffs, N.J.: 1925, rpt. Ann Arbor, Michigan: University of Michigan.

--------------------. *Thomas Hardy, The Novels and Stories*. Cambridge: Harvard University Press, 1949.

Florence Emily Hardy. *The Life of Thomas Hardy, 1840-1928*. London: Macmillan, 1962.

Robert B. Heilman. "Hardy's *Mayor*: Notes on Style." *Nineteenth Century Fiction* (1963-4).

Ward Hellstrom. "Hardy's Use of Setting in *Jude the Obscure*", *Victorian Newsletter*, no. 25 (Spring 64), 11-13.

J. Holloway. *The Victorian Sage: Studies in Argument*. London: Macmillan, 1953.

Irving Howe. *Thomas Hardy*. New York: Macmillan, 1967.

Roy Huss. "Social Change and Moral Decay in the Novels of Thomas Hardy", *Dalhousie Review*, 47, (1967-68), 28-44.

Lionel Johnson. *The Art of Thomas Hardy*. 1923; rpt. New York: Haskell House, 1966.

Philip Larkin. "Wanted: Good Hardy Critic." *Critical Quarterly*, VIII, (1966), 174-79.

William J. Matchett. "*The Woodlanders*, or Realism in Sheep's Clothing", *Nineteenth Century Fiction*, 9, (1954-5), 241-61.

Michael Millgate. *Thomas Hardy: His Career as a Novelist*. London: Bodley Head, 1971.

Roy Morrell. *Thomas Hardy: The Will and the Way*. Kuala Lumpur, University of Malaya Press, 1965.

Harold Orel. *Thomas Hardy's Epic-Drama: A Study of 'The Dynasts'*. New York: Greenwood Press, 1969.

John Paterson. *The Making of 'THE RETURN OF THE NATIVE'*. University of California Press, 1960.

F.B. Pinion. *A Hardy Companion: a Guide to the Works of Thomas Hardy and their Background*. London: Macmillan, 1968. ‐

W.R. Rutland. *Thomas Hardy, a Study of his Writings and their Background*. Oxford: Blackwell, 1938.

F.R. Southerington. *Hardy's Vision of Man*. London: Chatto and Windus, 1971.

Curtis C. Smith. "Natural Settings and Natural Characters in Hardy's *Desperate Remedies* and *A Pair of Blue Eyes*", *Thoth*, 8, (1967), 84-97.

J.I.M. Stewart. *Eight Modern Writers*. Oxford: University Press, 1963.

H.L. Weatherby. "Old-Fashioned Gods: Eliot on Lawrence and Hardy," *Sewanee Review*, Volume 9, 1967, 301-316.

Carl Jefferson Weber. *Hardy of Wessex: His Life and Literary Career*. (Rev. ed.) New York: Columbia University Press, 1965.

H.C. Webster. *On a Darkling Plain*. Chicago: University of Chicago Press, 1947.
R.J. White. *Thomas Hardy and History*. London: Macmillan, 1974.
Merryn Williams. *Thomas Hardy and Rural England*. London: Macmillan, 1972.
George Wing. *Hardy*. Edinburgh and London: Oliver and Boyd, 1963.
Morton Dauwen Zabel. "Hardy in Defense of his Art: The Aesthetic of Incongruity", *Southern Review*, VI, (1940).

2) H.G. Wells

Bernard Bergonzi. *The Early H.G. Wells*. Manchester: Manchester University Press, 1961.
Van Wyck Brooks. *The World of H.G. Wells*. St. Clair Shores, Michigan: Scholarly Press, 1970.
Christopher Caudwell. *Studies and Further Studies in a Dying Culture*. New York: Monthly Review Press, 1971.
Lovat Dickson. *H.G. Wells: His Turbulent Life and Times*. New York: Atheneum, 1969.
Leon Edel and N. Ray Gordon, editors. *Henry James and H.G. Wells*. Urbana: University of Illinois Press, 1958.
Camille Flammarion. *La Fin du Monde*. Paris: 1894.
Mark R. Hillegas. *The Future as Nightmare: H.G. Wells and the Anti-Utopians*. New York: Oxford University Press, 1967.
J. Kagarlitski. *The Life and Thought of H.G. Wells*. London: Sidgwick and Jackson, 1966.
Norman and Jeanne MacKenzie. *The Time Traveller: The Life of H.G. Wells*. London: Weidenfeld and Nicolson, 1973.
Norman Nicholson. *H.G. Wells*. London: Arthur Baxter, 1950.
Patrick Parrinder. *H.G. Wells*. Edinburgh: Oliver and Boyd, 1970.
Robert M. Philmus. *Into the Unknown: The Evolution of Science Fiction from Francis Godwin to H.G. Wells*. Berkeley: University of California Press, 1970.
--------------------. "*The Time Machine*; or The Fourth Dimension as Prophecy", *PMLA*, LXXXIV, (1969), pp. 530-535.
Ingwald Raknem. *H.G. Wells and His Critics*. London: Allen and Unwin, 1962.
W. Warren Wagar. *H.G. Wells and the World State*. New Haven: Yale University Press, 1961.
Robert P. Weeks. "Disentanglement as a Theme in H.G. Wells's Fiction", *Papers of the Michigan Academy of Science, Arts and Letters*, XXXIX (1954), pp. 439-444.
Anthony West. *Principles and Persuasions*. New York: Harcourt Brace, 1957.
Geoffrey West. *H.G. Wells: A Sketch for a Portrait*. London: Howe, 1930.
Jack Williamson. *H.G. Wells: Critic of Progress*. Baltimore: Mirage Press, 1973.

3) D.H. Lawrence

Richard Aldington. *D.H. Lawrence: Portrait of a Genius But*. New York: Duell, Sloan & Pearce, 1950.
Angelo Bertocci. "Symbolism in *Women in Love*." In *A D.H. Lawrence Miscellany*, edited by Harry T. Moore, pp. 83-102.
David Cavitch. *D.H. Lawrence and the New World*. New York: Oxford University Press, 1969.

275

Robert L. Chamberlain. "Pussum, Minette, and the Africo-Nordic Symbol in Lawrence's *Women in Love*." *PMLA*, 78 (1963), 407-16.

Jessie Chambers (pseud. E.T.). *D.H. Lawrence: A Personal Record*. London: Jonathan Cape Ltd., 1935.

L.D. Clark. *Dark Night of the Body: D.H. Lawrence's THE PLUMED SERPENT*. Austin: University of Texas Press, 1964.

Colin Clarke. *River of Dissolution: D.H. Lawrence and English Romanticism*. London: Routledge & Kegan Paul, 1969.

James C. Cowan. "The Function of Allusions and Symbols in Lawrence's *The Man Who Died*." *American Imago*, 17 (1950) 241-53.

G. Armour Craig. "D.H. Lawrence on Thinghood and Self-hood." *Massachusetts Review*, 1 (1959), 59-60.

Herman M. Daleski. *The Forked Flame: A Study of D.H. Lawrence*. Evanston, Illinois: Northwestern University, Press, 1965.

Roger Ebbatson. *Lawrence and the Nature Tradition*. New York: Humanities Press, 1980.

George Harry Ford. *Double Measure: A Study of the Novels and Stories of D.H. Lawrence*. New York: Holt, Rinehart and Winston, 1965.

Eugene Goodheart. *The Utopian Vision of D.H. Lawrence*. Chicago: The University of Chicago Press, 1963.

Baruch Hochman. *Another Ego: The Changing View of Self and Society in the Work of D.H. Lawrence*. Columbia: University of South Carolina Press, 1970.

Frederick J. Hoffman. "Lawrence's Quarrel with Freud", *Freudianism and the Literary Mind*. Baton Rouge: Louisiana State University Press, 1945.

Frederick J. Hoffman and Harry T. Moore, eds. *The Achievement of D.H. Lawrence*. Norman: University of Oklahoma Press, 1953.

Graham Hough. *The Dark Sun: A Study of D.H. Lawrence*. New York: Capricorn Books, 1956.

Frank Kermode. *D.H. Lawrence*. New York: Viking Press, 1973.

Jascha F. Kessler. "Descent in Darkness: The Myth of *The Plumed Serpent*". In *A D.H. Lawrence Miscellany* edited by Harry T. Moore, pp. 238-61.

--------------------. "D.H. Lawrence's Primitivism." *Texas Studies in Literature and Language*, 5 (1963), 467-88.

G. Wilson Knight. "Lawrence, Joyce, and Powys." *Essays in Criticism*, 11 (1961), 403-17.

Florence B. Leaver. "The Man-Nature Relationship of D.H. Lawrence's Novels." *University of Kansas City Review*, 19 (1953), 241-48.

F.R. Leavis. *D.H. Lawrence: Novelist*. New York: Alfred A. Knopf, 1956.

Harry T. Moore, ed. *A D.H. Lawrence Miscellany*. Carbondale: Southern Illinois University Press, 1959.

Harry T. Moore. *The Intelligent Heart: The Story of D.H. Lawrence*. New York: Farrar, Straus & Young, 1954.

Julian Moynahan. *The Deed of Life: The Novels and Tales of D.H. Lawrence*. Princeton, N.J.: Princeton University Press, 1963.

Marvin Mudrick. "The Originality of The Rainbow." In *A D.H. Lawrence Miscellany* edited by Harry T. Moore, pp. 56-82.

Edward Nehls, ed. *D.H. Lawrence: A Composite Biography*. 3 vols. Madison: University of Wisconsin Press, 1956-59.

Edward Nehls. "D.H. Lawrence: The Spirit of Place." In *The Achievement of D.H. Lawrence*, edited by Frederick J. Hoffman and Harry T. Moore, pp. 268-90.

George A. Panichas. *Adventure in Consciousness: The Meaning of D.H. Lawrence's Religious Quest*. The Hague: Mouton & Co., 1964.

R.E. Pritchard. *D.H. Lawrence: Body of Darkness*. London: Hutchinson University Library, 1971.

Philip Rieff. Introduction to *Psychoanalysis and the Unconscious and Fantasia of the Unconscious* by D.H. Lawrence. New York: The Viking Press, 1960.

Keith M. Sagar. *The Art of D.H. Lawrence*. Cambridge: University Press, 1966.

Scott Sanders. *D.H. Lawrence: The World of the Five Major Novels*. New York: The Viking Press, 1973.

Mark Schorer. "Lawrence and the Spirit of Place." in *A D.H. Lawrence Miscellany*, edited by Harry T. Moore, pp. 280-94.

Mark Spilka, ed. *D.H. Lawrence: A Collection of Critical Essays*. Englewood Cliffs, N.J.: Prentice-Hall, Inc., 1963.

Mark Spilka. *The Love Ethic of D.H. Lawrence*. London: Dennis Dobson, 1958.

Raney Stanford. "Thomas Hardy and Lawrence's *The White Peacock*." *Modern Fiction Studies*, (1959), 19-28.

John E. Stoll. *The Novels of D.H. Lawrence, A Search for Integration*. Columbia: University of Missouri Press, 1971.

Richard Swigg. *Lawrence, Hardy, and American Literature*. London: Oxford University Press, 1972.

E.W. Tedlock, Jr. *D.H. Lawrence, Artist and Rebel: A Study of Lawrence's Fiction*. Alberquerque: University of New Mexico Press, 1963.

--------------------. "D.H. Lawrence's Annotations of Ouspensky's *Tertium Organum*." *Texas Studies in Literature and Language*, 2 (1960), 206-18.

William York Tindall. *D.H. Lawrence and Susan His Cow*. New York: Columbia University Press, 1939.

--------------------. Introduction to *The Plumed Serpent*. New York: Alfred A. Knopf, Inc., 1951.

Father William Tiverton (pseud.) *D.H. Lawrence and Human Existence*. London: Rockliff Publishing Corporation Ltd., 1951.

Eliseo Vivas. *D.H. Lawrence: The Failure and Triumph of Art*. Evanston: Northwestern University Press, 1960.

Kingsley Widmer, "D.H. Lawrence and the Art of Nihilism", *Kenyon Review*, XX (Autumn, 1958), 604-616.

--------------------. "The Primitive Aesthetic: D.H. Lawrence." *Journal of Aesthetics and Art Criticism*, 17 (1959), 344-53.

Raymond Williams. "Lawrence and Tolstoy." *Critical Quarterly*, 2 (1960), 33-39.

Raymond Wright. "Lawrence's Non-Human Analogues." *Modern Language Notes*, 76 (1961), 426-32.

APPENDIX
Natural Space in Literature
Some Relevant Texts and Passages

The following books and passages further illustrate the perspectives on nature described in my text — chiefly in Part II, and include also instances not mentioned there. No attempt has been made to list every relevant passage known to me or even to refer to every passage discussed in the text. This outline is meant to be supplementary. In some longer works, where the passage referred to is not altogether obvious, I have indicated its character by means of a brief descriptive title, and given a chapter, section or line reference. Where there are many instances of the perspective in question, I have simply listed the title.

WILD NATURE, OR THE NATURAL SUBLIME

Wordsworth: "Tintern Abbey" (1795)
Wordsworth: "Unknown Modes of Being" from *The Prelude* (1799), first part, lines 119-129.
Wordsworth: "Types and Symbols of Eternity", *The Prelude* (1805), Book Sixth, lines 549-573.
Chateaubriand: "The Two Banks of the Mississippi", Prologue, *Atala* (1801)
Chateaubriand: "Two Perspectives of Nature," Chapter 12, of *Le Genie du Christianisme* (1802)
Shelley: "Mont Blanc" (1816)
Shelley: "The Cloud" (1818)
M. Shelley: Frankenstein meeting the monster in the alps, from *Frankenstein* (1818), Chapter Ten
Byron: "Darkness" (1816)
Byron: Childe Harold, Canto III, Lake Leman & etc. (1816)
Byron: Childe Harold, Canto III, "There is a Pleasure" & etc. (1818)
Leopardi: "*L'infinito*" (1819)
Lamartine: "*Le Lac*" (1820)
Bryant: "The Prairies" (1832)

Balzac: "A Passion in the Desert" (1832)

Cooper: Description of the virgin forest from Chapter One of *The Pathfinder* (1840)

Poe: The cliff and the maelstrom from "A Descent into the Maelstrom" (1841)

Stifter: The children on the mountain, from *Rock Crystal* (1843)

Ruskin: Panorama of Europe from *The Stones of Venice*, Vol. II, Chapter 6, (1851)

Arnold: Empedocles' last speech from "Empedocles on Etna" (1852)

Whitman: "The World Below the Brine" (1860)

Whitman: "Passage to India" (1871)

Whitman: "Patroling Barnegat" (1880)

Verne: The cemetery under the sea in Chapter Seventeen from *Twenty Thousand Leagues Under the Sea* (1870)

Holmes: "Nearing the Snow Line" (1870)

Hardy: Egdon Heath in Book First, Chapter One of *The Return of the Native* (1874)

Jefferies: *The Story of My Heart* (1883)

Tennyson: "Locksley Hall Sixty Years After" (1886)

Hamsun: *Pan* (1894)

Wells: *The Time Machine* (1894)

Wells: "The Star" (1897)

Wells: *The War of the Worlds* (1897)

Wells: *The First Men in the Moon* (1901)

Conrad: "Heart of Darkness" (1898-9)

Conrad: *Typhoon* (1903)

London: *The Call of the Wild* (1903)

London: "To Build a Fire" (1907)

Jensen: Spaceship Earth in "Christopher Columbus," Book III, Chapter Four of *The Long Journey* (1924)

Cather: The Blue Mesa in "Tom Outland's Story" from *The Professor's House* (1925)

Lawrence: The cabin in the mountains from *St. Mawr* (1925)

Stapledon: *Last and First Men* (1929)

Lewis: Ransom in space from *Out of the Silent Planet* (1938), Chapters Five and Six.

St. Exupéry: An aviator's view of earth from *Terre des Hommes* (1939)

Jeffers: "The Eye" (1948)

Kerouac: *Dharma Bums* (1958)

Snyder: "Piute Creek" (1959)

Snyder: "Above Pate Valley" (1959)

Lem: *Solaris* (1961)

Ballard: *The Drowned World* (1962)

Dillard: *Pilgrim at Tinker Creek* (1974)

THE IMAGE OF THE FIELD

Wordsworth: "The Ruined Cottage" (1797-9)
Wordsworth: "Michael" (1800)
Wordsworth: "Written in March" (1802)
Wordsworth: "The Solitary Reaper" (1805)
Keats: "To Autumn" (1819)
Cooper: *The Pioneers* (1823)
Clare: "The Fens" (about 1835)
Clare: "The Ploughboy" (about 1837)
Dröste-Hülsoff: *The Jew's Beech* (1841)
Gotthelf: *The Black Spider* (1842)
Turgenev: "Byezhin Prairie" (1851)
Thoreau: *Walden* (1854)
Whitman: "This Compost" (1856)
Whittier: "Snowbound" (1866)
Tolstoy: *Cossacks* (1862)
Tolstoy: *Anna Karenina* (1878)
Hardy: *Under the Greenwood Tree* (1872)
Hardy: *Far From the Madding Crowd* (1874)
Hardy: *Tess of the D'Urbervilles* (1891)
Jefferies: *The Gamekeeper at Home* (1878)
Jefferies: *Hodge and his Masters* (1880)
Jefferies: *The Life of the Fields* (1884)
Jefferies: *Amaryllis at the Fair* (1886)
Lanier: "The Waving of the Corn" (1876)
Zola: *Earth* (1886)
Strindberg: *The Natives of Hemso* (1887)
Garland: *Main-Travelled Roads* (1891)
Norris: *The Octopus* (1901)
Reymont: *The Peasants* (1904-9)
Hudson: *A Shepherd's Life* (1910)
Frost: *North of Boston* (1914)
Frost: *New Hampshire* (1923)
Lawrence: *The Rainbow* (1915)
Hamsum: *Growth of the Soil* (1918)
Cather: *O Pioneers!* (1912)
Cather: *My Antonia* (1918)
Rölvaag: *Giants in the Earth* (1927)
Giono: *Regain* (1930)
Grove: *Fruits of the Earth* (1933)
Silone: *Bread and Wine* (1936)
Faulkner: *The Hamlet* (1940)
Dinesen: "Sorrow Acre" (1942)
Buckler: *The Mountain and the Valley* (1952)
White: *The Tree of Man* (1955)

THE NATURAL PARADISE

Coleridge: "Kubla Khan" (1797-8)
Shelley: "Lines Written Among the Euganean Hills" (1818)

Shelley: Island Paradise from "Episychidion" (1821), lines 407-591.
Byron: Juan and Haidée episode from *Don Juan*, Canto II (1819)
Chateaubriand: "With the Savages", Chapter Eight fo *The Memoirs* (about 1815)
Clare: "Bushy Close" (about 1835)
Tennyson: "The Lotus Eaters" (1832/42)
Melville: The Polynesian Valley from *Typee* (1846)
Turgenev: "Kassian of Fair Strath" (1851)
Arnold: Song of Callicles lines 36-76, Act I, Scene Two of *Empedocles on Etna* (1852)
Thoreau: "Walking" (1862)
Fabre: "The Pond" from *The Life of the Fly* in *Souveniers Entomologiques* (1879 & ff)
Whitman: "A Sun-Bath-Nakedness" from *Specimen Days* (1882)
Twain: Huck and Jim by the river in Chapters Eight and Nine of *Huckleberry Finn* (1885)
Pater: Marius at the Aesculapium, Chapter Three of *Marius the Epicurean* (1885)
Yeats: "The Lake Isle of Innisfree" (1890/92)
Hudson: The forest in Chapters Two and Five of *Green Mansions* (1904)
Grahame: Pan's Island from Chapter Seven of *The Wind in the Willows* (1908)
Hemingway: Fishing at Burguete in Chapter Twelve of *The Sun Also Rises* (1926)
Hughes: Exeter Rocks in Chapter One of *A High Wind in Jamaica* (1929)
J.C. Powys: "Yellow Bracken", Chapter Seven of *Wind Solent* (1929)
Lewis: *Perelandra* (1942), Chapter One.
Simak: "Paradise", Chapter Five of *City* (1952)
Tolkien: "Lothlorien", Chapter Six of *The Fellowship of the Ring*, Part I (1954)
Lampedusa: " The Professor and the Siren" (1957)
Kerouac: *Dharma Bums* (1958)

MAN IN THE BIOSPHERE

D. Wordsworth: Grasmere Journal (1802)
Wordsworth: "The Green Linnet" (1803)
Wordsworth: "Yew Trees" (1803)
Clare: "The Nightingale's Nest" (1835-45)
Clare: "The Meadow Lake" (1835-45)
Clare: "Badger" (1835-45)
Hunt: "The Fish, the Man and the Spirit" (1835)
Melville: "The Grand Armada", Chapter LXXXVII of *Moby Dick* (1851)
Thoreau: The moose hunt from Chapter Two of *The Maine Woods* (1853-8)
Thoreau: *Walden* (1854)
Whitman: "Song of Myself" (1855)
Dickinson: "A Bird Came Down the Walk" (1862)
Dickinson: "A Narrow Fellow in the Grass" (1865)
Tolstoy: Episode of Laska, Part VI, Chapter Twelve of *Anna Karenina* (1878)
Hopkins: "Inversnaid" (1881)
Hardy: Clym on the Heath in Book Four, Chapter One of *The Return of the Native* (1874)
Hardy: "In a Wood" (1887)
Hardy: "Transformations" (1919)

282

Fabre: "The Burying Beetle" from *The Glowworm and Other Beetles* in *Souveniers Entomologiques* (1879 & ff)
Kipling: "The Law of the Jungle" (1895)
Roberts: *The Kindred of the Wild* (1902)
Hudson: The Pampas, Chapters Five and Six of *Far Away and Long Ago* (1918)
Moore: "The Fish" (1921)
Lawrence: "Snake" (1923)
Lawrence: The porpoises from *The Flying Fish* (1925)
Jeffers: "Hurt Hawks" (1928)
Campbell: "The Zebras" (1930)
Williams: "The Bull" (1934)
Frost: "Design" (1936)
Faulkner: *The Bear* (1942)
Leopold: *Sand County Almanac* (1949)
Hemingway: *The Old Man and the Sea* (1952)
Kazantzakis: Odysseus and Nature mingle, Book XVI of *The Odyssey: A Modern Sequel* (1958)
Hughes: "An Otter" (1960)
Snyder: *Riprap* (1959)
Snyder: *Myths and Texts* (1960)
Snyder: *Earth House Hold* (1969)
Dillard: *Pilgrim at Tinker Creek)* (1974)